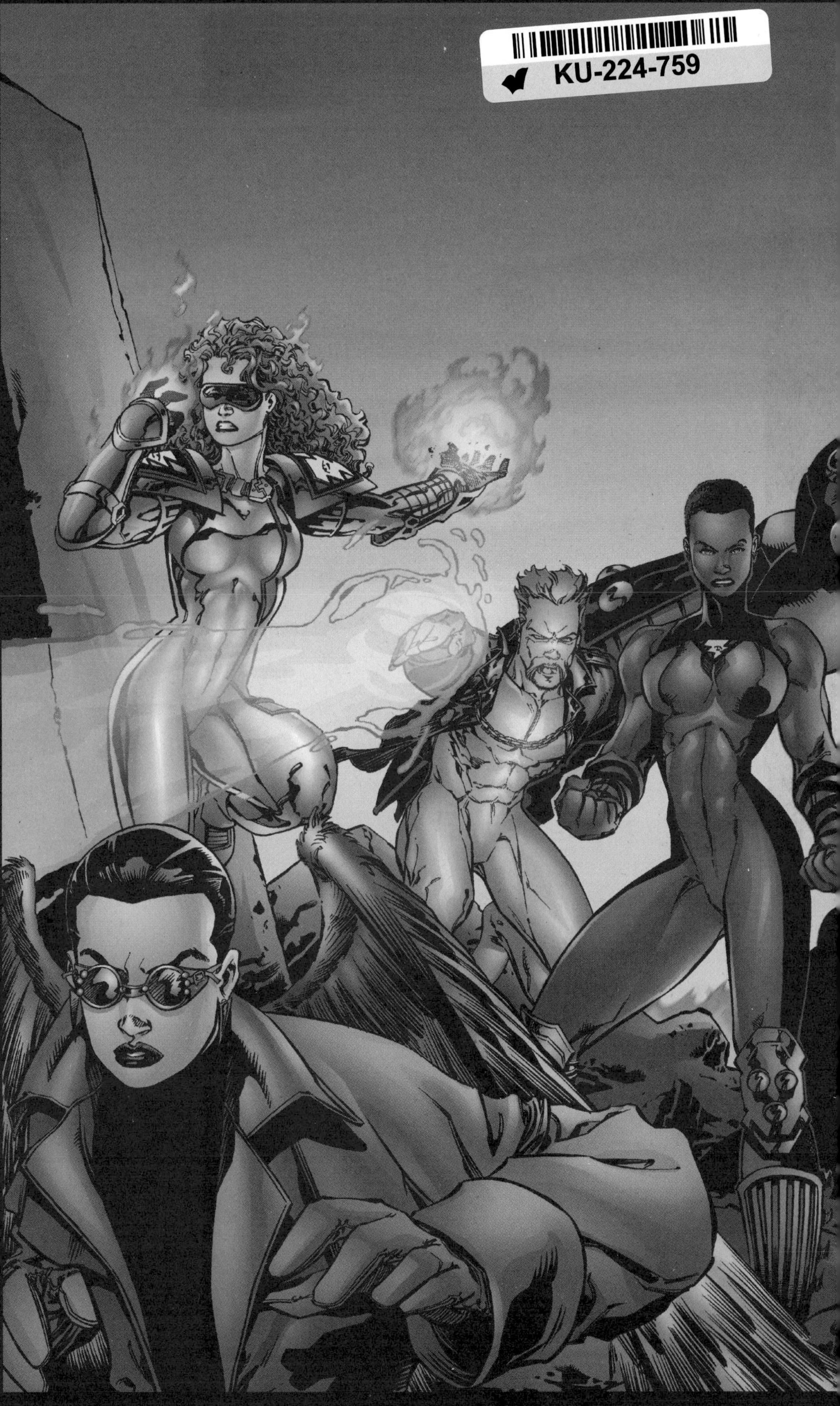

STORMWATCH

...MINAL ZONE

...Y: Warren Ellis
...LS: Oscar Jimenez
... Chuck Gibson
...RS: WildStorm FX
...RS: Clem Robins

CHANGE OR DIE

STORY: Warren Ellis
PENCILS: Tom Raney
INKS: Randy Elliott
COLORS: Gina Going - Laura DePuy
LETTERS: Bill O'Neil

STRANGE WEATHER

STORY: Warren Ellis
PENCILS: Oscar Jimenez - Michael Ryan
INKS: Jason Gorder - Mark McKenna - Richard Friend Eduardo Alpuente - Homage Studios
COLORS: Mike Rockwitz - WildStorm FX
LETTERS: Clem Robins

CREDITS

JENETTE KAHN President & Editor-in-... General Manager – WildStorm
SCOTT DUNBIER Group Editor RIC... ...UCH VP – Licensed Publishing
TERRI CUNNINGHAM V... ... – Manufacturing

Originally published in single magazine form as STORMWATCH #48 - #50, STORMWATCH PREVIEW #1, and STORMWATCH VOLUME TWO #1-#3.

PRINTED IN CANADA
DC Comics, a division of Warner Bros.– A Time Warner Entertainment Company

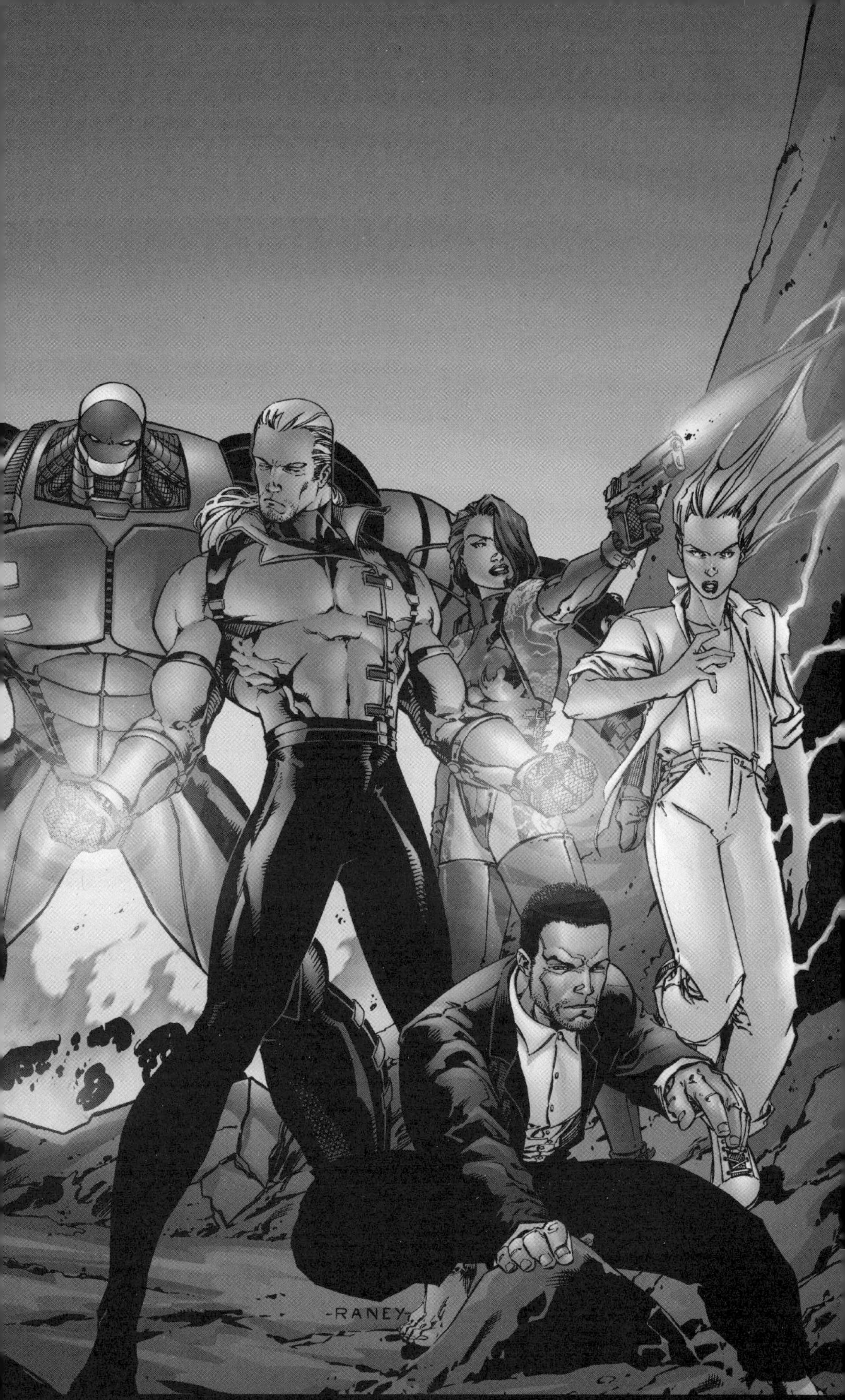
RANEY

CHANGE OR DIE

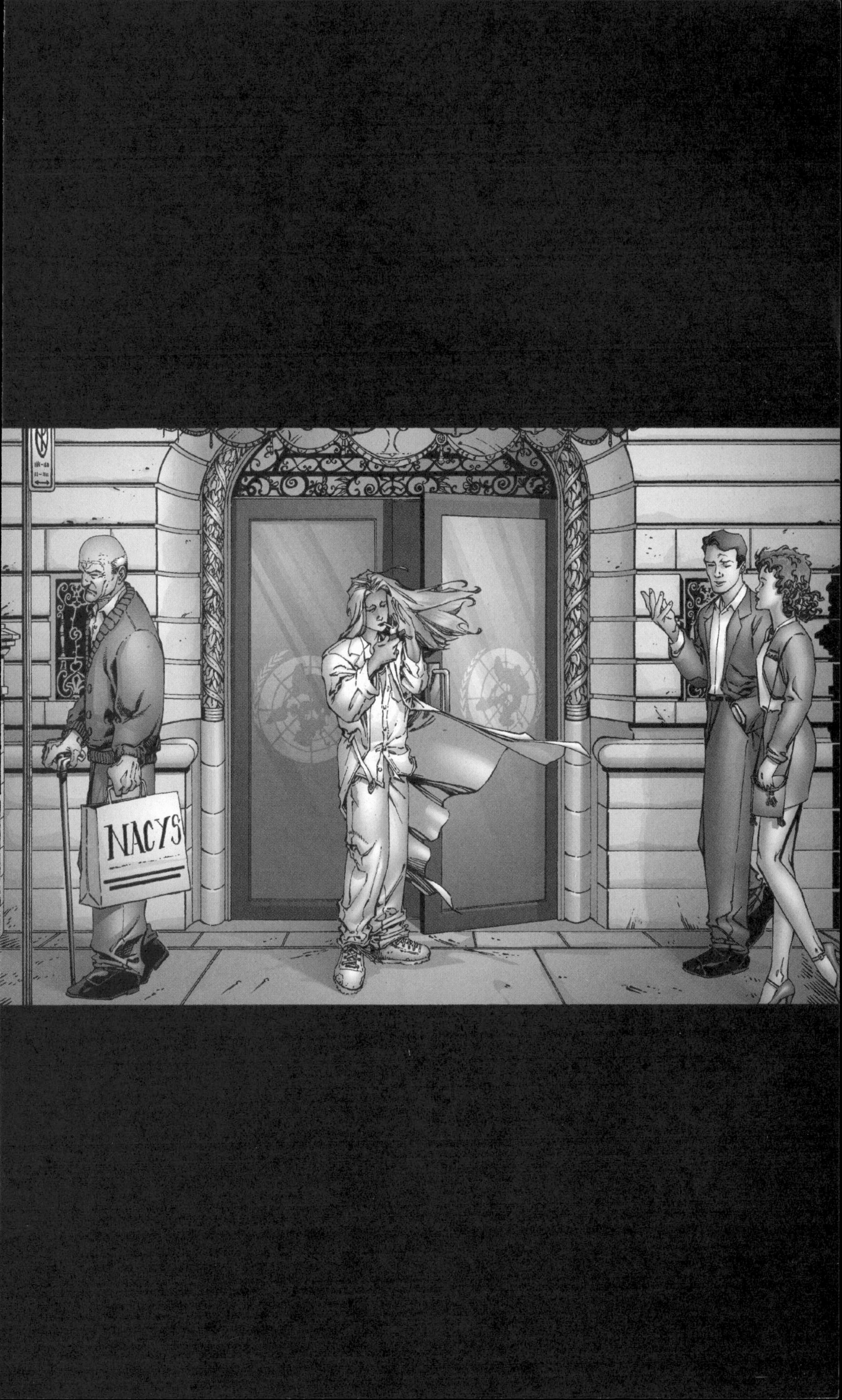
NACYS

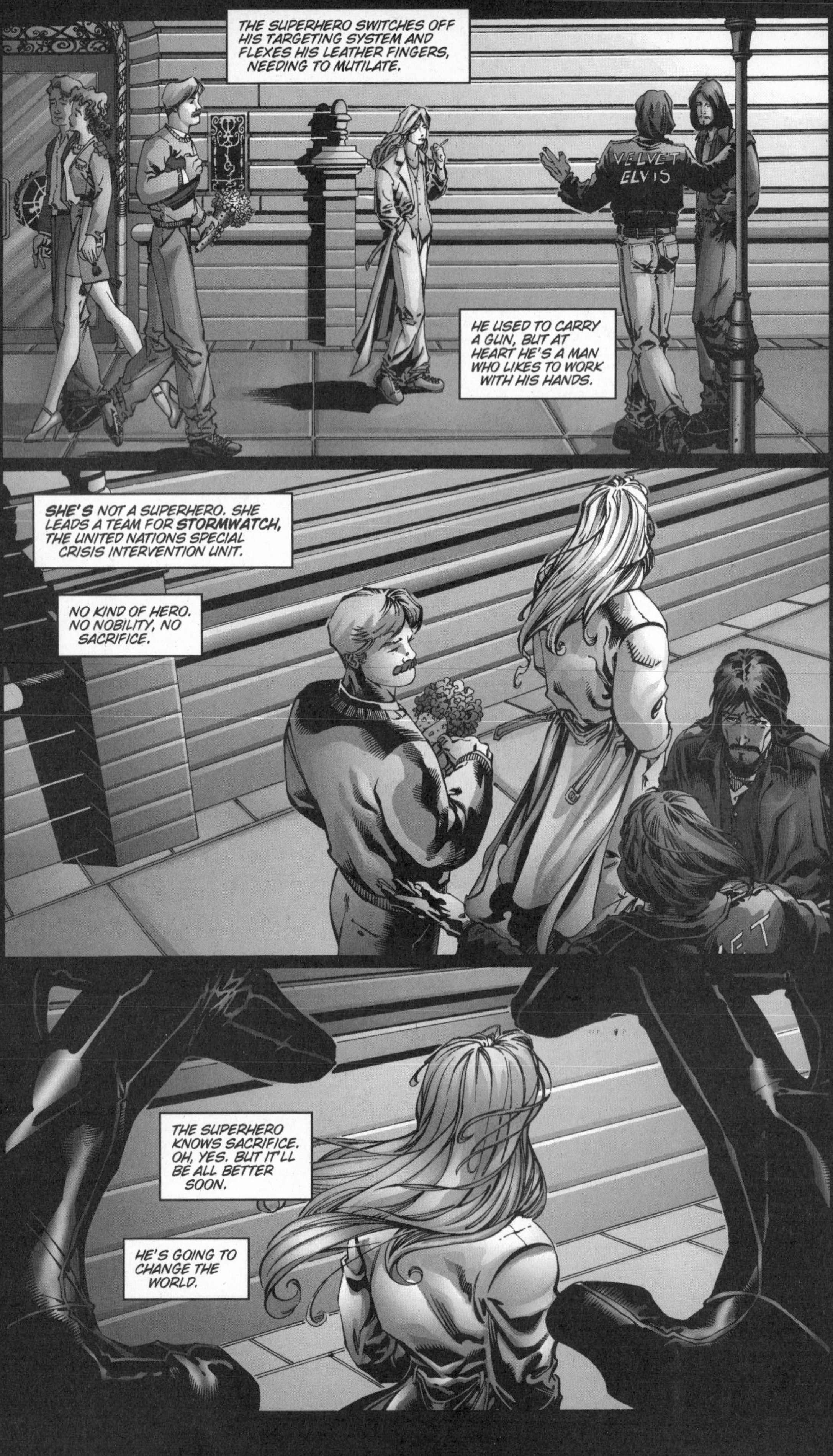
THE SUPERHERO SWITCHES OFF HIS TARGETING SYSTEM AND FLEXES HIS LEATHER FINGERS, NEEDING TO MUTILATE.
VELVET ELVIS
HE USED TO CARRY A GUN, BUT AT HEART HE'S A MAN WHO LIKES TO WORK WITH HIS HANDS.
SHE'S NOT A SUPERHERO. SHE LEADS A TEAM FOR STORMWATCH, THE UNITED NATIONS SPECIAL CRISIS INTERVENTION UNIT.
NO KIND OF HERO. NO NOBILITY, NO SACRIFICE.
THE SUPERHERO KNOWS SACRIFICE. OH, YES. BUT IT'LL BE ALL BETTER SOON.
HE'S GOING TO CHANGE THE WORLD.

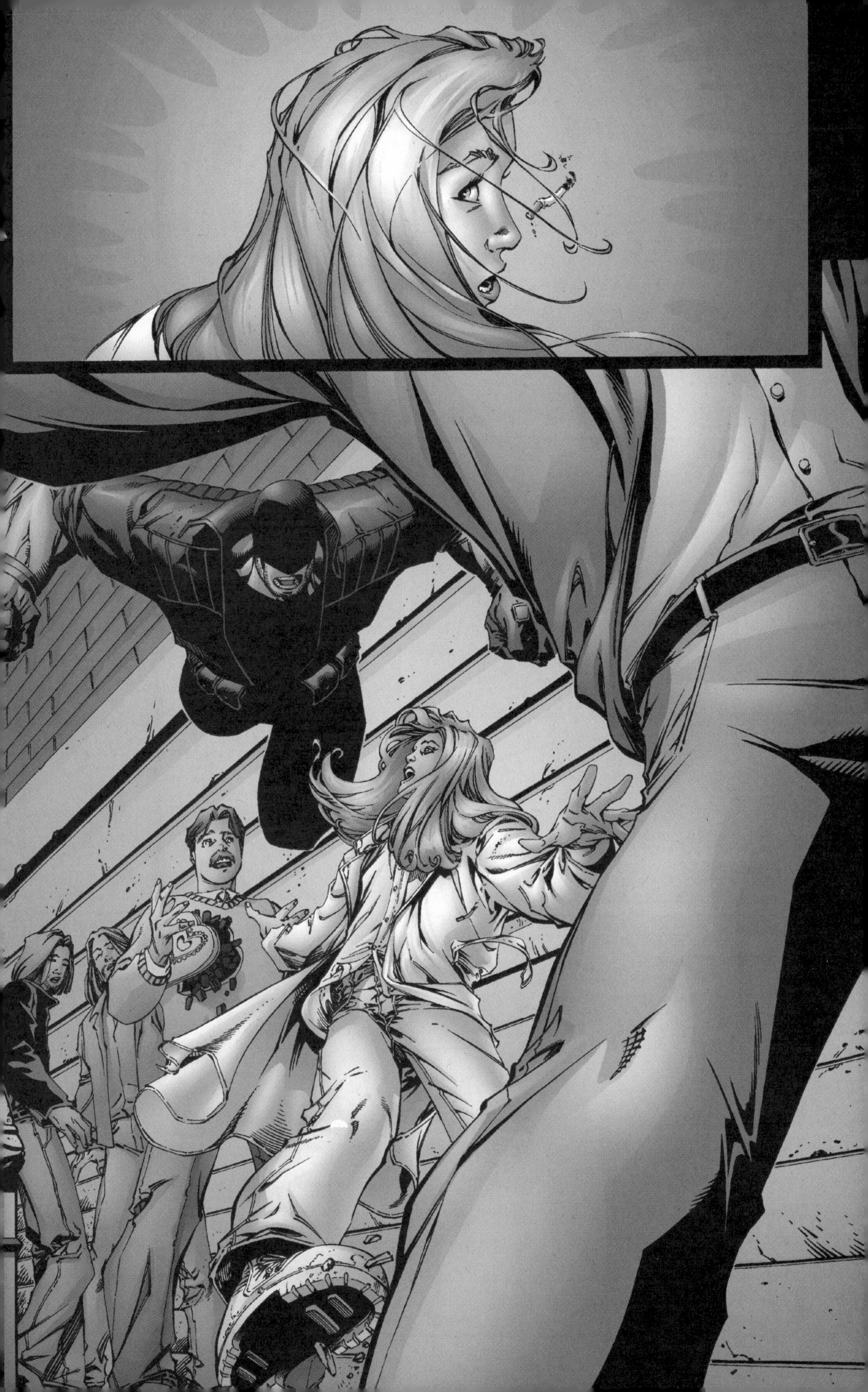

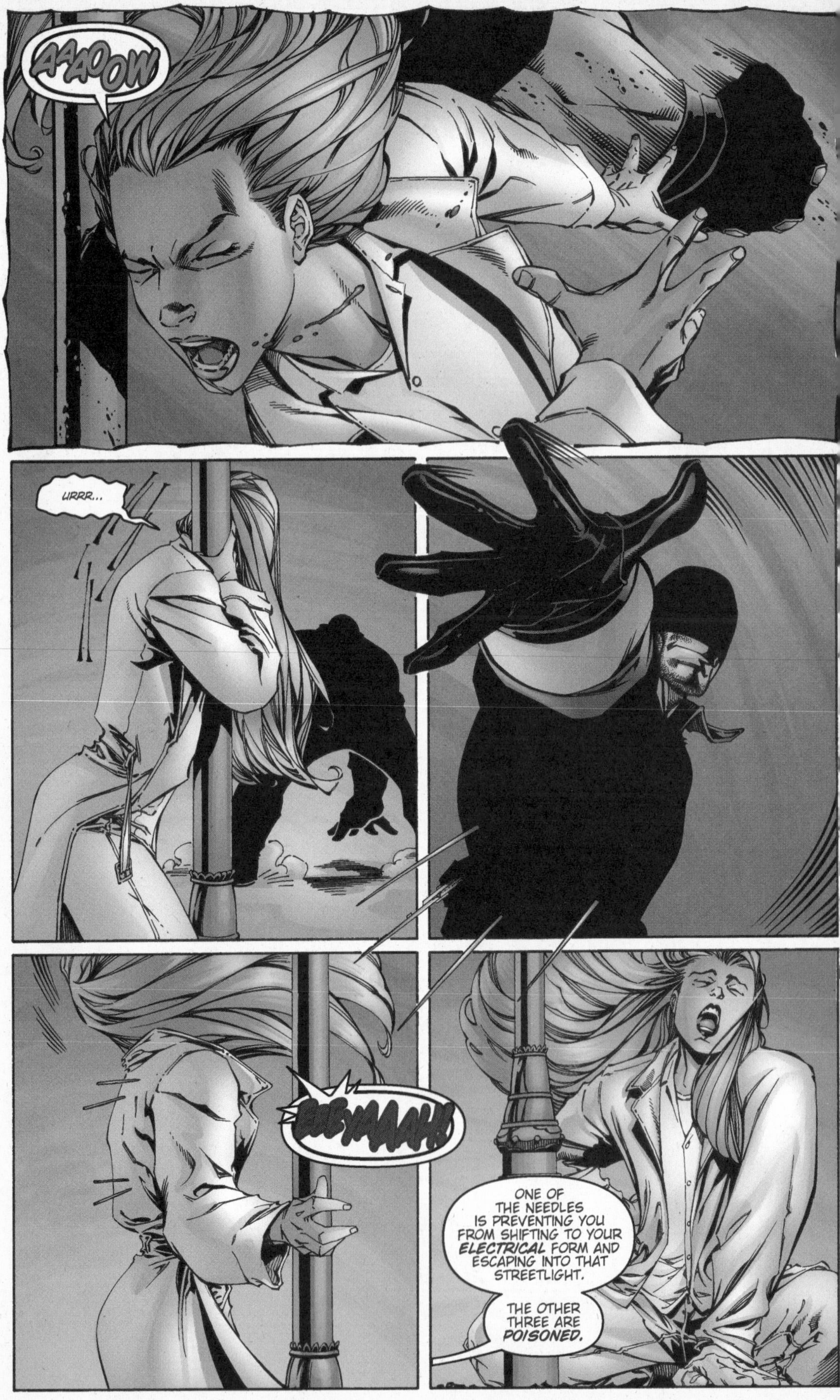
AAAOOW
URRR...
ONE OF THE NEEDLES IS PREVENTING YOU FROM SHIFTING TO YOUR ELECTRICAL FORM AND ESCAPING INTO THAT STREETLIGHT.
THE OTHER THREE ARE POISONED.

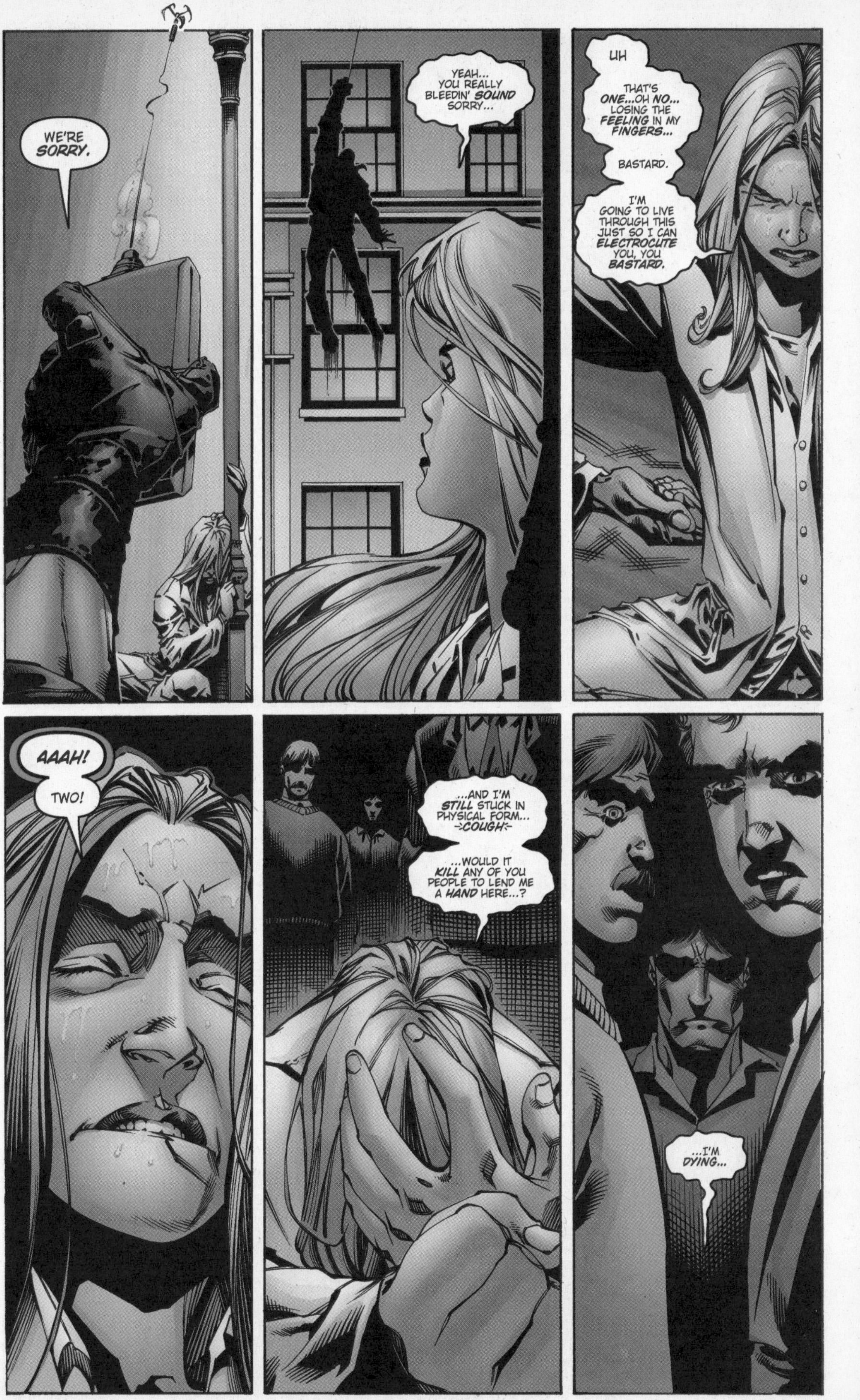
WE'RE SORRY.
YEAH... YOU REALLY BLEEDIN' SOUND SORRY...
UH
THAT'S ONE...OH NO... LOSING THE FEELING IN MY FINGERS...
BASTARD.
I'M GOING TO LIVE THROUGH THIS JUST SO I CAN ELECTROCUTE YOU, YOU BASTARD.
AAAH!
TWO!
...AND I'M STILL STUCK IN PHYSICAL FORM... -COUGH-
...WOULD IT KILL ANY OF YOU PEOPLE TO LEND ME A HAND HERE...?
...I'M DYING...

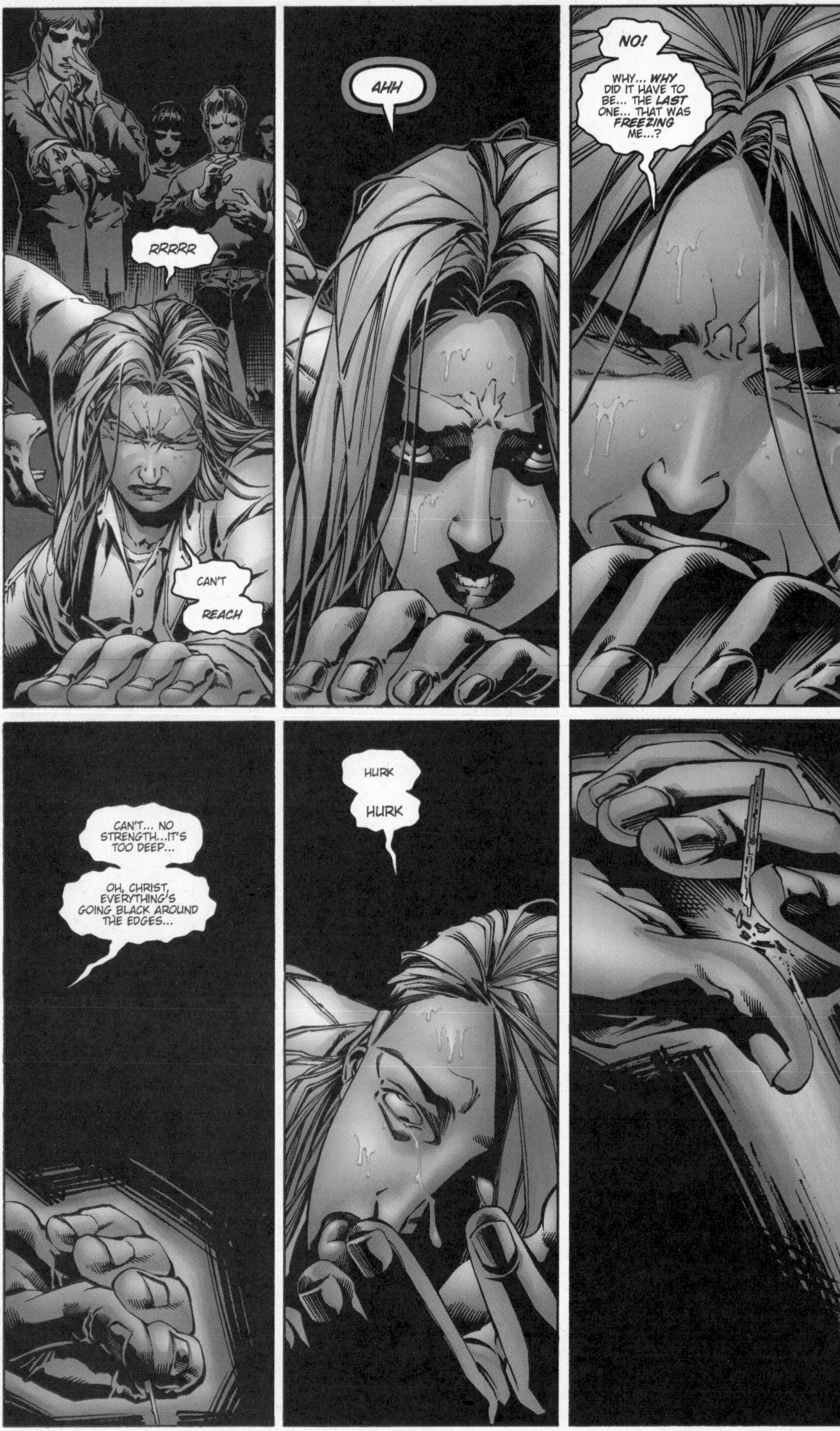
RRRRR
CAN'T
REACH
AHH
NO!
WHY... WHY DID IT HAVE TO BE... THE LAST ONE... THAT WAS FREEZING ME...?
CAN'T... NO STRENGTH...IT'S TOO DEEP...
OH, CHRIST, EVERYTHING'S GOING BLACK AROUND THE EDGES...
HURK
HURK

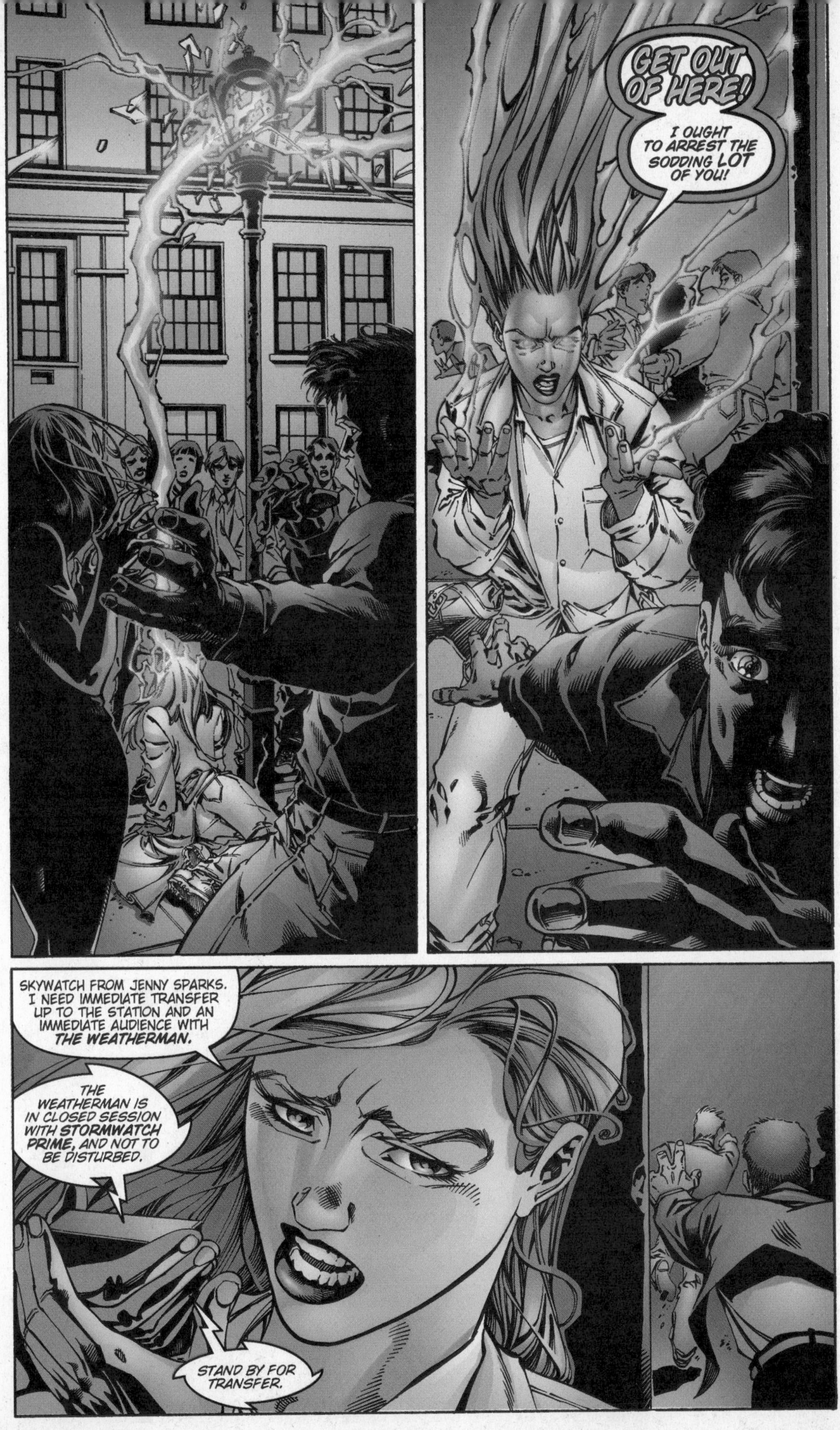
GET OUT OF HERE!
I OUGHT TO ARREST THE SODDING LOT OF YOU!
SKYWATCH FROM JENNY SPARKS. I NEED IMMEDIATE TRANSFER UP TO THE STATION AND AN IMMEDIATE AUDIENCE WITH THE WEATHERMAN.
THE WEATHERMAN IS IN CLOSED SESSION WITH STORMWATCH PRIME, AND NOT TO BE DISTURBED.
STAND BY FOR TRANSFER.

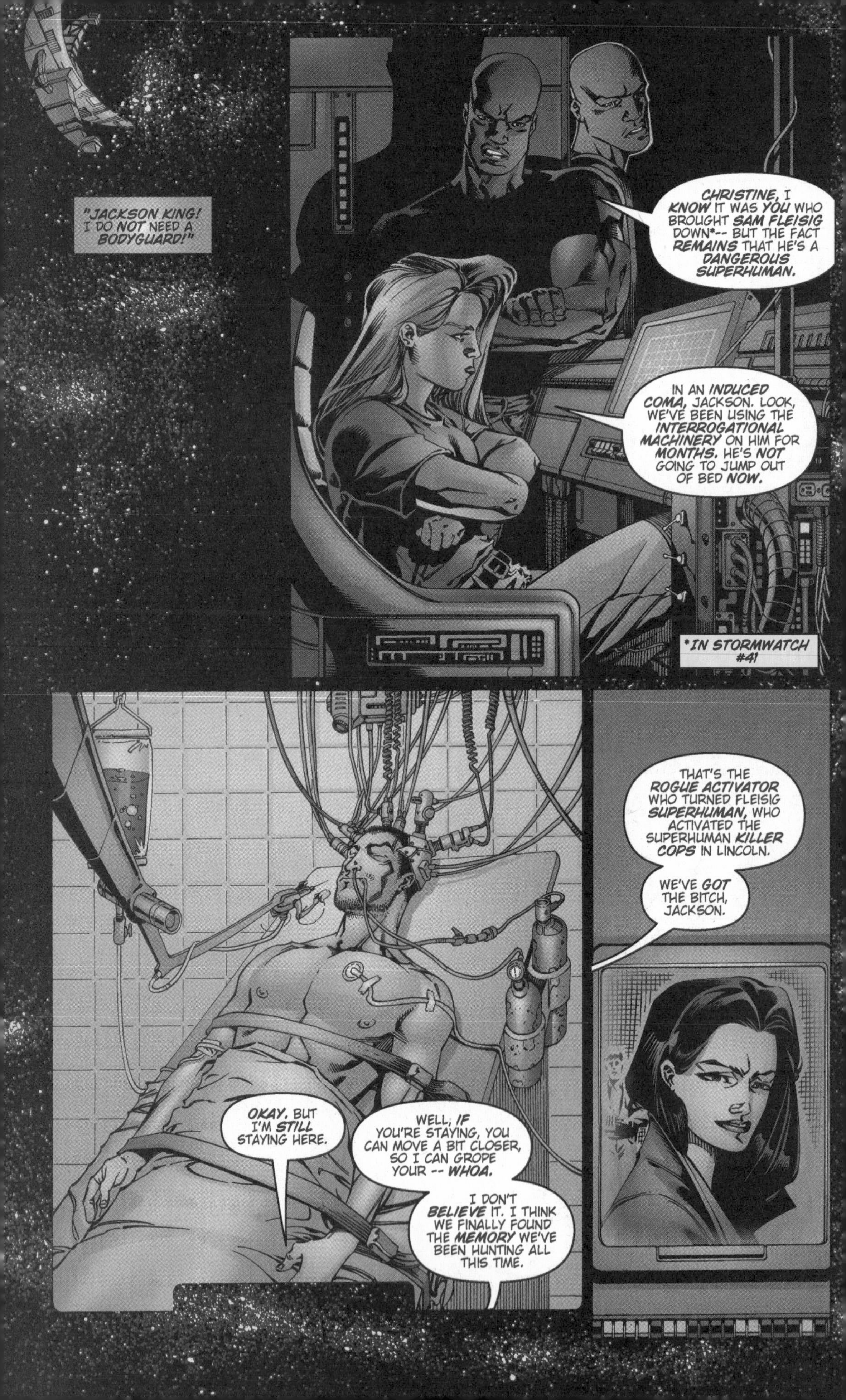
"JACKSON KING! I DO NOT NEED A BODYGUARD!"
CHRISTINE, I KNOW IT WAS YOU WHO BROUGHT SAM FLEISIG DOWN*-- BUT THE FACT REMAINS THAT HE'S A DANGEROUS SUPERHUMAN.
IN AN INDUCED COMA, JACKSON. LOOK, WE'VE BEEN USING THE INTERROGATIONAL MACHINERY ON HIM FOR MONTHS. HE'S NOT GOING TO JUMP OUT OF BED NOW.
*IN STORMWATCH #41
OKAY. BUT I'M STILL STAYING HERE.
WELL, IF YOU'RE STAYING, YOU CAN MOVE A BIT CLOSER, SO I CAN GROPE YOUR -- WHOA.
I DON'T BELIEVE IT. I THINK WE FINALLY FOUND THE MEMORY WE'VE BEEN HUNTING ALL THIS TIME.
THAT'S THE ROGUE ACTIVATOR WHO TURNED FLEISIG SUPERHUMAN, WHO ACTIVATED THE SUPERHUMAN KILLER COPS IN LINCOLN.
WE'VE GOT THE BITCH, JACKSON.

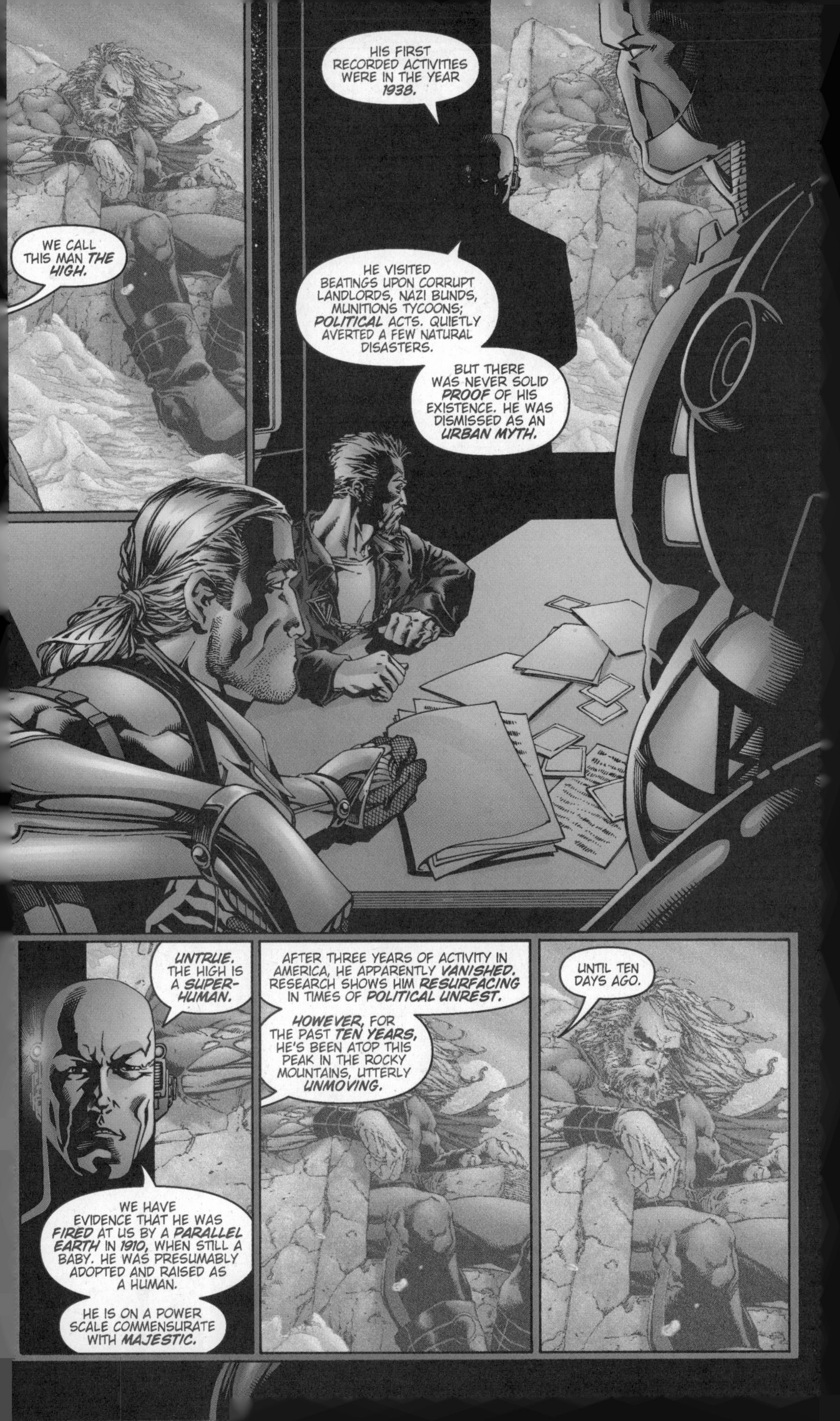

WE CALL THIS MAN THE HIGH.
HIS FIRST RECORDED ACTIVITIES WERE IN THE YEAR 1938.
HE VISITED BEATINGS UPON CORRUPT LANDLORDS, NAZI BUNDS, MUNITIONS TYCOONS; POLITICAL ACTS. QUIETLY AVERTED A FEW NATURAL DISASTERS.
BUT THERE WAS NEVER SOLID PROOF OF HIS EXISTENCE. HE WAS DISMISSED AS AN URBAN MYTH.
UNTRUE. THE HIGH IS A SUPER-HUMAN.
WE HAVE EVIDENCE THAT HE WAS FIRED AT US BY A PARALLEL EARTH IN 1910, WHEN STILL A BABY. HE WAS PRESUMABLY ADOPTED AND RAISED AS A HUMAN.
HE IS ON A POWER SCALE COMMENSURATE WITH MAJESTIC.
AFTER THREE YEARS OF ACTIVITY IN AMERICA, HE APPARENTLY VANISHED. RESEARCH SHOWS HIM RESURFACING IN TIMES OF POLITICAL UNREST.
HOWEVER, FOR THE PAST TEN YEARS, HE'S BEEN ATOP THIS PEAK IN THE ROCKY MOUNTAINS, UTTERLY UNMOVING.
UNTIL TEN DAYS AGO.

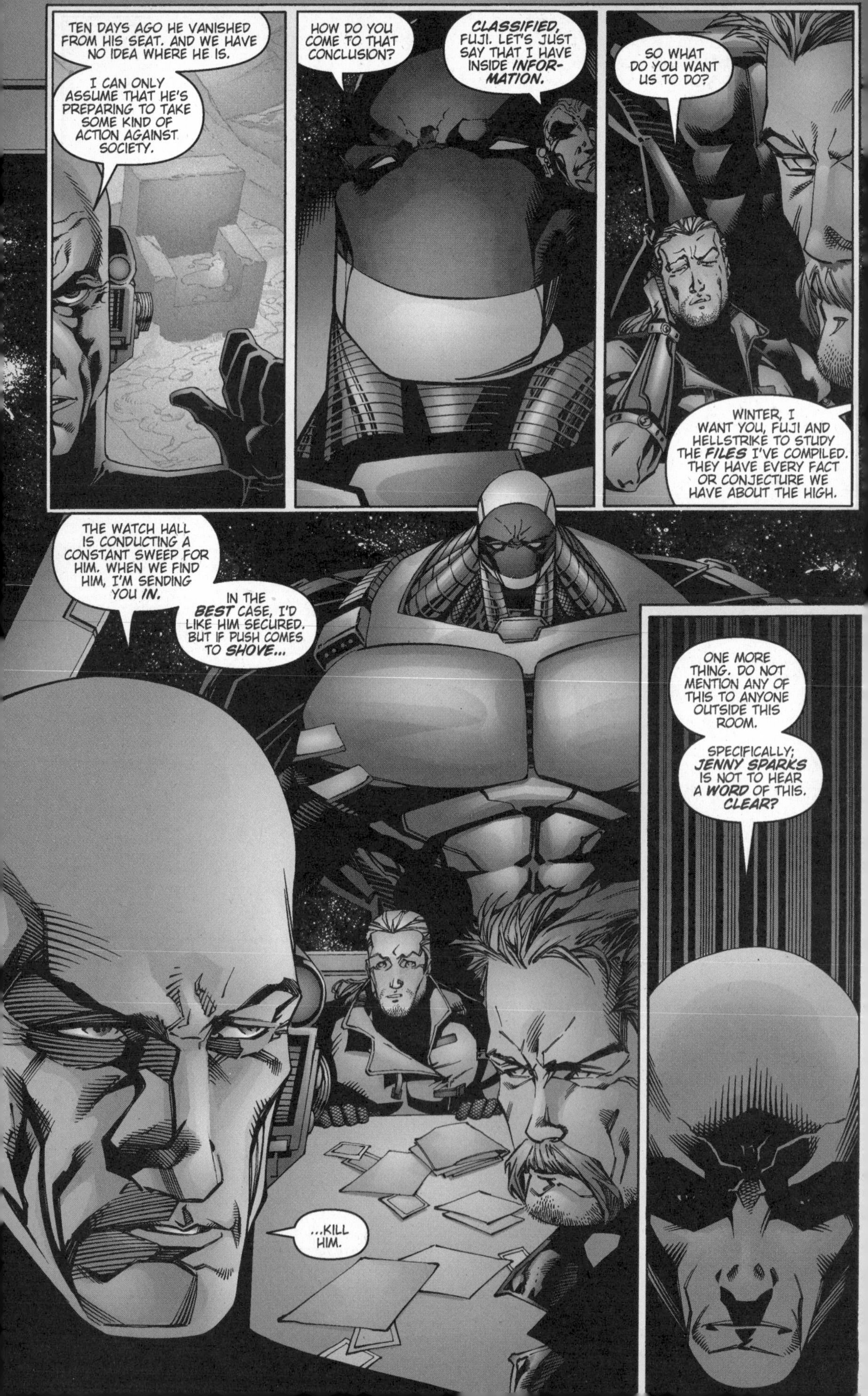
TEN DAYS AGO HE VANISHED FROM HIS SEAT. AND WE HAVE NO IDEA WHERE HE IS.
I CAN ONLY ASSUME THAT HE'S PREPARING TO TAKE SOME KIND OF ACTION AGAINST SOCIETY.
HOW DO YOU COME TO THAT CONCLUSION?
CLASSIFIED, FUJI. LET'S JUST SAY THAT I HAVE INSIDE INFORMATION.
SO WHAT DO YOU WANT US TO DO?
WINTER, I WANT YOU, FUJI AND HELLSTRIKE TO STUDY THE FILES I'VE COMPILED. THEY HAVE EVERY FACT OR CONJECTURE WE HAVE ABOUT THE HIGH.
THE WATCH HALL IS CONDUCTING A CONSTANT SWEEP FOR HIM. WHEN WE FIND HIM, I'M SENDING YOU IN.
IN THE BEST CASE, I'D LIKE HIM SECURED. BUT IF PUSH COMES TO SHOVE...
...KILL HIM.
ONE MORE THING. DO NOT MENTION ANY OF THIS TO ANYONE OUTSIDE THIS ROOM.
SPECIFICALLY; JENNY SPARKS IS NOT TO HEAR A WORD OF THIS. CLEAR?

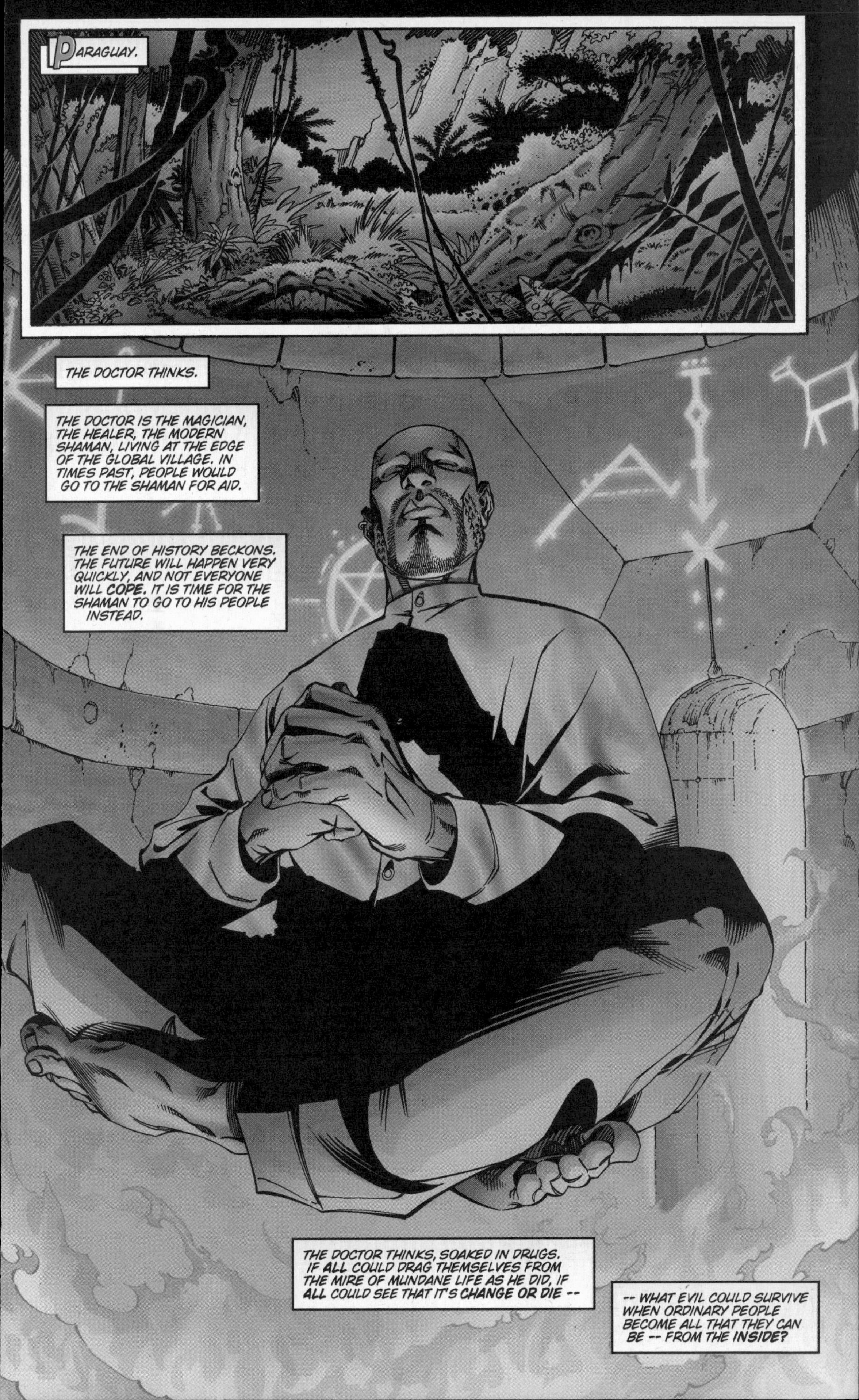
PARAGUAY.
THE DOCTOR THINKS.
THE DOCTOR IS THE MAGICIAN, THE HEALER, THE MODERN SHAMAN, LIVING AT THE EDGE OF THE GLOBAL VILLAGE. IN TIMES PAST, PEOPLE WOULD GO TO THE SHAMAN FOR AID.
THE END OF HISTORY BECKONS. THE FUTURE WILL HAPPEN VERY QUICKLY, AND NOT EVERYONE WILL COPE. IT IS TIME FOR THE SHAMAN TO GO TO HIS PEOPLE INSTEAD.
THE DOCTOR THINKS, SOAKED IN DRUGS. IF ALL COULD DRAG THEMSELVES FROM THE MIRE OF MUNDANE LIFE AS HE DID, IF ALL COULD SEE THAT IT'S CHANGE OR DIE --
-- WHAT EVIL COULD SURVIVE WHEN ORDINARY PEOPLE BECOME ALL THAT THEY CAN BE -- FROM THE INSIDE?

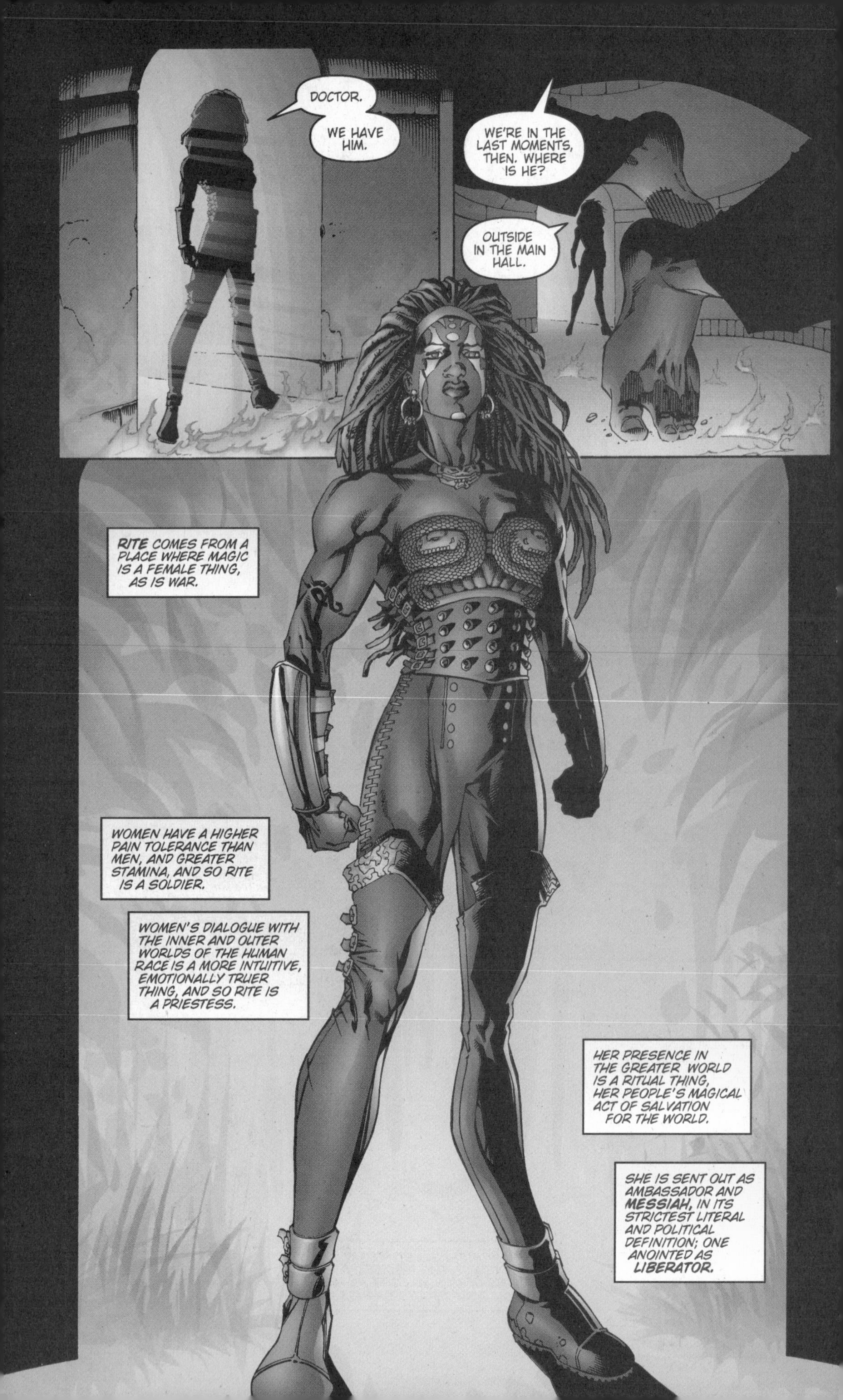
DOCTOR.
WE HAVE HIM.
WE'RE IN THE LAST MOMENTS, THEN. WHERE IS HE?
OUTSIDE IN THE MAIN HALL.
RITE COMES FROM A PLACE WHERE MAGIC IS A FEMALE THING, AS IS WAR.
WOMEN HAVE A HIGHER PAIN TOLERANCE THAN MEN, AND GREATER STAMINA, AND SO RITE IS A SOLDIER.
WOMEN'S DIALOGUE WITH THE INNER AND OUTER WORLDS OF THE HUMAN RACE IS A MORE INTUITIVE, EMOTIONALLY TRUER THING, AND SO RITE IS A PRIESTESS.
HER PRESENCE IN THE GREATER WORLD IS A RITUAL THING, HER PEOPLE'S MAGICAL ACT OF SALVATION FOR THE WORLD.
SHE IS SENT OUT AS AMBASSADOR AND MESSIAH, IN ITS STRICTEST LITERAL AND POLITICAL DEFINITION; ONE ANOINTED AS LIBERATOR.

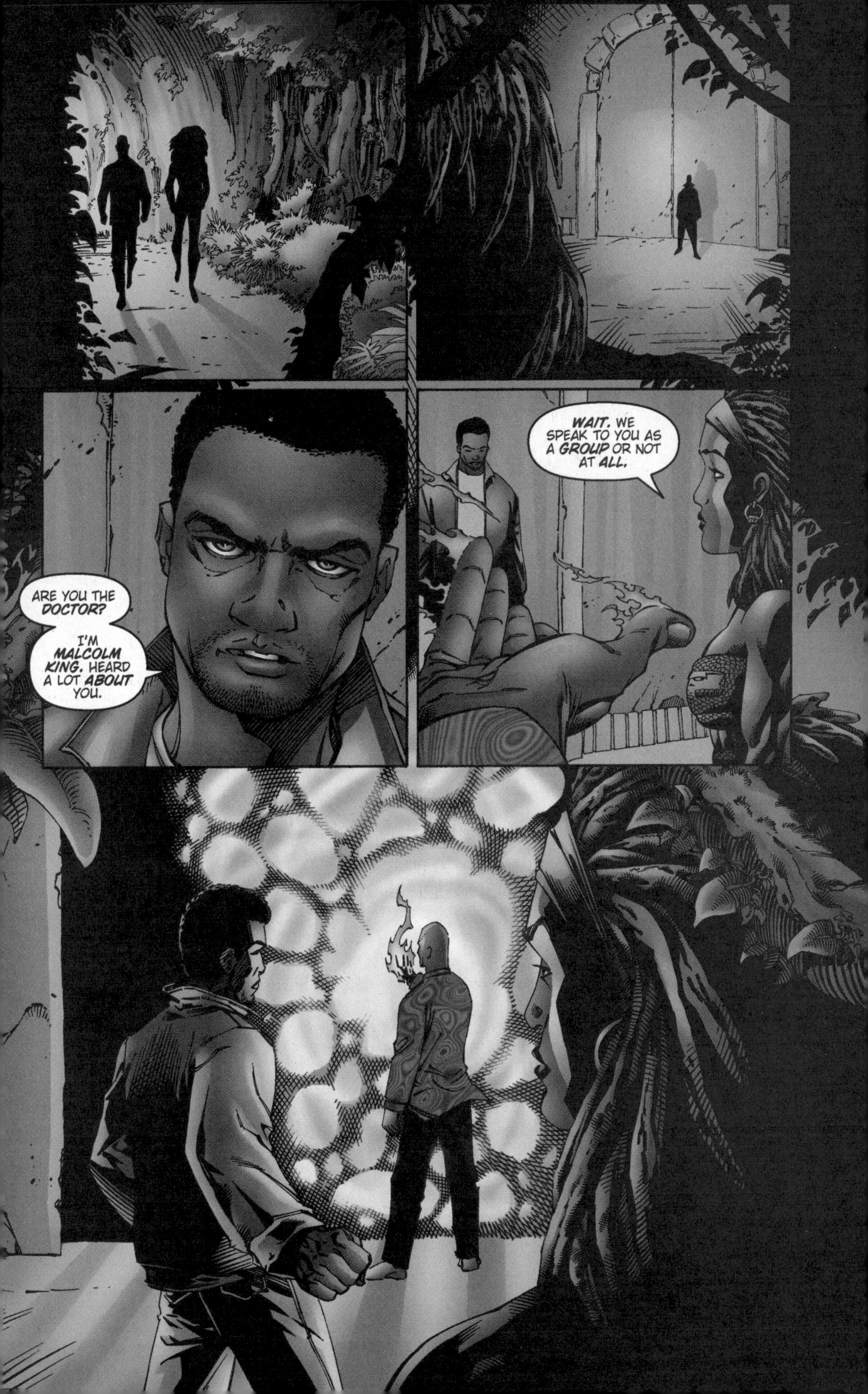
ARE YOU THE DOCTOR?
I'M MALCOLM KING. HEARD A LOT ABOUT YOU.
WAIT. WE SPEAK TO YOU AS A GROUP OR NOT AT ALL.

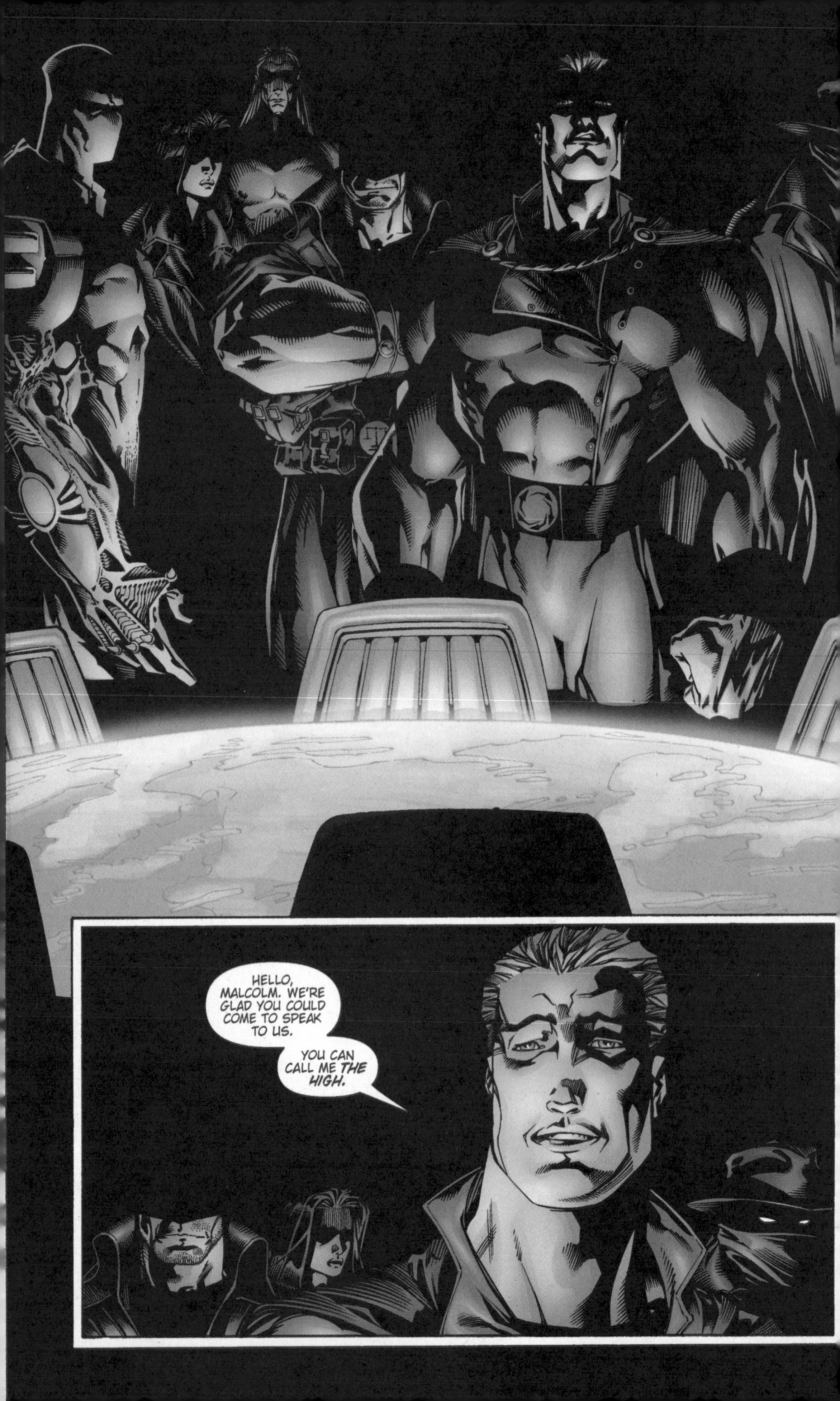
HELLO, MALCOLM. WE'RE GLAD YOU COULD COME TO SPEAK TO US.
YOU CAN CALL ME THE HIGH.

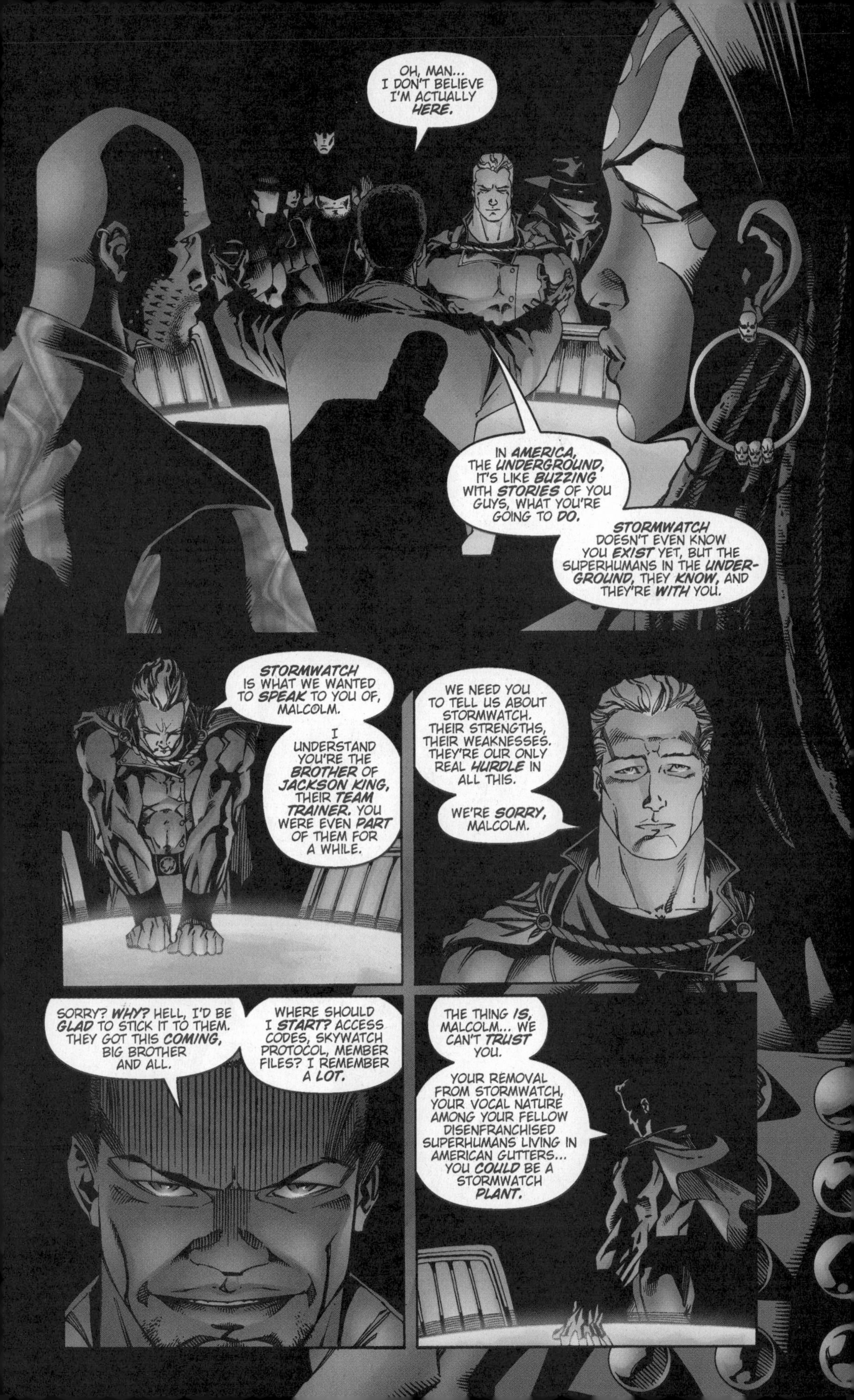

OH, MAN... I DON'T BELIEVE I'M ACTUALLY HERE.
IN AMERICA, THE UNDERGROUND, IT'S LIKE BUZZING WITH STORIES OF YOU GUYS, WHAT YOU'RE GOING TO DO.
STORMWATCH DOESN'T EVEN KNOW YOU EXIST YET, BUT THE SUPERHUMANS IN THE UNDER-GROUND, THEY KNOW, AND THEY'RE WITH YOU.
STORMWATCH IS WHAT WE WANTED TO SPEAK TO YOU OF, MALCOLM.
I UNDERSTAND YOU'RE THE BROTHER OF JACKSON KING, THEIR TEAM TRAINER. YOU WERE EVEN PART OF THEM FOR A WHILE.
WE NEED YOU TO TELL US ABOUT STORMWATCH. THEIR STRENGTHS, THEIR WEAKNESSES. THEY'RE OUR ONLY REAL HURDLE IN ALL THIS.
WE'RE SORRY, MALCOLM.
SORRY? WHY? HELL, I'D BE GLAD TO STICK IT TO THEM. THEY GOT THIS COMING, BIG BROTHER AND ALL.
WHERE SHOULD I START? ACCESS CODES, SKYWATCH PROTOCOL, MEMBER FILES? I REMEMBER A LOT.
THE THING IS, MALCOLM... WE CAN'T TRUST YOU.
YOUR REMOVAL FROM STORMWATCH, YOUR VOCAL NATURE AMONG YOUR FELLOW DISENFRANCHISED SUPERHUMANS LIVING IN AMERICAN GUTTERS... YOU COULD BE A STORMWATCH PLANT.

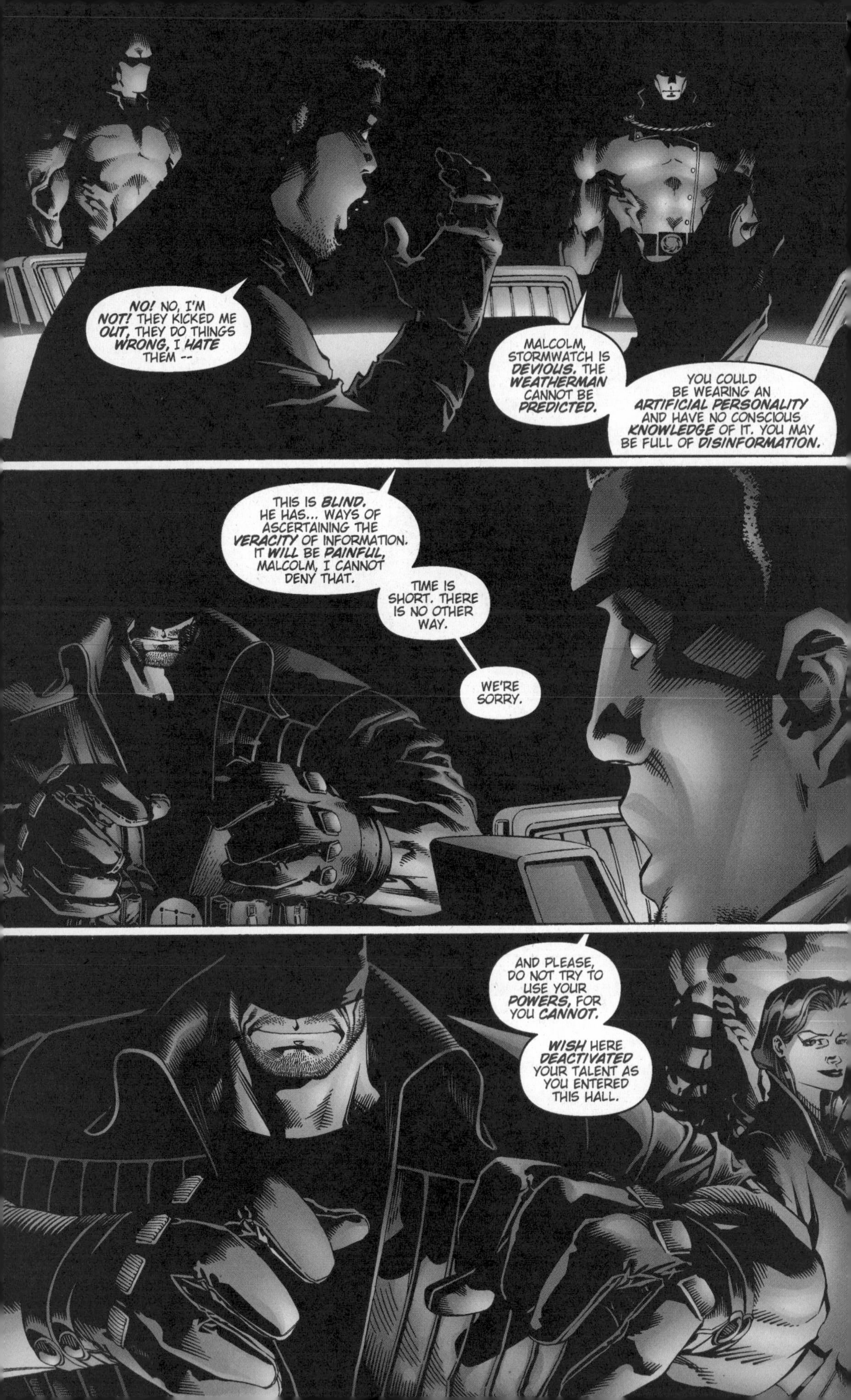
NO! NO, I'M NOT! THEY KICKED ME OUT, THEY DO THINGS WRONG, I HATE THEM --
MALCOLM, STORMWATCH IS DEVIOUS. THE WEATHERMAN CANNOT BE PREDICTED.
YOU COULD BE WEARING AN ARTIFICIAL PERSONALITY AND HAVE NO CONSCIOUS KNOWLEDGE OF IT. YOU MAY BE FULL OF DISINFORMATION.
THIS IS BLIND. HE HAS... WAYS OF ASCERTAINING THE VERACITY OF INFORMATION. IT WILL BE PAINFUL, MALCOLM, I CANNOT DENY THAT.
TIME IS SHORT. THERE IS NO OTHER WAY.
WE'RE SORRY.
AND PLEASE, DO NOT TRY TO USE YOUR POWERS, FOR YOU CANNOT.
WISH HERE DEACTIVATED YOUR TALENT AS YOU ENTERED THIS HALL.

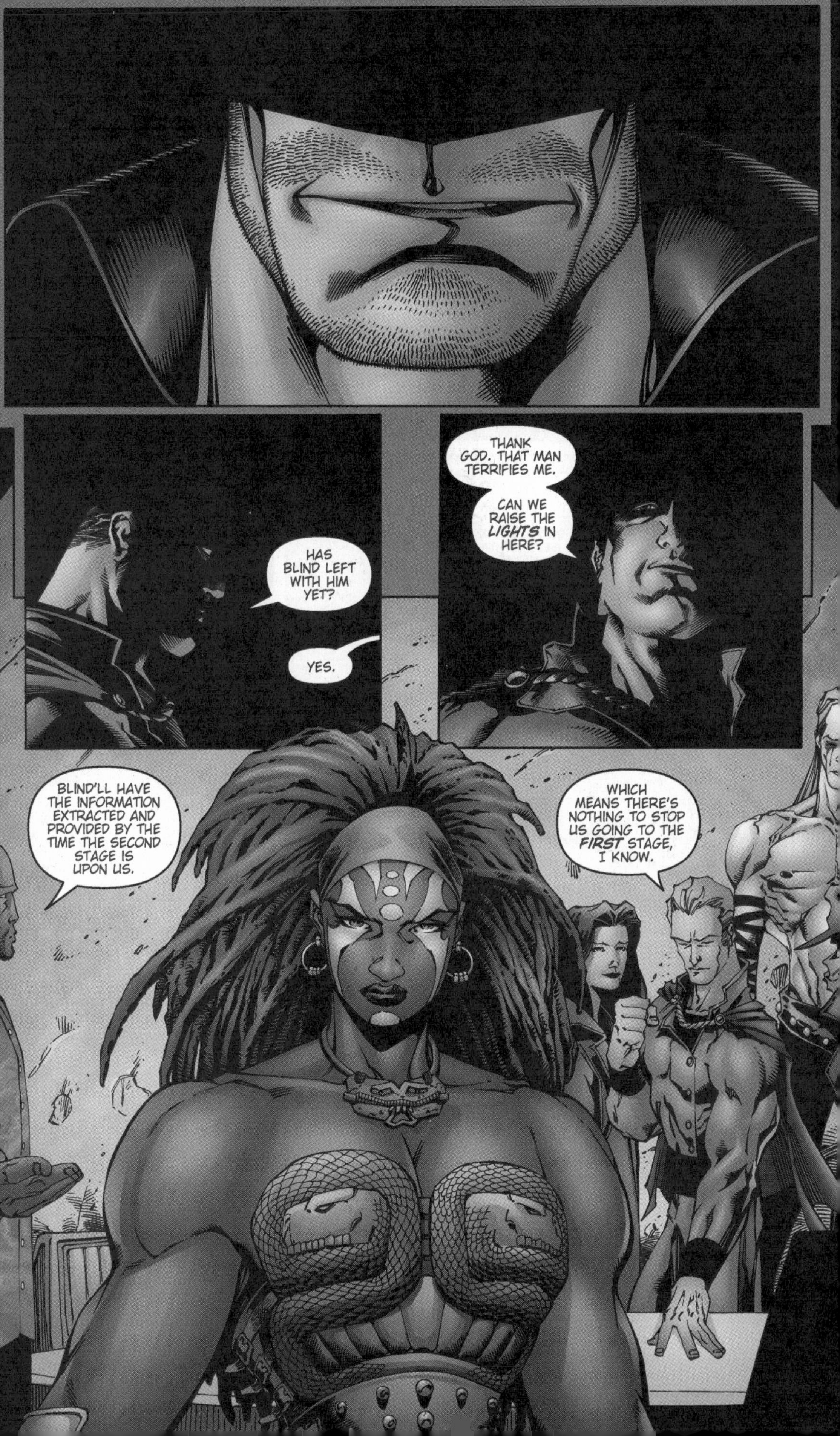
HAS BLIND LEFT WITH HIM YET?
YES.
THANK GOD. THAT MAN TERRIFIES ME.
CAN WE RAISE THE LIGHTS IN HERE?
BLIND'LL HAVE THE INFORMATION EXTRACTED AND PROVIDED BY THE TIME THE SECOND STAGE IS UPON US.
WHICH MEANS THERE'S NOTHING TO STOP US GOING TO THE FIRST STAGE, I KNOW.

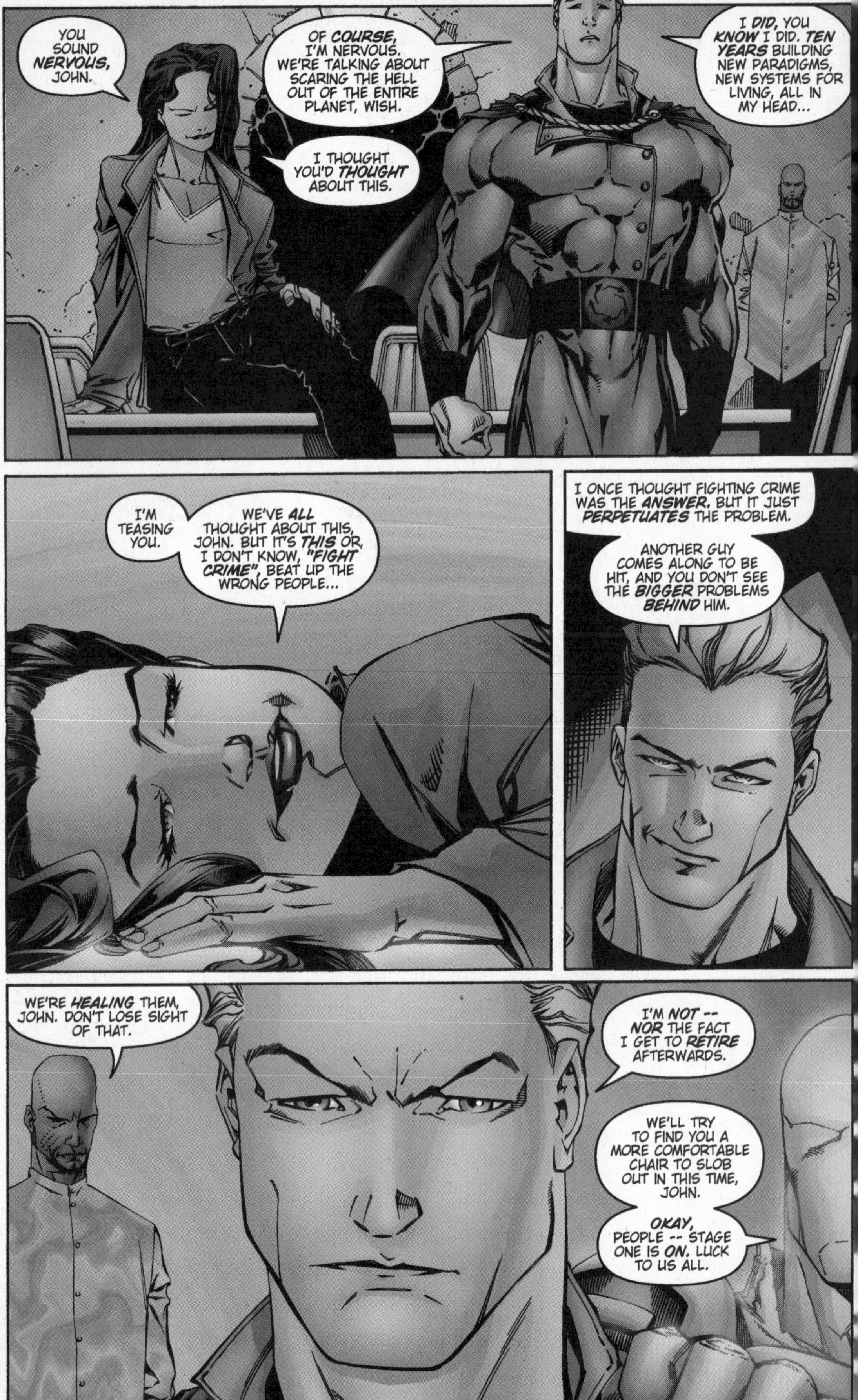
YOU SOUND NERVOUS, JOHN.
OF COURSE, I'M NERVOUS. WE'RE TALKING ABOUT SCARING THE HELL OUT OF THE ENTIRE PLANET, WISH.
I THOUGHT YOU'D THOUGHT ABOUT THIS.
I DID, YOU KNOW I DID. TEN YEARS BUILDING NEW PARADIGMS, NEW SYSTEMS FOR LIVING, ALL IN MY HEAD...
I'M TEASING YOU.
WE'VE ALL THOUGHT ABOUT THIS, JOHN. BUT IT'S THIS OR, I DON'T KNOW, "FIGHT CRIME", BEAT UP THE WRONG PEOPLE...
I ONCE THOUGHT FIGHTING CRIME WAS THE ANSWER. BUT IT JUST PERPETUATES THE PROBLEM.
ANOTHER GUY COMES ALONG TO BE HIT, AND YOU DON'T SEE THE BIGGER PROBLEMS BEHIND HIM.
WE'RE HEALING THEM, JOHN. DON'T LOSE SIGHT OF THAT.
I'M NOT -- NOR THE FACT I GET TO RETIRE AFTERWARDS.
WE'LL TRY TO FIND YOU A MORE COMFORTABLE CHAIR TO SLOB OUT IN THIS TIME, JOHN.
OKAY, PEOPLE -- STAGE ONE IS ON. LUCK TO US ALL.

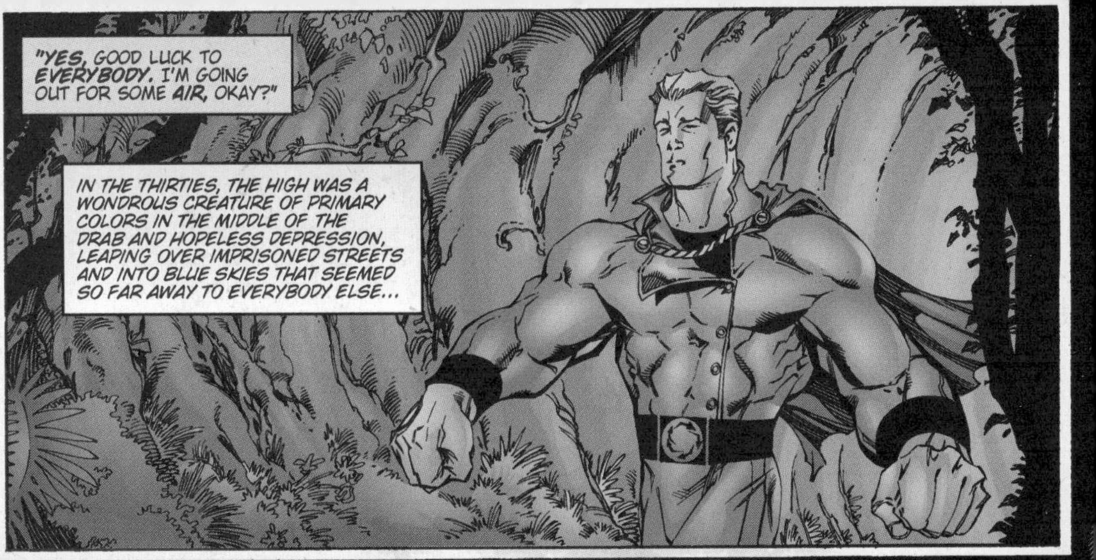
"YES, GOOD LUCK TO EVERYBODY. I'M GOING OUT FOR SOME AIR, OKAY?"
IN THE THIRTIES, THE HIGH WAS A WONDROUS CREATURE OF PRIMARY COLORS IN THE MIDDLE OF THE DRAB AND HOPELESS DEPRESSION, LEAPING OVER IMPRISONED STREETS AND INTO BLUE SKIES THAT SEEMED SO FAR AWAY TO EVERYBODY ELSE...

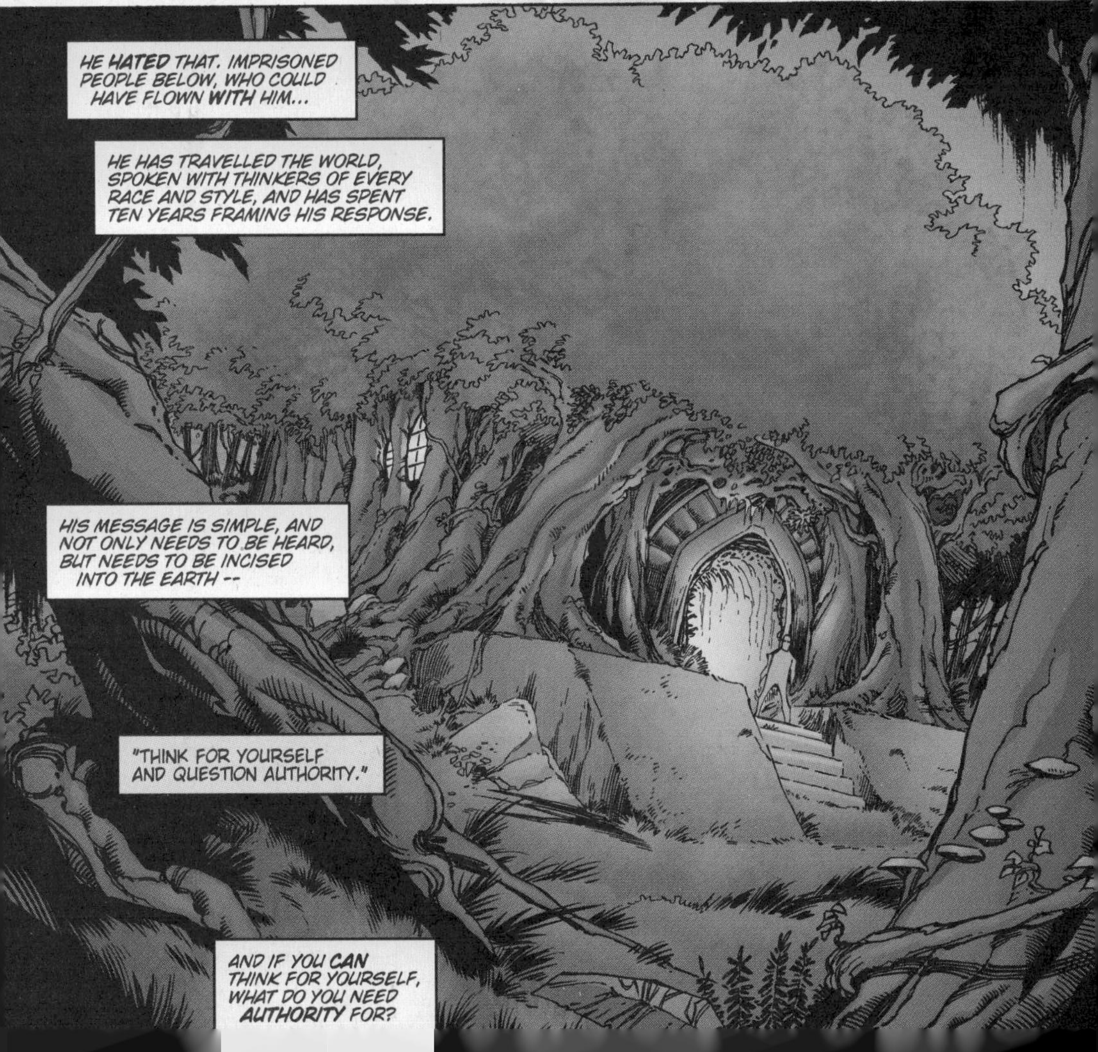
HE HATED THAT. IMPRISONED PEOPLE BELOW, WHO COULD HAVE FLOWN WITH HIM...
HE HAS TRAVELLED THE WORLD, SPOKEN WITH THINKERS OF EVERY RACE AND STYLE, AND HAS SPENT TEN YEARS FRAMING HIS RESPONSE.
HIS MESSAGE IS SIMPLE, AND NOT ONLY NEEDS TO BE HEARD, BUT NEEDS TO BE INCISED INTO THE EARTH --
"THINK FOR YOURSELF AND QUESTION AUTHORITY."
AND IF YOU CAN THINK FOR YOURSELF, WHAT DO YOU NEED AUTHORITY FOR?

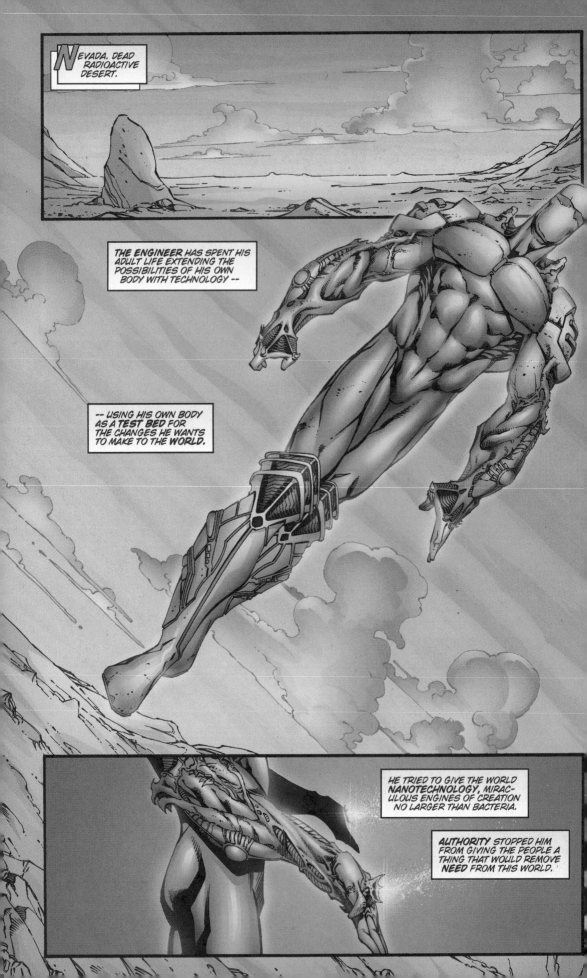

NEVADA. DEAD RADIOACTIVE DESERT.

THE ENGINEER HAS SPENT HIS ADULT LIFE EXTENDING THE POSSIBILITIES OF HIS OWN BODY WITH TECHNOLOGY --

-- USING HIS OWN BODY AS A TEST BED FOR THE CHANGES HE WANTS TO MAKE TO THE WORLD.

HE TRIED TO GIVE THE WORLD NANOTECHNOLOGY, MIRACULOUS ENGINES OF CREATION NO LARGER THAN BACTERIA.

AUTHORITY STOPPED HIM FROM GIVING THE PEOPLE A THING THAT WOULD REMOVE NEED FROM THIS WORLD.

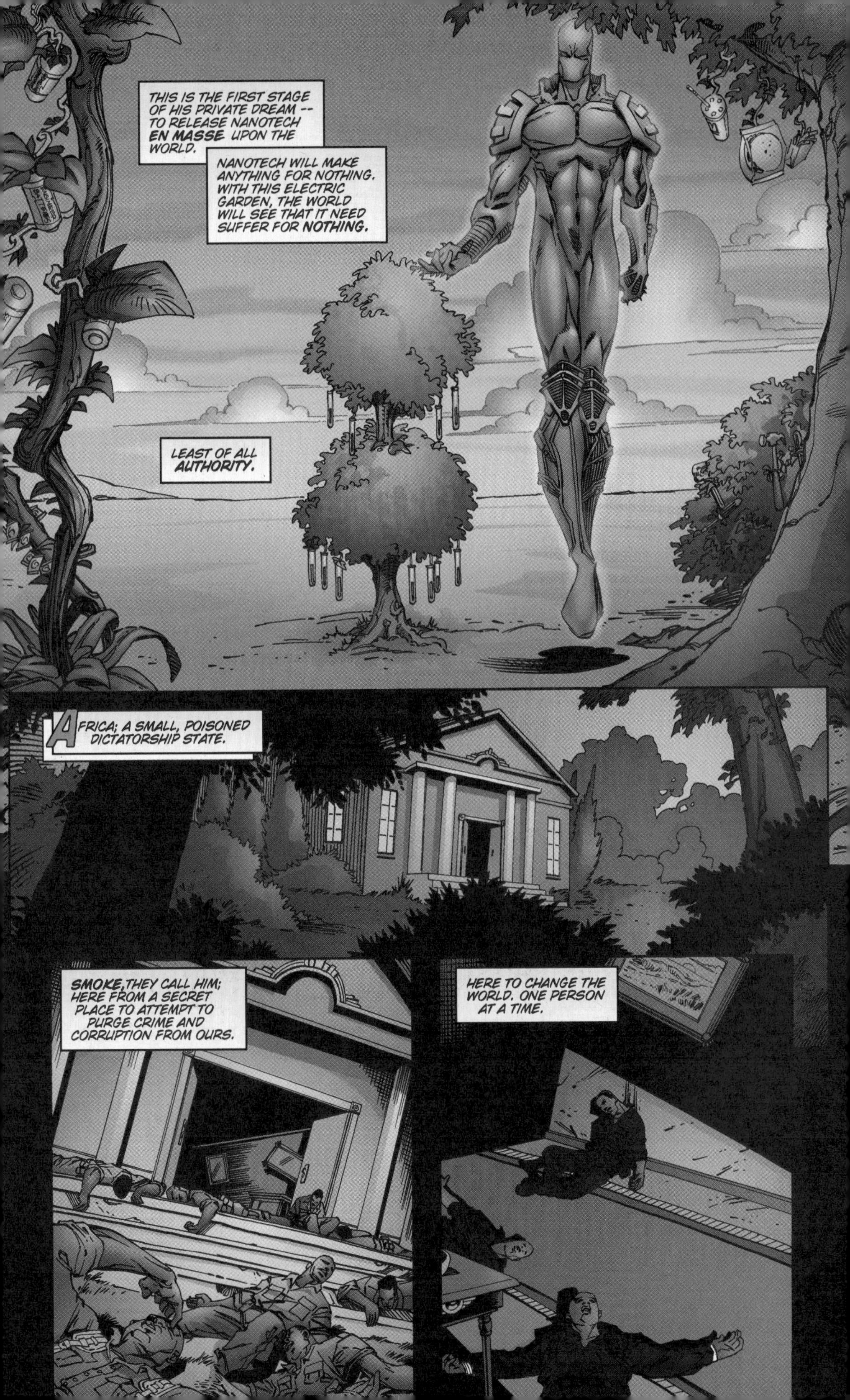
THIS IS THE FIRST STAGE OF HIS PRIVATE DREAM -- TO RELEASE NANOTECH **EN MASSE** UPON THE WORLD.
NANOTECH WILL MAKE ANYTHING FOR NOTHING. WITH THIS ELECTRIC GARDEN, THE WORLD WILL SEE THAT IT NEED SUFFER FOR **NOTHING**.
LEAST OF ALL **AUTHORITY**.
AFRICA; A SMALL, POISONED DICTATORSHIP STATE.
SMOKE, THEY CALL HIM; HERE FROM A SECRET PLACE TO ATTEMPT TO PURGE CRIME AND CORRUPTION FROM OURS.
HERE TO CHANGE THE WORLD. ONE PERSON AT A TIME.

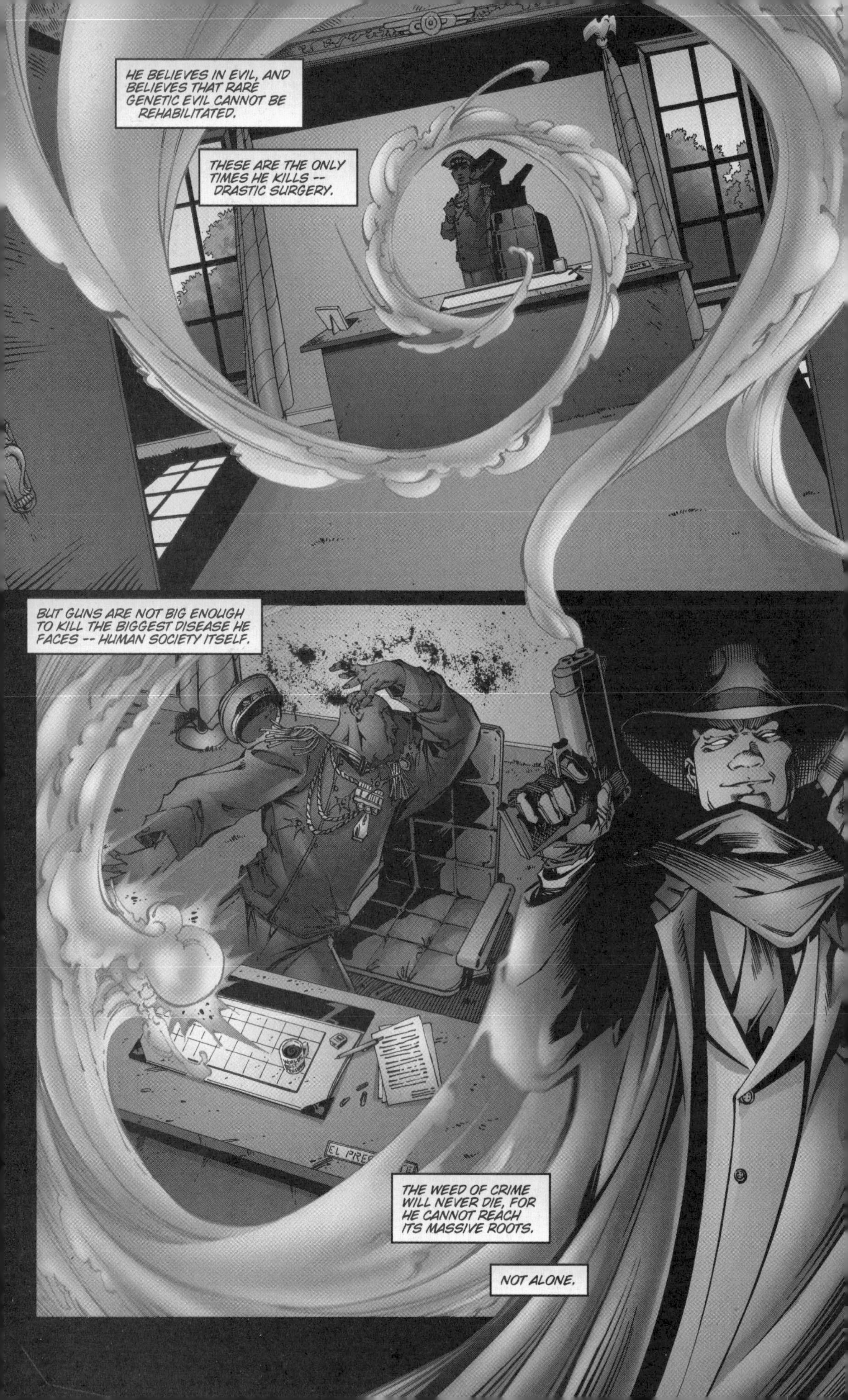
HE BELIEVES IN EVIL, AND BELIEVES THAT RARE GENETIC EVIL CANNOT BE REHABILITATED.
THESE ARE THE ONLY TIMES HE KILLS -- DRASTIC SURGERY.
BUT GUNS ARE NOT BIG ENOUGH TO KILL THE BIGGEST DISEASE HE FACES -- HUMAN SOCIETY ITSELF.
THE WEED OF CRIME WILL NEVER DIE, FOR HE CANNOT REACH ITS MASSIVE ROOTS.
NOT ALONE.

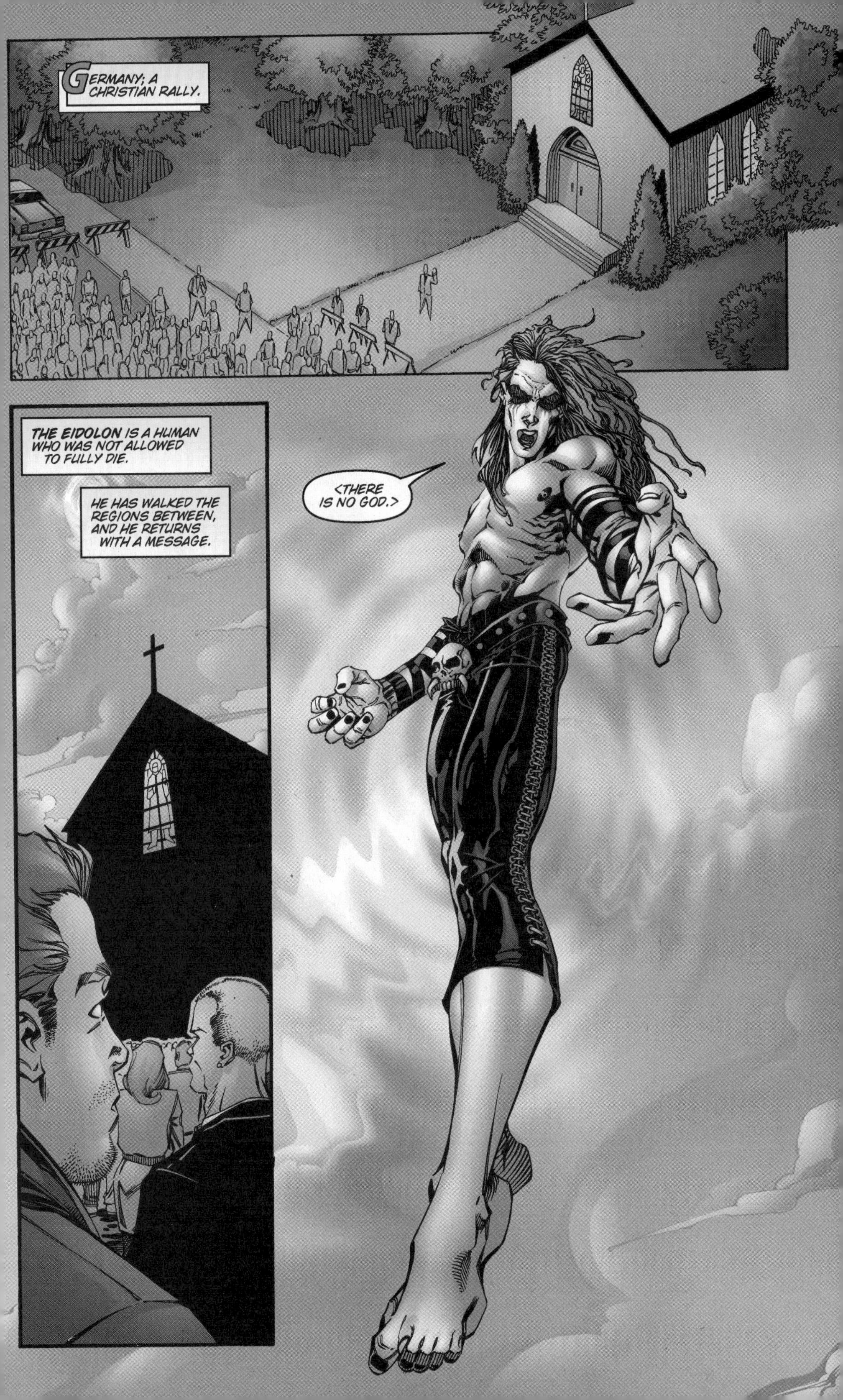
GERMANY; A CHRISTIAN RALLY.
THE EIDOLON IS A HUMAN WHO WAS NOT ALLOWED TO FULLY DIE.
HE HAS WALKED THE REGIONS BETWEEN, AND HE RETURNS WITH A MESSAGE.
<THERE IS NO GOD.>

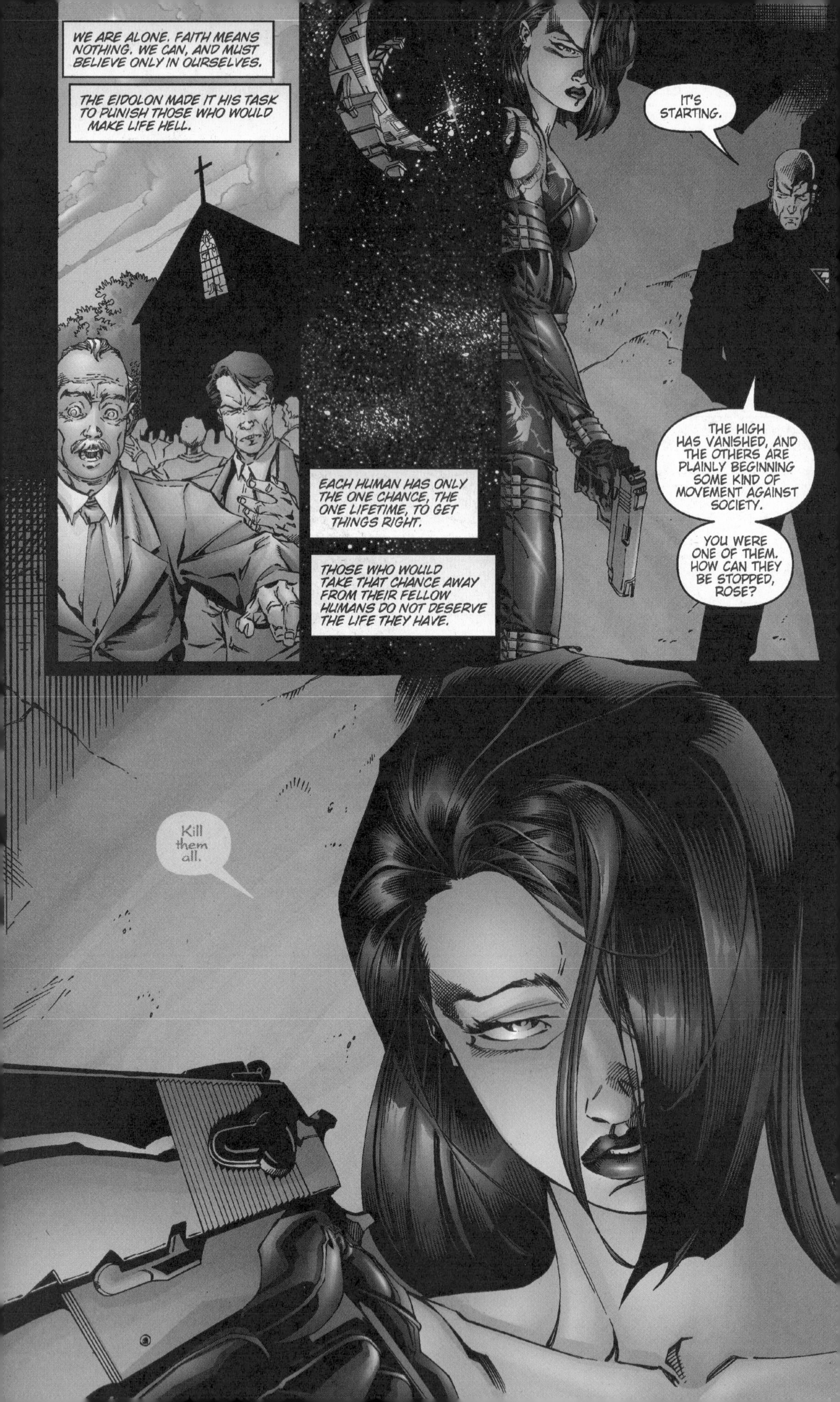
WE ARE ALONE. FAITH MEANS NOTHING. WE CAN, AND MUST BELIEVE ONLY IN OURSELVES.
THE EIDOLON MADE IT HIS TASK TO PUNISH THOSE WHO WOULD MAKE LIFE HELL.
EACH HUMAN HAS ONLY THE ONE CHANCE, THE ONE LIFETIME, TO GET THINGS RIGHT.
THOSE WHO WOULD TAKE THAT CHANCE AWAY FROM THEIR FELLOW HUMANS DO NOT DESERVE THE LIFE THEY HAVE.
IT'S STARTING.
THE HIGH HAS VANISHED, AND THE OTHERS ARE PLAINLY BEGINNING SOME KIND OF MOVEMENT AGAINST SOCIETY.
YOU WERE ONE OF THEM. HOW CAN THEY BE STOPPED, ROSE?
Kill them all.

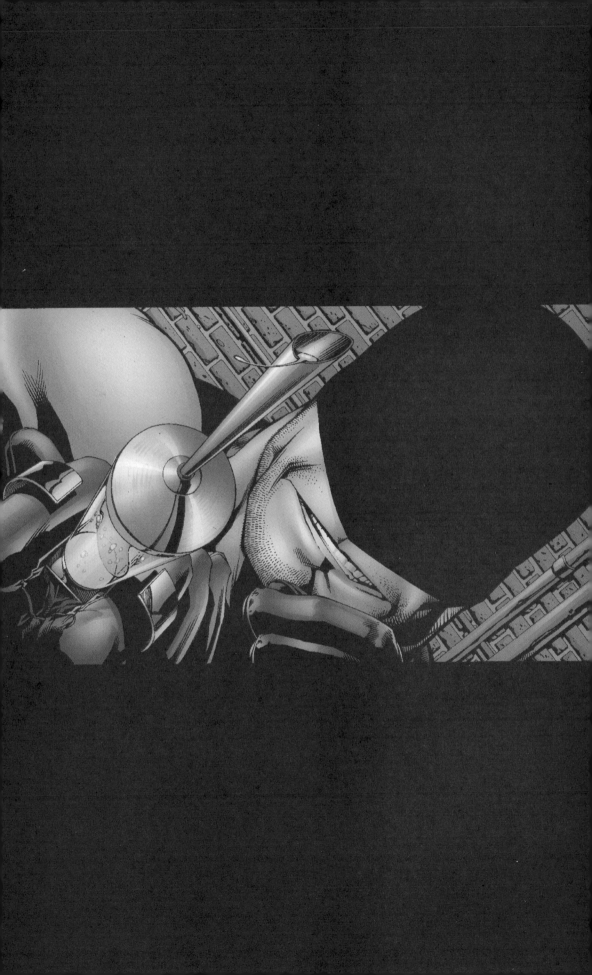

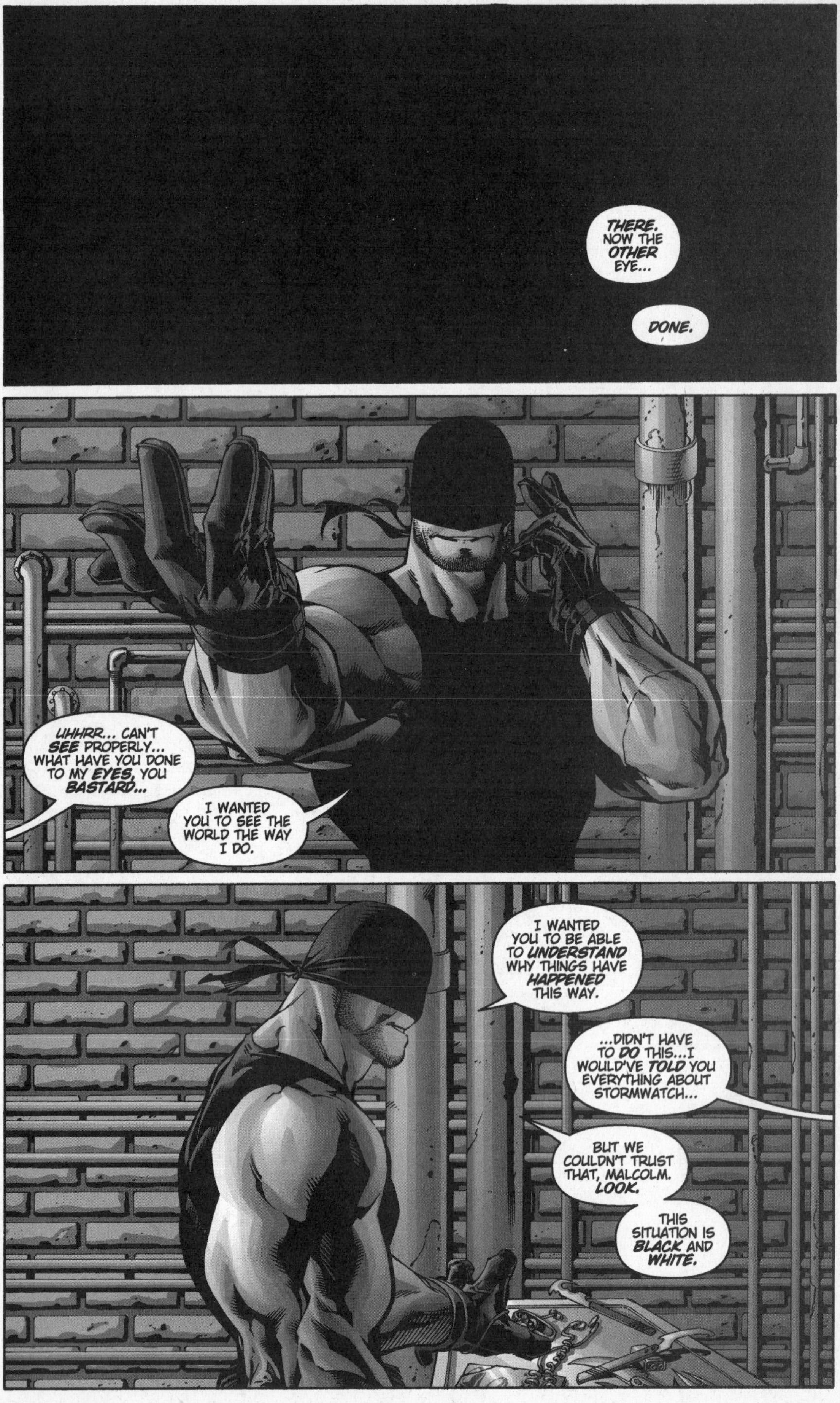

THERE. NOW THE OTHER EYE...
DONE.
UHHRR... CAN'T SEE PROPERLY... WHAT HAVE YOU DONE TO MY EYES, YOU BASTARD...
I WANTED YOU TO SEE THE WORLD THE WAY I DO.
I WANTED YOU TO BE ABLE TO UNDERSTAND WHY THINGS HAVE HAPPENED THIS WAY.
...DIDN'T HAVE TO DO THIS...I WOULD'VE TOLD YOU EVERYTHING ABOUT STORMWATCH...
BUT WE COULDN'T TRUST THAT, MALCOLM. LOOK.
THIS SITUATION IS BLACK AND WHITE.

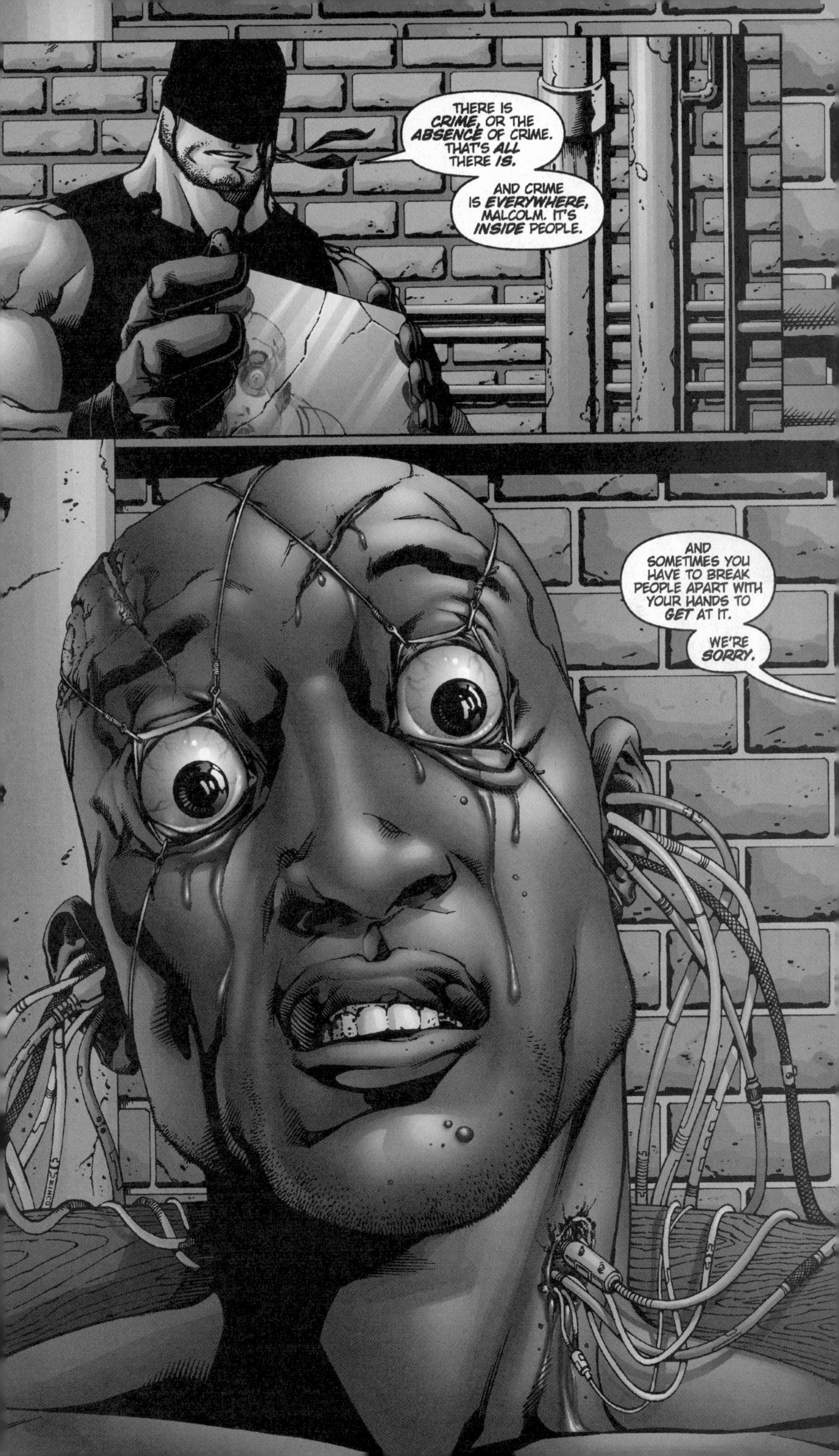
THERE IS CRIME, OR THE ABSENCE OF CRIME. THAT'S ALL THERE IS.
AND CRIME IS EVERYWHERE, MALCOLM. IT'S INSIDE PEOPLE.
AND SOMETIMES YOU HAVE TO BREAK PEOPLE APART WITH YOUR HANDS TO GET AT IT.
WE'RE SORRY.

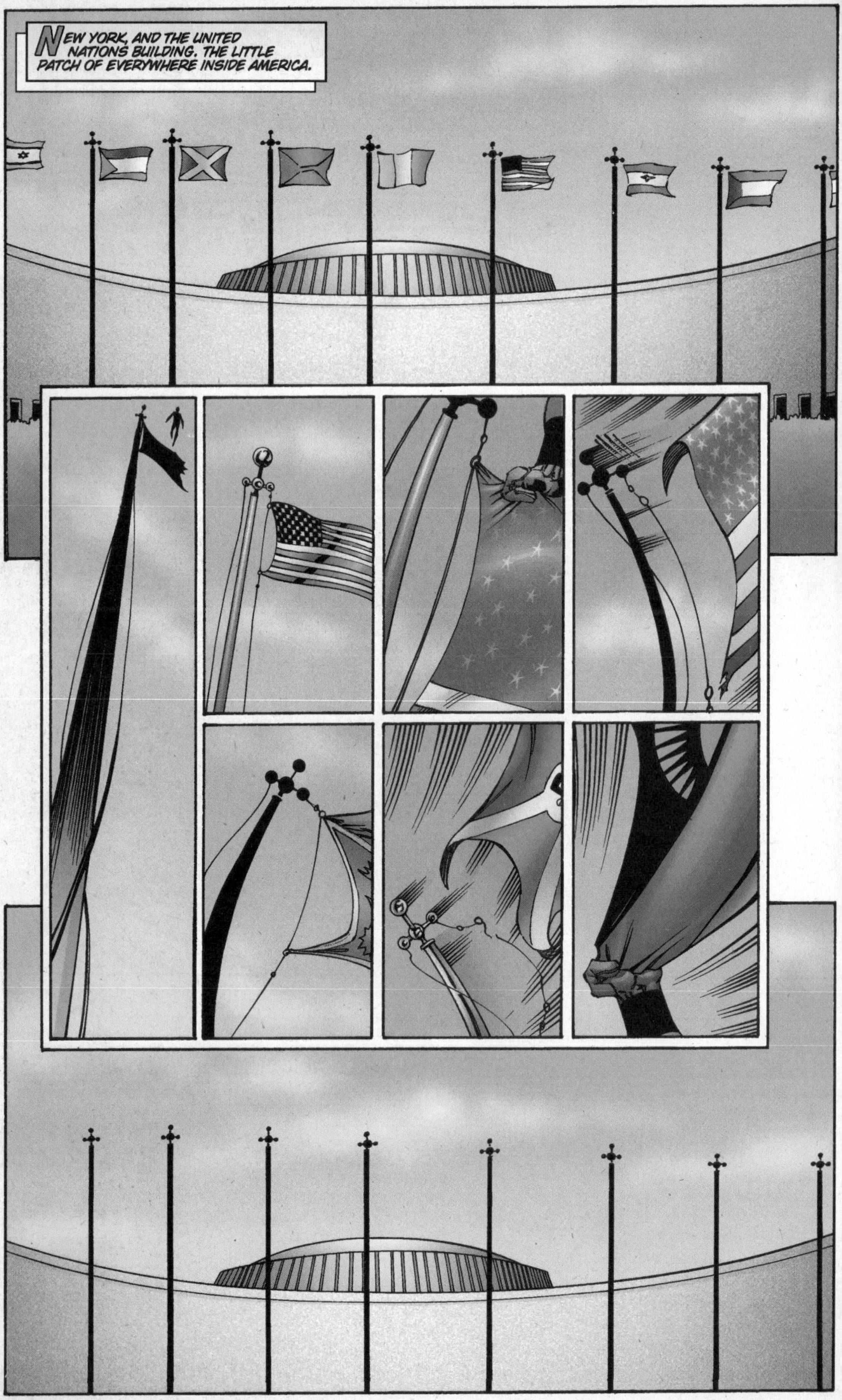
NEW YORK, AND THE UNITED NATIONS BUILDING. THE LITTLE PATCH OF EVERYWHERE INSIDE AMERICA.

PRINTED IN CANADA

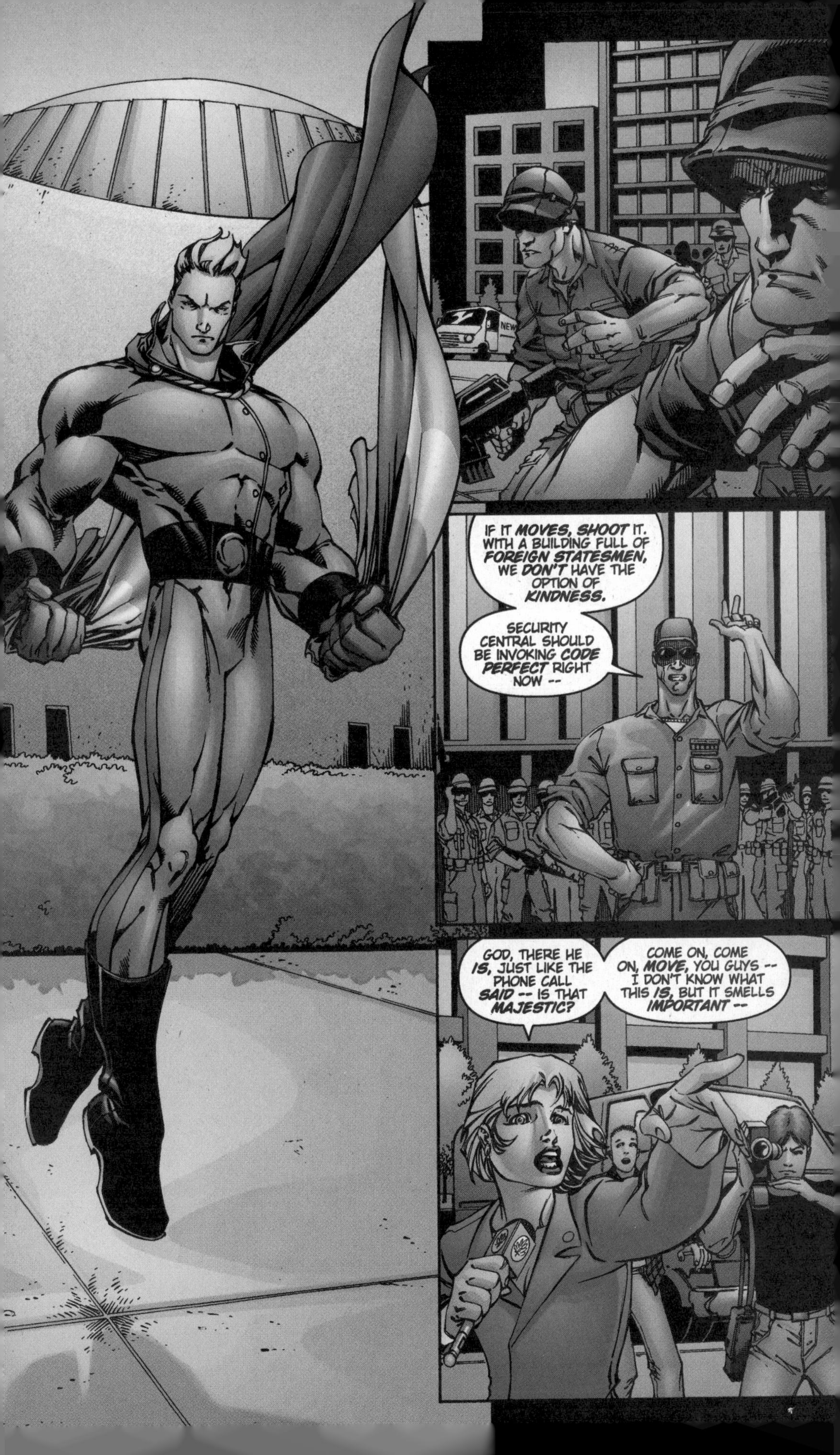

IF IT MOVES, SHOOT IT. WITH A BUILDING FULL OF FOREIGN STATESMEN, WE DON'T HAVE THE OPTION OF KINDNESS.
SECURITY CENTRAL SHOULD BE INVOKING CODE PERFECT RIGHT NOW --
GOD, THERE HE IS, JUST LIKE THE PHONE CALL SAID -- IS THAT MAJESTIC?
COME ON, COME ON, MOVE, YOU GUYS -- I DON'T KNOW WHAT THIS IS, BUT IT SMELLS IMPORTANT --

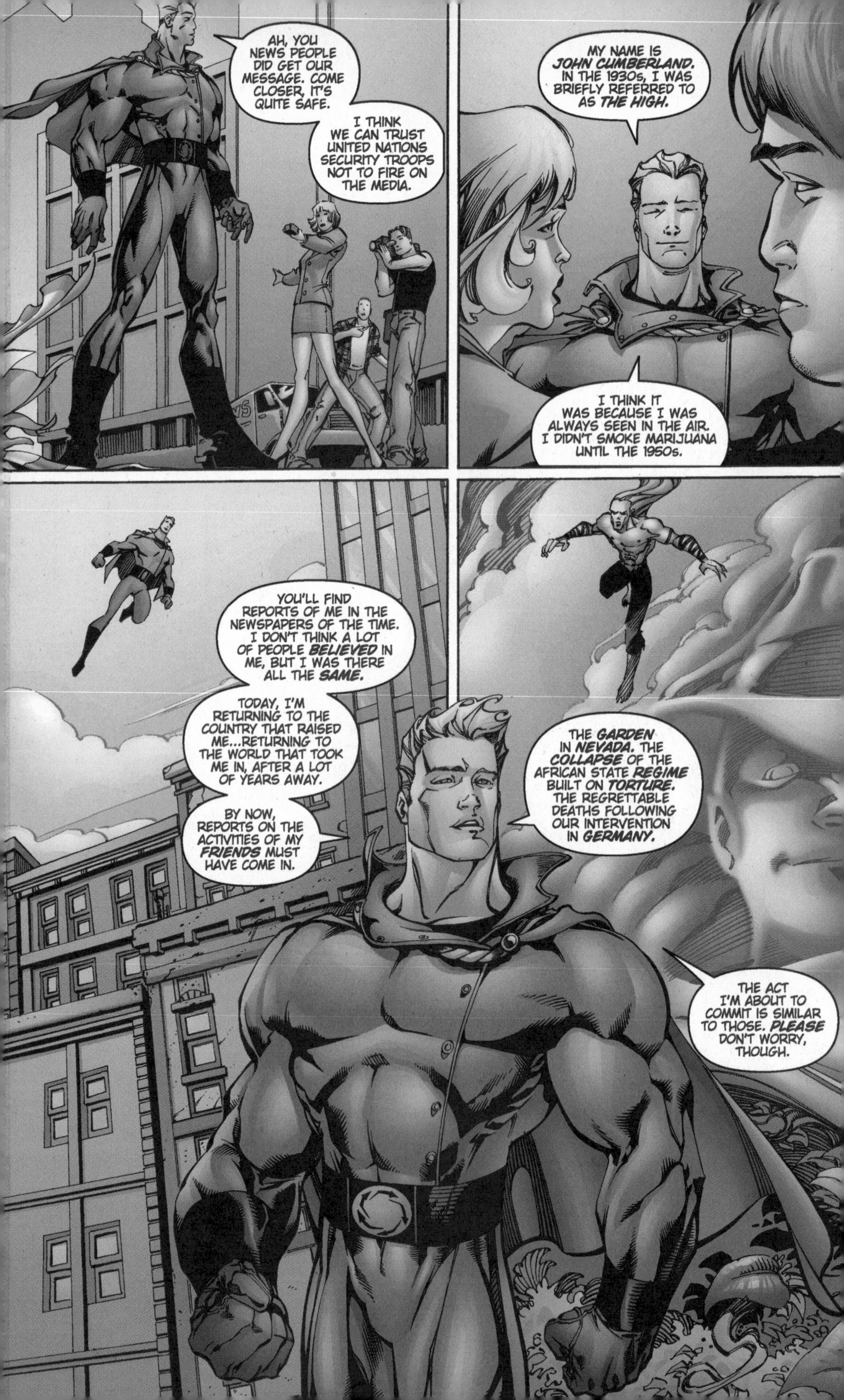
AH, YOU NEWS PEOPLE DID GET OUR MESSAGE. COME CLOSER, IT'S QUITE SAFE.
I THINK WE CAN TRUST UNITED NATIONS SECURITY TROOPS NOT TO FIRE ON THE MEDIA.
MY NAME IS JOHN CUMBERLAND. IN THE 1930s, I WAS BRIEFLY REFERRED TO AS THE HIGH.
I THINK IT WAS BECAUSE I WAS ALWAYS SEEN IN THE AIR. I DIDN'T SMOKE MARIJUANA UNTIL THE 1950s.
YOU'LL FIND REPORTS OF ME IN THE NEWSPAPERS OF THE TIME. I DON'T THINK A LOT OF PEOPLE BELIEVED IN ME, BUT I WAS THERE ALL THE SAME.
TODAY, I'M RETURNING TO THE COUNTRY THAT RAISED ME...RETURNING TO THE WORLD THAT TOOK ME IN, AFTER A LOT OF YEARS AWAY.
BY NOW, REPORTS ON THE ACTIVITIES OF MY FRIENDS MUST HAVE COME IN.
THE GARDEN IN NEVADA. THE COLLAPSE OF THE AFRICAN STATE REGIME BUILT ON TORTURE. THE REGRETTABLE DEATHS FOLLOWING OUR INTERVENTION IN GERMANY.
THE ACT I'M ABOUT TO COMMIT IS SIMILAR TO THOSE. PLEASE DON'T WORRY, THOUGH.

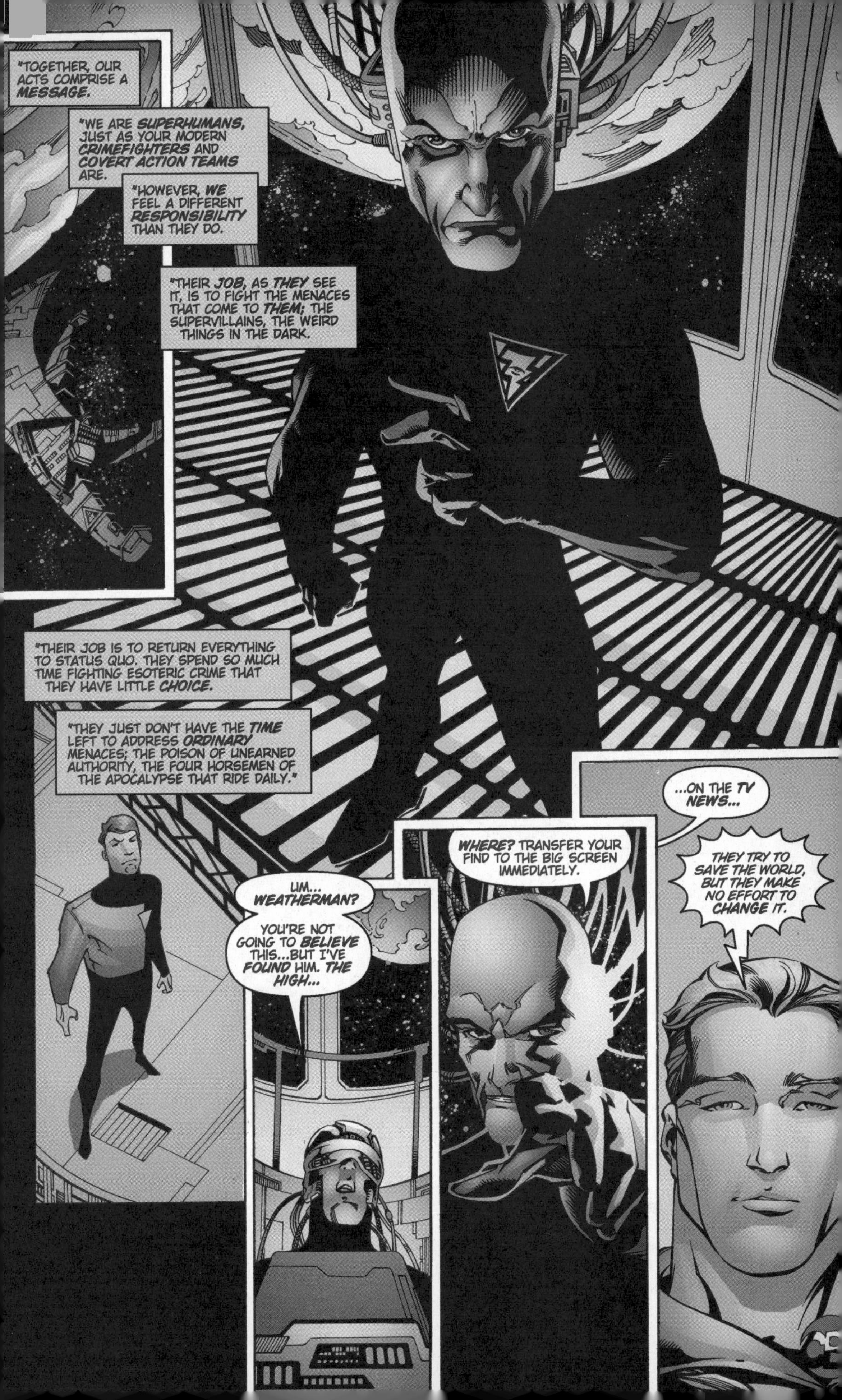
"TOGETHER, OUR ACTS COMPRISE A MESSAGE.
"WE ARE SUPERHUMANS, JUST AS YOUR MODERN CRIMEFIGHTERS AND COVERT ACTION TEAMS ARE.
"HOWEVER, WE FEEL A DIFFERENT RESPONSIBILITY THAN THEY DO.
"THEIR JOB, AS THEY SEE IT, IS TO FIGHT THE MENACES THAT COME TO THEM; THE SUPERVILLAINS, THE WEIRD THINGS IN THE DARK.
"THEIR JOB IS TO RETURN EVERYTHING TO STATUS QUO. THEY SPEND SO MUCH TIME FIGHTING ESOTERIC CRIME THAT THEY HAVE LITTLE CHOICE.
"THEY JUST DON'T HAVE THE TIME LEFT TO ADDRESS ORDINARY MENACES; THE POISON OF UNEARNED AUTHORITY, THE FOUR HORSEMEN OF THE APOCALYPSE THAT RIDE DAILY."
UM... WEATHERMAN?
YOU'RE NOT GOING TO BELIEVE THIS...BUT I'VE FOUND HIM. THE HIGH...
WHERE? TRANSFER YOUR FIND TO THE BIG SCREEN IMMEDIATELY.
...ON THE TV NEWS...
THEY TRY TO SAVE THE WORLD, BUT THEY MAKE NO EFFORT TO CHANGE IT.

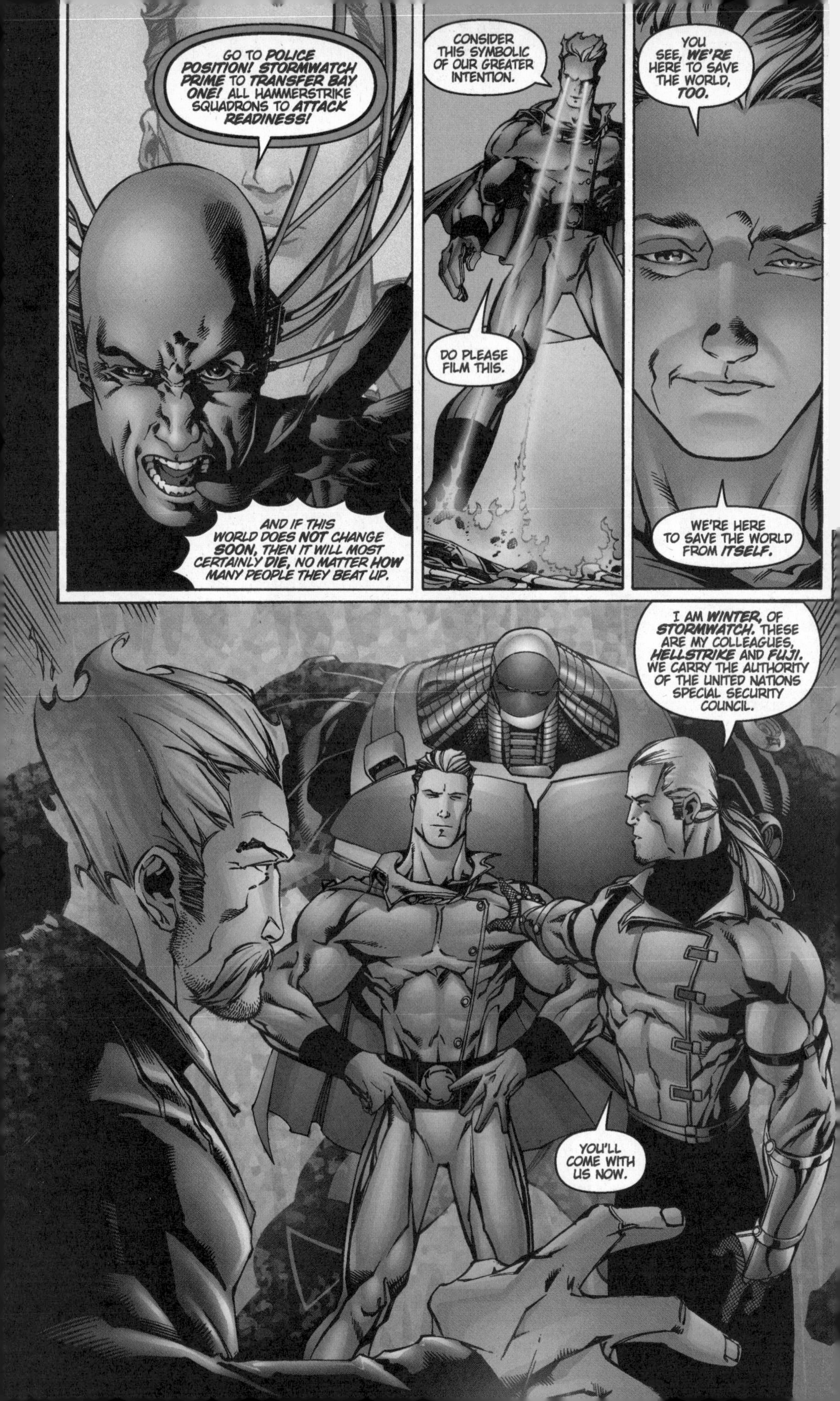
GO TO POLICE POSITION! STORMWATCH PRIME TO TRANSFER BAY ONE! ALL HAMMERSTRIKE SQUADRONS TO ATTACK READINESS!
AND IF THIS WORLD DOES NOT CHANGE SOON, THEN IT WILL MOST CERTAINLY DIE, NO MATTER HOW MANY PEOPLE THEY BEAT UP.
CONSIDER THIS SYMBOLIC OF OUR GREATER INTENTION.
DO PLEASE FILM THIS.
YOU SEE, WE'RE HERE TO SAVE THE WORLD, TOO.
WE'RE HERE TO SAVE THE WORLD FROM ITSELF.
I AM WINTER, OF STORMWATCH. THESE ARE MY COLLEAGUES, HELLSTRIKE AND FUJI. WE CARRY THE AUTHORITY OF THE UNITED NATIONS SPECIAL SECURITY COUNCIL.
YOU'LL COME WITH US NOW.

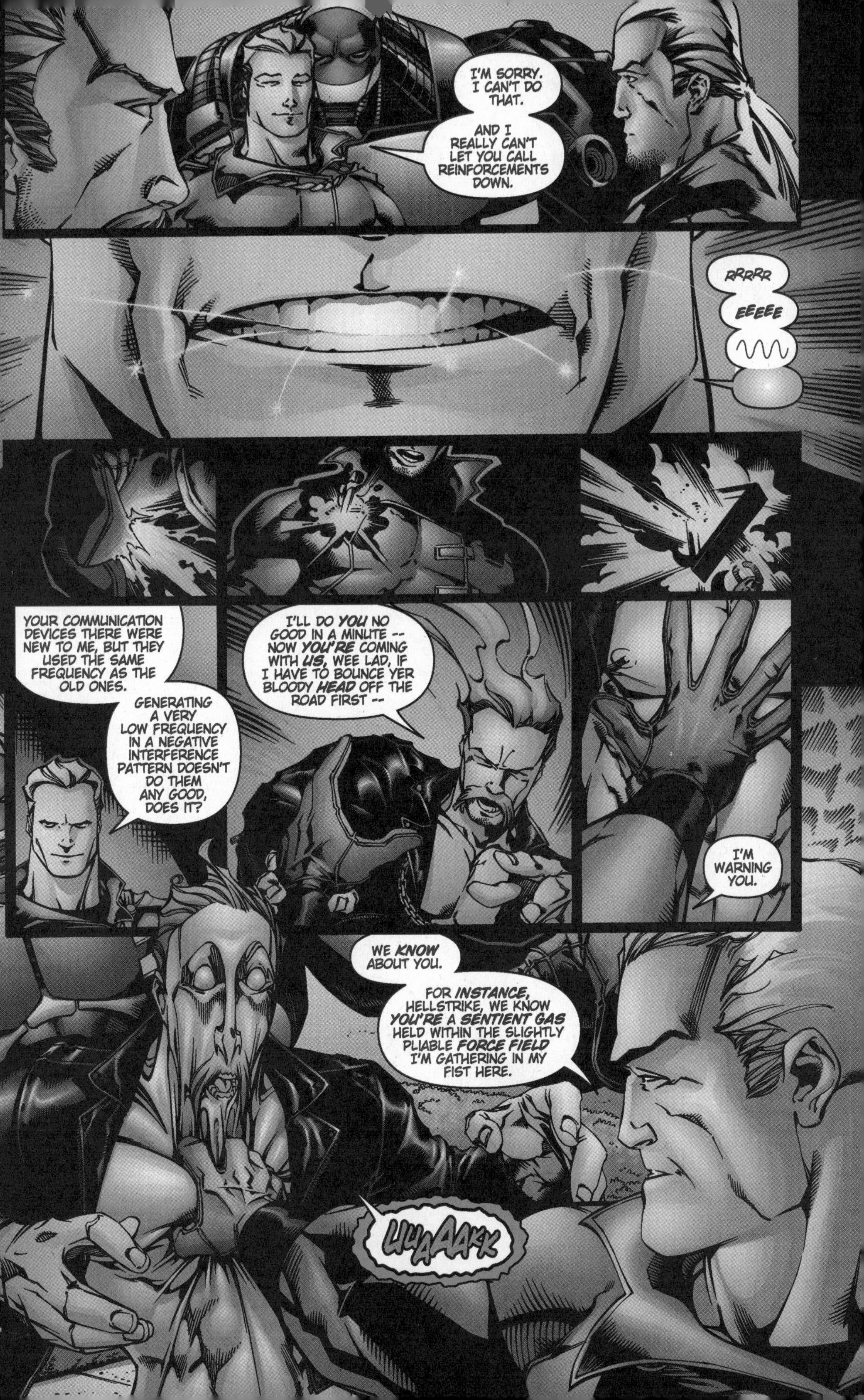
I'M SORRY. I CAN'T DO THAT.
AND I REALLY CAN'T LET YOU CALL REINFORCEMENTS DOWN.
RRRRR
EEEEE
YOUR COMMUNICATION DEVICES THERE WERE NEW TO ME, BUT THEY USED THE SAME FREQUENCY AS THE OLD ONES.
GENERATING A VERY LOW FREQUENCY IN A NEGATIVE INTERFERENCE PATTERN DOESN'T DO THEM ANY GOOD, DOES IT?
I'LL DO YOU NO GOOD IN A MINUTE -- NOW YOU'RE COMING WITH US, WEE LAD, IF I HAVE TO BOUNCE YER BLOODY HEAD OFF THE ROAD FIRST --
I'M WARNING YOU.
WE KNOW ABOUT YOU.
FOR INSTANCE, HELLSTRIKE, WE KNOW YOU'RE A SENTIENT GAS HELD WITHIN THE SLIGHTLY PLIABLE FORCE FIELD I'M GATHERING IN MY FIST HERE.
UUAAAKK

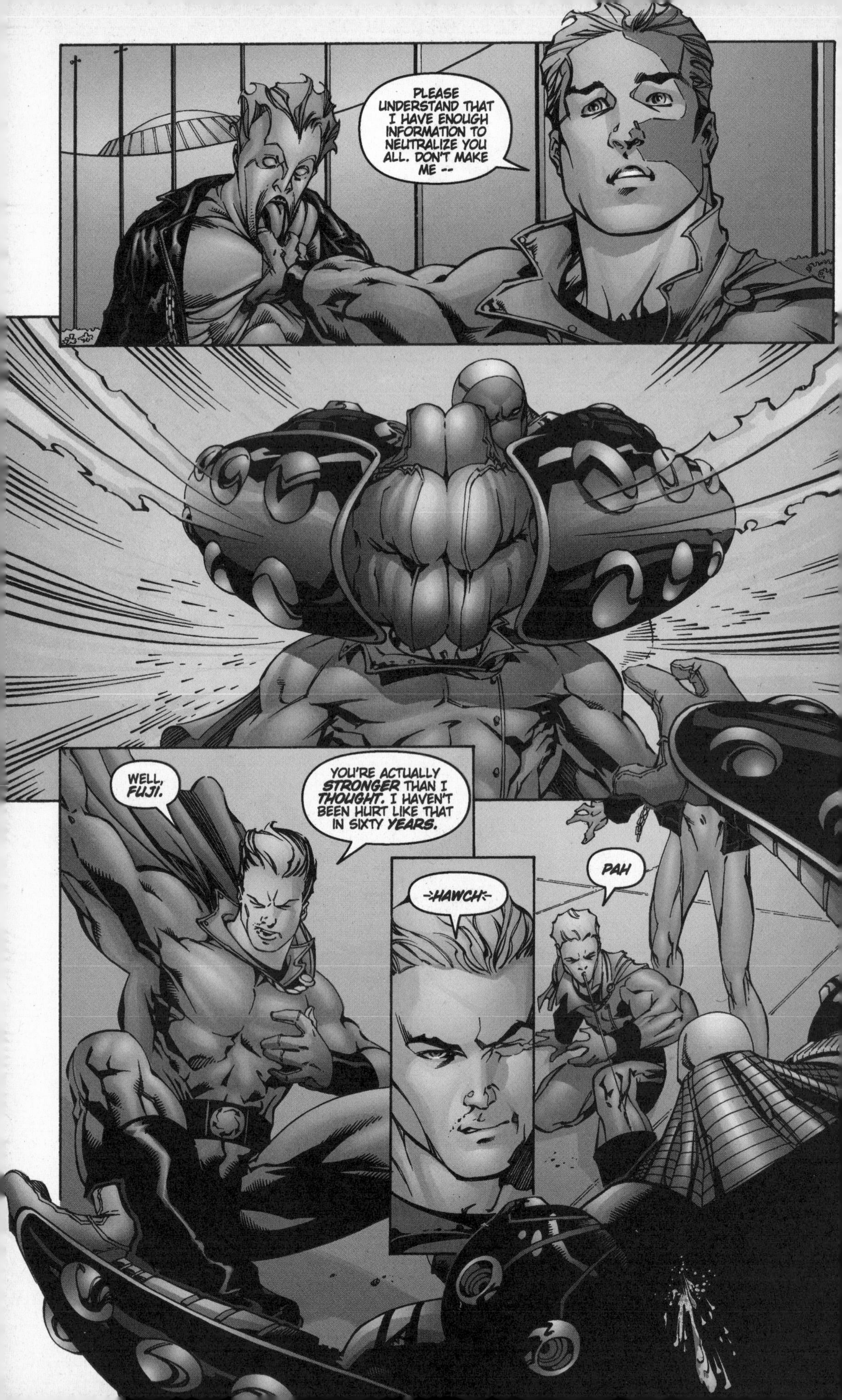

PLEASE UNDERSTAND THAT I HAVE ENOUGH INFORMATION TO NEUTRALIZE YOU ALL. DON'T MAKE ME --
WELL, FUJI.
YOU'RE ACTUALLY STRONGER THAN I THOUGHT. I HAVEN'T BEEN HURT LIKE THAT IN SIXTY YEARS.
-HAWCH-
PAH

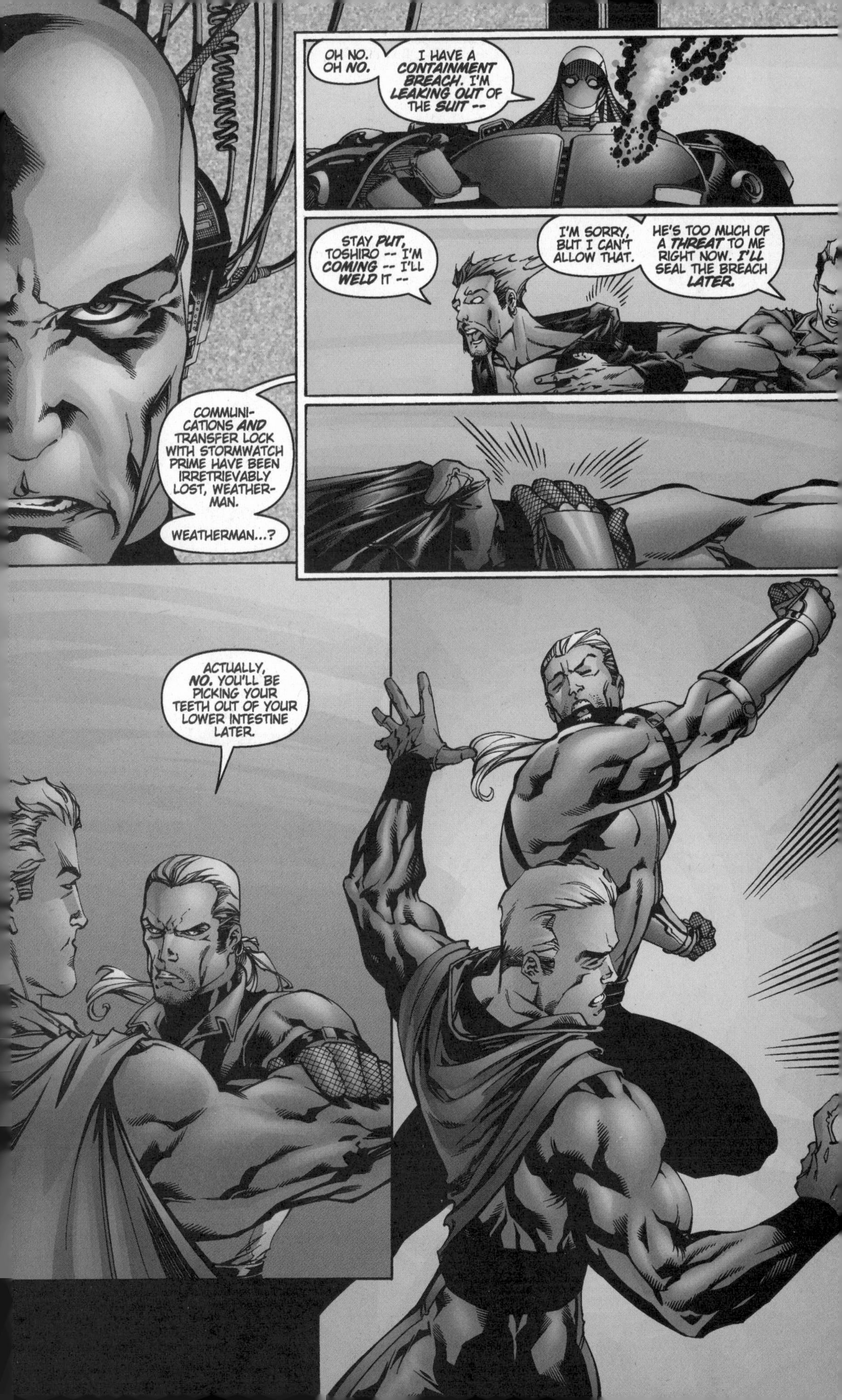
OH NO. OH NO.
I HAVE A CONTAINMENT BREACH. I'M LEAKING OUT OF THE SUIT --
STAY PUT, TOSHIRO -- I'M COMING -- I'LL WELD IT --
I'M SORRY, BUT I CAN'T ALLOW THAT.
HE'S TOO MUCH OF A THREAT TO ME RIGHT NOW. I'LL SEAL THE BREACH LATER.
COMMUNI-CATIONS AND TRANSFER LOCK WITH STORMWATCH PRIME HAVE BEEN IRRETRIEVABLY LOST, WEATHER-MAN.
WEATHERMAN...?
ACTUALLY, NO. YOU'LL BE PICKING YOUR TEETH OUT OF YOUR LOWER INTESTINE LATER.

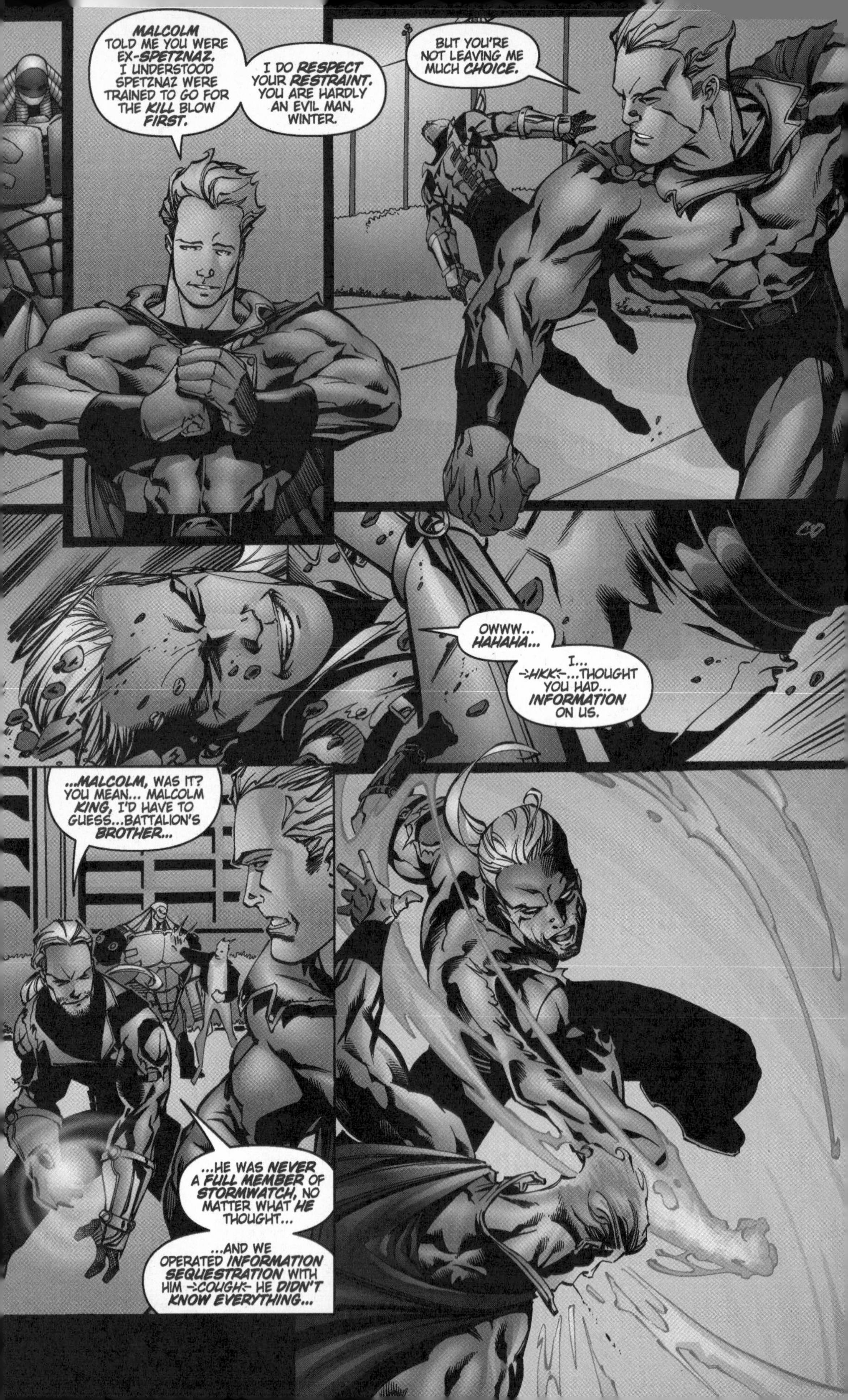
MALCOLM TOLD ME YOU WERE EX-SPETZNAZ. I UNDERSTOOD SPETZNAZ WERE TRAINED TO GO FOR THE KILL BLOW FIRST.
I DO RESPECT YOUR RESTRAINT. YOU ARE HARDLY AN EVIL MAN, WINTER.
BUT YOU'RE NOT LEAVING ME MUCH CHOICE.
OWWW... HAHAHA...
I... ->HKK<-...THOUGHT YOU HAD... INFORMATION ON US.
...MALCOLM, WAS IT? YOU MEAN... MALCOLM KING, I'D HAVE TO GUESS...BATTALION'S BROTHER...
...HE WAS NEVER A FULL MEMBER OF STORMWATCH, NO MATTER WHAT HE THOUGHT...
...AND WE OPERATED INFORMATION SEQUESTRATION WITH HIM ->COUGH<- HE DIDN'T KNOW EVERYTHING...

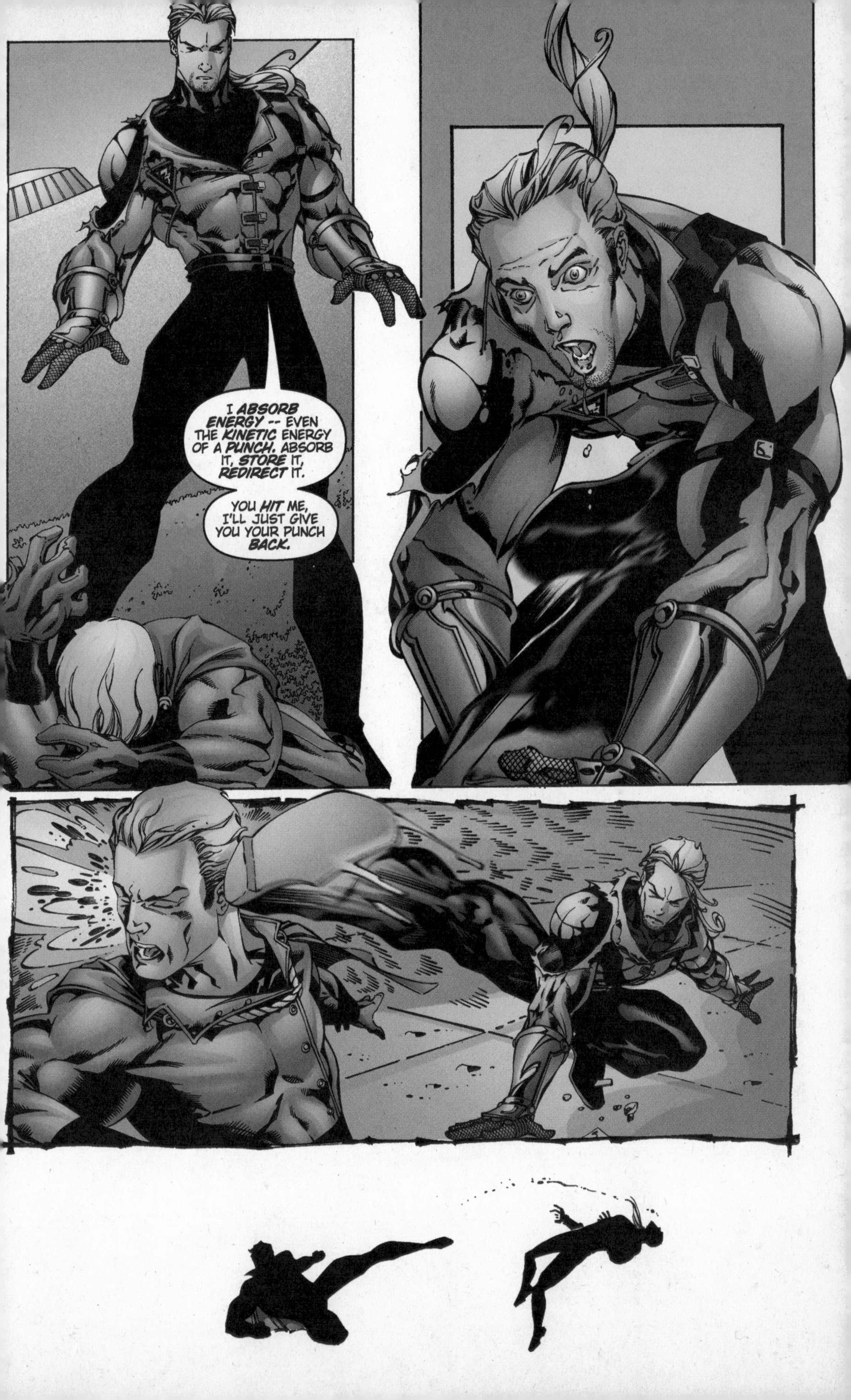
I ABSORB ENERGY -- EVEN THE KINETIC ENERGY OF A PUNCH. ABSORB IT, STORE IT, REDIRECT IT.
YOU HIT ME, I'LL JUST GIVE YOU YOUR PUNCH BACK.

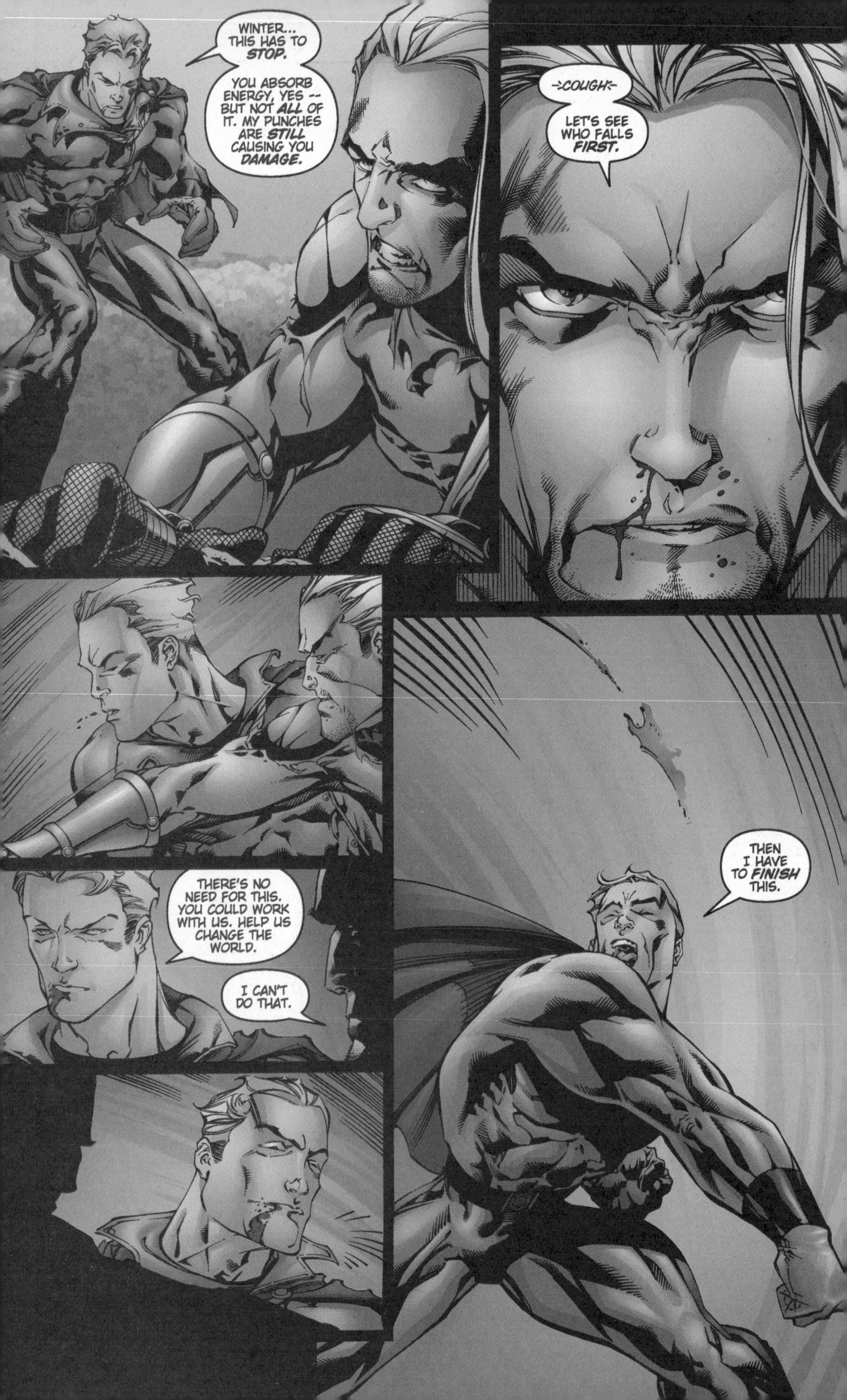
WINTER... THIS HAS TO STOP.
YOU ABSORB ENERGY, YES -- BUT NOT ALL OF IT. MY PUNCHES ARE STILL CAUSING YOU DAMAGE.
-COUGH-
LET'S SEE WHO FALLS FIRST.
THERE'S NO NEED FOR THIS. YOU COULD WORK WITH US. HELP US CHANGE THE WORLD.
I CAN'T DO THAT.
THEN I HAVE TO FINISH THIS.

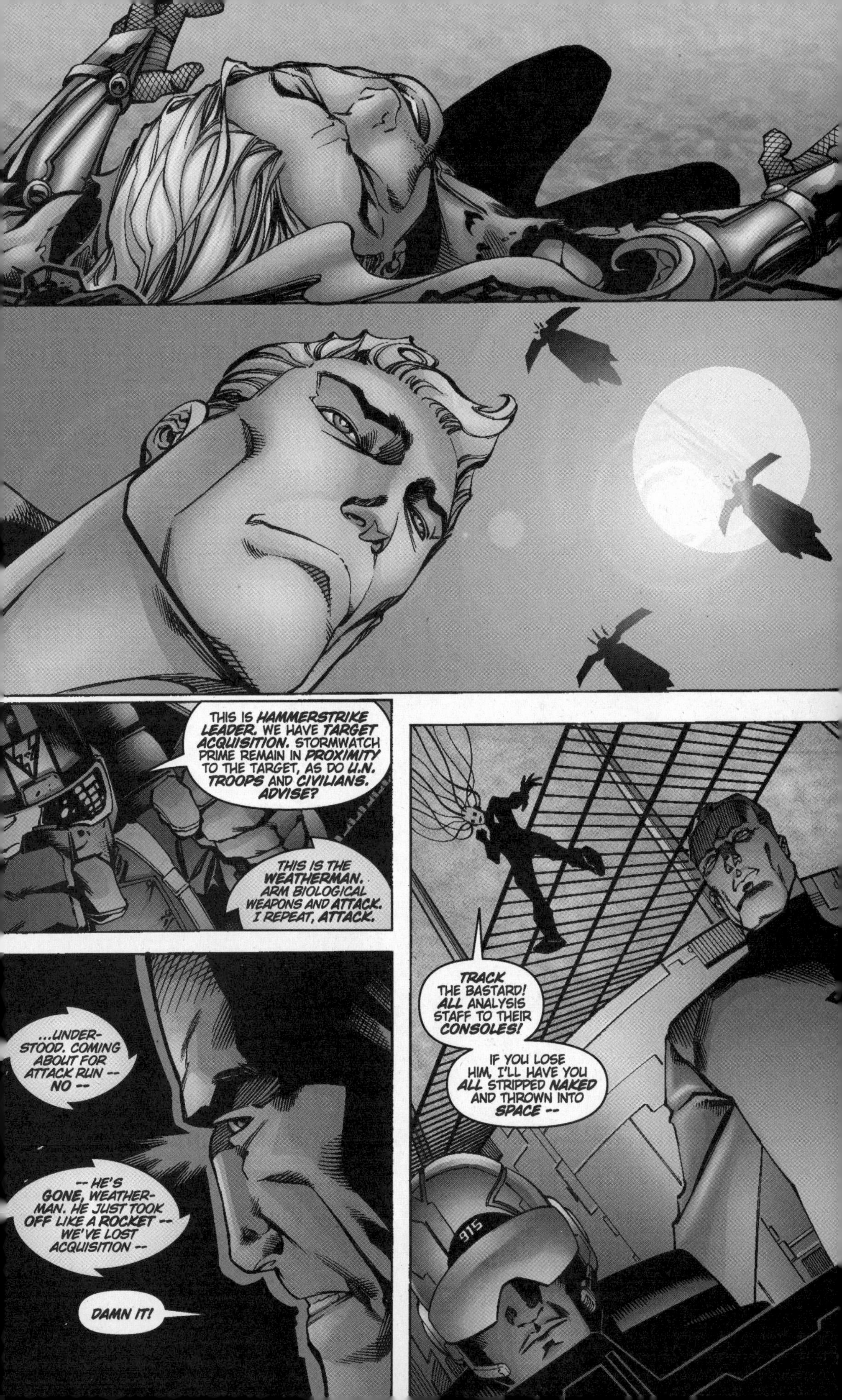
THIS IS HAMMERSTRIKE LEADER. WE HAVE TARGET ACQUISITION. STORMWATCH PRIME REMAIN IN PROXIMITY TO THE TARGET, AS DO U.N. TROOPS AND CIVILIANS. ADVISE?
THIS IS THE WEATHERMAN. ARM BIOLOGICAL WEAPONS AND ATTACK. I REPEAT, ATTACK.
...UNDER-STOOD. COMING ABOUT FOR ATTACK RUN -- NO --
-- HE'S GONE, WEATHER-MAN. HE JUST TOOK OFF LIKE A ROCKET -- WE'VE LOST ACQUISITION --
DAMN IT!
TRACK THE BASTARD! ALL ANALYSIS STAFF TO THEIR CONSOLES!
IF YOU LOSE HIM, I'LL HAVE YOU ALL STRIPPED NAKED AND THROWN INTO SPACE --

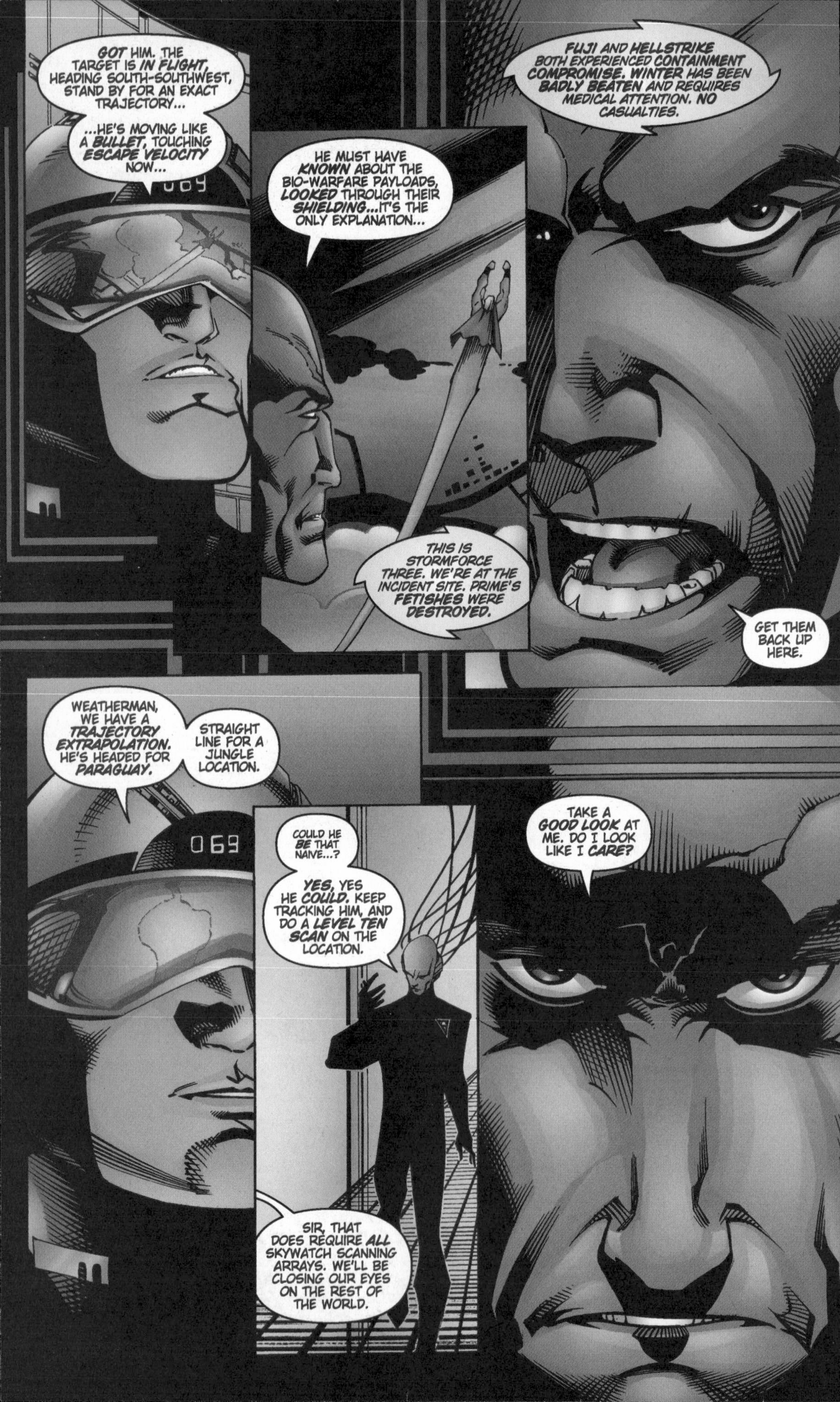
GOT HIM. THE TARGET IS IN FLIGHT, HEADING SOUTH-SOUTHWEST, STAND BY FOR AN EXACT TRAJECTORY...
...HE'S MOVING LIKE A BULLET, TOUCHING ESCAPE VELOCITY NOW...
069
HE MUST HAVE KNOWN ABOUT THE BIO-WARFARE PAYLOADS, LOOKED THROUGH THEIR SHIELDING...IT'S THE ONLY EXPLANATION...
FUJI AND HELLSTRIKE BOTH EXPERIENCED CONTAINMENT COMPROMISE. WINTER HAS BEEN BADLY BEATEN AND REQUIRES MEDICAL ATTENTION. NO CASUALTIES.
THIS IS STORMFORCE THREE. WE'RE AT THE INCIDENT SITE. PRIME'S FETISHES WERE DESTROYED.
GET THEM BACK UP HERE.
WEATHERMAN, WE HAVE A TRAJECTORY EXTRAPOLATION. HE'S HEADED FOR PARAGUAY.
STRAIGHT LINE FOR A JUNGLE LOCATION.
069
COULD HE BE THAT NAIVE...?
YES, YES HE COULD. KEEP TRACKING HIM, AND DO A LEVEL TEN SCAN ON THE LOCATION.
TAKE A GOOD LOOK AT ME. DO I LOOK LIKE I CARE?
SIR, THAT DOES REQUIRE ALL SKYWATCH SCANNING ARRAYS. WE'LL BE CLOSING OUR EYES ON THE REST OF THE WORLD.

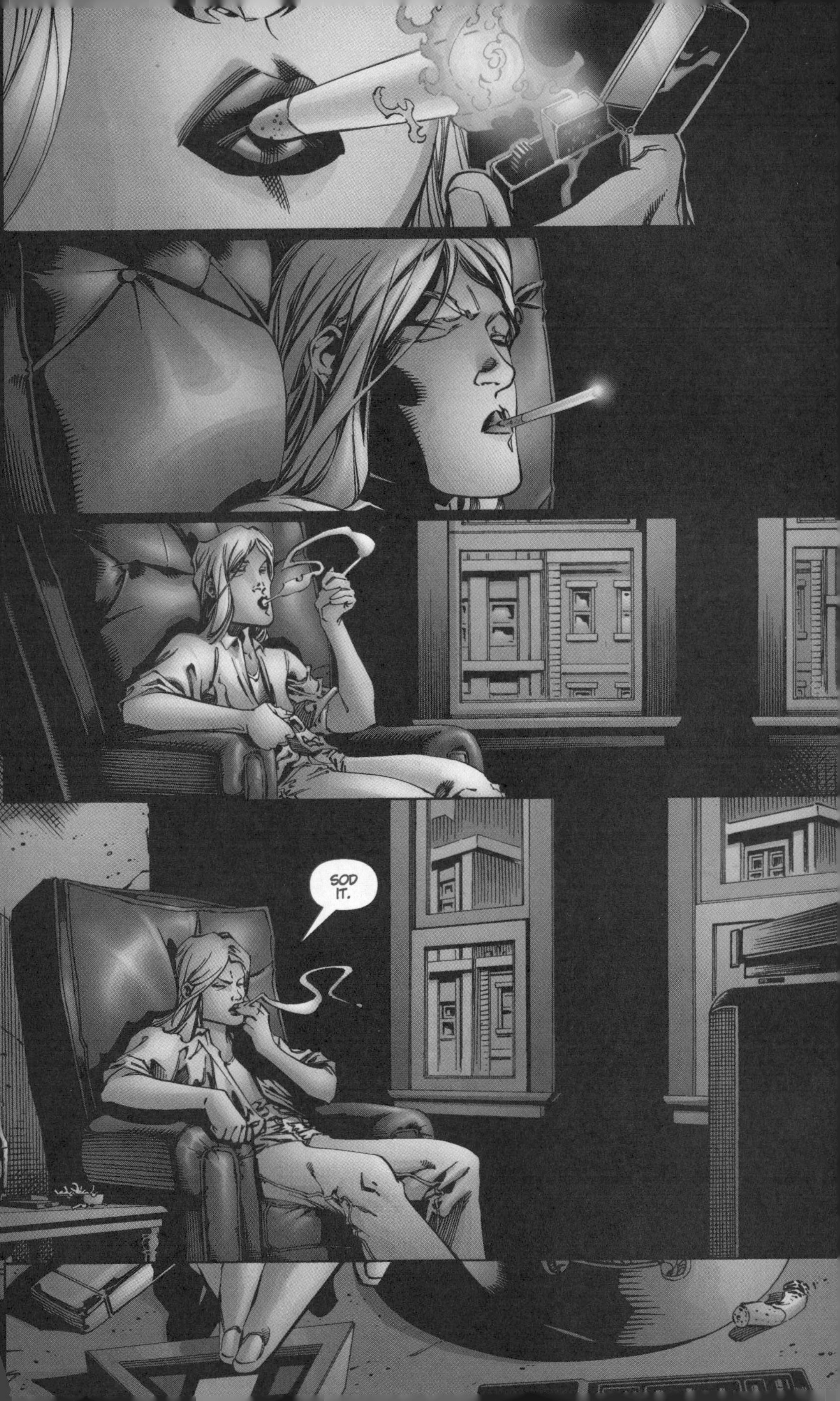
SOD IT.

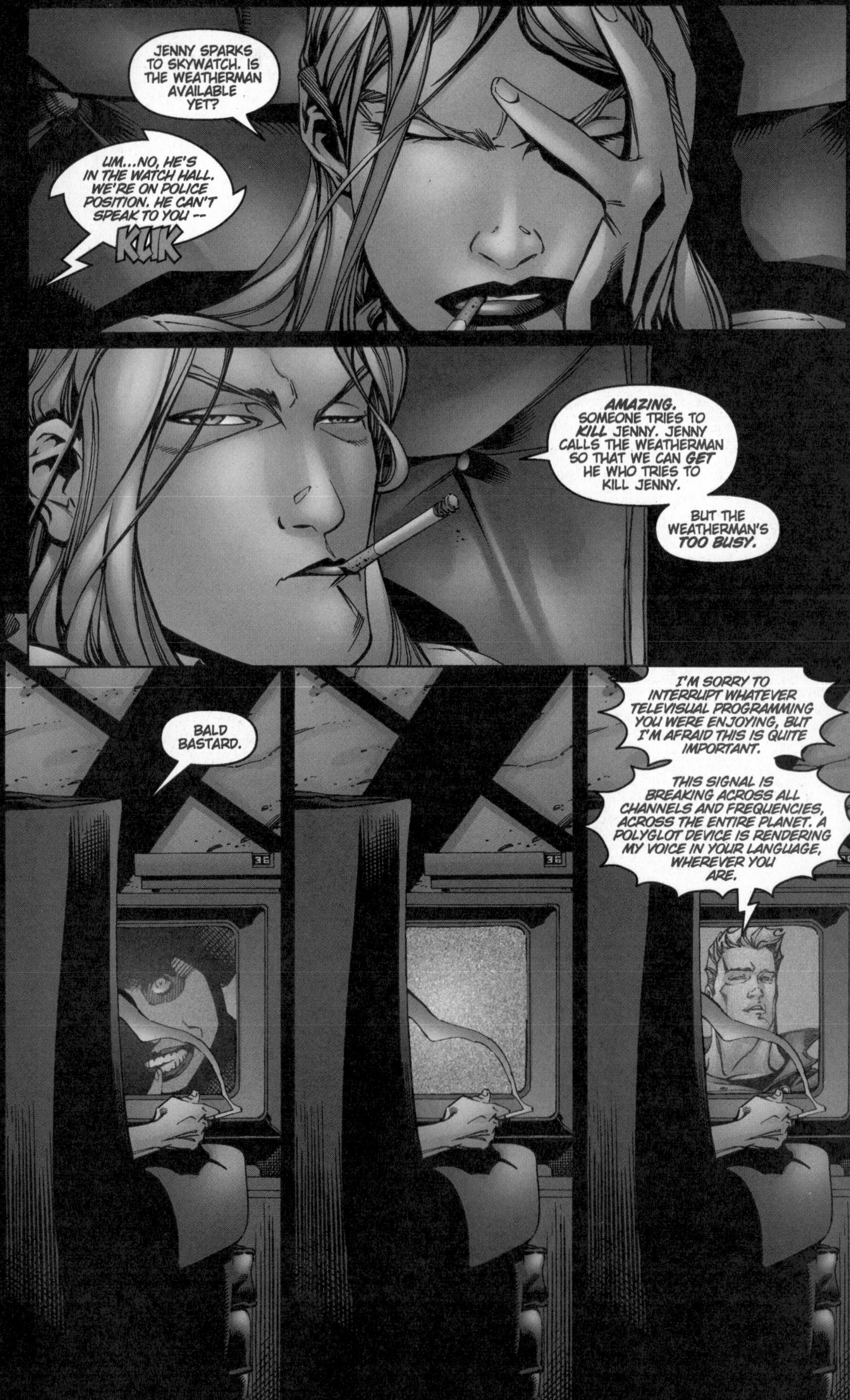
JENNY SPARKS TO SKYWATCH. IS THE WEATHERMAN AVAILABLE YET?
UM...NO, HE'S IN THE WATCH HALL. WE'RE ON POLICE POSITION. HE CAN'T SPEAK TO YOU --
KLIK
AMAZING. SOMEONE TRIES TO KILL JENNY. JENNY CALLS THE WEATHERMAN SO THAT WE CAN GET HE WHO TRIES TO KILL JENNY.
BUT THE WEATHERMAN'S TOO BUSY.
BALD BASTARD.
I'M SORRY TO INTERRUPT WHATEVER TELEVISUAL PROGRAMMING YOU WERE ENJOYING, BUT I'M AFRAID THIS IS QUITE IMPORTANT.
THIS SIGNAL IS BREAKING ACROSS ALL CHANNELS AND FREQUENCIES, ACROSS THE ENTIRE PLANET. A POLYGLOT DEVICE IS RENDERING MY VOICE IN YOUR LANGUAGE, WHEREVER YOU ARE.

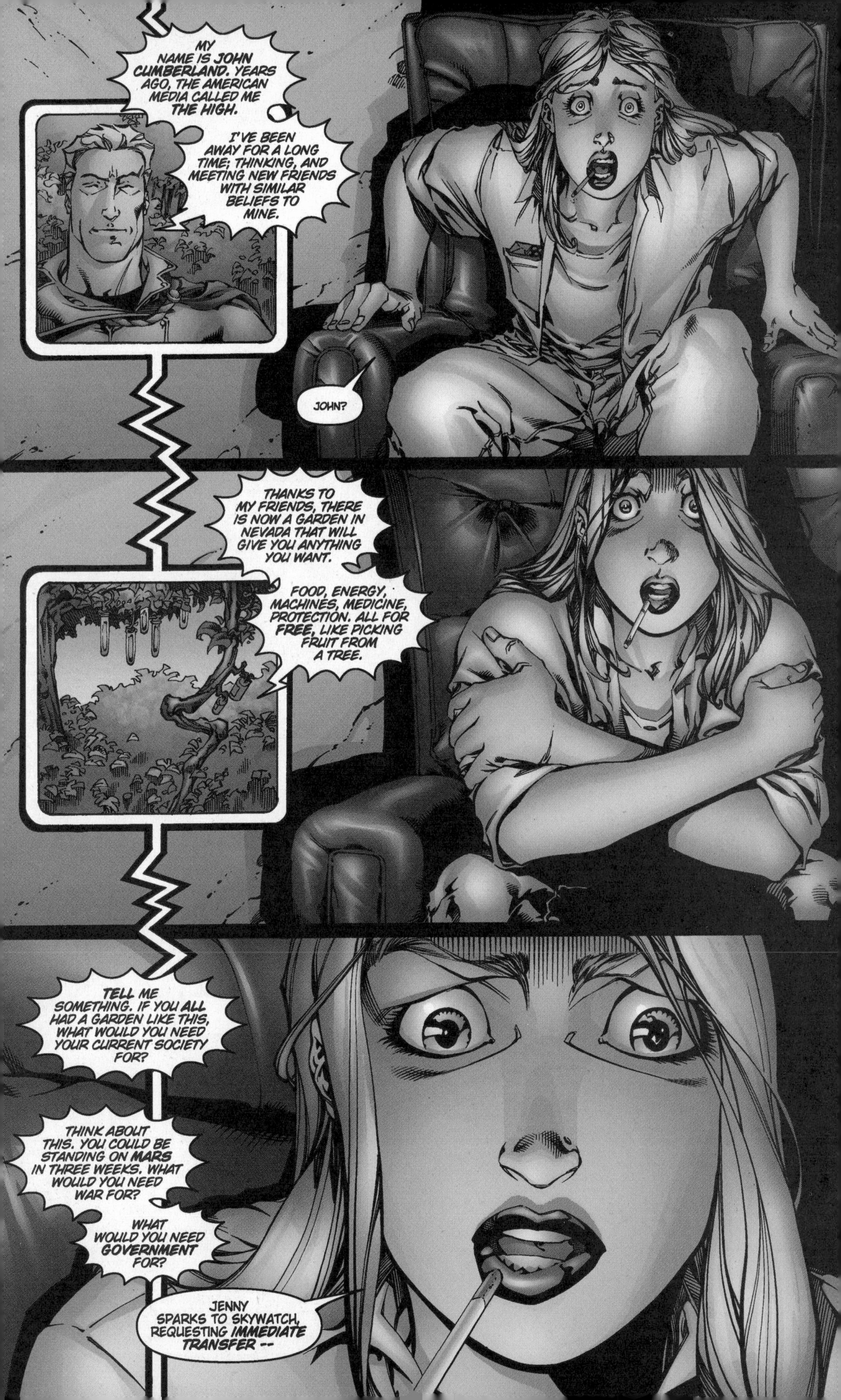
MY NAME IS JOHN CUMBERLAND. YEARS AGO, THE AMERICAN MEDIA CALLED ME THE HIGH.
I'VE BEEN AWAY FOR A LONG TIME; THINKING, AND MEETING NEW FRIENDS WITH SIMILAR BELIEFS TO MINE.
JOHN?
THANKS TO MY FRIENDS, THERE IS NOW A GARDEN IN NEVADA THAT WILL GIVE YOU ANYTHING YOU WANT.
FOOD, ENERGY, MACHINES, MEDICINE, PROTECTION. ALL FOR FREE, LIKE PICKING FRUIT FROM A TREE.
TELL ME SOMETHING. IF YOU ALL HAD A GARDEN LIKE THIS, WHAT WOULD YOU NEED YOUR CURRENT SOCIETY FOR?
THINK ABOUT THIS. YOU COULD BE STANDING ON MARS IN THREE WEEKS. WHAT WOULD YOU NEED WAR FOR?
WHAT WOULD YOU NEED GOVERNMENT FOR?
JENNY SPARKS TO SKYWATCH, REQUESTING IMMEDIATE TRANSFER --

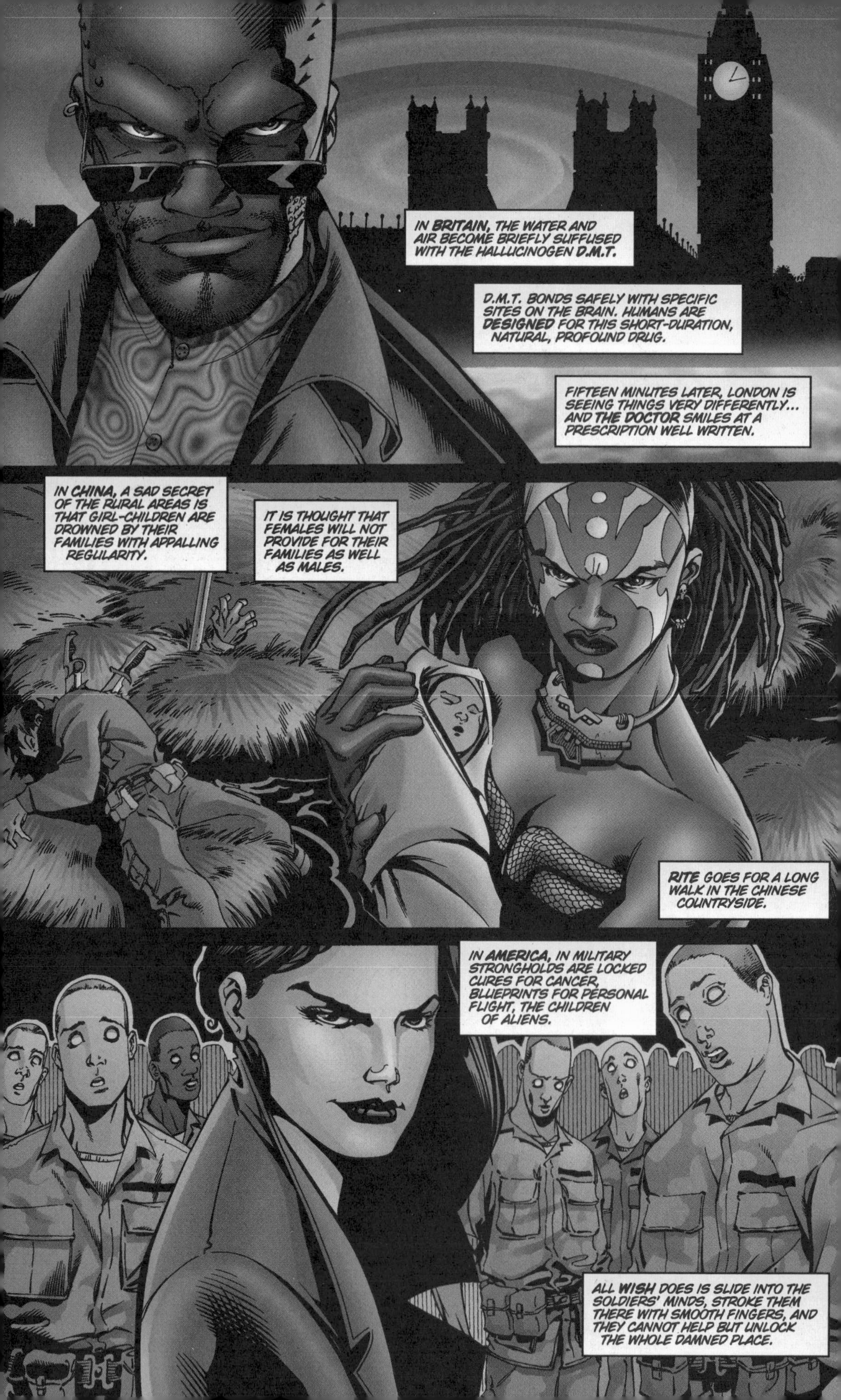
IN BRITAIN, THE WATER AND AIR BECOME BRIEFLY SUFFUSED WITH THE HALLUCINOGEN D.M.T.
D.M.T. BONDS SAFELY WITH SPECIFIC SITES ON THE BRAIN. HUMANS ARE DESIGNED FOR THIS SHORT-DURATION, NATURAL, PROFOUND DRUG.
FIFTEEN MINUTES LATER, LONDON IS SEEING THINGS VERY DIFFERENTLY... AND THE DOCTOR SMILES AT A PRESCRIPTION WELL WRITTEN.
IN CHINA, A SAD SECRET OF THE RURAL AREAS IS THAT GIRL-CHILDREN ARE DROWNED BY THEIR FAMILIES WITH APPALLING REGULARITY.
IT IS THOUGHT THAT FEMALES WILL NOT PROVIDE FOR THEIR FAMILIES AS WELL AS MALES.
RITE GOES FOR A LONG WALK IN THE CHINESE COUNTRYSIDE.
IN AMERICA, IN MILITARY STRONGHOLDS ARE LOCKED CURES FOR CANCER, BLUEPRINTS FOR PERSONAL FLIGHT, THE CHILDREN OF ALIENS.
ALL WISH DOES IS SLIDE INTO THE SOLDIERS' MINDS, STROKE THEM THERE WITH SMOOTH FINGERS, AND THEY CANNOT HELP BUT UNLOCK THE WHOLE DAMNED PLACE.

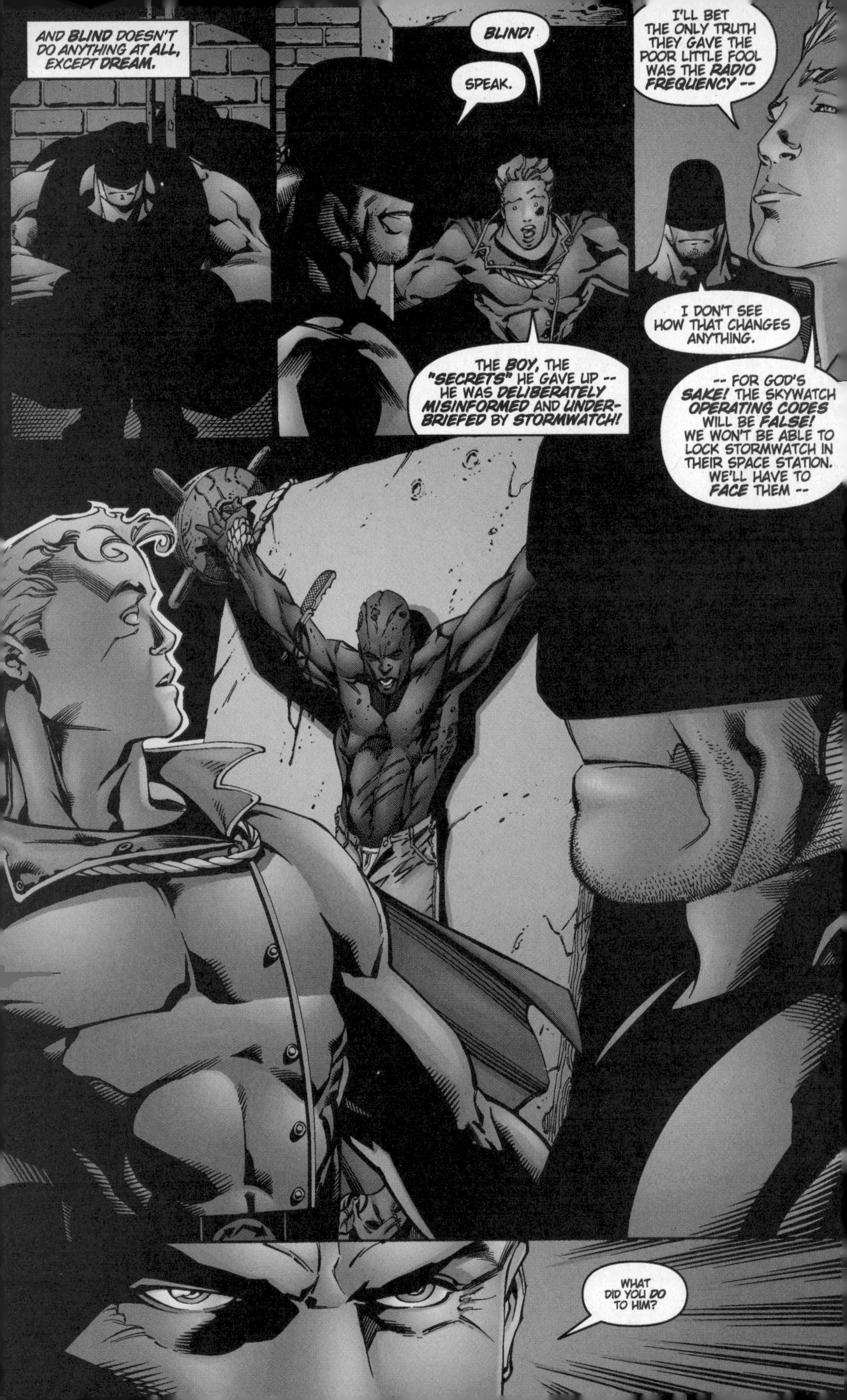
AND BLIND DOESN'T DO ANYTHING AT ALL, EXCEPT DREAM.
BLIND!
SPEAK.
THE BOY, THE "SECRETS" HE GAVE UP -- HE WAS DELIBERATELY MISINFORMED AND UNDER-BRIEFED BY STORMWATCH!
I'LL BET THE ONLY TRUTH THEY GAVE THE POOR LITTLE FOOL WAS THE RADIO FREQUENCY --
I DON'T SEE HOW THAT CHANGES ANYTHING.
-- FOR GOD'S SAKE! THE SKYWATCH OPERATING CODES WILL BE FALSE! WE WON'T BE ABLE TO LOCK STORMWATCH IN THEIR SPACE STATION. WE'LL HAVE TO FACE THEM --
WHAT DID YOU DO TO HIM?

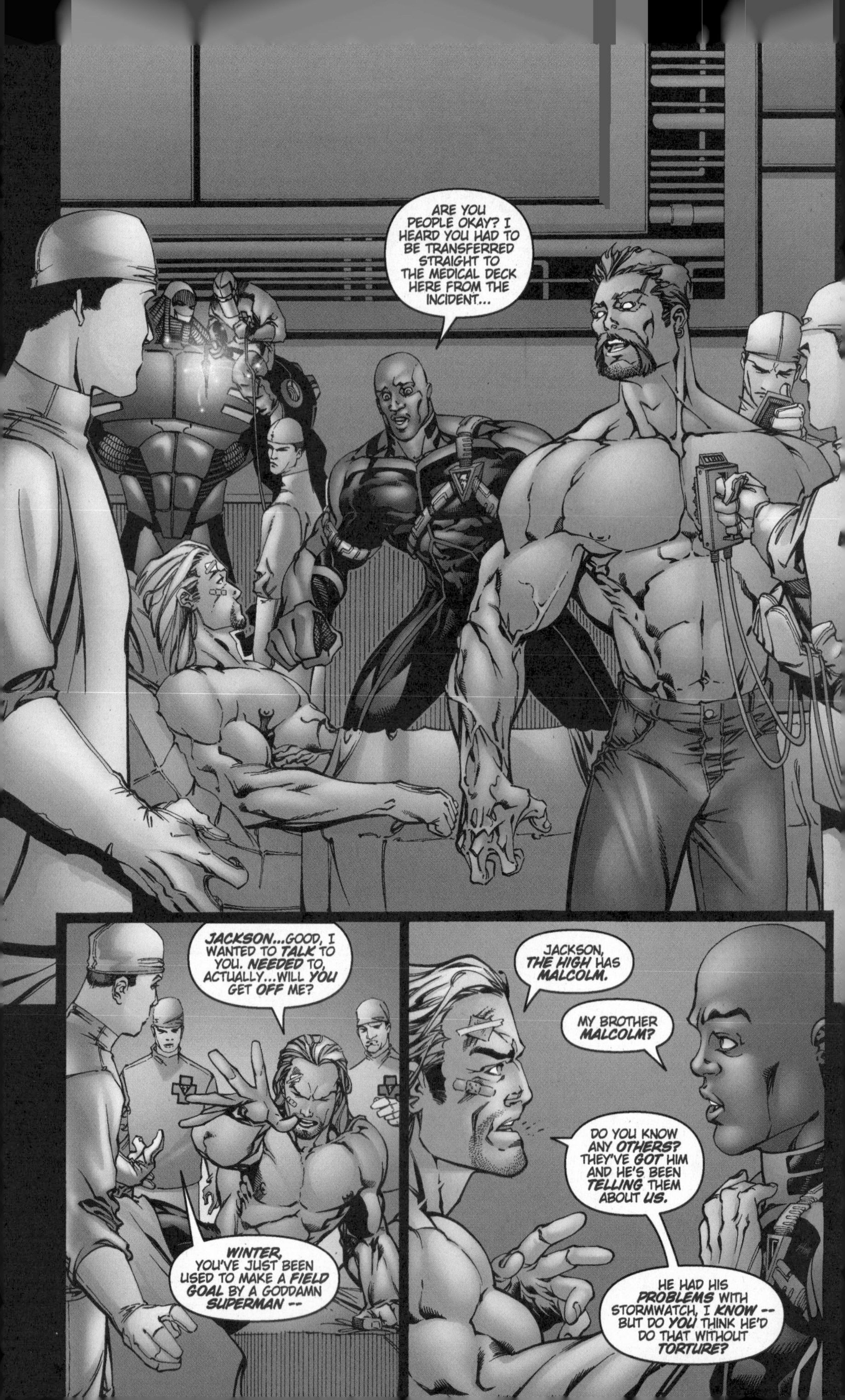
ARE YOU PEOPLE OKAY? I HEARD YOU HAD TO BE TRANSFERRED STRAIGHT TO THE MEDICAL DECK HERE FROM THE INCIDENT...
JACKSON...GOOD, I WANTED TO TALK TO YOU. NEEDED TO, ACTUALLY...WILL YOU GET OFF ME?
WINTER, YOU'VE JUST BEEN USED TO MAKE A FIELD GOAL BY A GODDAMN SUPERMAN --
JACKSON, THE HIGH HAS MALCOLM.
MY BROTHER MALCOLM?
DO YOU KNOW ANY OTHERS? THEY'VE GOT HIM AND HE'S BEEN TELLING THEM ABOUT US.
HE HAD HIS PROBLEMS WITH STORMWATCH, I KNOW -- BUT DO YOU THINK HE'D DO THAT WITHOUT TORTURE?

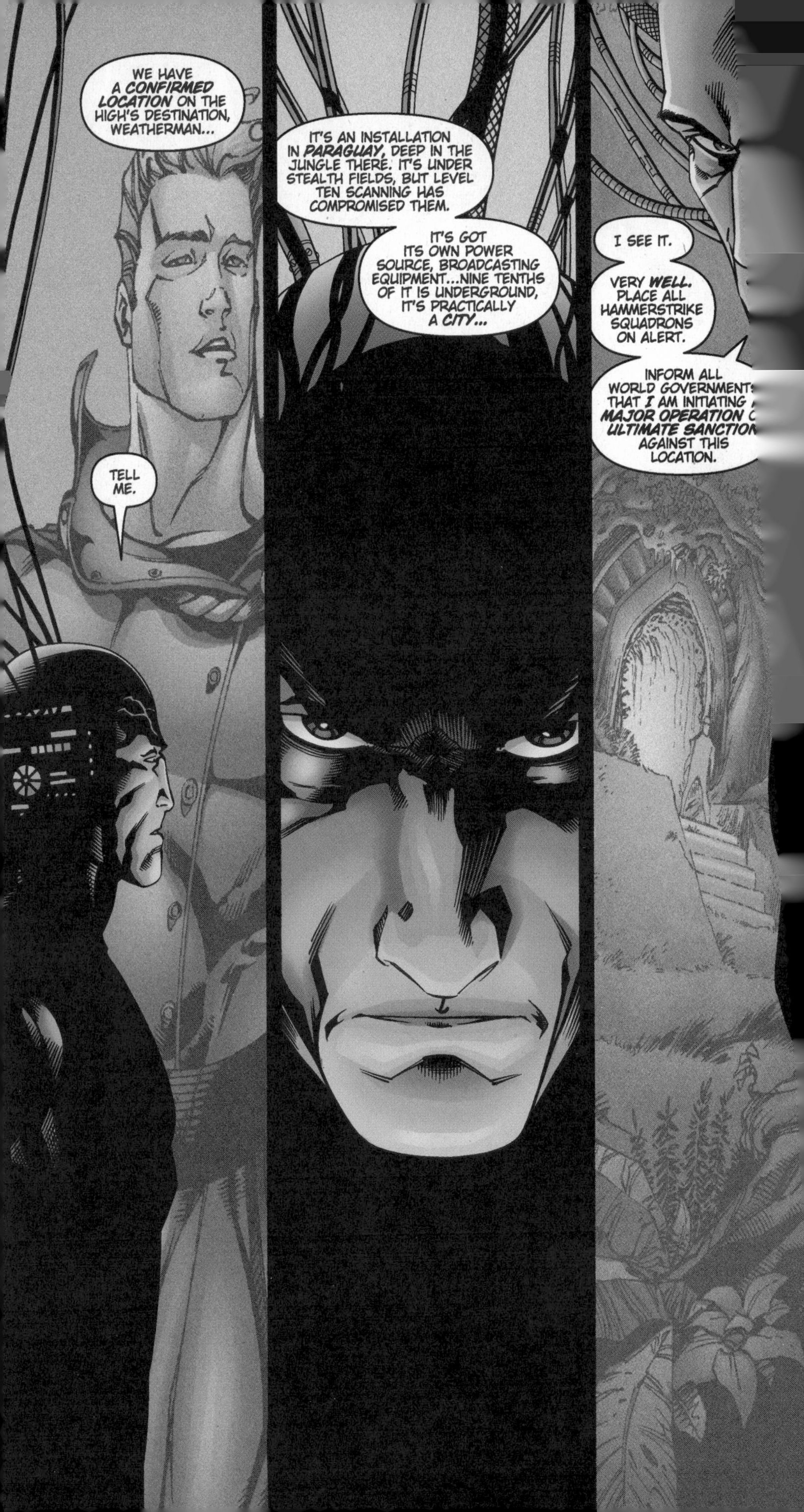
WE HAVE A CONFIRMED LOCATION ON THE HIGH'S DESTINATION, WEATHERMAN...
TELL ME.
IT'S AN INSTALLATION IN PARAGUAY, DEEP IN THE JUNGLE THERE. IT'S UNDER STEALTH FIELDS, BUT LEVEL TEN SCANNING HAS COMPROMISED THEM.
IT'S GOT ITS OWN POWER SOURCE, BROADCASTING EQUIPMENT...NINE TENTHS OF IT IS UNDERGROUND, IT'S PRACTICALLY A CITY...
I SEE IT.
VERY WELL. PLACE ALL HAMMERSTRIKE SQUADRONS ON ALERT.
INFORM ALL WORLD GOVERNMENTS THAT I AM INITIATING A MAJOR OPERATION OF ULTIMATE SANCTION AGAINST THIS LOCATION.

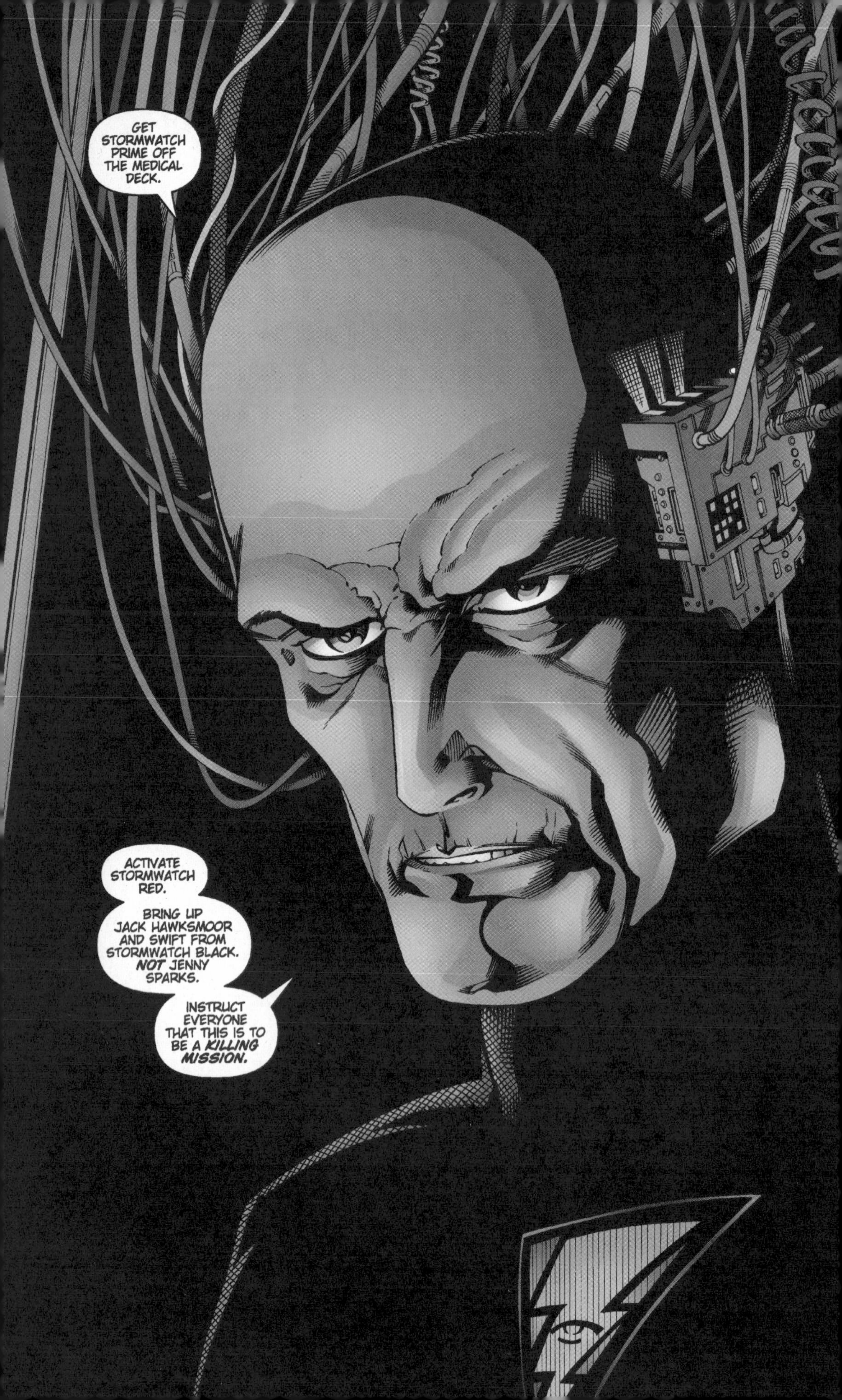
GET STORMWATCH PRIME OFF THE MEDICAL DECK.
ACTIVATE STORMWATCH RED.
BRING UP JACK HAWKSMOOR AND SWIFT FROM STORMWATCH BLACK. *NOT* JENNY SPARKS.
INSTRUCT EVERYONE THAT THIS IS TO BE A *KILLING MISSION.*

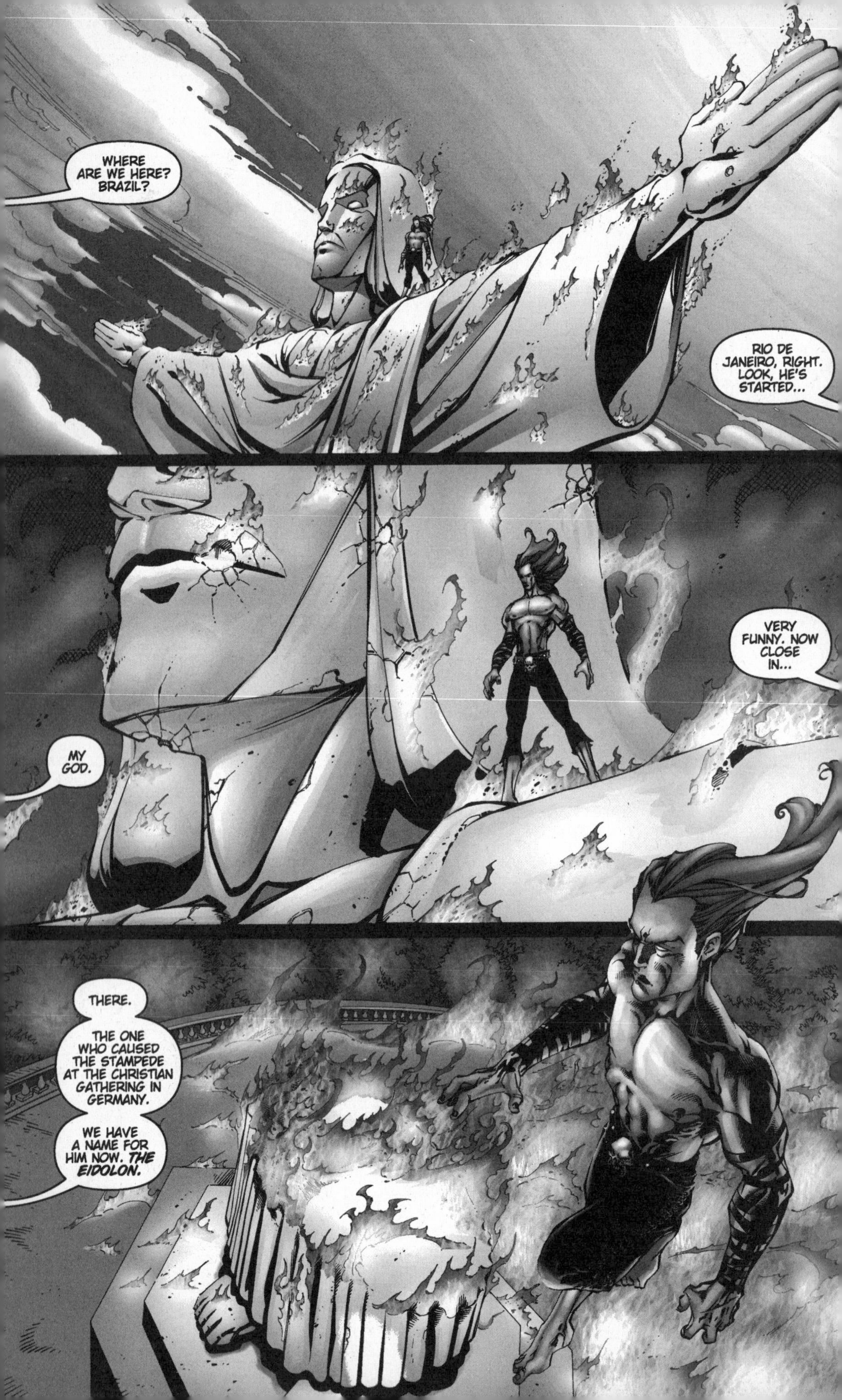

WHERE ARE WE HERE? BRAZIL?
RIO DE JANEIRO, RIGHT. LOOK, HE'S STARTED...
VERY FUNNY. NOW CLOSE IN...
MY GOD.
THERE.
THE ONE WHO CAUSED THE STAMPEDE AT THE CHRISTIAN GATHERING IN GERMANY.
WE HAVE A NAME FOR HIM NOW. *THE EIDOLON.*

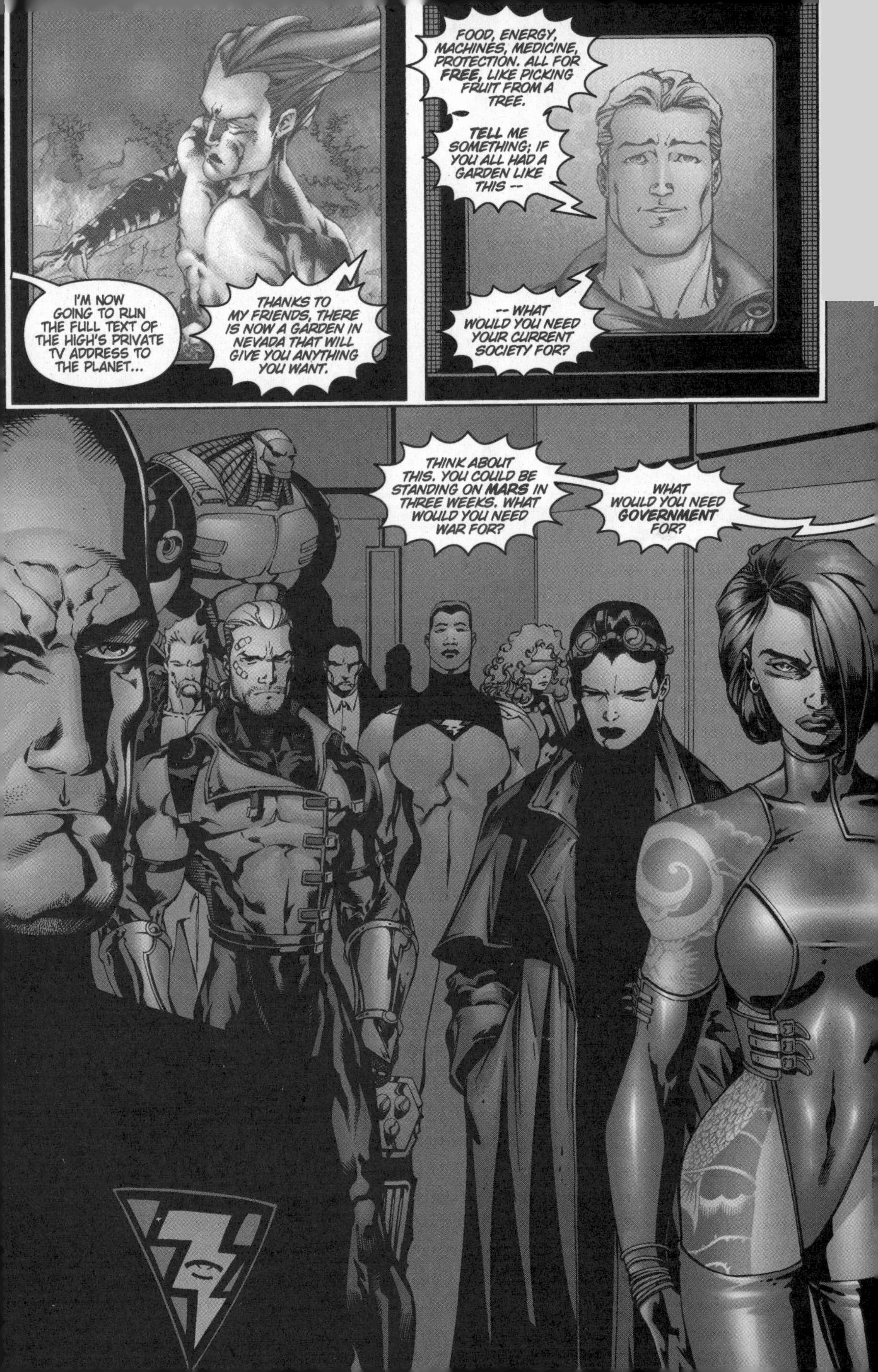
I'M NOW GOING TO RUN THE FULL TEXT OF THE HIGH'S PRIVATE TV ADDRESS TO THE PLANET...
THANKS TO MY FRIENDS, THERE IS NOW A GARDEN IN NEVADA THAT WILL GIVE YOU ANYTHING YOU WANT.
FOOD, ENERGY, MACHINES, MEDICINE, PROTECTION. ALL FOR FREE, LIKE PICKING FRUIT FROM A TREE.
TELL ME SOMETHING; IF YOU ALL HAD A GARDEN LIKE THIS --
-- WHAT WOULD YOU NEED YOUR CURRENT SOCIETY FOR?
THINK ABOUT THIS. YOU COULD BE STANDING ON MARS IN THREE WEEKS. WHAT WOULD YOU NEED WAR FOR?
WHAT WOULD YOU NEED GOVERNMENT FOR?

WE'RE HERE TO PRESENT YOU WITH THESE QUESTIONS, AND THE TOOLS FOR SOLVING THEM.

THE WEATHERMAN'S PRIVATE MEMORY JOURNAL: I find myself studying my team during the tape.

I GUESS, IN SOME WAYS, THIS DOESN'T SEEM SO STRANGE.

THE WORLD IS GROWING USED TO COSTUMED CRIMEFIGHTERS, SPECIAL MEN AND WOMEN WHO SEEM TO HOLD YOUR WORLD IN THEIR HANDS.

WINTER, the field leader, was given a beating by The High, the speaker. The High also disabled FUJI and HELLSTRIKE. Hate radiates from them.

WHAT WE'RE DOING IS HANDING THAT WORLD BACK TO YOU.

FIGHTING CRIME IS NO GOOD UNLESS YOU LOOK PAST CRIME, TO ITS ROOT.

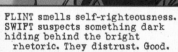

JACK HAWKSMOOR, a creature designed for life in cities, allows intrigue to override his irritation with his medics.

SAVING THE WORLD IS NO GOOD IF WE LEAVE IT THE WAY WE FOUND IT.

FLINT smells self-righteousness. SWIFT suspects something dark hiding behind the bright rhetoric. They distrust. Good.

IT IS OUR INTENT TO HAND YOU A SAVED WORLD, TO OFFER YOU TOOLS THAT WILL MAKE YOU GREAT. AND THEN -- YOU WILL NEVER SEE US AGAIN.

FAHRENHEIT is the only American on this field team. I wonder if that doesn't make her susceptible to The High's carefully managed idealism.

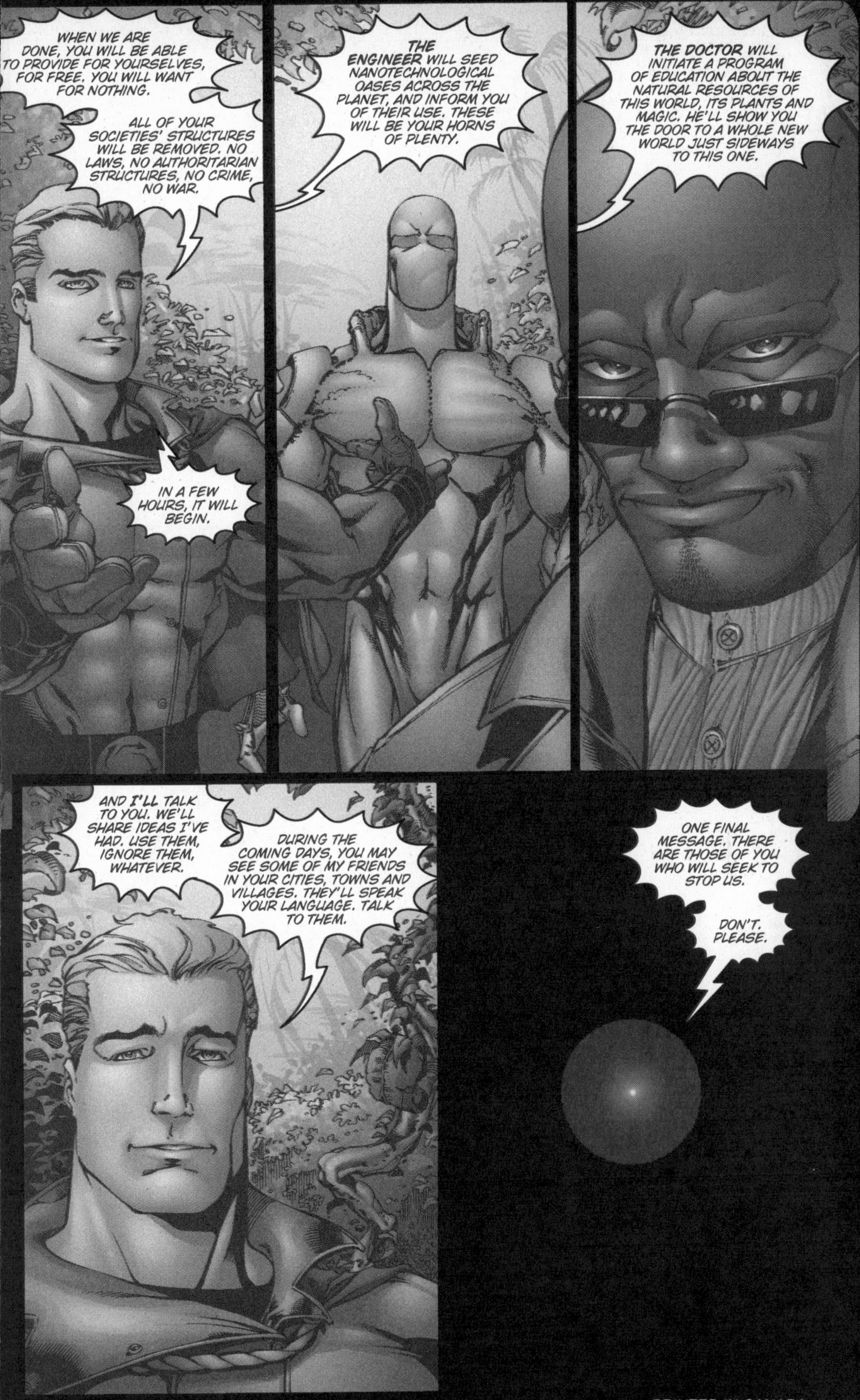
WHEN WE ARE DONE, YOU WILL BE ABLE TO PROVIDE FOR YOURSELVES, FOR FREE. YOU WILL WANT FOR NOTHING.
ALL OF YOUR SOCIETIES' STRUCTURES WILL BE REMOVED. NO LAWS, NO AUTHORITARIAN STRUCTURES, NO CRIME, NO WAR.
IN A FEW HOURS, IT WILL BEGIN.
THE ENGINEER WILL SEED NANOTECHNOLOGICAL OASES ACROSS THE PLANET, AND INFORM YOU OF THEIR USE. THESE WILL BE YOUR HORNS OF PLENTY.
THE DOCTOR WILL INITIATE A PROGRAM OF EDUCATION ABOUT THE NATURAL RESOURCES OF THIS WORLD, ITS PLANTS AND MAGIC. HE'LL SHOW YOU THE DOOR TO A WHOLE NEW WORLD JUST SIDEWAYS TO THIS ONE.
AND I'LL TALK TO YOU. WE'LL SHARE IDEAS I'VE HAD. USE THEM, IGNORE THEM, WHATEVER.
DURING THE COMING DAYS, YOU MAY SEE SOME OF MY FRIENDS IN YOUR CITIES, TOWNS AND VILLAGES. THEY'LL SPEAK YOUR LANGUAGE. TALK TO THEM.
ONE FINAL MESSAGE. THERE ARE THOSE OF YOU WHO WILL SEEK TO STOP US.
DON'T. PLEASE.

PRINTED IN CANADA

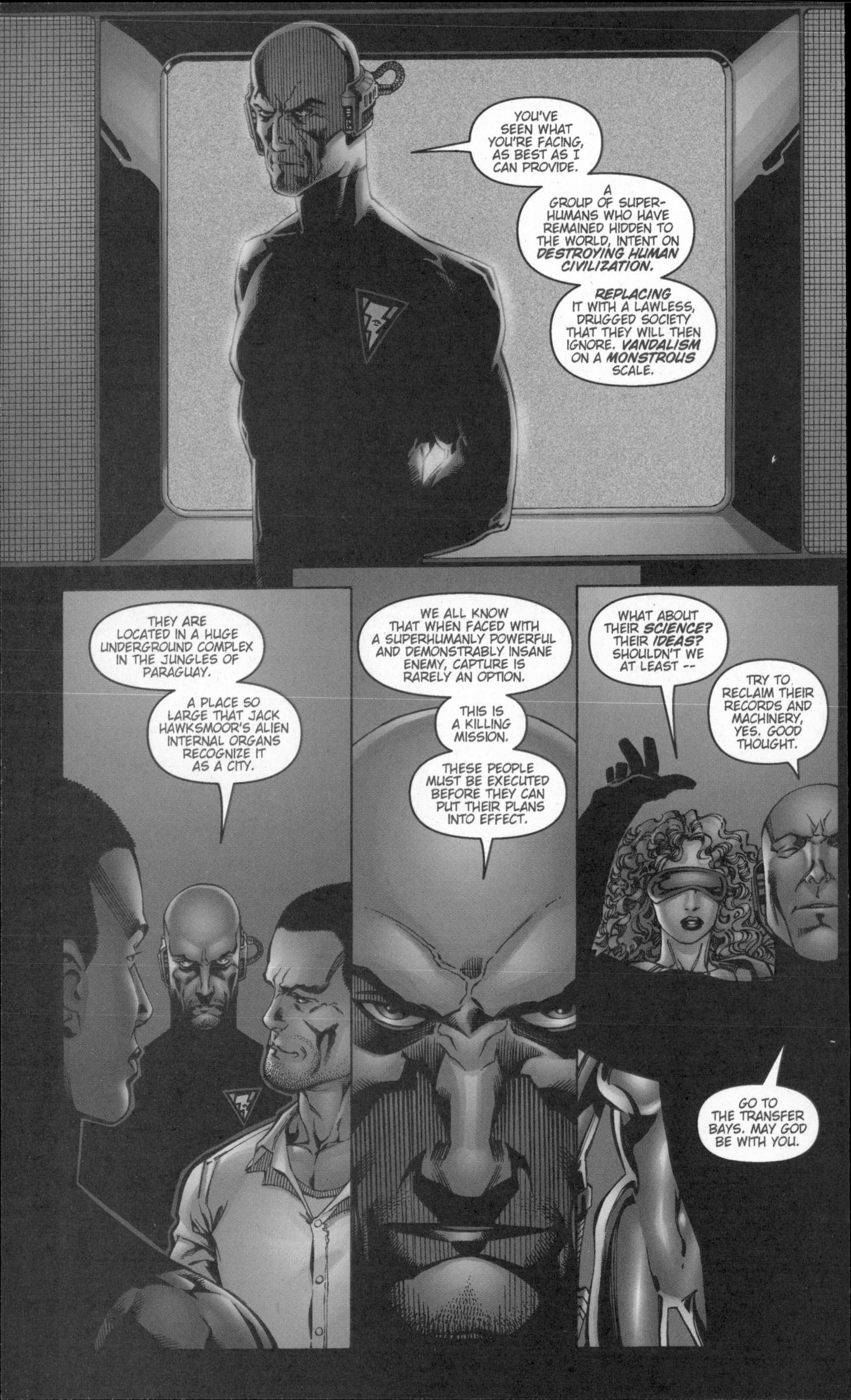
YOU'VE SEEN WHAT YOU'RE FACING, AS BEST AS I CAN PROVIDE.
A GROUP OF SUPER-HUMANS WHO HAVE REMAINED HIDDEN TO THE WORLD, INTENT ON DESTROYING HUMAN CIVILIZATION.
REPLACING IT WITH A LAWLESS, DRUGGED SOCIETY THAT THEY WILL THEN IGNORE. VANDALISM ON A MONSTROUS SCALE.
THEY ARE LOCATED IN A HUGE UNDERGROUND COMPLEX IN THE JUNGLES OF PARAGUAY.
A PLACE SO LARGE THAT JACK HAWKSMOOR'S ALIEN INTERNAL ORGANS RECOGNIZE IT AS A CITY.
WE ALL KNOW THAT WHEN FACED WITH A SUPERHUMANLY POWERFUL AND DEMONSTRABLY INSANE ENEMY, CAPTURE IS RARELY AN OPTION.
THIS IS A KILLING MISSION.
THESE PEOPLE MUST BE EXECUTED BEFORE THEY CAN PUT THEIR PLANS INTO EFFECT.
WHAT ABOUT THEIR SCIENCE? THEIR IDEAS? SHOULDN'T WE AT LEAST --
TRY TO RECLAIM THEIR RECORDS AND MACHINERY, YES. GOOD THOUGHT.
GO TO THE TRANSFER BAYS. MAY GOD BE WITH YOU.

BASTARDS...

...THOSE BASTARDS...

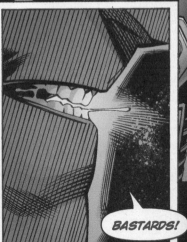

BASTARDS!

WEATHER-MAN, JENNY SPARKS IS ON BOARD AGAIN, DEMANDING TO SEE YOU.

...

TELL HER TO WAIT, DAMNIT.

...DAMN IT...

...I WON'T HAVE THEM CHANGING THE WORLD. NOT YET. NOT LIKE THIS. NOT...

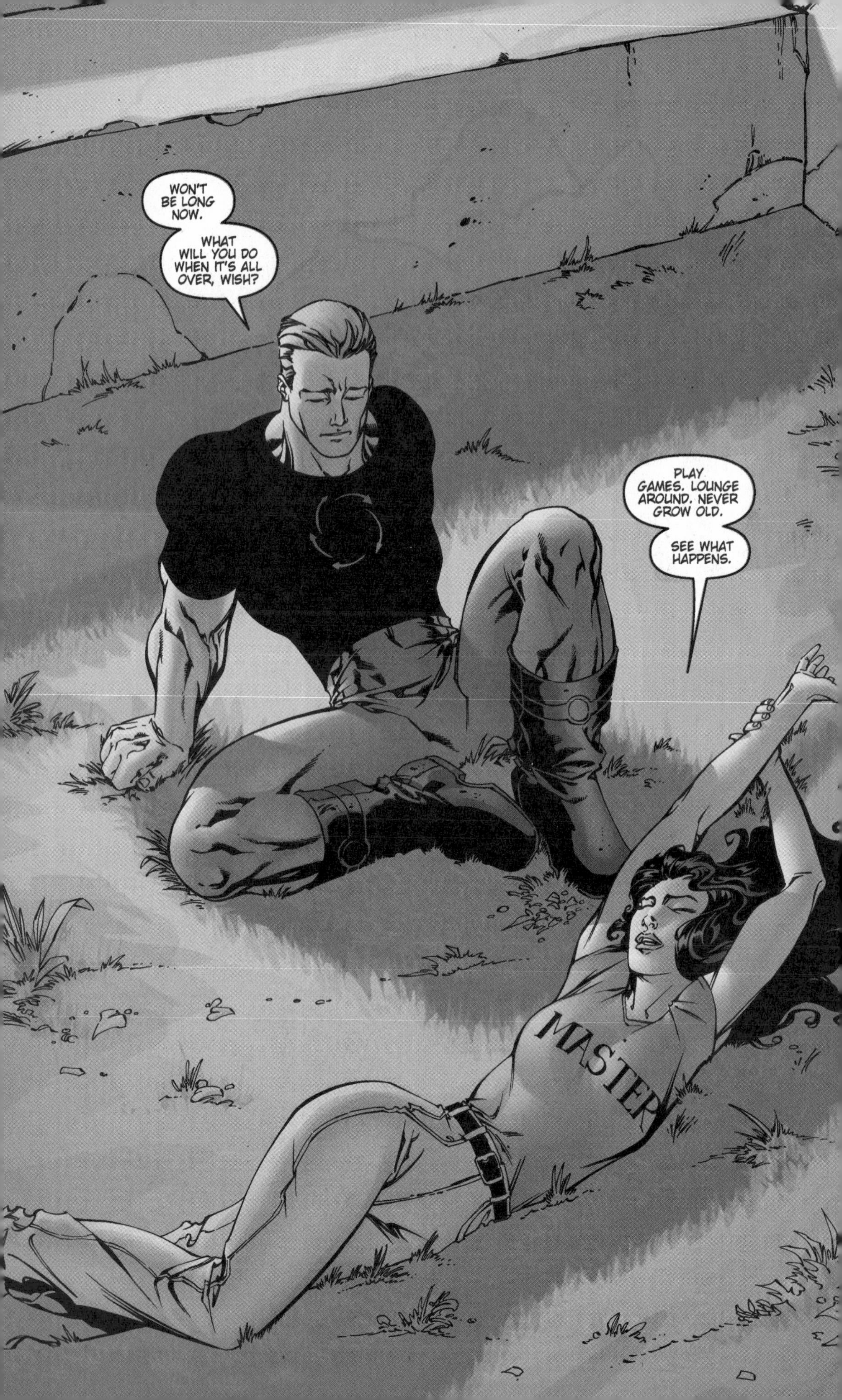
WON'T BE LONG NOW.
WHAT WILL YOU DO WHEN IT'S ALL OVER, WISH?
PLAY GAMES. LOUNGE AROUND. NEVER GROW OLD.
SEE WHAT HAPPENS.
MASTER

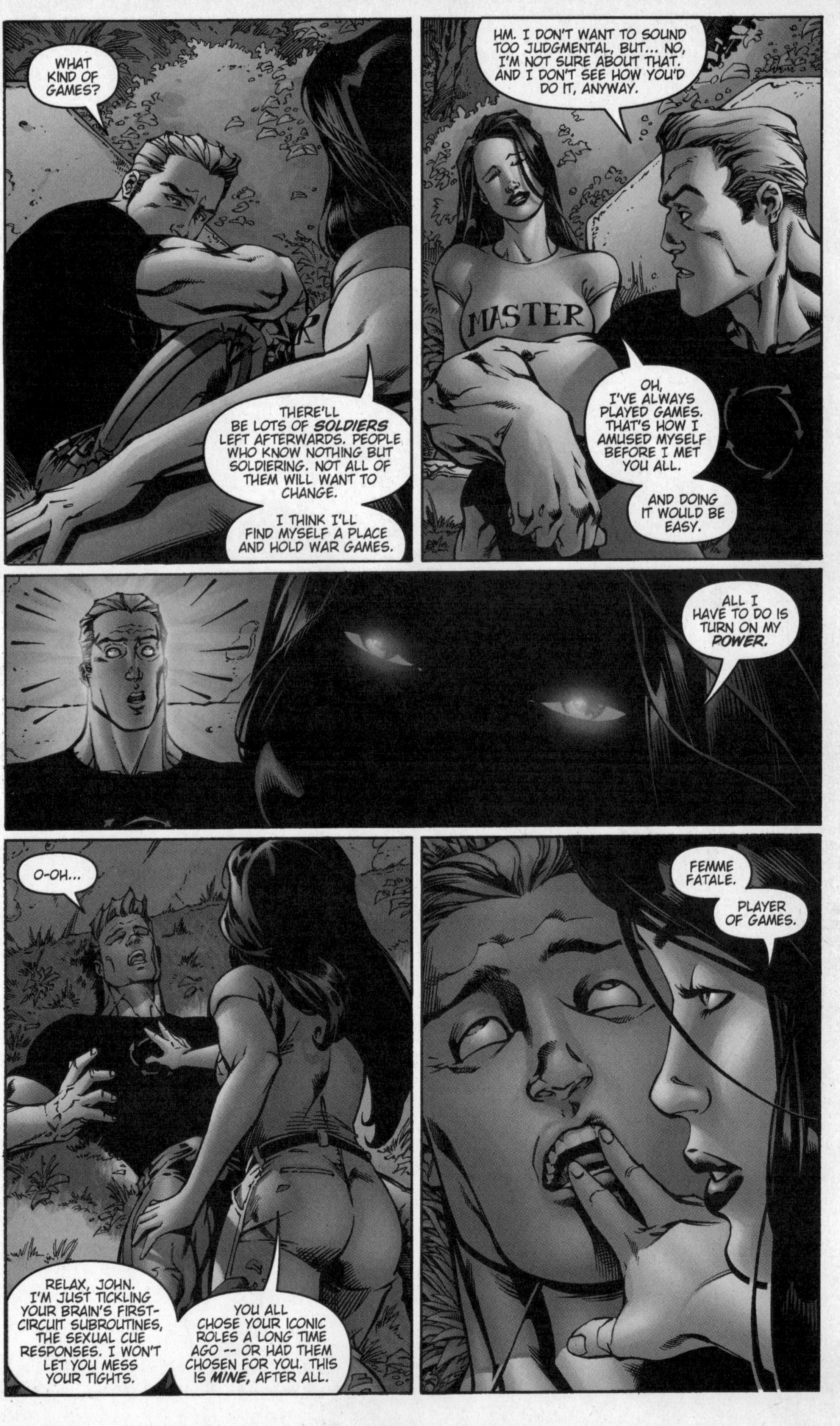
WHAT KIND OF GAMES?
THERE'LL BE LOTS OF SOLDIERS LEFT AFTERWARDS. PEOPLE WHO KNOW NOTHING BUT SOLDIERING. NOT ALL OF THEM WILL WANT TO CHANGE.
I THINK I'LL FIND MYSELF A PLACE AND HOLD WAR GAMES.
HM. I DON'T WANT TO SOUND TOO JUDGMENTAL, BUT... NO, I'M NOT SURE ABOUT THAT. AND I DON'T SEE HOW YOU'D DO IT, ANYWAY.
MASTER
OH, I'VE ALWAYS PLAYED GAMES. THAT'S HOW I AMUSED MYSELF BEFORE I MET YOU ALL.
AND DOING IT WOULD BE EASY.
ALL I HAVE TO DO IS TURN ON MY POWER.
O-OH...
RELAX, JOHN. I'M JUST TICKLING YOUR BRAIN'S FIRST-CIRCUIT SUBROUTINES, THE SEXUAL CUE RESPONSES. I WON'T LET YOU MESS YOUR TIGHTS.
YOU ALL CHOSE YOUR ICONIC ROLES A LONG TIME AGO -- OR HAD THEM CHOSEN FOR YOU. THIS IS MINE, AFTER ALL.
FEMME FATALE.
PLAYER OF GAMES.

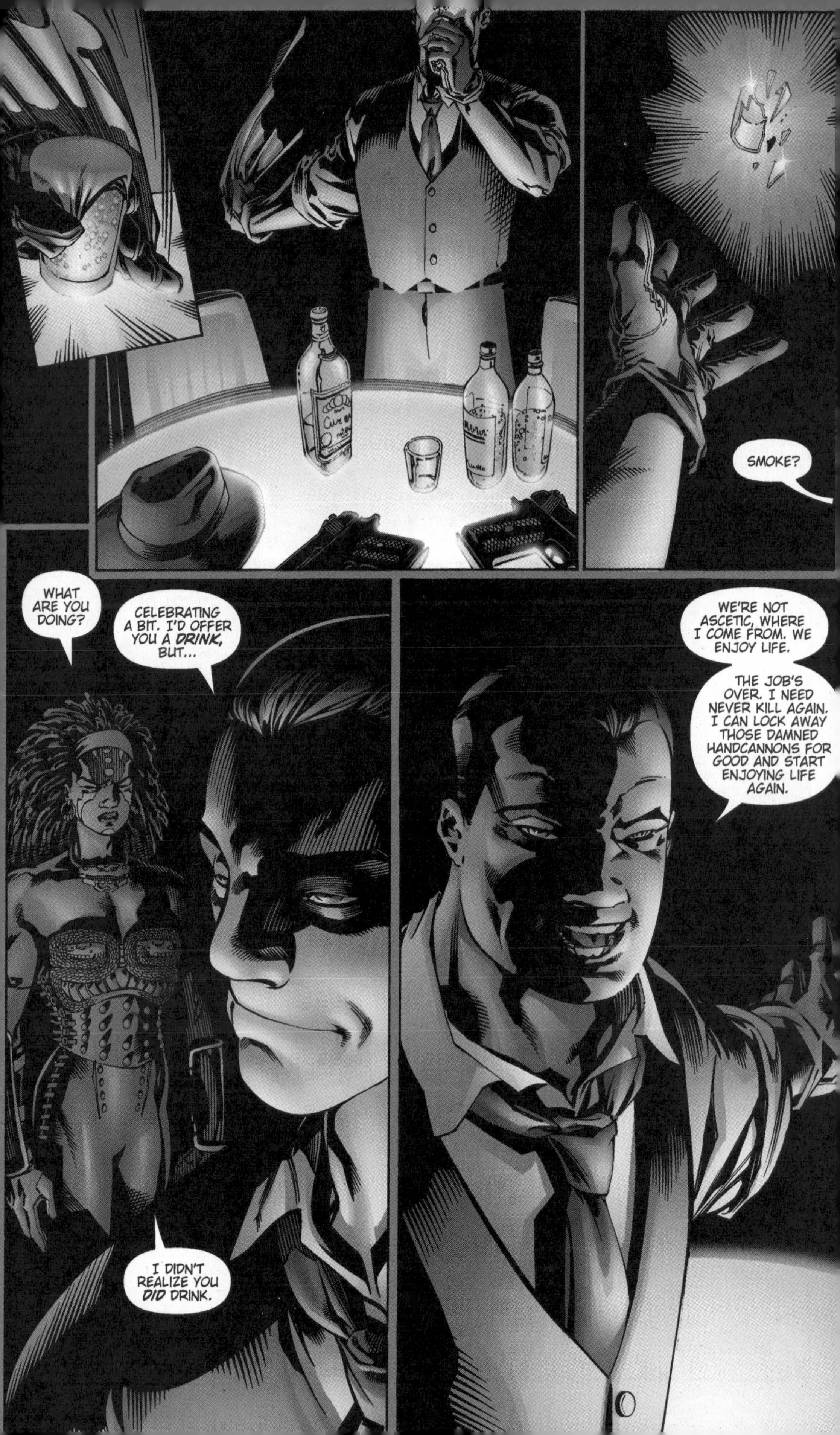
SMOKE?
WHAT ARE YOU DOING?
CELEBRATING A BIT. I'D OFFER YOU A ***DRINK,*** BUT...
I DIDN'T REALIZE YOU ***DID*** DRINK.
WE'RE NOT ASCETIC, WHERE I COME FROM. WE ENJOY LIFE.
THE JOB'S OVER. I NEED NEVER KILL AGAIN. I CAN LOCK AWAY THOSE DAMNED HANDCANNONS FOR GOOD AND START ENJOYING LIFE AGAIN.

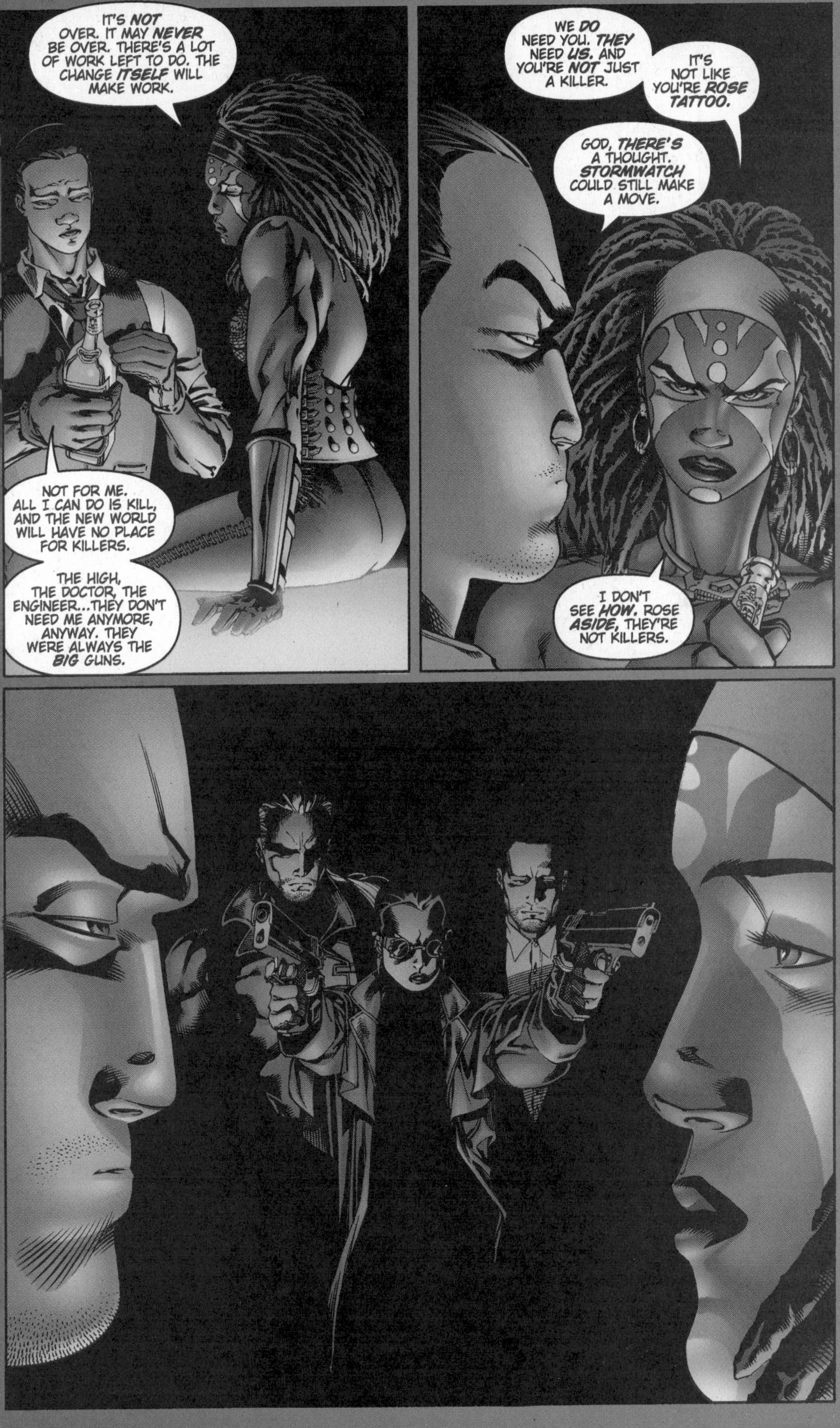

IT'S NOT OVER. IT MAY NEVER BE OVER. THERE'S A LOT OF WORK LEFT TO DO. THE CHANGE ITSELF WILL MAKE WORK.
NOT FOR ME. ALL I CAN DO IS KILL, AND THE NEW WORLD WILL HAVE NO PLACE FOR KILLERS.
THE HIGH, THE DOCTOR, THE ENGINEER...THEY DON'T NEED ME ANYMORE, ANYWAY. THEY WERE ALWAYS THE BIG GUNS.
WE DO NEED YOU. THEY NEED US. AND YOU'RE NOT JUST A KILLER.
IT'S NOT LIKE YOU'RE ROSE TATTOO.
GOD, THERE'S A THOUGHT. STORMWATCH COULD STILL MAKE A MOVE.
I DON'T SEE HOW. ROSE ASIDE, THEY'RE NOT KILLERS.

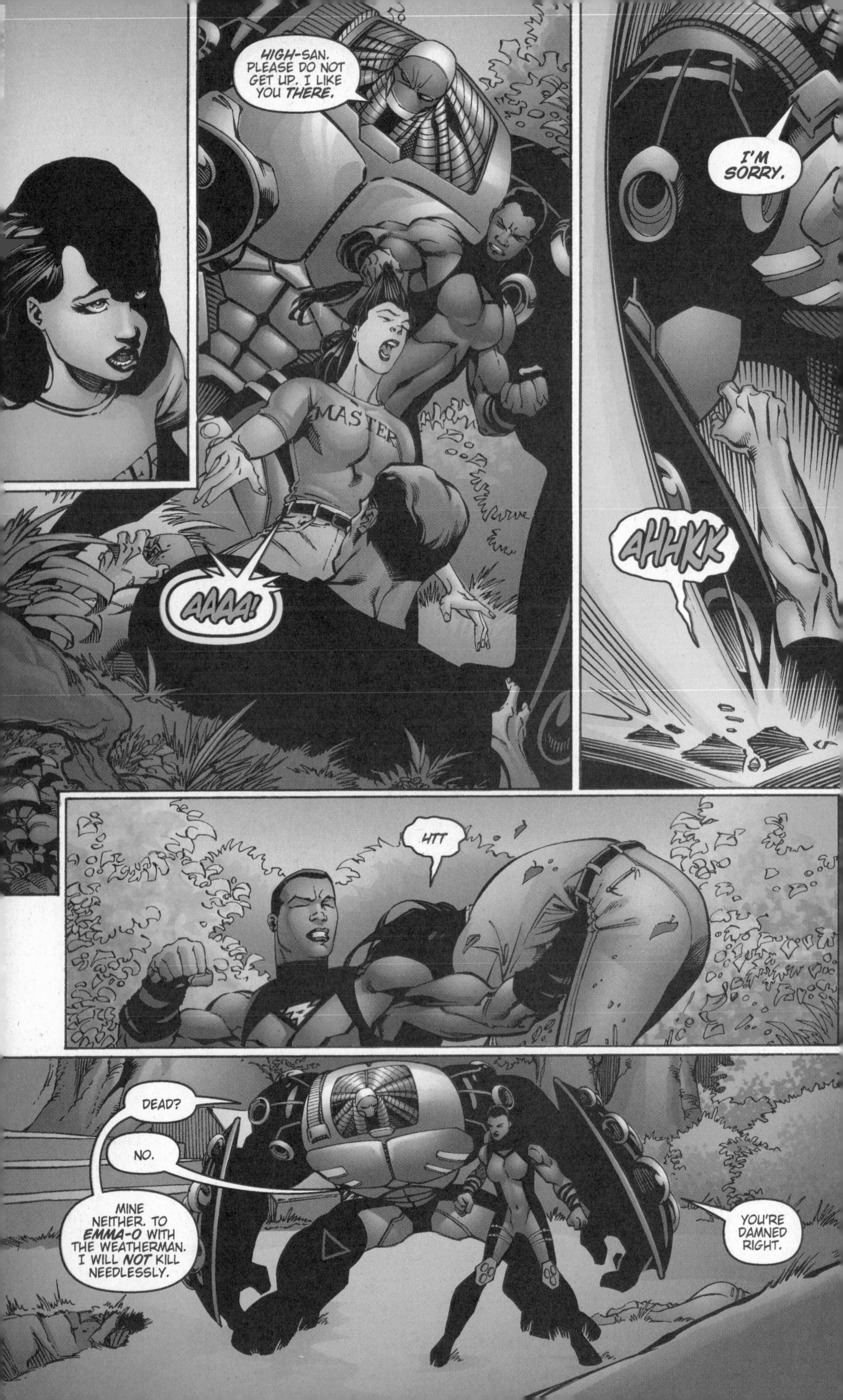

HIGH-SAN. PLEASE DO NOT GET UP. I LIKE YOU THERE.
MASTER
AAAA!
I'M SORRY.
AHHKK
UTT
DEAD?
NO.
MINE NEITHER. TO EMMA-O WITH THE WEATHERMAN. I WILL NOT KILL NEEDLESSLY.
YOU'RE DAMNED RIGHT.

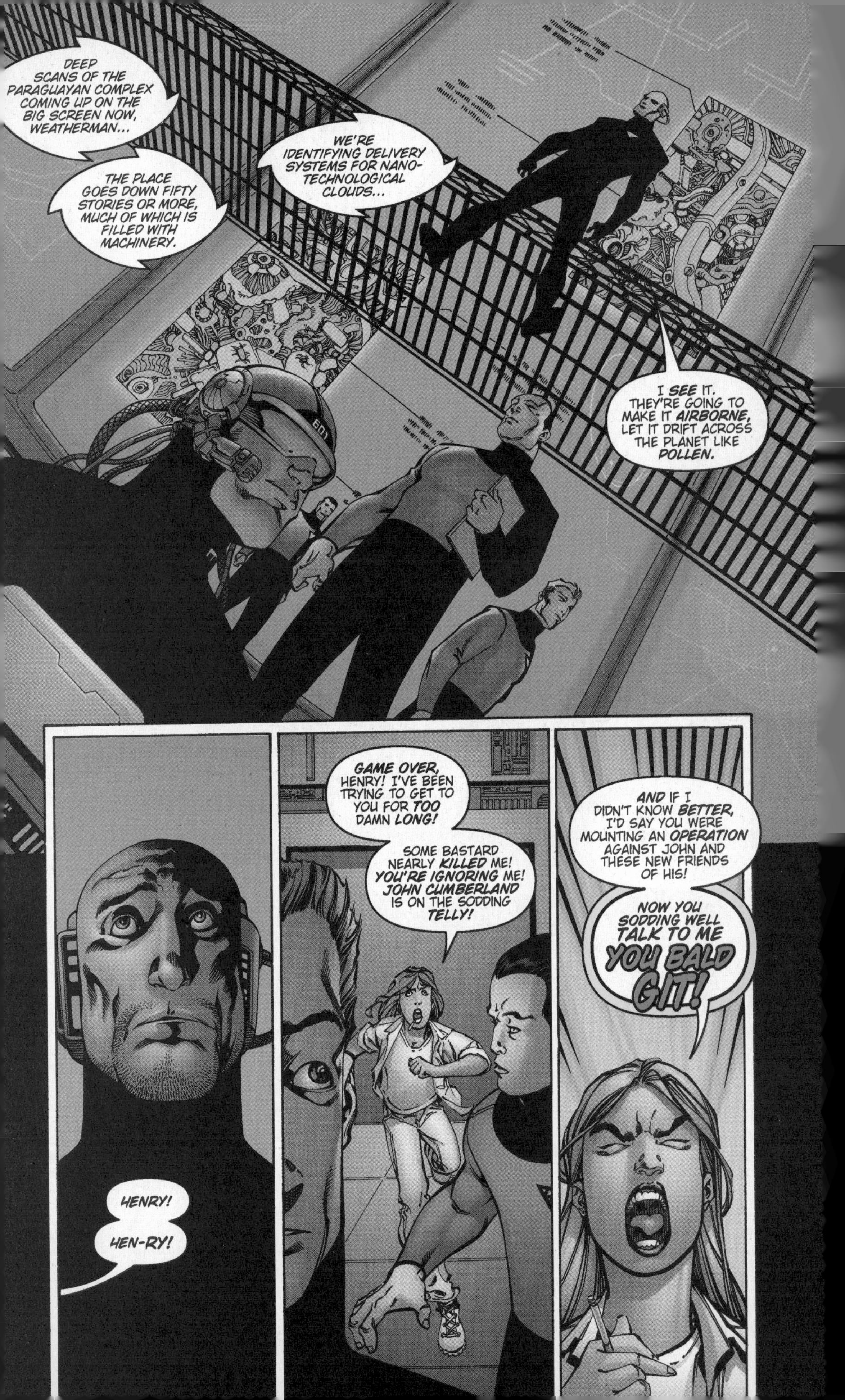
DEEP SCANS OF THE PARAGUAYAN COMPLEX COMING UP ON THE BIG SCREEN NOW, WEATHERMAN...
THE PLACE GOES DOWN FIFTY STORIES OR MORE, MUCH OF WHICH IS FILLED WITH MACHINERY.
WE'RE IDENTIFYING DELIVERY SYSTEMS FOR NANO-TECHNOLOGICAL CLOUDS...
I SEE IT. THEY'RE GOING TO MAKE IT AIRBORNE, LET IT DRIFT ACROSS THE PLANET LIKE POLLEN.
HENRY!
HEN-RY!
GAME OVER, HENRY! I'VE BEEN TRYING TO GET TO YOU FOR TOO DAMN LONG!
SOME BASTARD NEARLY KILLED ME! YOU'RE IGNORING ME! JOHN CUMBERLAND IS ON THE SODDING TELLY!
AND IF I DIDN'T KNOW BETTER, I'D SAY YOU WERE MOUNTING AN OPERATION AGAINST JOHN AND THESE NEW FRIENDS OF HIS!
NOW YOU SODDING WELL TALK TO ME YOU BALD GIT!

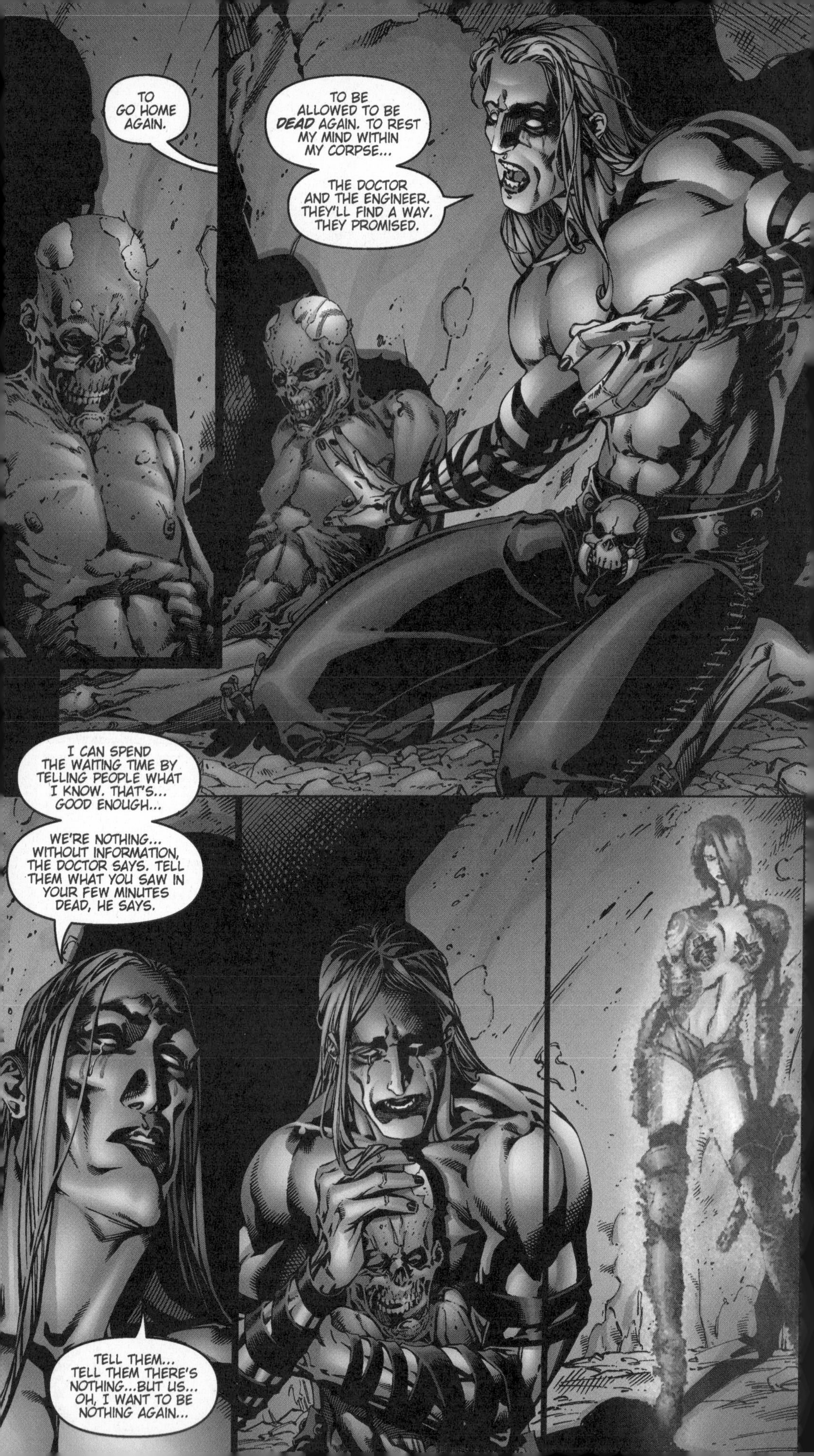
TO GO HOME AGAIN.
TO BE ALLOWED TO BE DEAD AGAIN. TO REST MY MIND WITHIN MY CORPSE...
THE DOCTOR AND THE ENGINEER. THEY'LL FIND A WAY. THEY PROMISED.
I CAN SPEND THE WAITING TIME BY TELLING PEOPLE WHAT I KNOW. THAT'S... GOOD ENOUGH...
WE'RE NOTHING... WITHOUT INFORMATION, THE DOCTOR SAYS. TELL THEM WHAT YOU SAW IN YOUR FEW MINUTES DEAD, HE SAYS.
TELL THEM... TELL THEM THERE'S NOTHING...BUT US... OH, I WANT TO BE NOTHING AGAIN...

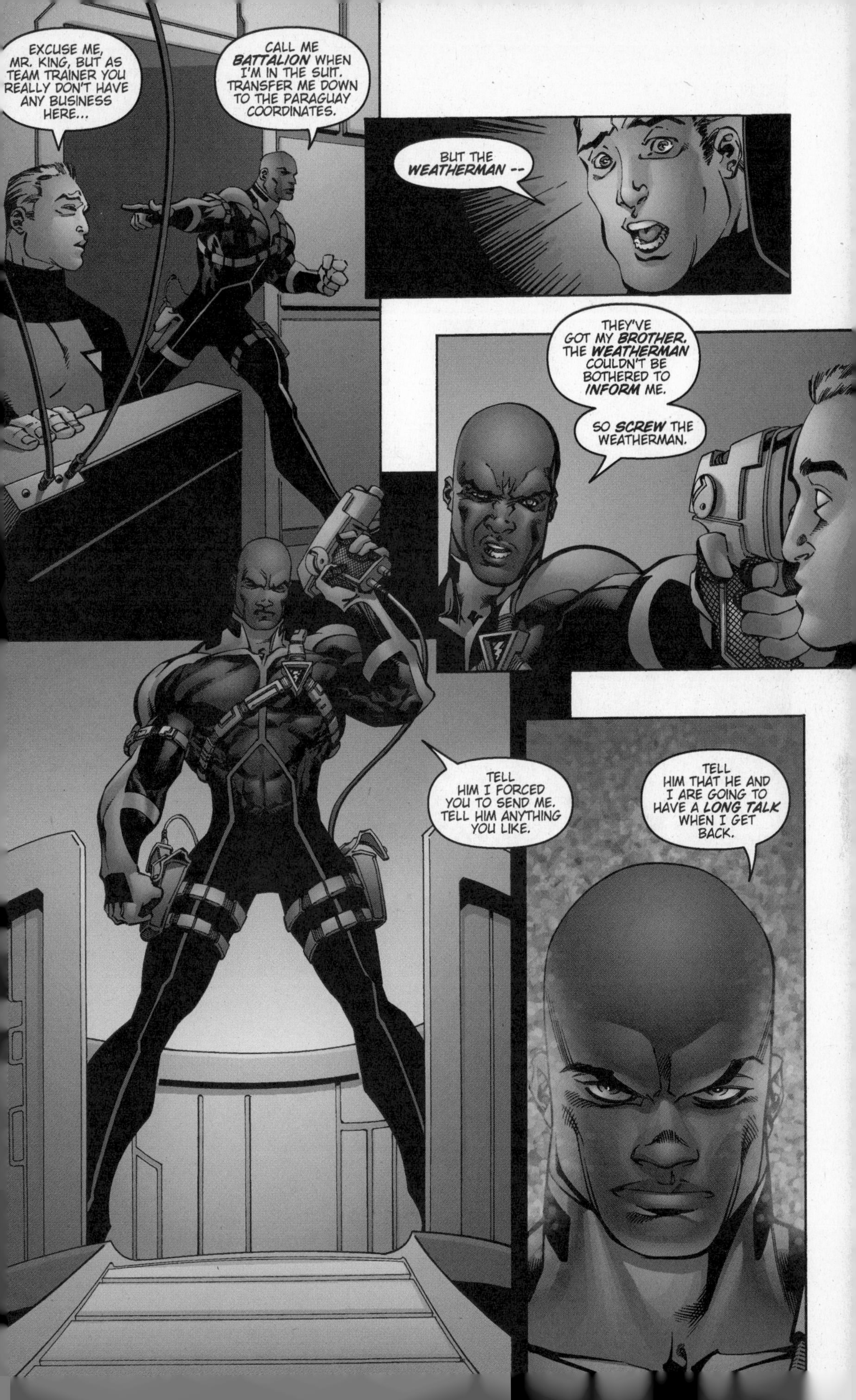
EXCUSE ME, MR. KING, BUT AS TEAM TRAINER YOU REALLY DON'T HAVE ANY BUSINESS HERE...
CALL ME BATTALION WHEN I'M IN THE SUIT. TRANSFER ME DOWN TO THE PARAGUAY COORDINATES.
BUT THE WEATHERMAN --
THEY'VE GOT MY BROTHER. THE WEATHERMAN COULDN'T BE BOTHERED TO INFORM ME.
SO SCREW THE WEATHERMAN.
TELL HIM I FORCED YOU TO SEND ME. TELL HIM ANYTHING YOU LIKE.
TELL HIM THAT HE AND I ARE GOING TO HAVE A LONG TALK WHEN I GET BACK.

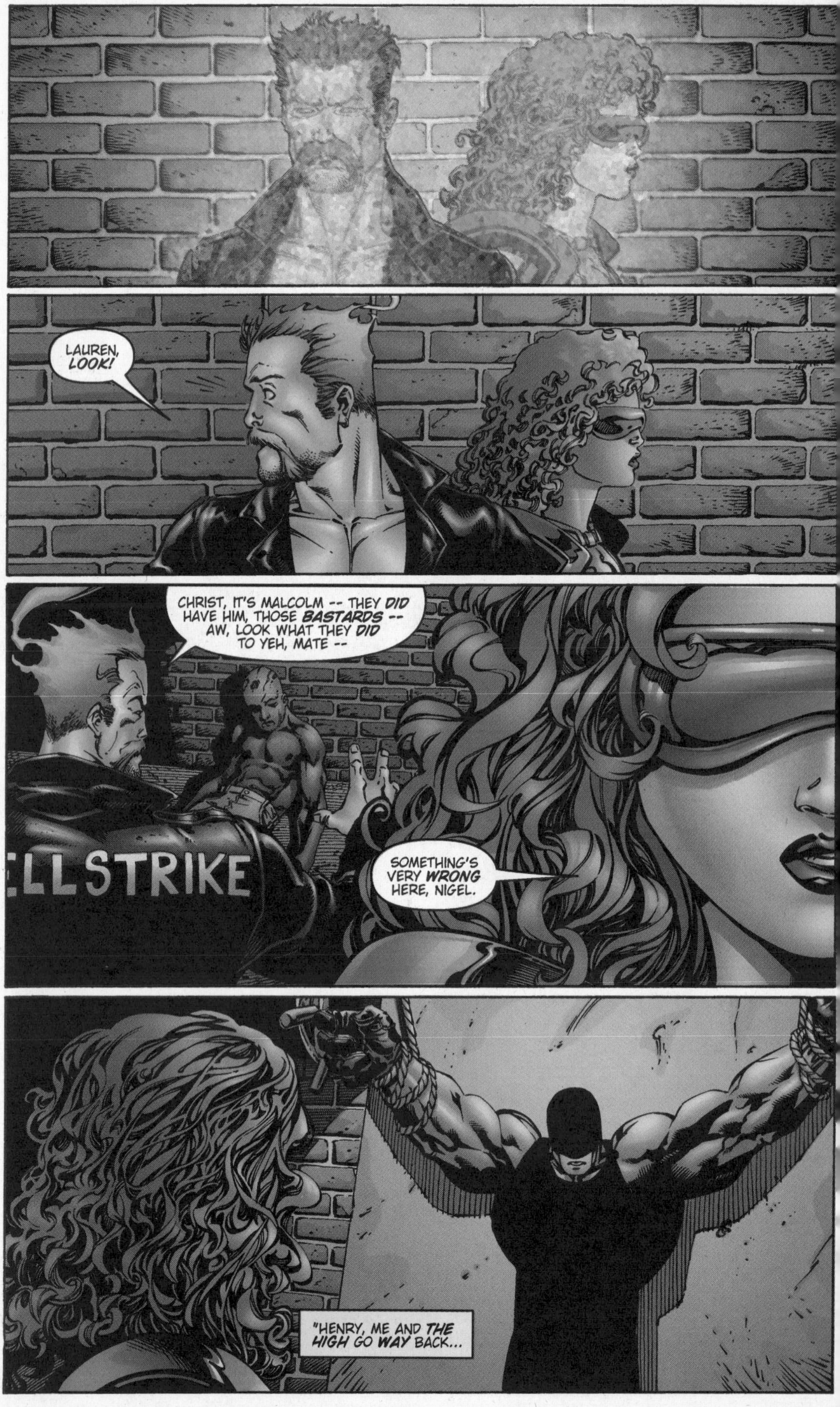
LAUREN, LOOK!
CHRIST, IT'S MALCOLM -- THEY DID HAVE HIM, THOSE BASTARDS -- AW, LOOK WHAT THEY DID TO YEH, MATE --
ELLSTRIKE
SOMETHING'S VERY WRONG HERE, NIGEL.
"HENRY, ME AND THE HIGH GO WAY BACK...

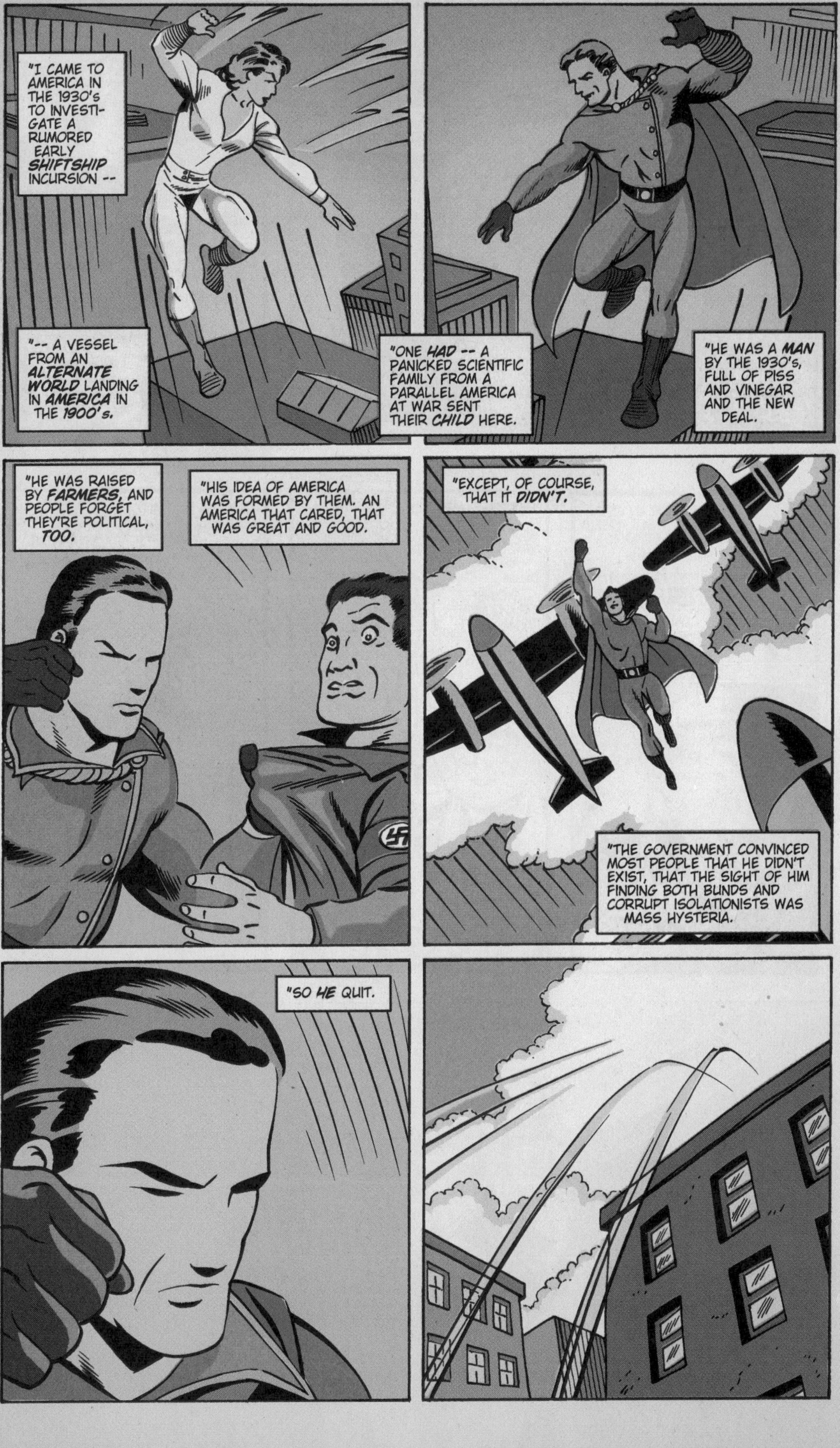
"I CAME TO AMERICA IN THE 1930's TO INVESTI-GATE A RUMORED EARLY SHIFTSHIP INCURSION --
"-- A VESSEL FROM AN ALTERNATE WORLD LANDING IN AMERICA IN THE 1900's.
"ONE HAD -- A PANICKED SCIENTIFIC FAMILY FROM A PARALLEL AMERICA AT WAR SENT THEIR CHILD HERE.
"HE WAS A MAN BY THE 1930's, FULL OF PISS AND VINEGAR AND THE NEW DEAL.
"HE WAS RAISED BY FARMERS, AND PEOPLE FORGET THEY'RE POLITICAL, TOO.
"HIS IDEA OF AMERICA WAS FORMED BY THEM. AN AMERICA THAT CARED, THAT WAS GREAT AND GOOD.
"EXCEPT, OF COURSE, THAT IT DIDN'T.
"THE GOVERNMENT CONVINCED MOST PEOPLE THAT HE DIDN'T EXIST, THAT THE SIGHT OF HIM FINDING BOTH BUNDS AND CORRUPT ISOLATIONISTS WAS MASS HYSTERIA.
"SO HE QUIT.

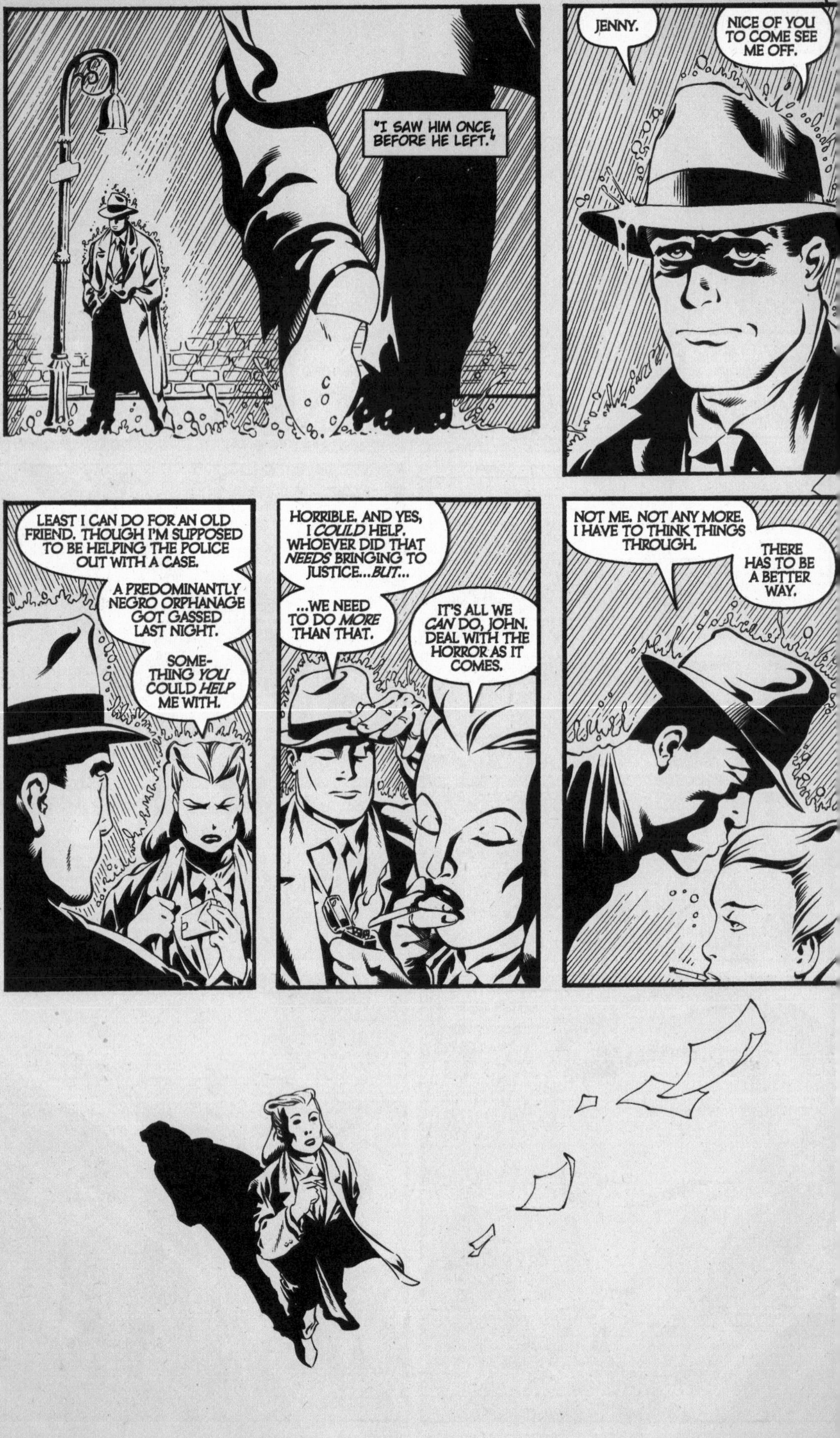

"I SAW HIM ONCE, BEFORE HE LEFT."
JENNY.
NICE OF YOU TO COME SEE ME OFF.
LEAST I CAN DO FOR AN OLD FRIEND. THOUGH I'M SUPPOSED TO BE HELPING THE POLICE OUT WITH A CASE.
A PREDOMINANTLY NEGRO ORPHANAGE GOT GASSED LAST NIGHT.
SOME-THING YOU COULD HELP ME WITH.
HORRIBLE. AND YES, I COULD HELP. WHOEVER DID THAT NEEDS BRINGING TO JUSTICE... BUT...
...WE NEED TO DO MORE THAN THAT.
IT'S ALL WE CAN DO, JOHN. DEAL WITH THE HORROR AS IT COMES.
NOT ME. NOT ANY MORE. I HAVE TO THINK THINGS THROUGH.
THERE HAS TO BE A BETTER WAY.

I KNOW. I KNOW *ALL* OF THIS, JENNY.

YOU... DO?

THEN *WHY* ARE YOU RUNNING AN *OPERATION* HERE? WHY AREN'T YOU *TALKING* TO HIM AND HIS PEOPLE?

FOR GOD'S SAKE, HE'S BEEN THINKING ABOUT HOW TO FIX THIS PLANET FOR *DECADES*. SHARE IDEAS WITH HIM, HENRY.

THIS IS *PRECISELY* WHY I DID NOT WANT YOU INVOLVED WITH THIS OP. YOU'RE MUDDYING THINGS.

YEAH, RIGHT. NOW *LISTEN* -- HOW DO YOU KNOW ABOUT JOHN?

ROSE TATTOO TOLD ME.

ROSE TATTOO DOESN'T *SPEAK*.

OH, YES SHE *DOES*. SHE'S ALWAYS SPOKEN TO *ME*.

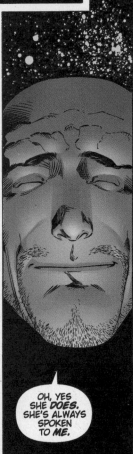

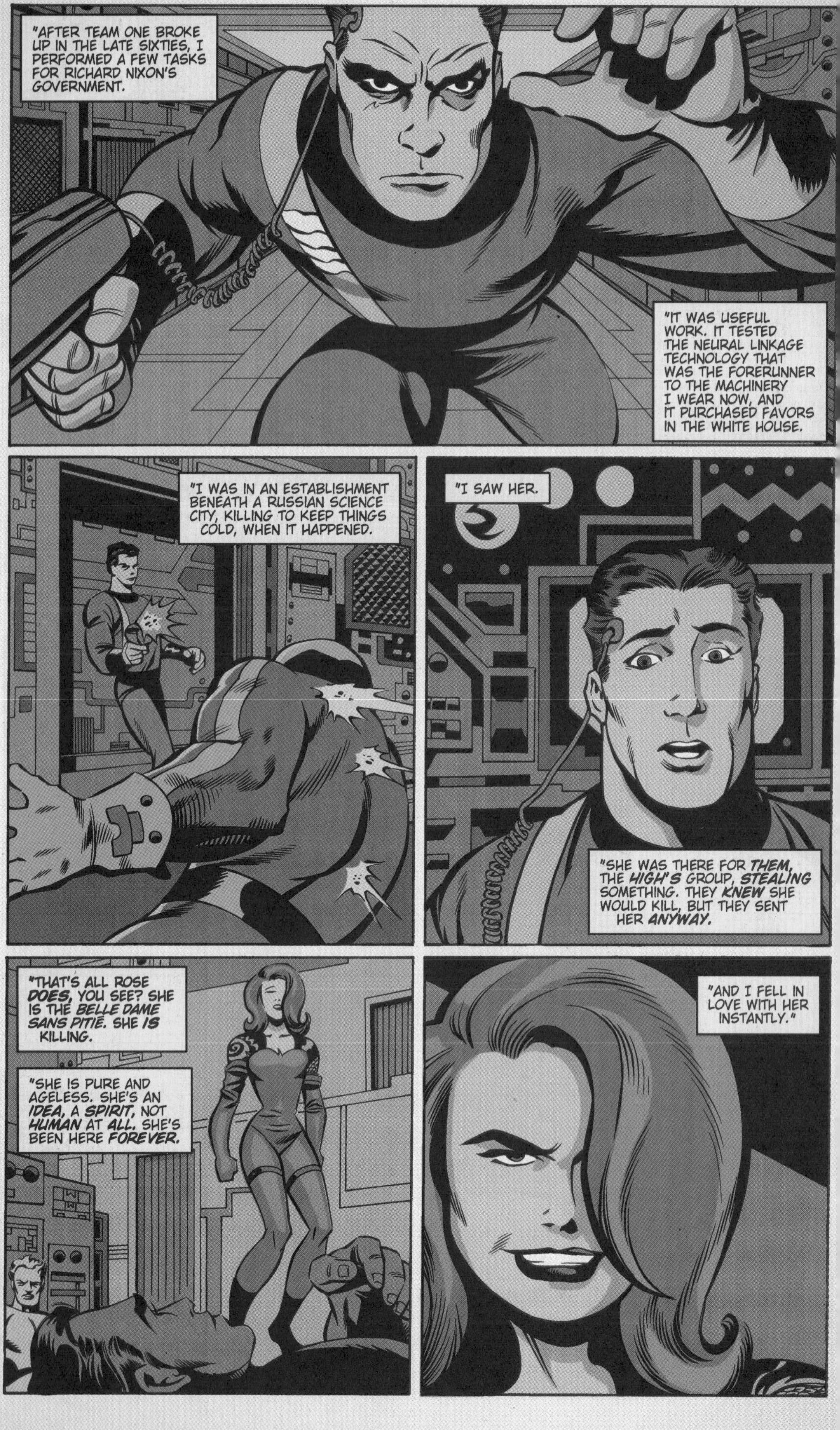
"AFTER TEAM ONE BROKE UP IN THE LATE SIXTIES, I PERFORMED A FEW TASKS FOR RICHARD NIXON'S GOVERNMENT.
"IT WAS USEFUL WORK. IT TESTED THE NEURAL LINKAGE TECHNOLOGY THAT WAS THE FORERUNNER TO THE MACHINERY I WEAR NOW, AND IT PURCHASED FAVORS IN THE WHITE HOUSE.
"I WAS IN AN ESTABLISHMENT BENEATH A RUSSIAN SCIENCE CITY, KILLING TO KEEP THINGS COLD, WHEN IT HAPPENED.
"I SAW HER.
"SHE WAS THERE FOR *THEM*, THE *HIGH'S* GROUP, *STEALING* SOMETHING. THEY *KNEW* SHE WOULD KILL, BUT THEY SENT HER *ANYWAY*.
"THAT'S ALL ROSE *DOES*, YOU SEE? SHE IS THE *BELLE DAME SANS PITIÉ*. SHE *IS* KILLING.
"SHE IS PURE AND AGELESS. SHE'S AN *IDEA*, A *SPIRIT*, NOT *HUMAN* AT *ALL*. SHE'S BEEN HERE *FOREVER*.
"AND I FELL IN LOVE WITH HER INSTANTLY."

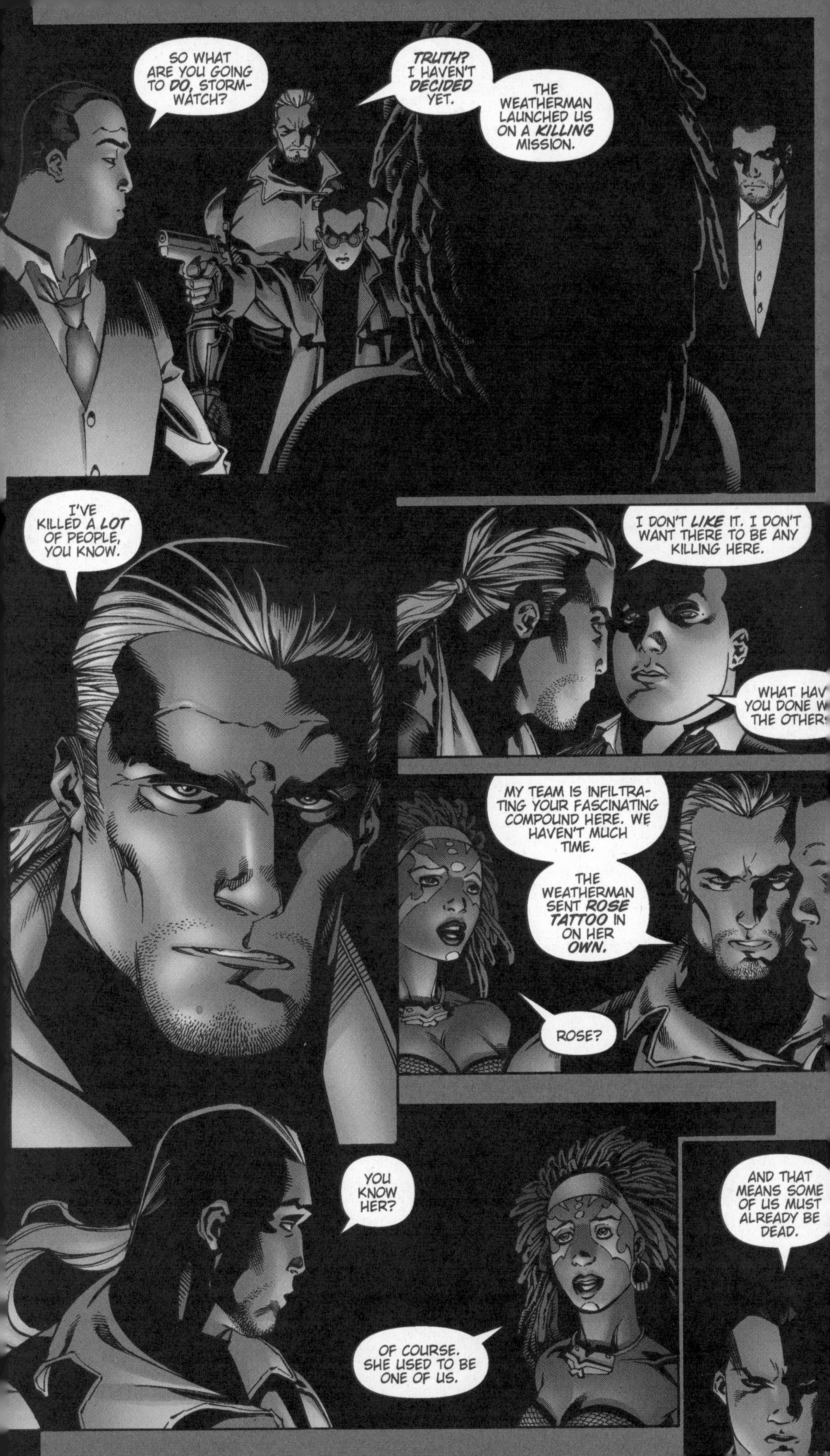
SO WHAT ARE YOU GOING TO DO, STORM-WATCH?
TRUTH? I HAVEN'T DECIDED YET.
THE WEATHERMAN LAUNCHED US ON A KILLING MISSION.
I'VE KILLED A LOT OF PEOPLE, YOU KNOW.
I DON'T LIKE IT. I DON'T WANT THERE TO BE ANY KILLING HERE.
WHAT HAV YOU DONE W THE OTHERS
MY TEAM IS INFILTRA-TING YOUR FASCINATING COMPOUND HERE. WE HAVEN'T MUCH TIME.
THE WEATHERMAN SENT ROSE TATTOO IN ON HER OWN.
ROSE?
YOU KNOW HER?
OF COURSE. SHE USED TO BE ONE OF US.
AND THAT MEANS SOME OF US MUST ALREADY BE DEAD.

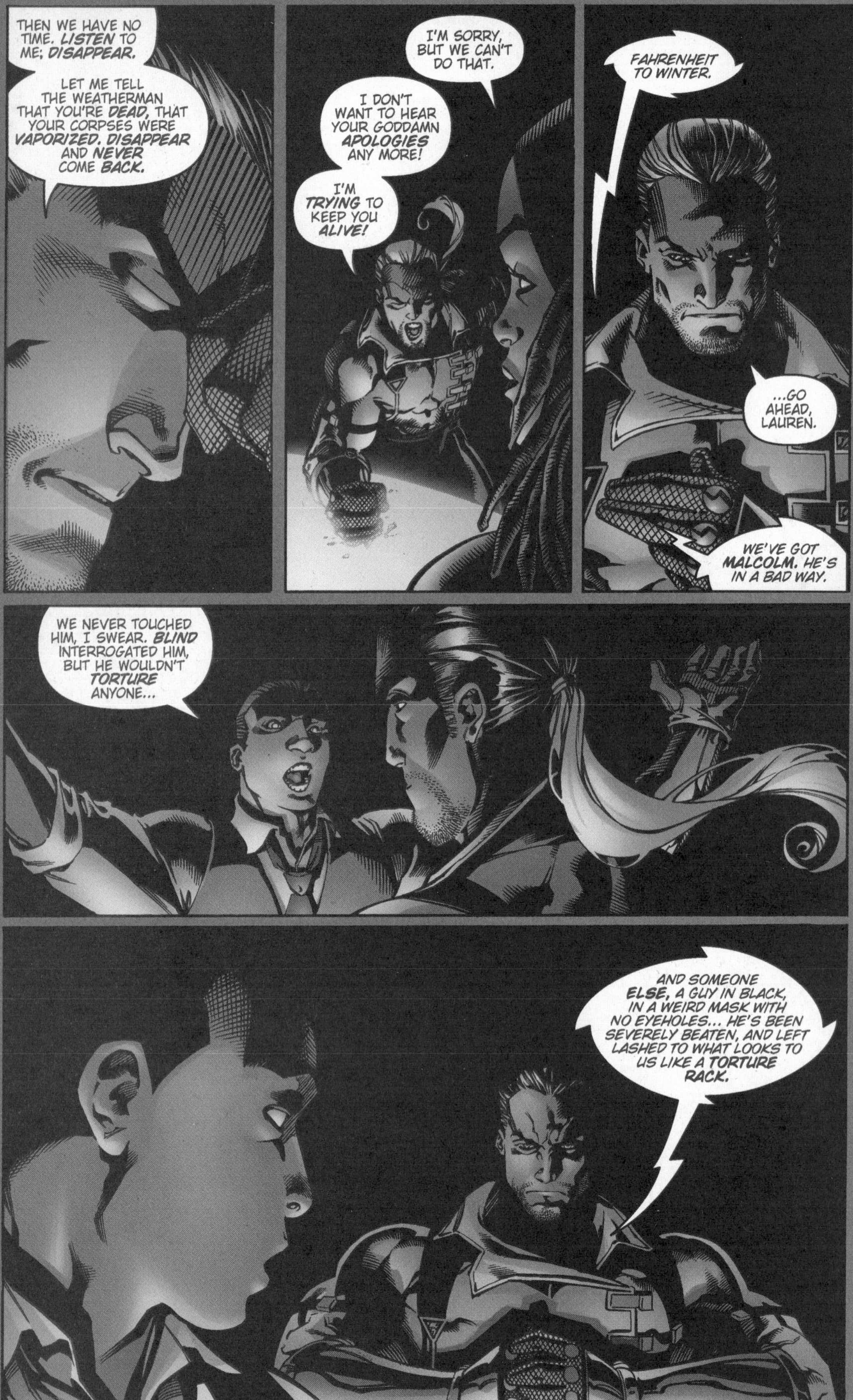
THEN WE HAVE NO TIME. LISTEN TO ME; DISAPPEAR.
LET ME TELL THE WEATHERMAN THAT YOU'RE DEAD, THAT YOUR CORPSES WERE VAPORIZED. DISAPPEAR AND NEVER COME BACK.
I'M SORRY, BUT WE CAN'T DO THAT.
I DON'T WANT TO HEAR YOUR GODDAMN APOLOGIES ANY MORE!
I'M TRYING TO KEEP YOU ALIVE!
FAHRENHEIT TO WINTER.
...GO AHEAD, LAUREN.
WE'VE GOT MALCOLM. HE'S IN A BAD WAY.
WE NEVER TOUCHED HIM, I SWEAR. BLIND INTERROGATED HIM, BUT HE WOULDN'T TORTURE ANYONE...
AND SOMEONE ELSE, A GUY IN BLACK, IN A WEIRD MASK WITH NO EYEHOLES... HE'S BEEN SEVERELY BEATEN, AND LEFT LASHED TO WHAT LOOKS TO US LIKE A TORTURE RACK.

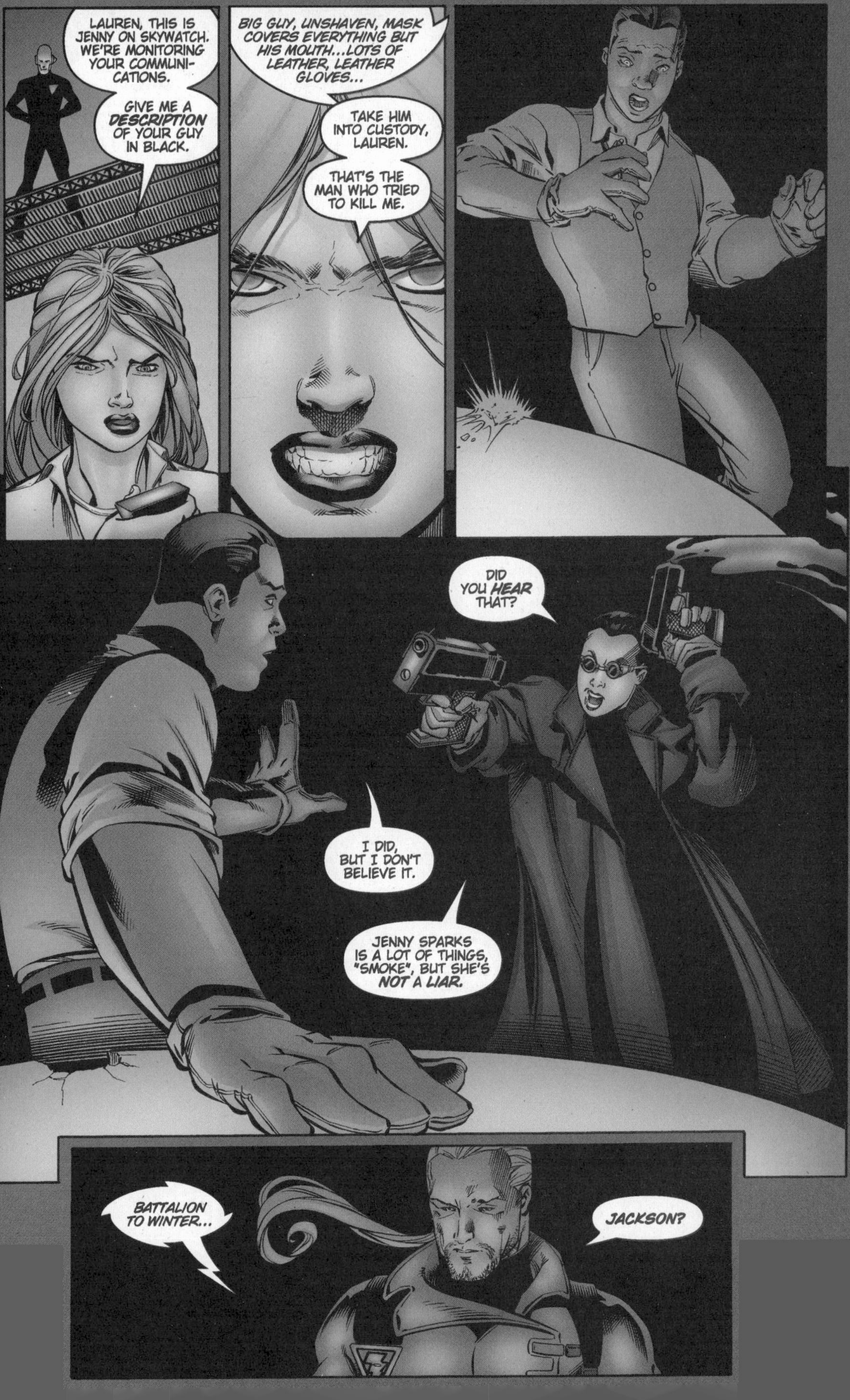
LAUREN, THIS IS JENNY ON SKYWATCH. WE'RE MONITORING YOUR COMMUNI-CATIONS.
GIVE ME A DESCRIPTION OF YOUR GUY IN BLACK.
BIG GUY, UNSHAVEN, MASK COVERS EVERYTHING BUT HIS MOUTH...LOTS OF LEATHER, LEATHER GLOVES...
TAKE HIM INTO CUSTODY, LAUREN.
THAT'S THE MAN WHO TRIED TO KILL ME.
DID YOU HEAR THAT?
I DID, BUT I DON'T BELIEVE IT.
JENNY SPARKS IS A LOT OF THINGS, "SMOKE", BUT SHE'S NOT A LIAR.
BATTALION TO WINTER...
JACKSON?

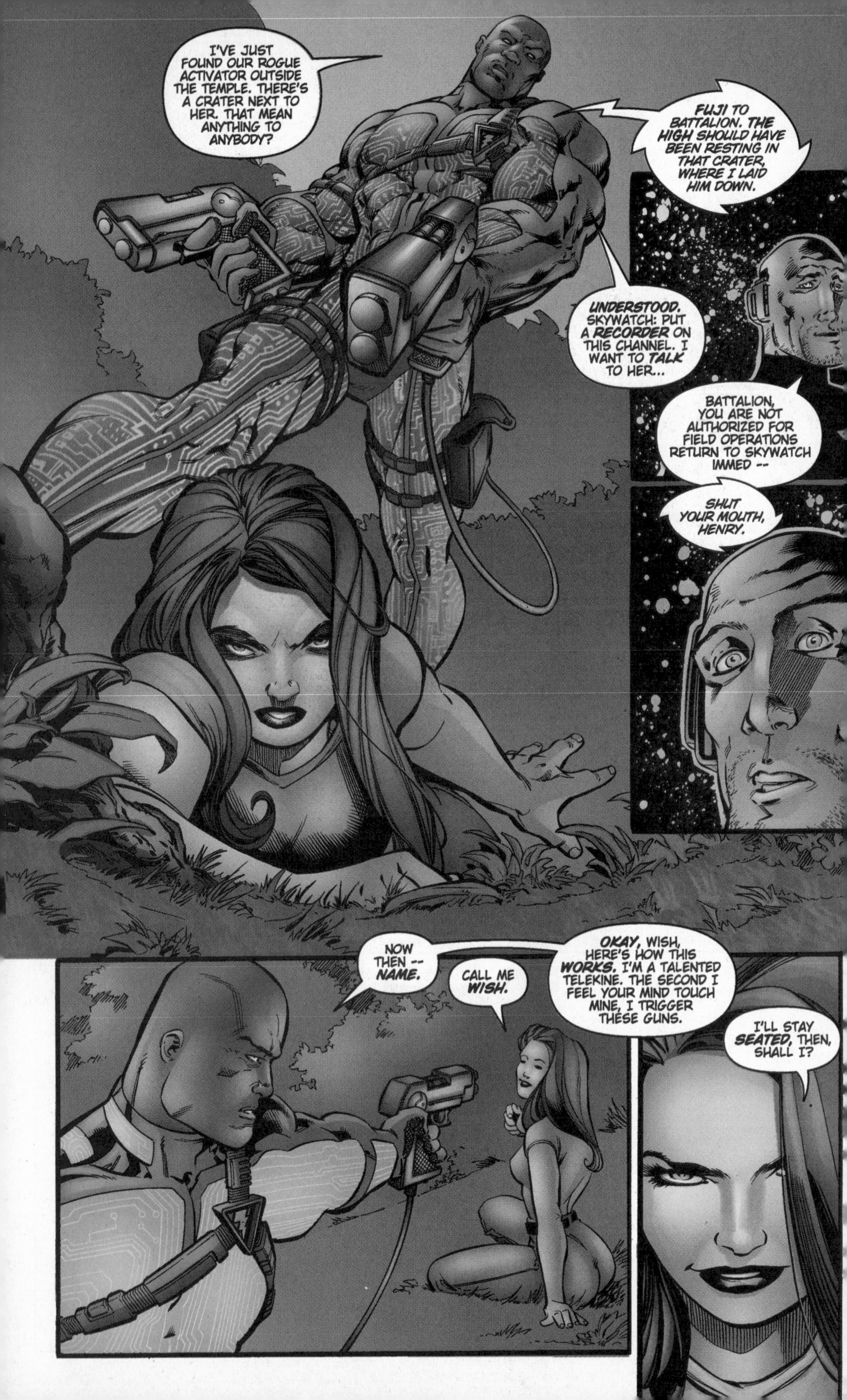
I'VE JUST FOUND OUR ROGUE ACTIVATOR OUTSIDE THE TEMPLE. THERE'S A CRATER NEXT TO HER. THAT MEAN ANYTHING TO ANYBODY?
FUJI TO BATTALION. THE HIGH SHOULD HAVE BEEN RESTING IN THAT CRATER, WHERE I LAID HIM DOWN.
UNDERSTOOD. SKYWATCH: PUT A RECORDER ON THIS CHANNEL. I WANT TO TALK TO HER...
BATTALION, YOU ARE NOT AUTHORIZED FOR FIELD OPERATIONS RETURN TO SKYWATCH IMMED --
SHUT YOUR MOUTH, HENRY.
NOW THEN -- NAME.
CALL ME WISH.
OKAY, WISH, HERE'S HOW THIS WORKS. I'M A TALENTED TELEKINE. THE SECOND I FEEL YOUR MIND TOUCH MINE, I TRIGGER THESE GUNS.
I'LL STAY SEATED, THEN, SHALL I?

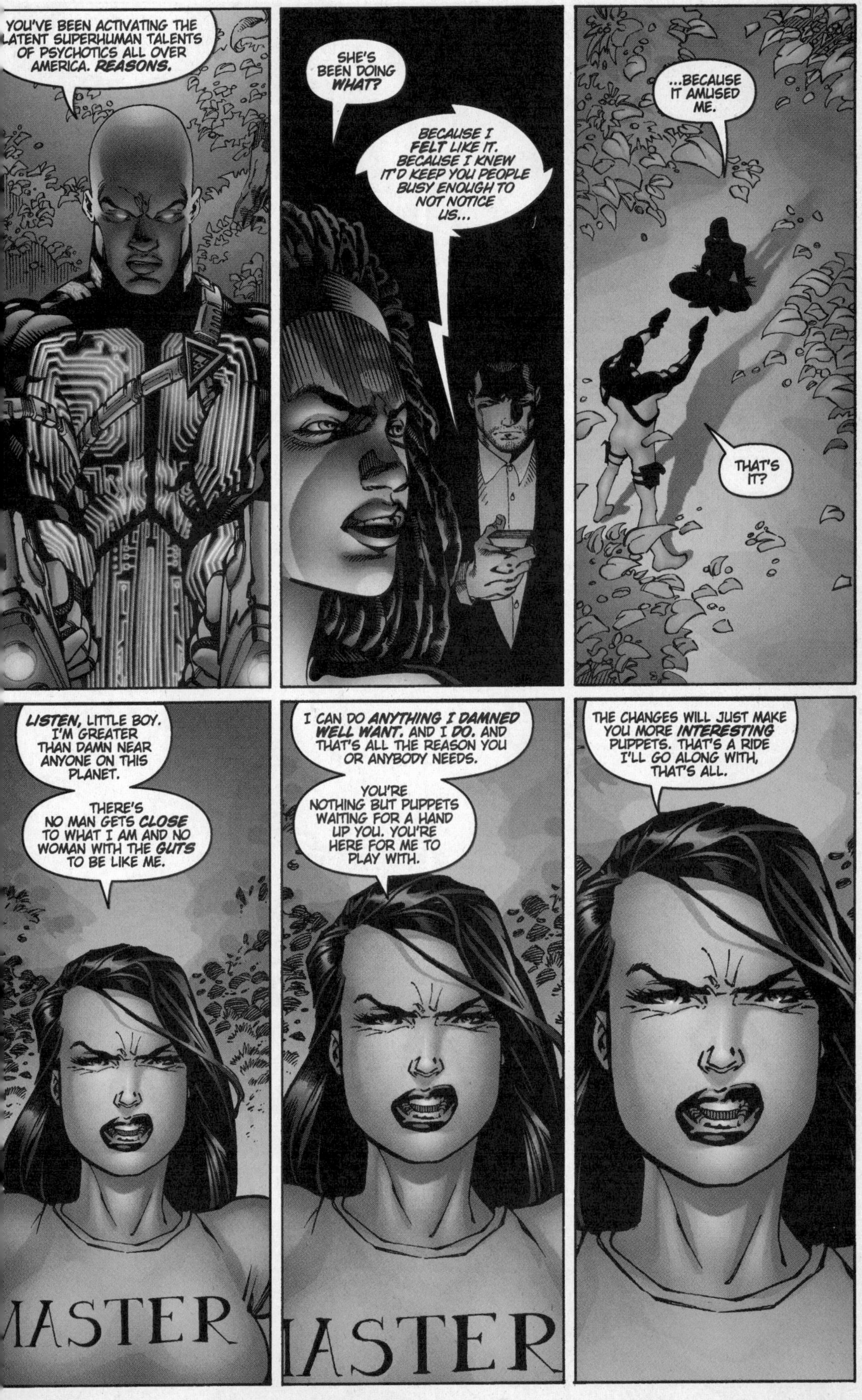

YOU'VE BEEN ACTIVATING THE LATENT SUPERHUMAN TALENTS OF PSYCHOTICS ALL OVER AMERICA. REASONS.
SHE'S BEEN DOING WHAT?
BECAUSE I FELT LIKE IT. BECAUSE I KNEW IT'D KEEP YOU PEOPLE BUSY ENOUGH TO NOT NOTICE US...
...BECAUSE IT AMUSED ME.
THAT'S IT?
LISTEN, LITTLE BOY. I'M GREATER THAN DAMN NEAR ANYONE ON THIS PLANET.
THERE'S NO MAN GETS CLOSE TO WHAT I AM AND NO WOMAN WITH THE GUTS TO BE LIKE ME.
MASTER
I CAN DO ANYTHING I DAMNED WELL WANT. AND I DO. AND THAT'S ALL THE REASON YOU OR ANYBODY NEEDS.
YOU'RE NOTHING BUT PUPPETS WAITING FOR A HAND UP YOU. YOU'RE HERE FOR ME TO PLAY WITH.
MASTER
THE CHANGES WILL JUST MAKE YOU MORE INTERESTING PUPPETS. THAT'S A RIDE I'LL GO ALONG WITH, THAT'S ALL.

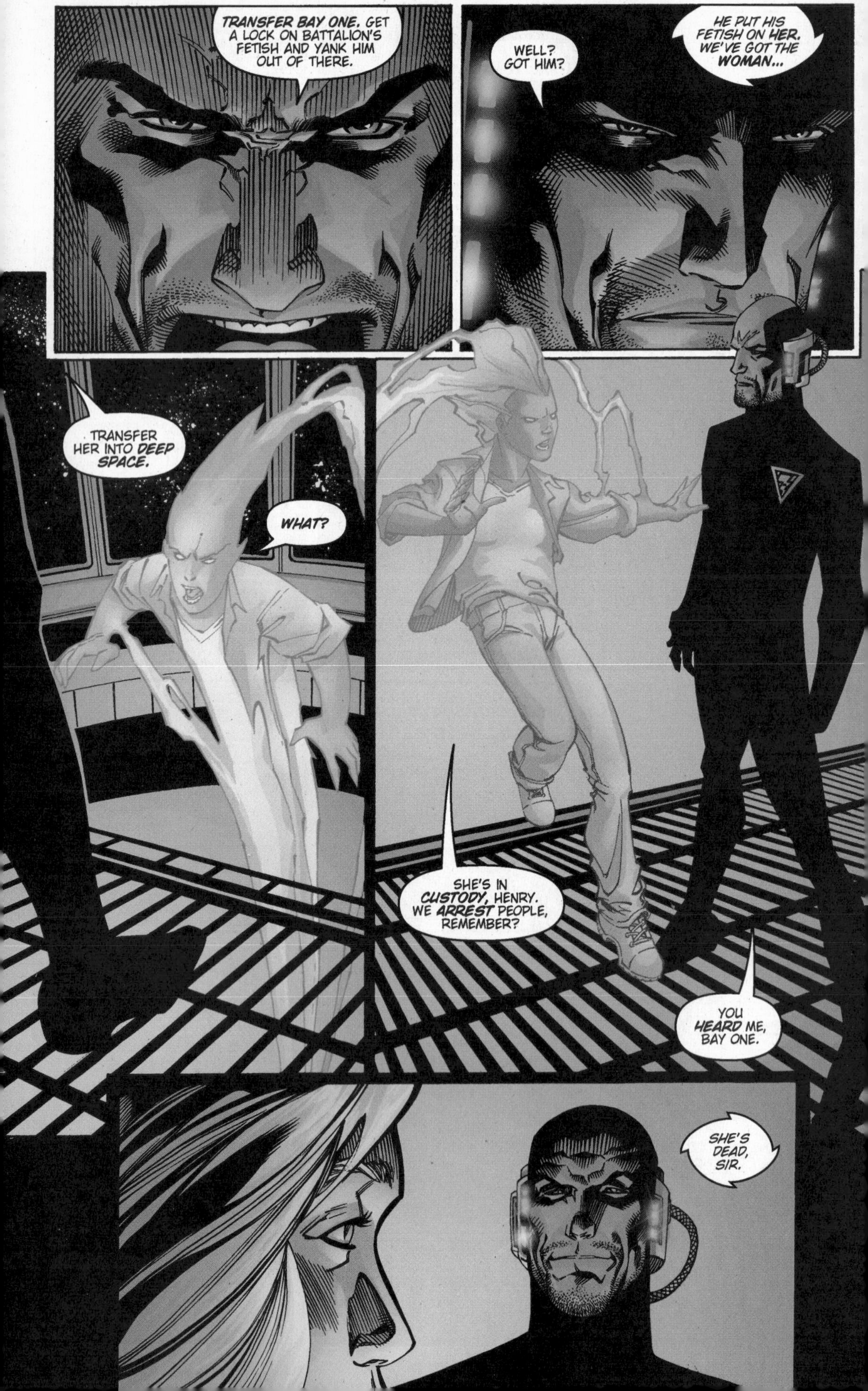
TRANSFER BAY ONE. GET A LOCK ON BATTALION'S FETISH AND YANK HIM OUT OF THERE.
WELL? GOT HIM?
HE PUT HIS FETISH ON HER. WE'VE GOT THE WOMAN...
TRANSFER HER INTO DEEP SPACE.
WHAT?
SHE'S IN CUSTODY, HENRY. WE ARREST PEOPLE, REMEMBER?
YOU HEARD ME, BAY ONE.
SHE'S DEAD, SIR.

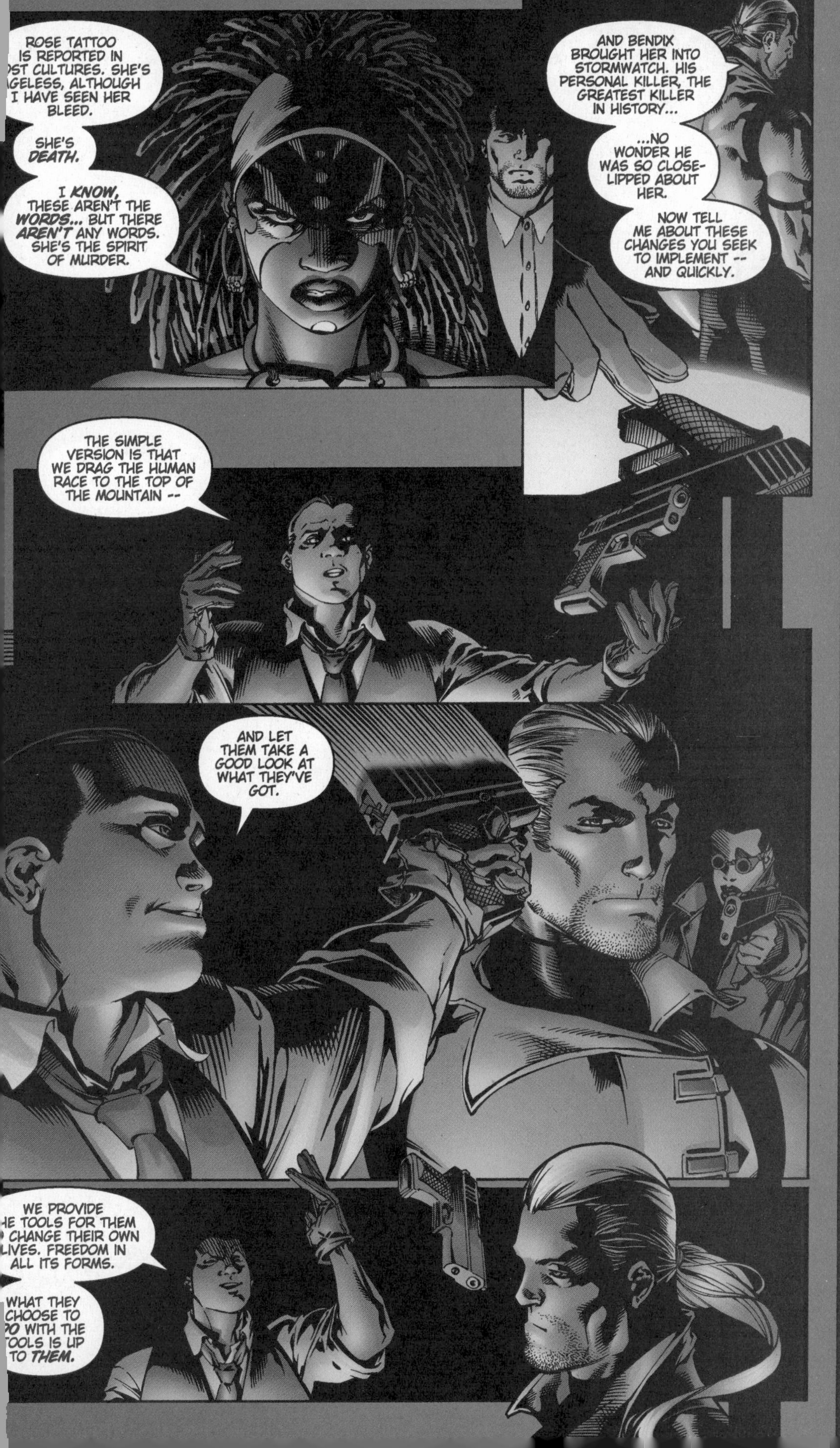
ROSE TATTOO IS REPORTED IN OST CULTURES. SHE'S AGELESS, ALTHOUGH I HAVE SEEN HER BLEED.
SHE'S *DEATH.*
I *KNOW,* THESE AREN'T THE *WORDS...* BUT THERE *AREN'T* ANY WORDS. SHE'S THE SPIRIT OF MURDER.
AND BENDIX BROUGHT HER INTO STORMWATCH. HIS PERSONAL KILLER, THE GREATEST KILLER IN HISTORY...
...NO WONDER HE WAS SO CLOSE-LIPPED ABOUT HER.
NOW TELL ME ABOUT THESE CHANGES YOU SEEK TO IMPLEMENT -- AND QUICKLY.
THE SIMPLE VERSION IS THAT WE DRAG THE HUMAN RACE TO THE TOP OF THE MOUNTAIN --
AND LET THEM TAKE A GOOD LOOK AT WHAT THEY'VE GOT.
WE PROVIDE HE TOOLS FOR THEM O CHANGE THEIR OWN LIVES. FREEDOM IN ALL ITS FORMS.
WHAT THEY CHOOSE TO *DO* WITH THE TOOLS IS UP TO *THEM.*

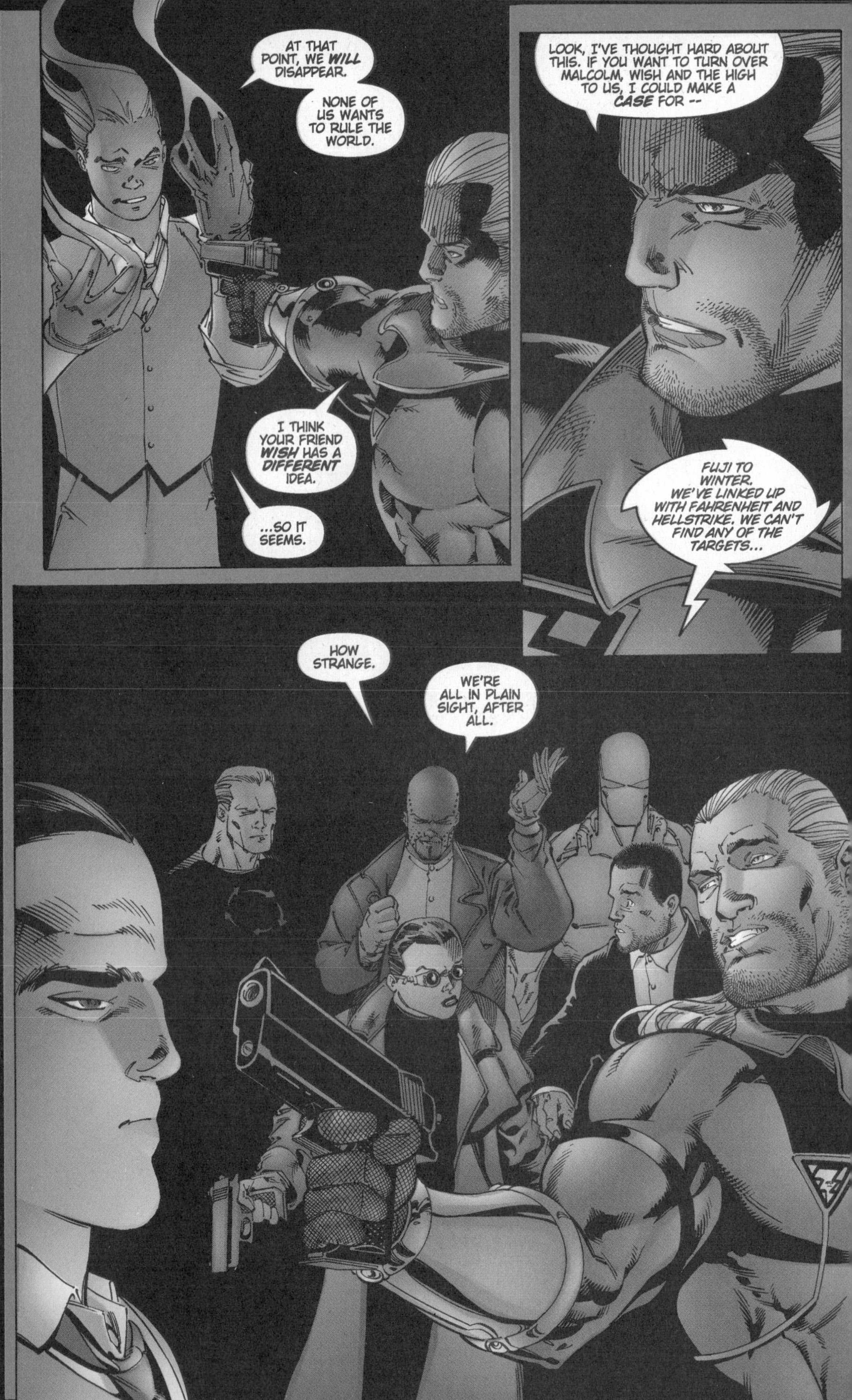
AT THAT POINT, WE WILL DISAPPEAR.
NONE OF US WANTS TO RULE THE WORLD.
I THINK YOUR FRIEND WISH HAS A DIFFERENT IDEA.
...SO IT SEEMS.
LOOK, I'VE THOUGHT HARD ABOUT THIS. IF YOU WANT TO TURN OVER MALCOLM, WISH AND THE HIGH TO US, I COULD MAKE A CASE FOR --
FUJI TO WINTER. WE'VE LINKED UP WITH FAHRENHEIT AND HELLSTRIKE. WE CAN'T FIND ANY OF THE TARGETS...
HOW STRANGE.
WE'RE ALL IN PLAIN SIGHT, AFTER ALL.

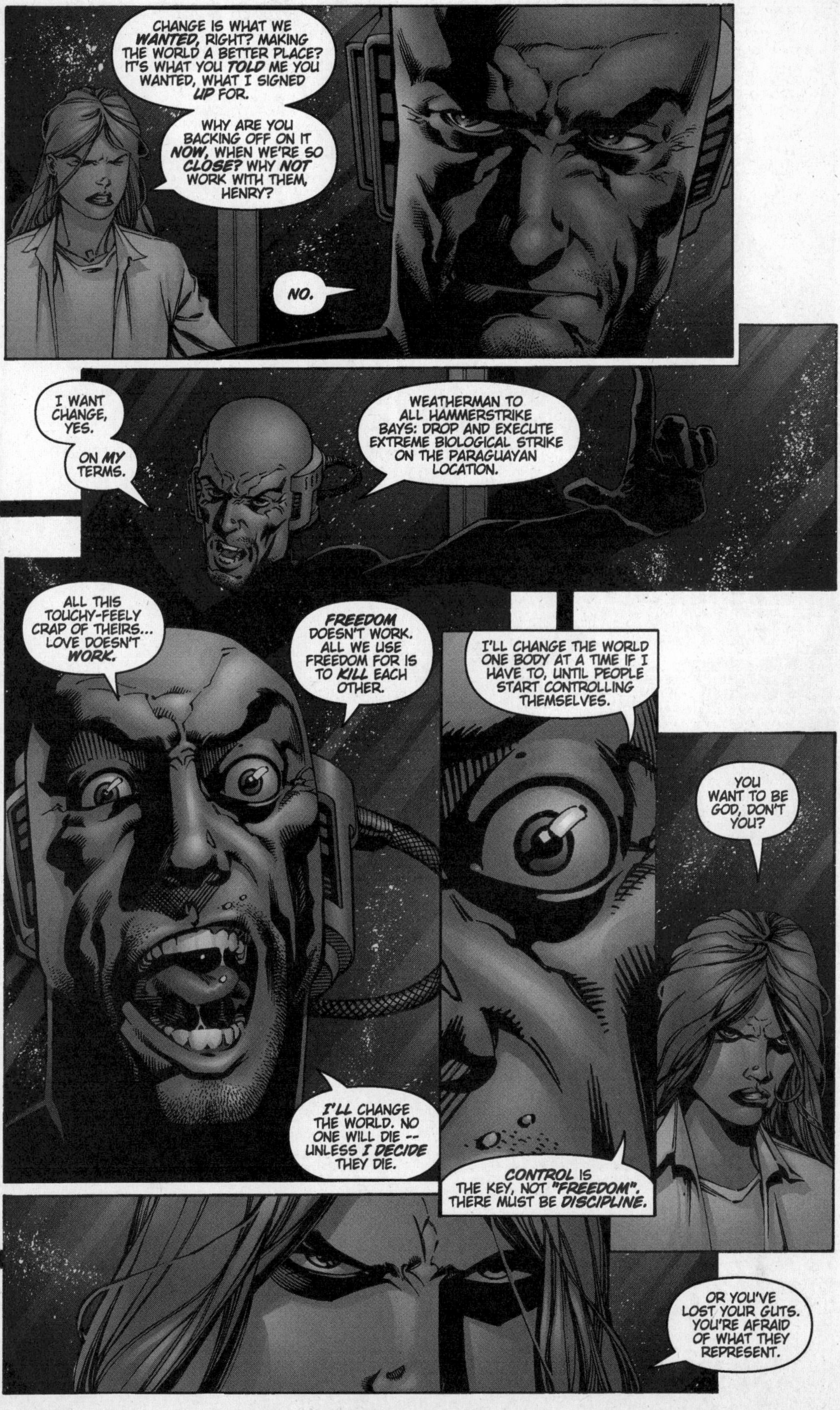

CHANGE IS WHAT WE WANTED, RIGHT? MAKING THE WORLD A BETTER PLACE? IT'S WHAT YOU TOLD ME YOU WANTED, WHAT I SIGNED UP FOR.
WHY ARE YOU BACKING OFF ON IT NOW, WHEN WE'RE SO CLOSE? WHY NOT WORK WITH THEM, HENRY?
NO.
I WANT CHANGE, YES.
ON MY TERMS.
WEATHERMAN TO ALL HAMMERSTRIKE BAYS: DROP AND EXECUTE EXTREME BIOLOGICAL STRIKE ON THE PARAGUAYAN LOCATION.
ALL THIS TOUCHY-FEELY CRAP OF THEIRS... LOVE DOESN'T WORK.
FREEDOM DOESN'T WORK. ALL WE USE FREEDOM FOR IS TO KILL EACH OTHER.
I'LL CHANGE THE WORLD. NO ONE WILL DIE -- UNLESS I DECIDE THEY DIE.
I'LL CHANGE THE WORLD ONE BODY AT A TIME IF I HAVE TO, UNTIL PEOPLE START CONTROLLING THEMSELVES.
CONTROL IS THE KEY, NOT "FREEDOM". THERE MUST BE DISCIPLINE.
YOU WANT TO BE GOD, DON'T YOU?
OR YOU'VE LOST YOUR GUTS. YOU'RE AFRAID OF WHAT THEY REPRESENT.

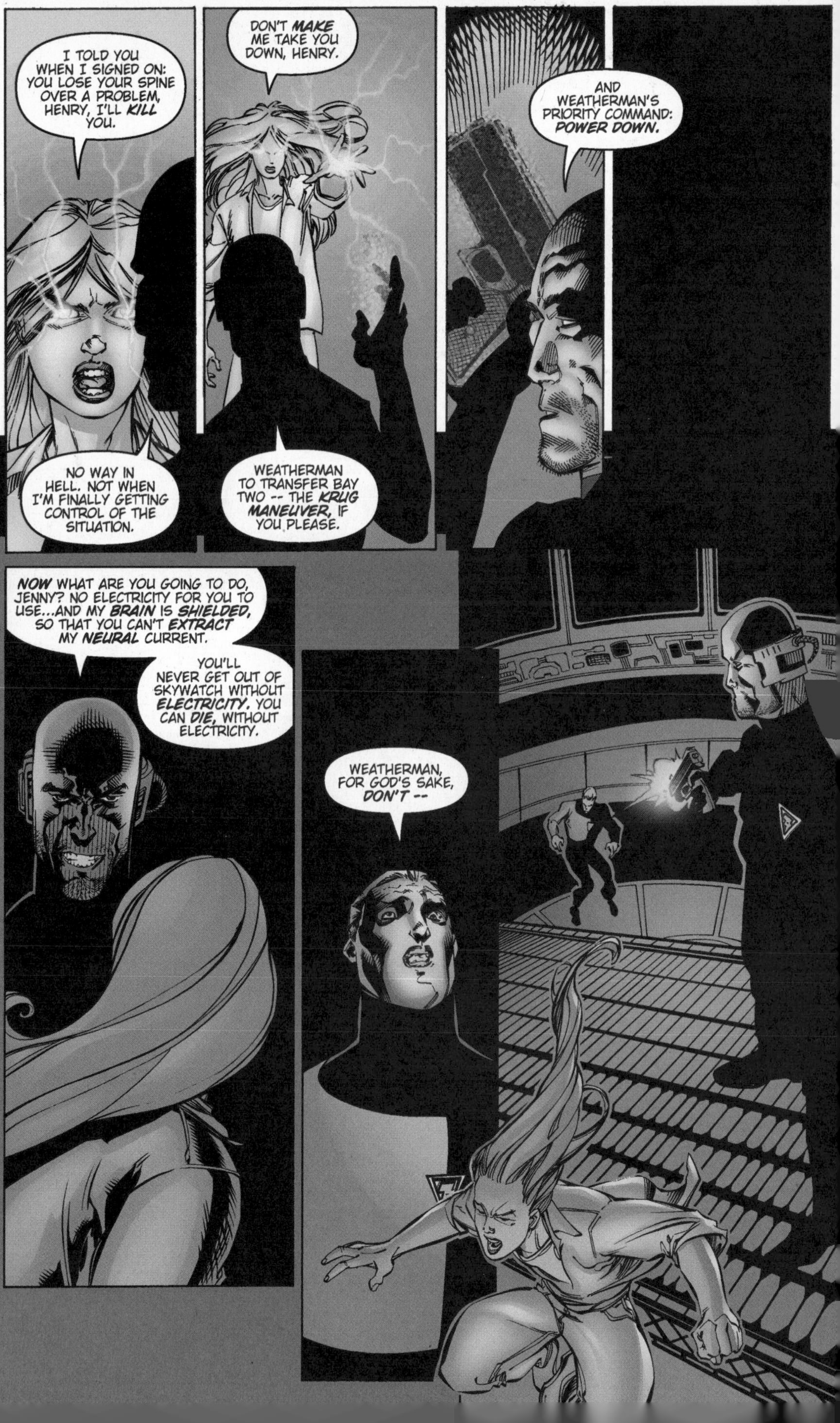
I TOLD YOU WHEN I SIGNED ON: YOU LOSE YOUR SPINE OVER A PROBLEM, HENRY, I'LL KILL YOU.
NO WAY IN HELL. NOT WHEN I'M FINALLY GETTING CONTROL OF THE SITUATION.
DON'T MAKE ME TAKE YOU DOWN, HENRY.
WEATHERMAN TO TRANSFER BAY TWO -- THE KRUG MANEUVER, IF YOU PLEASE.
AND WEATHERMAN'S PRIORITY COMMAND: POWER DOWN.
NOW WHAT ARE YOU GOING TO DO, JENNY? NO ELECTRICITY FOR YOU TO USE...AND MY BRAIN IS SHIELDED, SO THAT YOU CAN'T EXTRACT MY NEURAL CURRENT.
YOU'LL NEVER GET OUT OF SKYWATCH WITHOUT ELECTRICITY. YOU CAN DIE, WITHOUT ELECTRICITY.
WEATHERMAN, FOR GOD'S SAKE, DON'T --

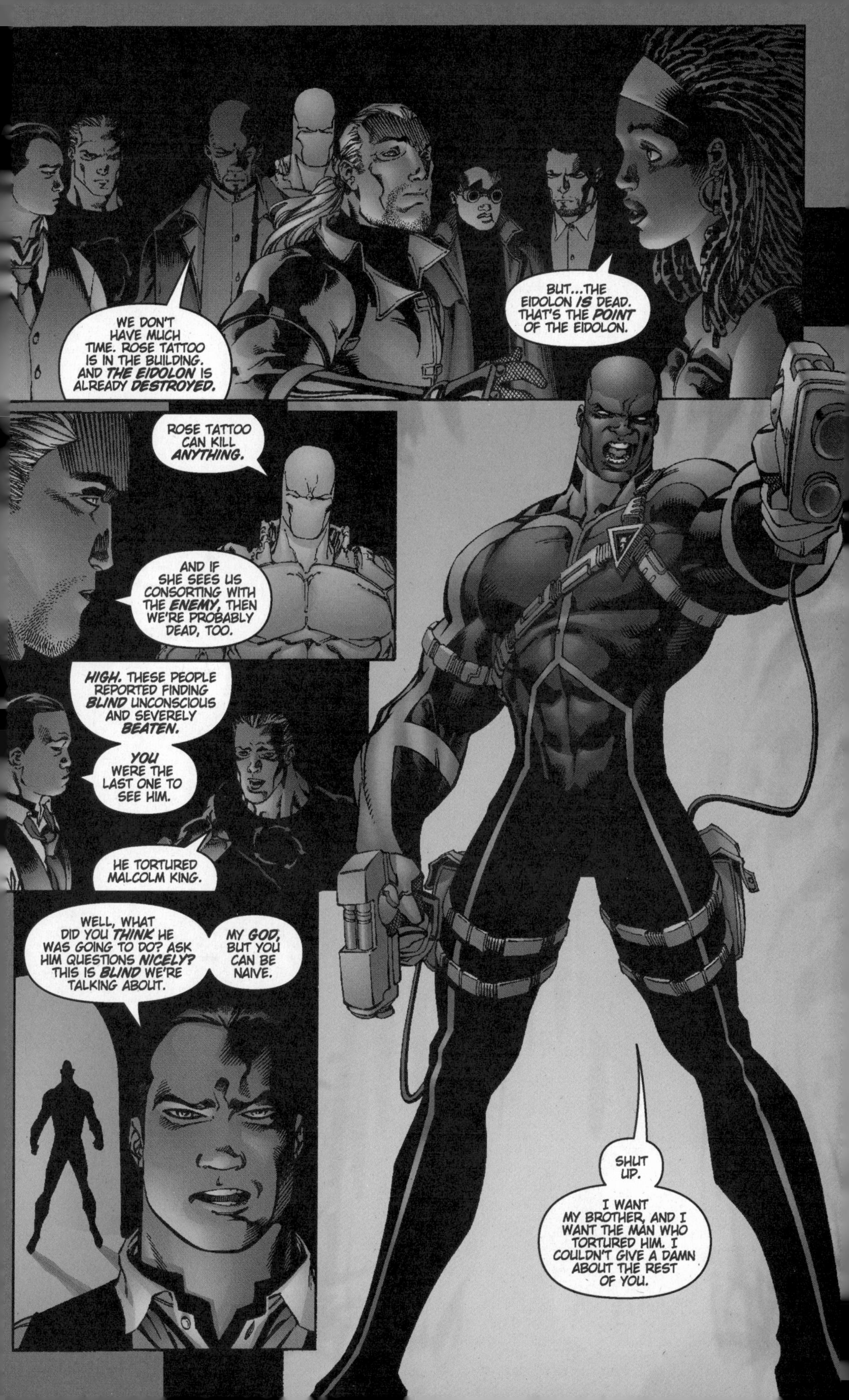

WE DON'T HAVE MUCH TIME. ROSE TATTOO IS IN THE BUILDING. AND *THE EIDOLON* IS ALREADY *DESTROYED.*
BUT...THE EIDOLON *IS* DEAD. THAT'S THE *POINT* OF THE EIDOLON.
ROSE TATTOO CAN KILL *ANYTHING.*
AND IF SHE SEES US CONSORTING WITH THE *ENEMY,* THEN WE'RE PROBABLY DEAD, TOO.
HIGH. THESE PEOPLE REPORTED FINDING *BLIND* UNCONSCIOUS AND SEVERELY *BEATEN.*
YOU WERE THE LAST ONE TO SEE HIM.
HE TORTURED MALCOLM KING.
WELL, WHAT DID YOU *THINK* HE WAS GOING TO DO? ASK HIM QUESTIONS *NICELY?* THIS IS *BLIND* WE'RE TALKING ABOUT.
MY *GOD,* BUT YOU CAN BE NAIVE.
SHUT UP.
I WANT MY BROTHER, AND I WANT THE MAN WHO TORTURED HIM. I COULDN'T GIVE A DAMN ABOUT THE REST OF YOU.

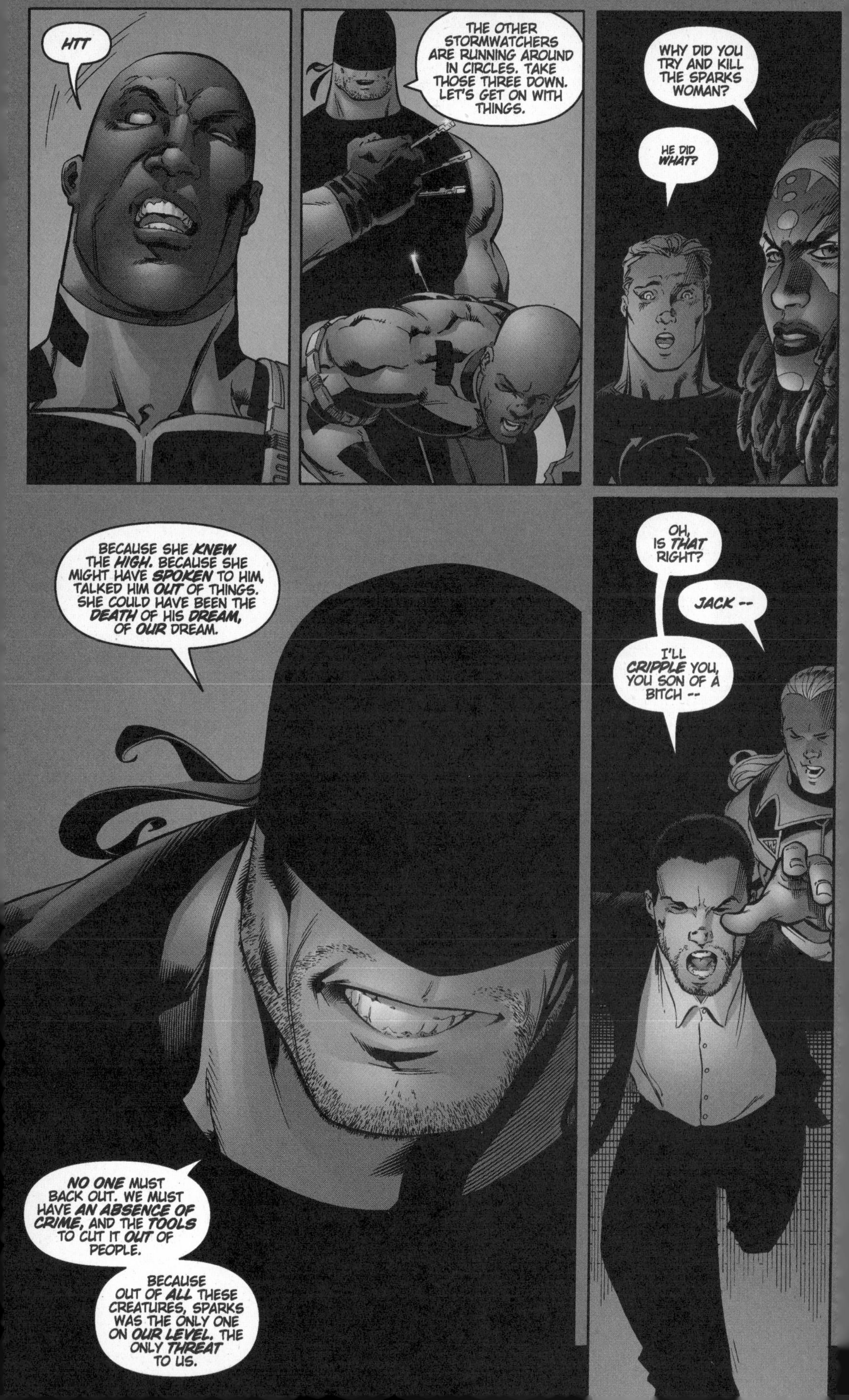
HTT
THE OTHER STORMWATCHERS ARE RUNNING AROUND IN CIRCLES. TAKE THOSE THREE DOWN. LET'S GET ON WITH THINGS.
WHY DID YOU TRY AND KILL THE SPARKS WOMAN?
HE DID WHAT?
BECAUSE SHE KNEW THE HIGH. BECAUSE SHE MIGHT HAVE SPOKEN TO HIM, TALKED HIM OUT OF THINGS. SHE COULD HAVE BEEN THE DEATH OF HIS DREAM, OF OUR DREAM.
NO ONE MUST BACK OUT. WE MUST HAVE AN ABSENCE OF CRIME, AND THE TOOLS TO CUT IT OUT OF PEOPLE.
BECAUSE OUT OF ALL THESE CREATURES, SPARKS WAS THE ONLY ONE ON OUR LEVEL. THE ONLY THREAT TO US.
OH, IS THAT RIGHT?
JACK --
I'LL CRIPPLE YOU, YOU SON OF A BITCH --

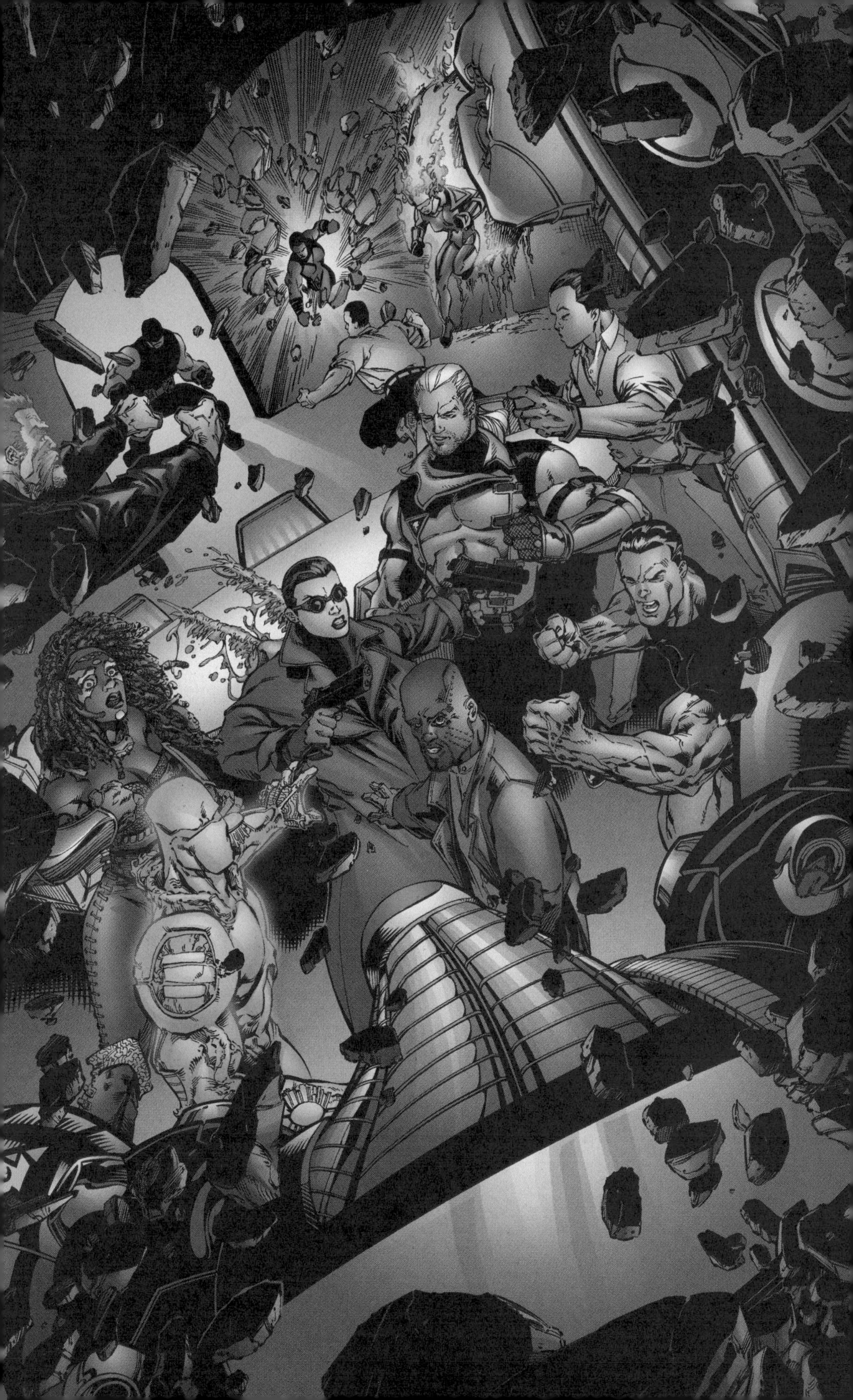

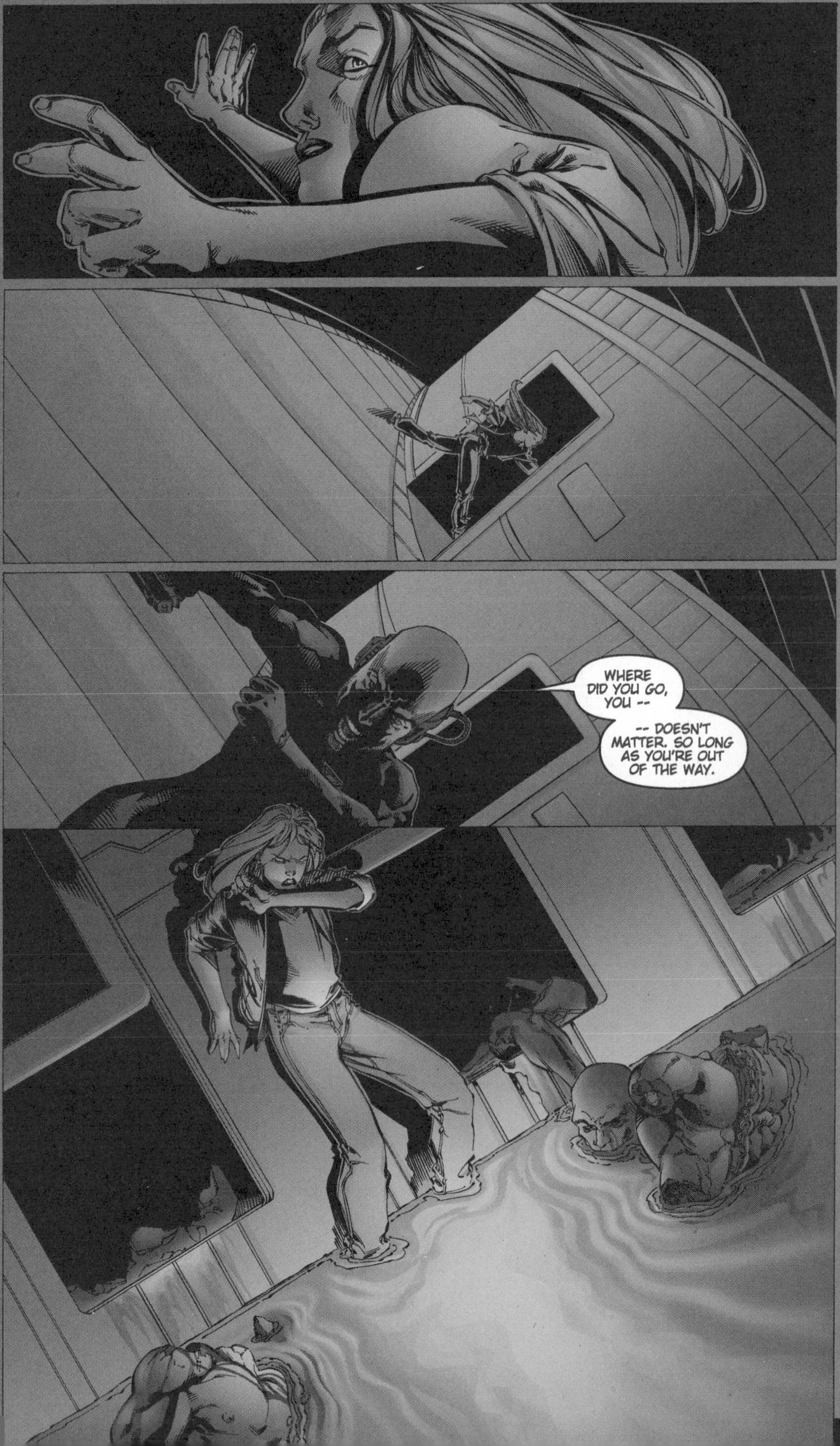
WHERE DID YOU GO, YOU --
-- DOESN'T MATTER. SO LONG AS YOU'RE OUT OF THE WAY.

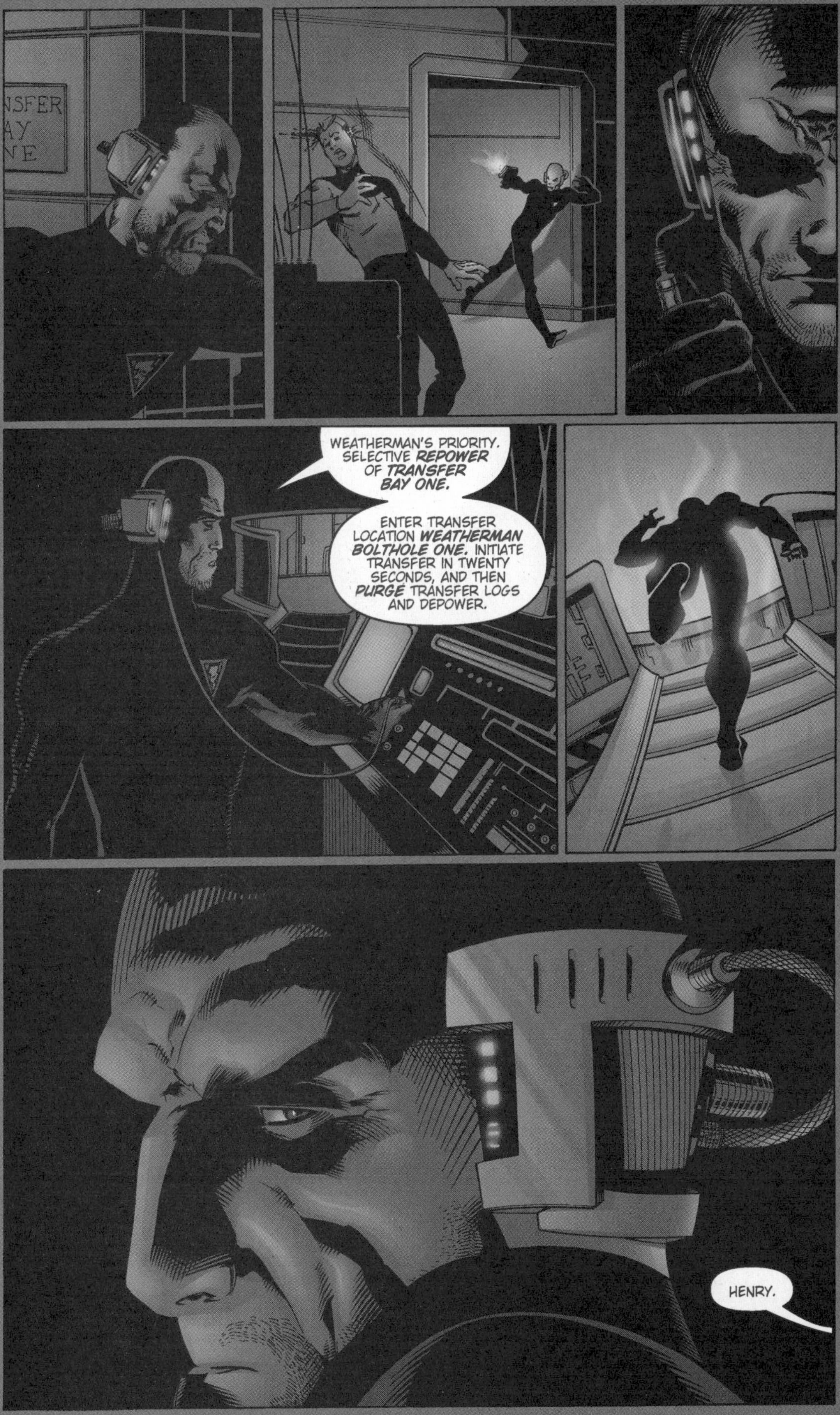
NSFER
AY
NE
WEATHERMAN'S PRIORITY. SELECTIVE REPOWER OF TRANSFER BAY ONE.
ENTER TRANSFER LOCATION WEATHERMAN BOLTHOLE ONE. INITIATE TRANSFER IN TWENTY SECONDS, AND THEN PURGE TRANSFER LOGS AND DEPOWER.
HENRY.

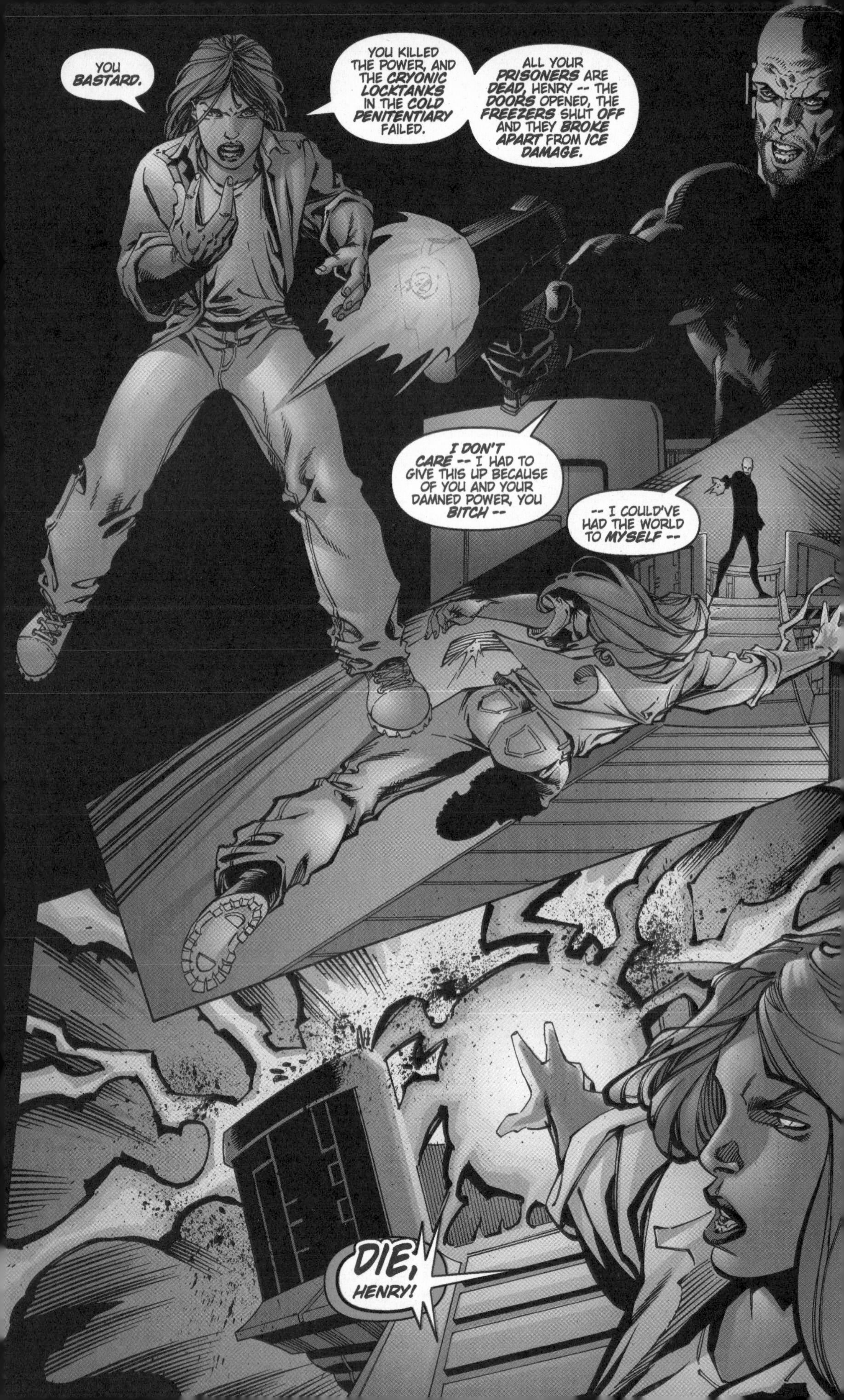
YOU BASTARD.
YOU KILLED THE POWER, AND THE CRYONIC LOCKTANKS IN THE COLD PENITENTIARY FAILED.
ALL YOUR PRISONERS ARE DEAD, HENRY -- THE DOORS OPENED, THE FREEZERS SHUT OFF AND THEY BROKE APART FROM ICE DAMAGE.
I DON'T CARE -- I HAD TO GIVE THIS UP BECAUSE OF YOU AND YOUR DAMNED POWER, YOU BITCH --
-- I COULD'VE HAD THE WORLD TO MYSELF --
DIE, HENRY!

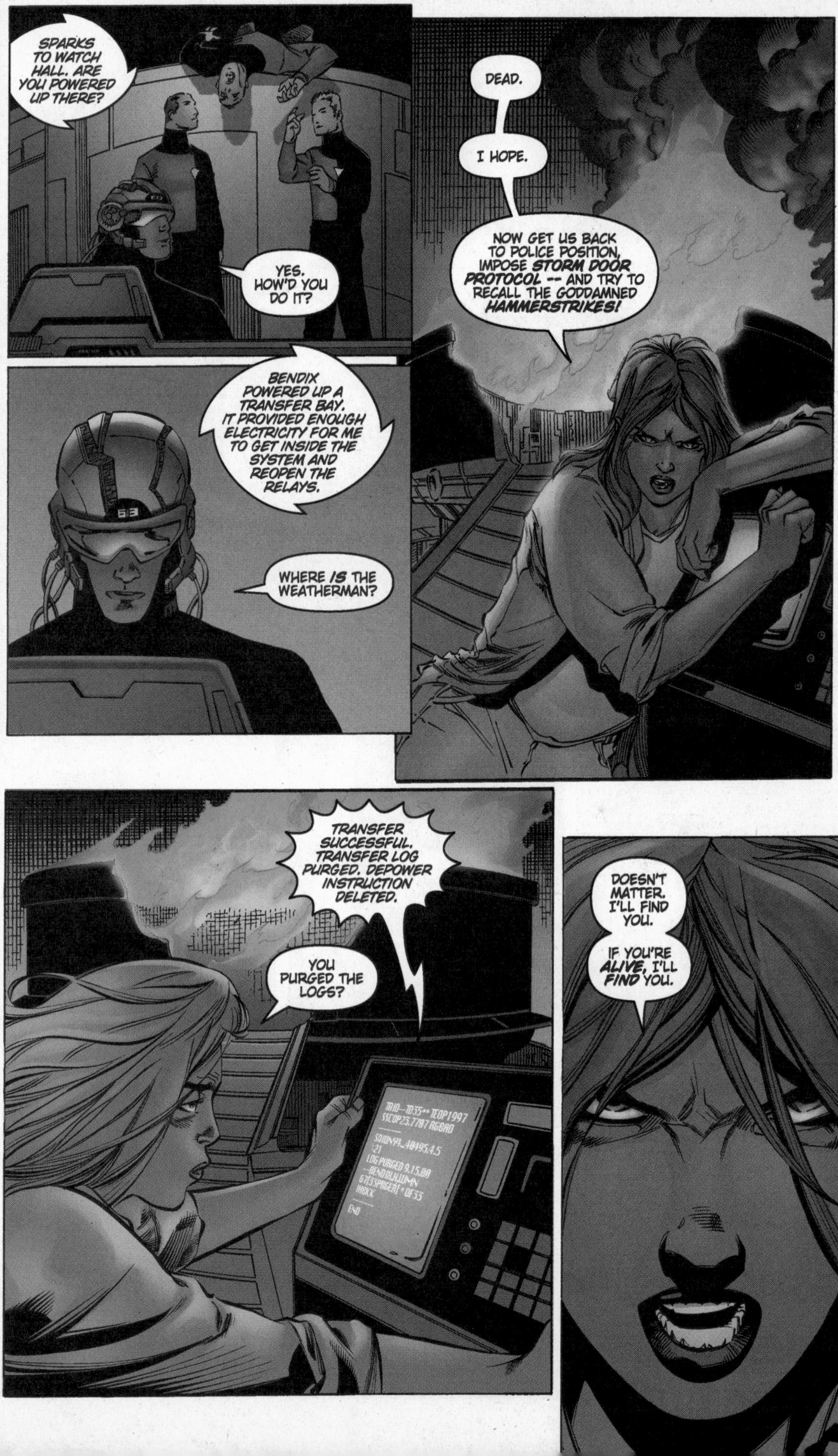

SPARKS TO WATCH HALL. ARE YOU POWERED UP THERE?
YES. HOW'D YOU DO IT?
BENDIX POWERED UP A TRANSFER BAY. IT PROVIDED ENOUGH ELECTRICITY FOR ME TO GET INSIDE THE SYSTEM AND REOPEN THE RELAYS.
WHERE *IS* THE WEATHERMAN?
DEAD.
I HOPE.
NOW GET US BACK TO POLICE POSITION, IMPOSE **STORM DOOR PROTOCOL** -- AND TRY TO RECALL THE GODDAMNED **HAMMERSTRIKES!**
TRANSFER SUCCESSFUL. TRANSFER LOG PURGED. DEPOWER INSTRUCTION DELETED.
YOU PURGED THE LOGS?
DOESN'T MATTER. I'LL FIND YOU.
IF YOU'RE *ALIVE*, I'LL *FIND* YOU.

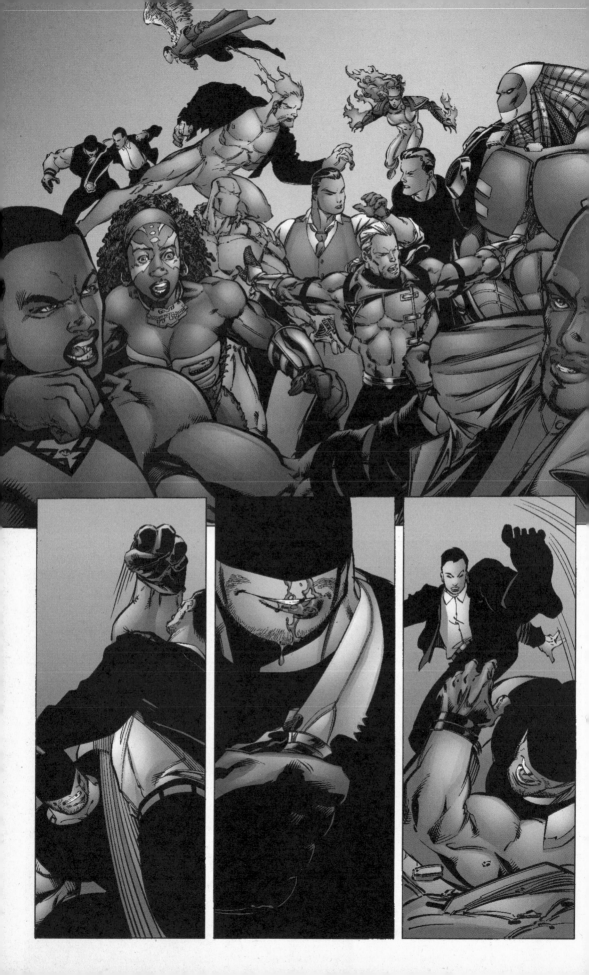

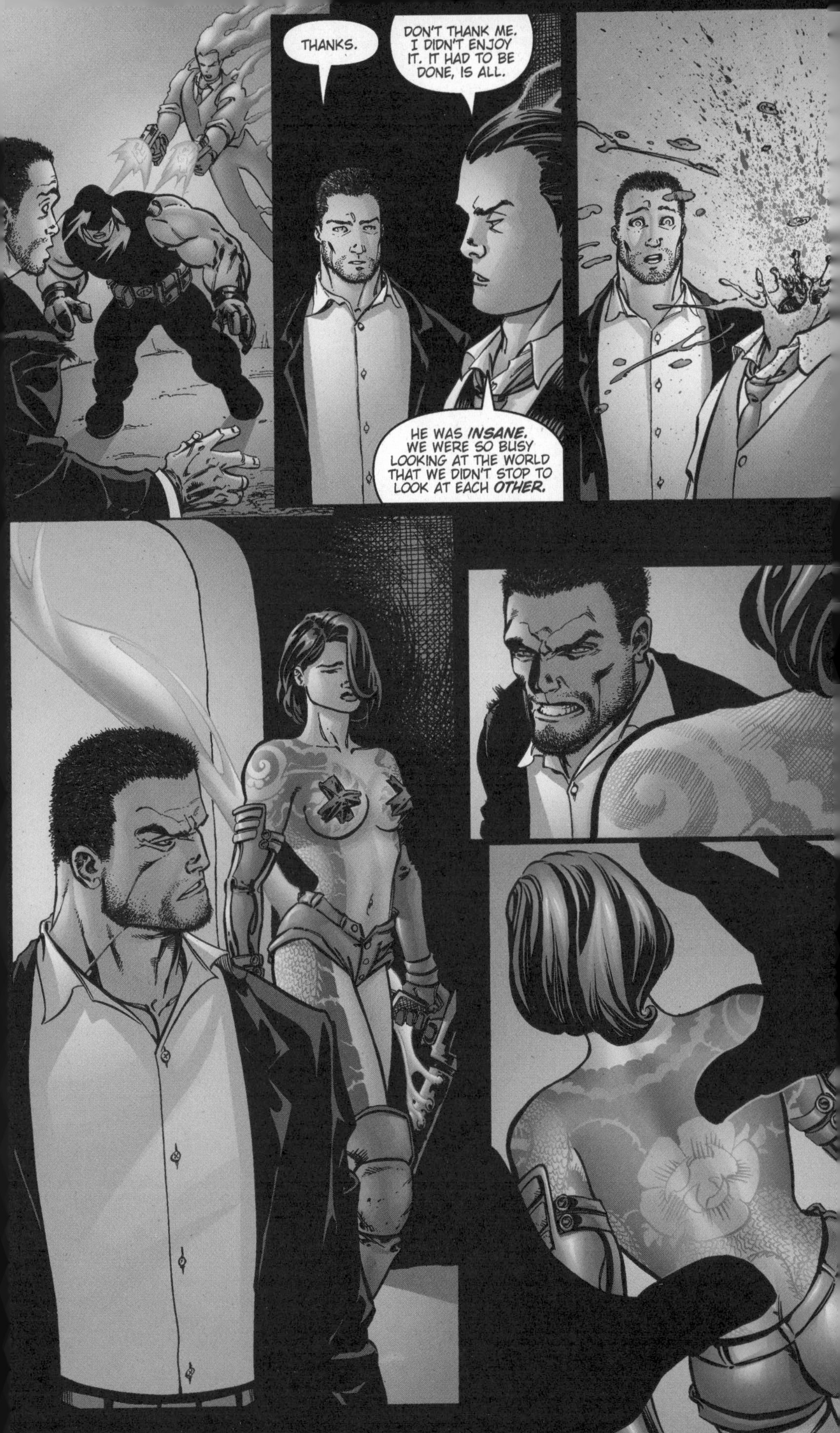
THANKS.
DON'T THANK ME. I DIDN'T ENJOY IT. IT HAD TO BE DONE, IS ALL.
HE WAS INSANE. WE WERE SO BUSY LOOKING AT THE WORLD THAT WE DIDN'T STOP TO LOOK AT EACH OTHER.

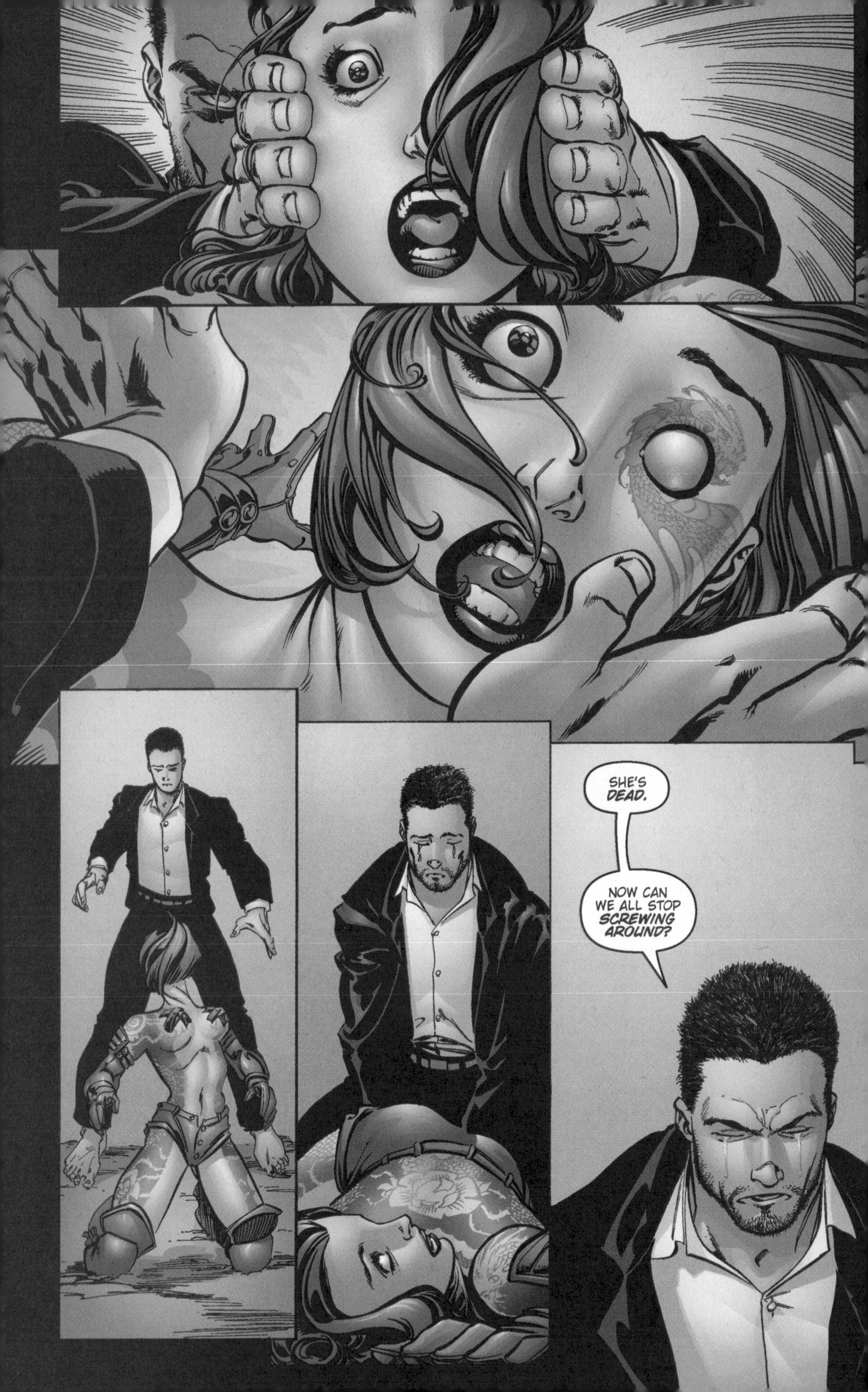
SHE'S DEAD.
NOW CAN WE ALL STOP SCREWING AROUND?

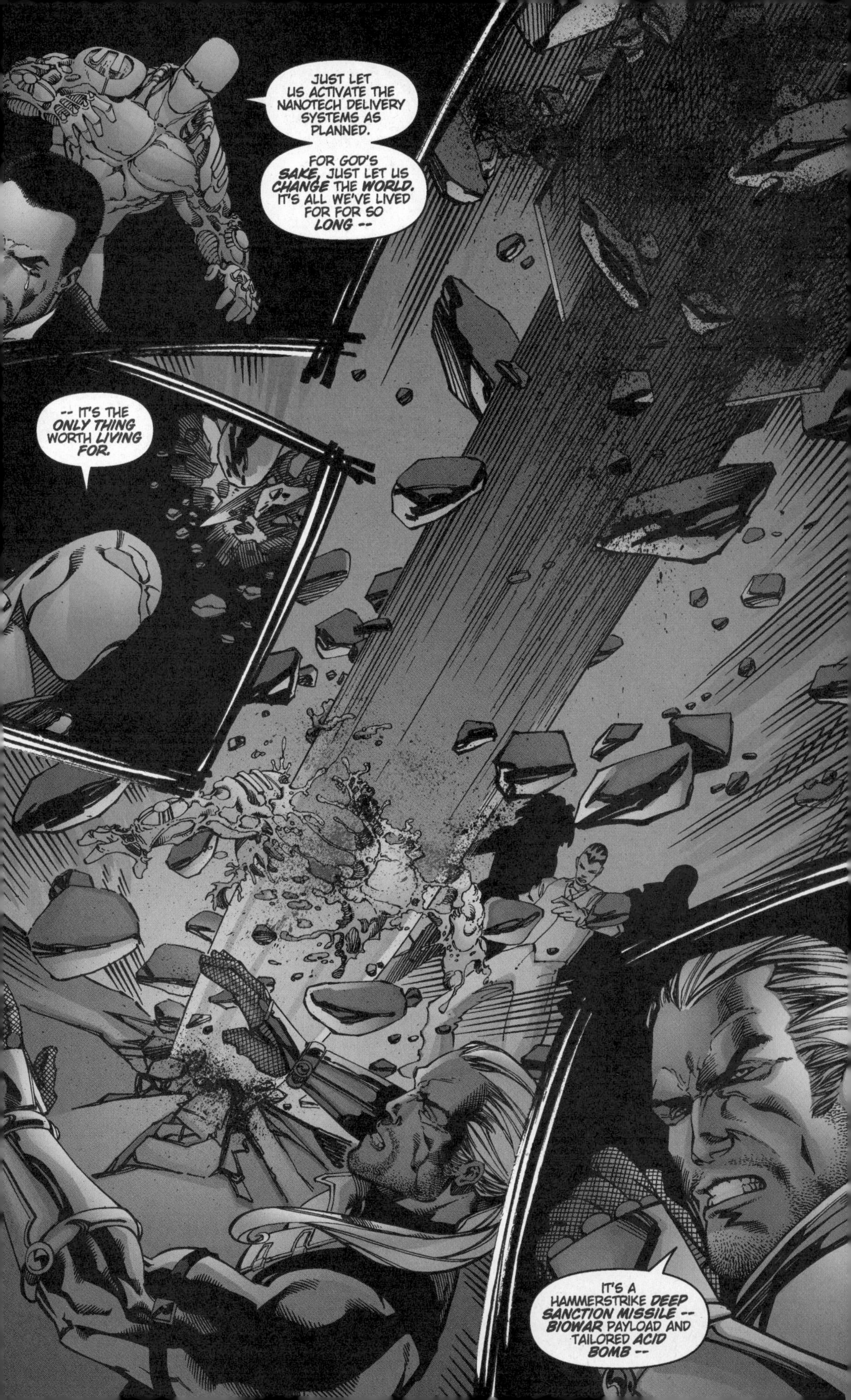
JUST LET US ACTIVATE THE NANOTECH DELIVERY SYSTEMS AS PLANNED.
FOR GOD'S SAKE, JUST LET US CHANGE THE WORLD. IT'S ALL WE'VE LIVED FOR FOR SO LONG --
-- IT'S THE ONLY THING WORTH LIVING FOR.
IT'S A HAMMERSTRIKE DEEP SANCTION MISSILE -- BIOWAR PAYLOAD AND TAILORED ACID BOMB --

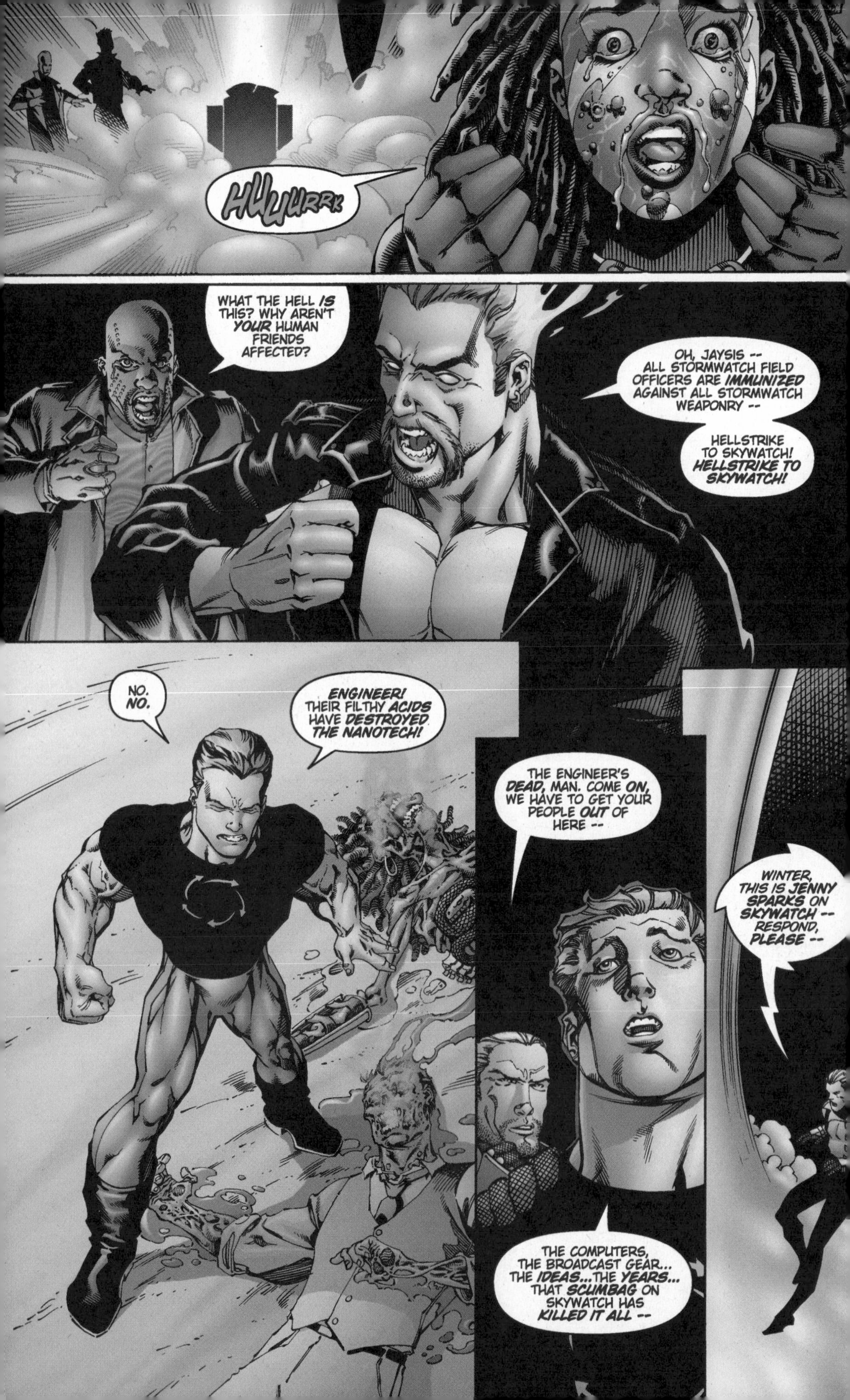
HUUURRK
WHAT THE HELL *IS* THIS? WHY AREN'T *YOUR* HUMAN FRIENDS AFFECTED?
OH, JAYSIS -- ALL STORMWATCH FIELD OFFICERS ARE *IMMUNIZED* AGAINST ALL STORMWATCH WEAPONRY --
HELLSTRIKE TO SKYWATCH! *HELLSTRIKE TO SKYWATCH!*
NO. *NO.*
ENGINEER! THEIR FILTHY *ACIDS* HAVE *DESTROYED THE NANOTECH!*
THE ENGINEER'S *DEAD*, MAN. COME *ON*, WE HAVE TO GET YOUR PEOPLE *OUT* OF HERE --
WINTER, THIS IS *JENNY SPARKS* ON *SKYWATCH* -- RESPOND, *PLEASE* --
THE COMPUTERS, THE BROADCAST GEAR... THE *IDEAS*... THE *YEARS*... THAT *SCUMBAG* ON SKYWATCH HAS *KILLED IT ALL* --

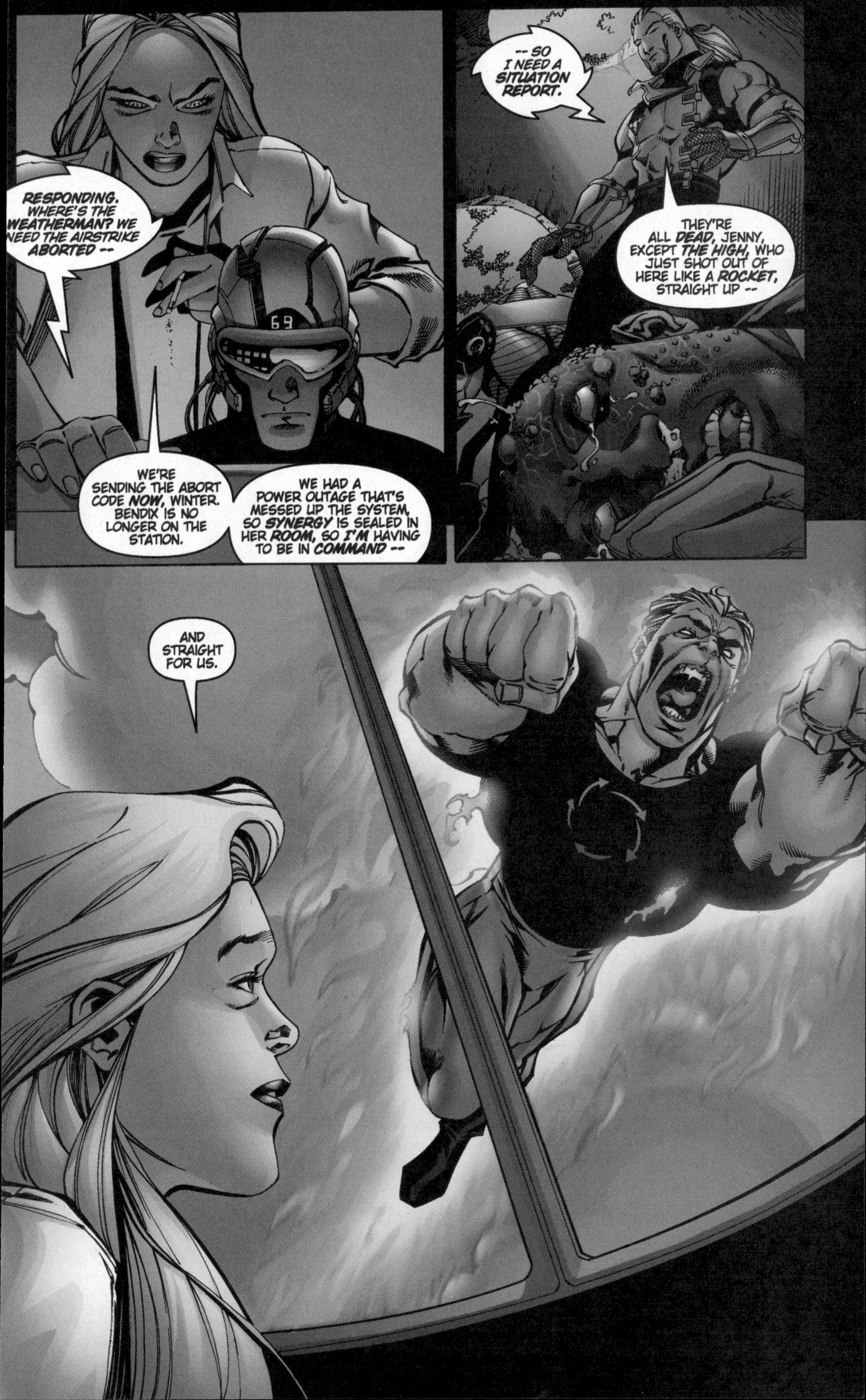
RESPONDING. WHERE'S THE WEATHERMAN? WE NEED THE AIRSTRIKE ABORTED --
WE'RE SENDING THE ABORT CODE NOW, WINTER. BENDIX IS NO LONGER ON THE STATION.
WE HAD A POWER OUTAGE THAT'S MESSED UP THE SYSTEM, SO SYNERGY IS SEALED IN HER ROOM, SO I'M HAVING TO BE IN COMMAND --
-- SO I NEED A SITUATION REPORT.
THEY'RE ALL DEAD, JENNY, EXCEPT THE HIGH, WHO JUST SHOT OUT OF HERE LIKE A ROCKET, STRAIGHT UP --
AND STRAIGHT FOR US.

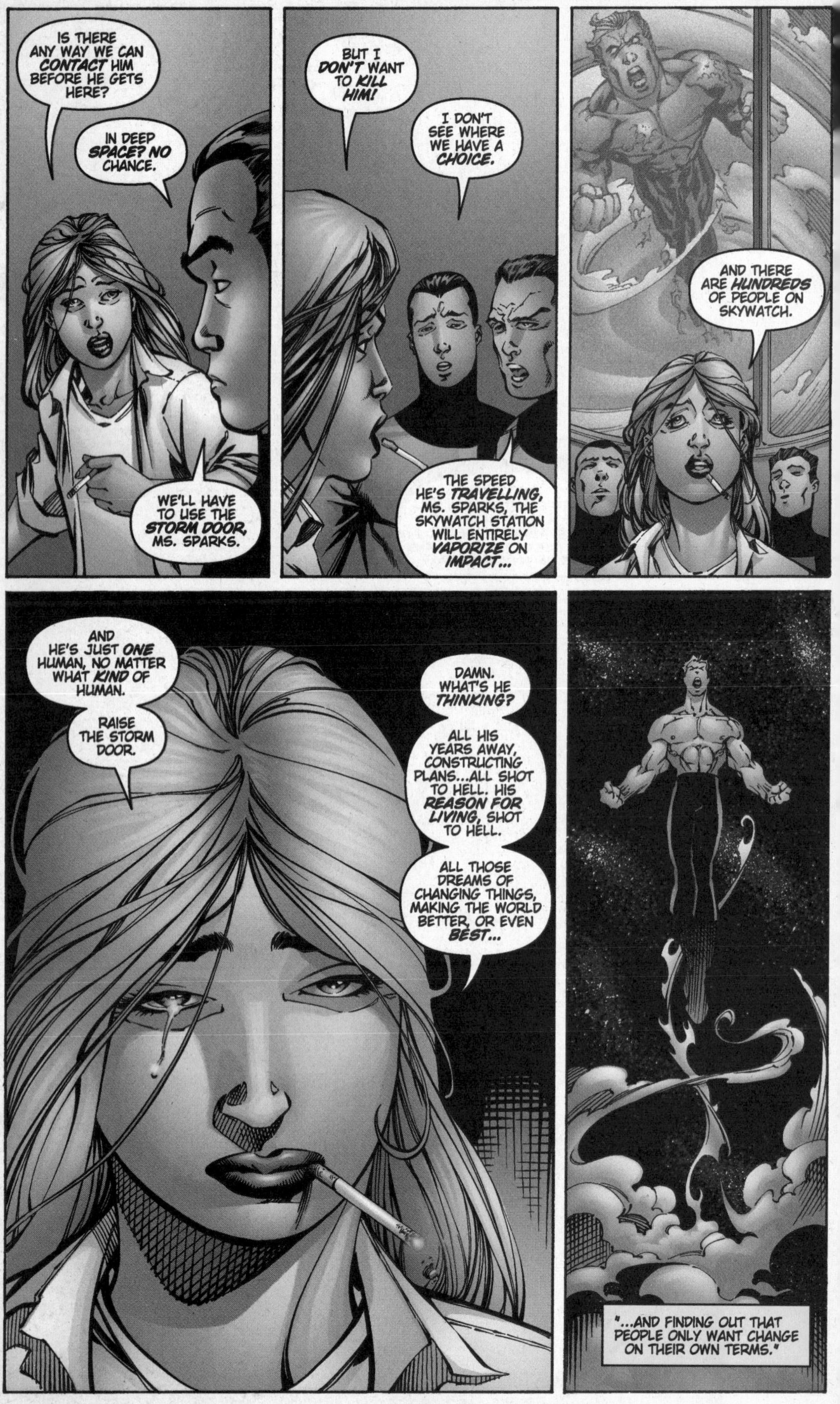
IS THERE ANY WAY WE CAN CONTACT HIM BEFORE HE GETS HERE?
IN DEEP SPACE? NO CHANCE.
WE'LL HAVE TO USE THE STORM DOOR, MS. SPARKS.
BUT I DON'T WANT TO KILL HIM!
I DON'T SEE WHERE WE HAVE A CHOICE.
THE SPEED HE'S TRAVELLING, MS. SPARKS, THE SKYWATCH STATION WILL ENTIRELY VAPORIZE ON IMPACT...
AND THERE ARE HUNDREDS OF PEOPLE ON SKYWATCH.
AND HE'S JUST ONE HUMAN, NO MATTER WHAT KIND OF HUMAN.
RAISE THE STORM DOOR.
DAMN. WHAT'S HE THINKING?
ALL HIS YEARS AWAY, CONSTRUCTING PLANS...ALL SHOT TO HELL. HIS REASON FOR LIVING, SHOT TO HELL.
ALL THOSE DREAMS OF CHANGING THINGS, MAKING THE WORLD BETTER, OR EVEN BEST...
"...AND FINDING OUT THAT PEOPLE ONLY WANT CHANGE ON THEIR OWN TERMS."

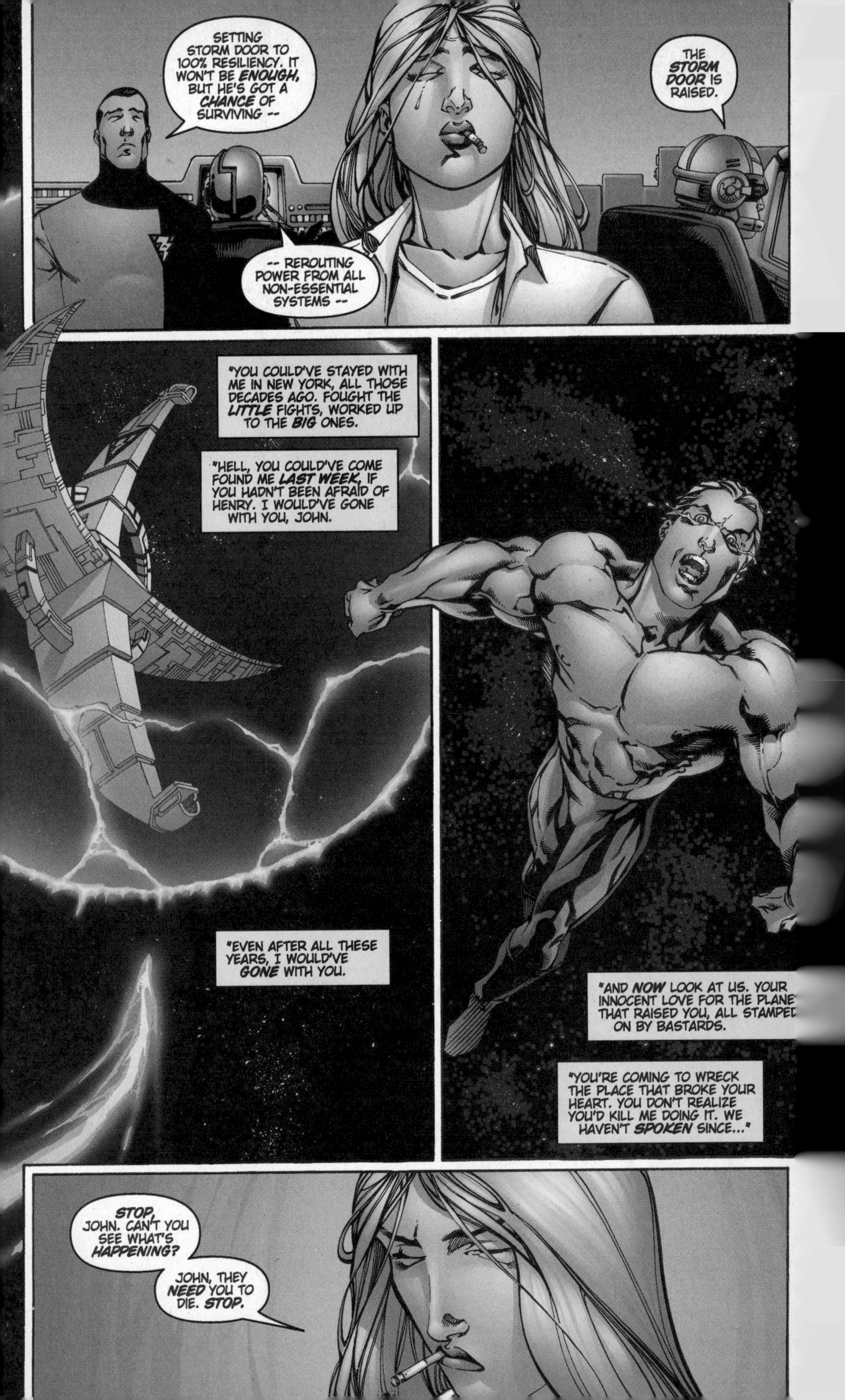
SETTING STORM DOOR TO 100% RESILIENCY. IT WON'T BE ENOUGH, BUT HE'S GOT A CHANCE OF SURVIVING --
-- REROUTING POWER FROM ALL NON-ESSENTIAL SYSTEMS --
THE STORM DOOR IS RAISED.
"YOU COULD'VE STAYED WITH ME IN NEW YORK, ALL THOSE DECADES AGO. FOUGHT THE LITTLE FIGHTS, WORKED UP TO THE BIG ONES.
"HELL, YOU COULD'VE COME FOUND ME LAST WEEK, IF YOU HADN'T BEEN AFRAID OF HENRY. I WOULD'VE GONE WITH YOU, JOHN.
"EVEN AFTER ALL THESE YEARS, I WOULD'VE GONE WITH YOU.
"AND NOW LOOK AT US. YOUR INNOCENT LOVE FOR THE PLANET THAT RAISED YOU, ALL STAMPED ON BY BASTARDS.
"YOU'RE COMING TO WRECK THE PLACE THAT BROKE YOUR HEART. YOU DON'T REALIZE YOU'D KILL ME DOING IT. WE HAVEN'T SPOKEN SINCE..."
STOP, JOHN. CAN'T YOU SEE WHAT'S HAPPENING?
JOHN, THEY NEED YOU TO DIE. STOP.

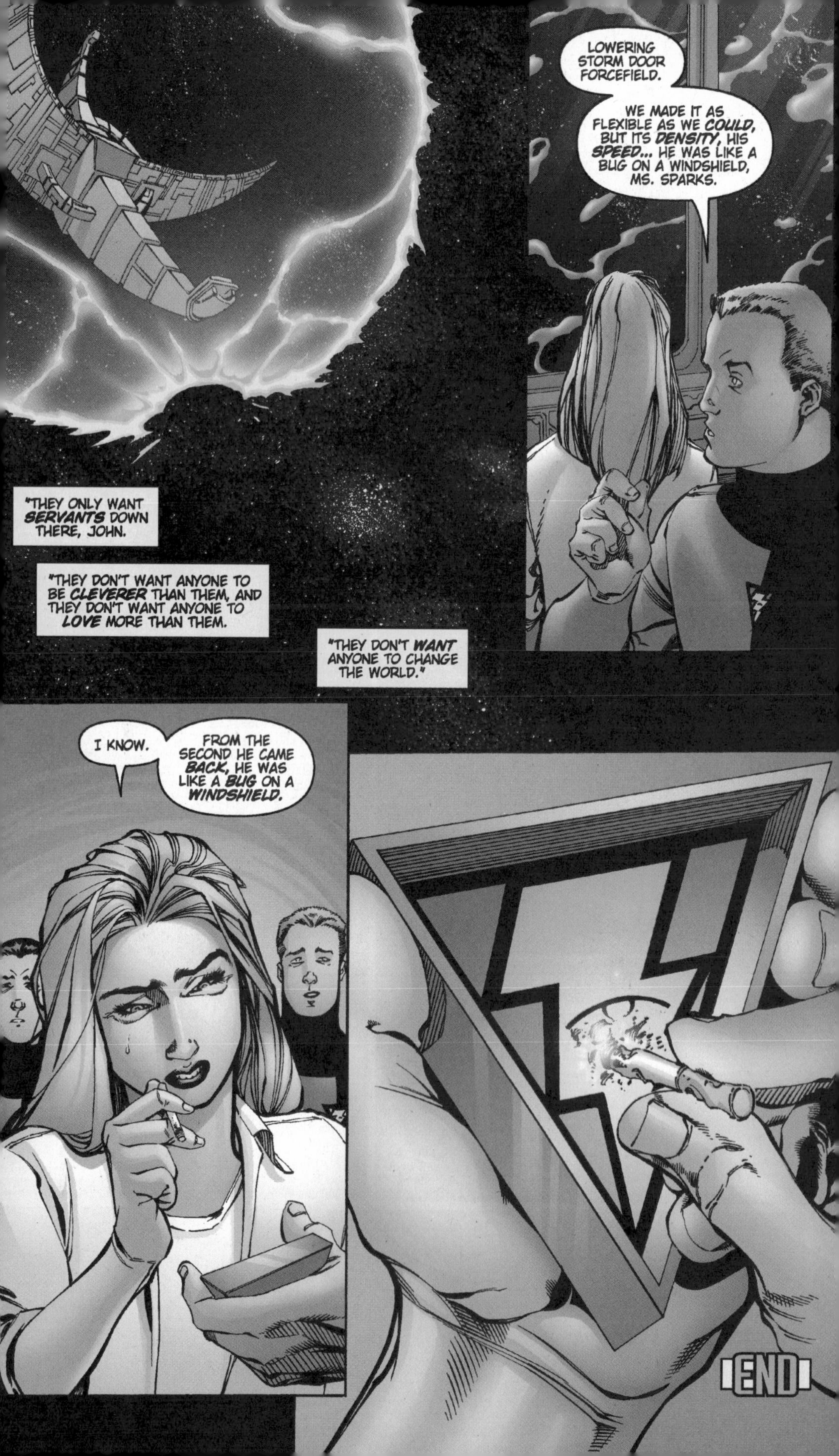
"THEY ONLY WANT SERVANTS DOWN THERE, JOHN.
"THEY DON'T WANT ANYONE TO BE CLEVERER THAN THEM, AND THEY DON'T WANT ANYONE TO LOVE MORE THAN THEM.
"THEY DON'T WANT ANYONE TO CHANGE THE WORLD."
LOWERING STORM DOOR FORCEFIELD.
WE MADE IT AS FLEXIBLE AS WE COULD, BUT ITS DENSITY, HIS SPEED... HE WAS LIKE A BUG ON A WINDSHIELD, MS. SPARKS.
I KNOW.
FROM THE SECOND HE CAME BACK, HE WAS LIKE A BUG ON A WINDSHIELD.
END

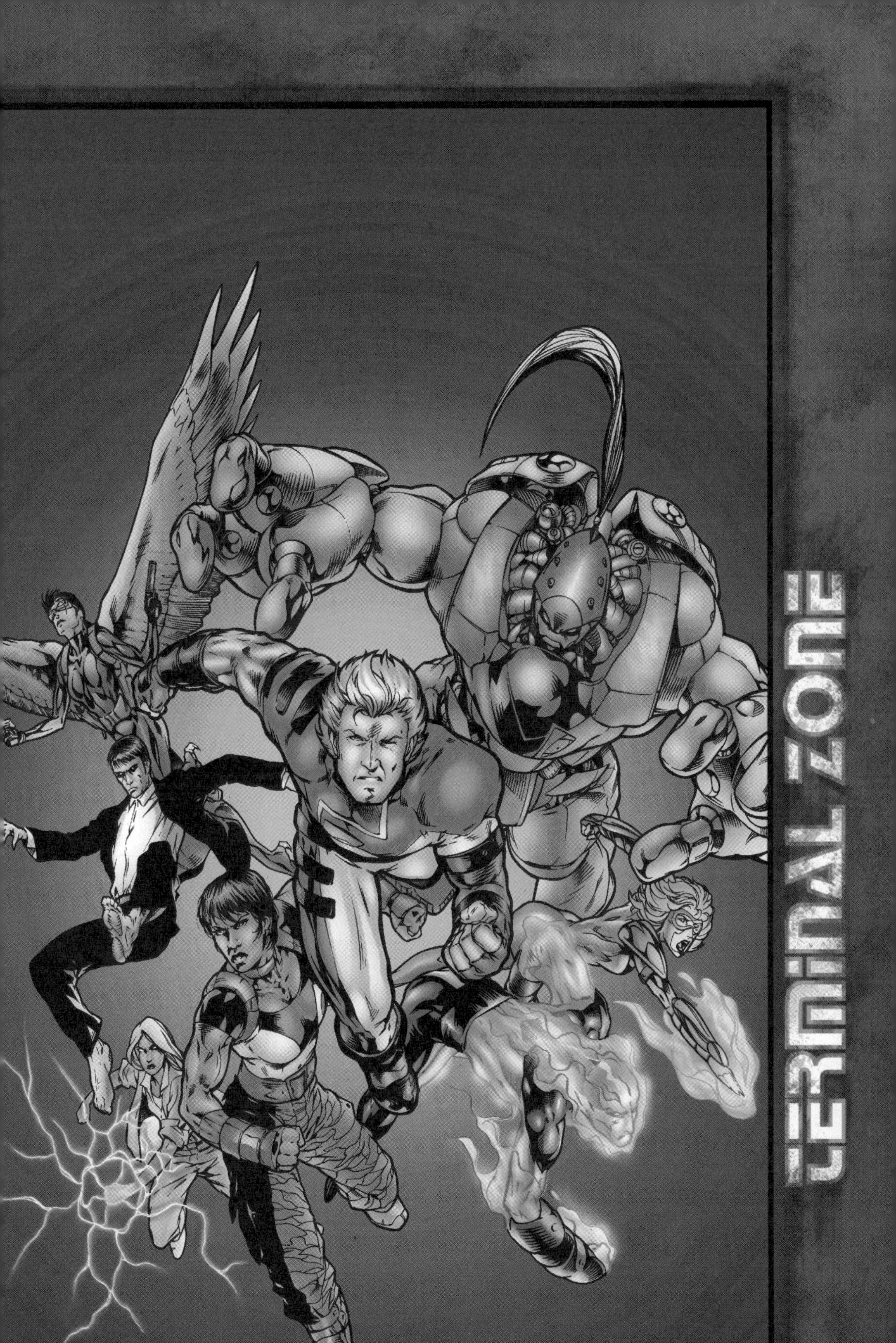
TERMINAL ZONE

ART BY OSCAR JIMENEZ & CHUCK GIBSON. COLOR BY WILDSTORM FX

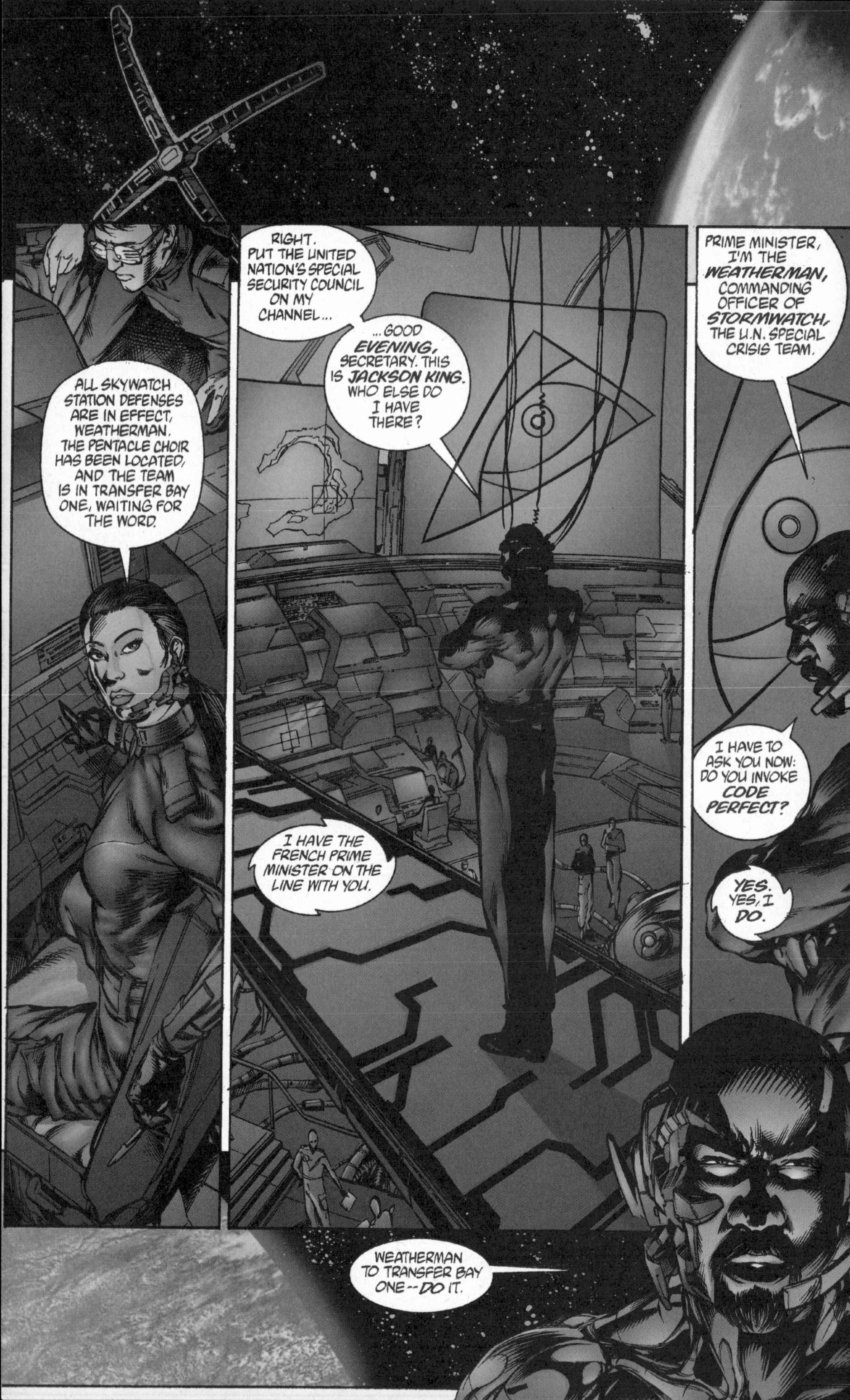
ALL SKYWATCH STATION DEFENSES ARE IN EFFECT, WEATHERMAN. THE PENTACLE CHOIR HAS BEEN LOCATED, AND THE TEAM IS IN TRANSFER BAY ONE, WAITING FOR THE WORD.
RIGHT. PUT THE UNITED NATION'S SPECIAL SECURITY COUNCIL ON MY CHANNEL...
...GOOD EVENING, SECRETARY. THIS IS JACKSON KING. WHO ELSE DO I HAVE THERE?
I HAVE THE FRENCH PRIME MINISTER ON THE LINE WITH YOU.
PRIME MINISTER, I'M THE WEATHERMAN, COMMANDING OFFICER OF STORMWATCH, THE U.N. SPECIAL CRISIS TEAM.
I HAVE TO ASK YOU NOW: DO YOU INVOKE CODE PERFECT?
YES. YES, I DO.
WEATHERMAN TO TRANSFER BAY ONE--DO IT.

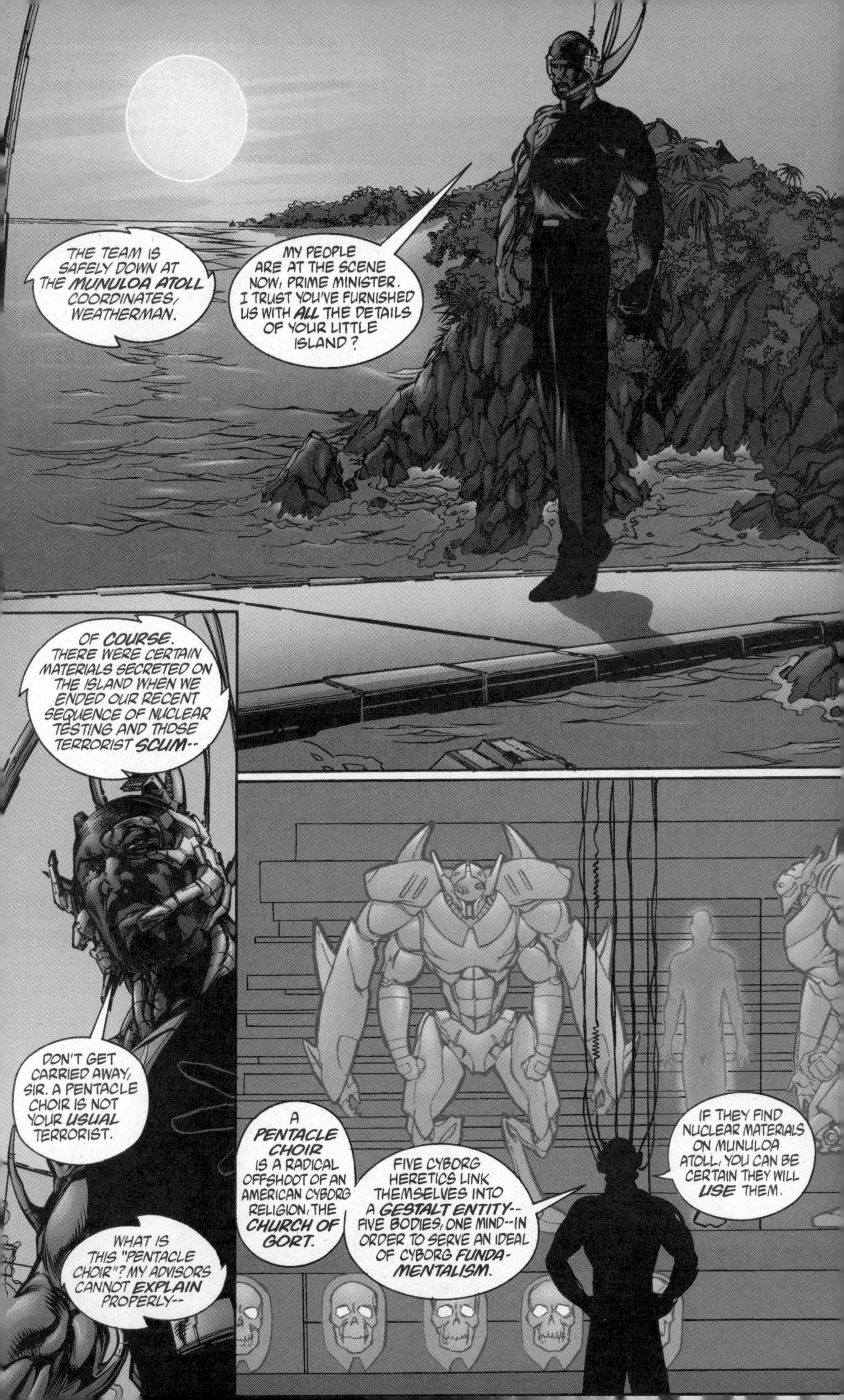
THE TEAM IS SAFELY DOWN AT THE MUNULOA ATOLL COORDINATES, WEATHERMAN.
MY PEOPLE ARE AT THE SCENE NOW, PRIME MINISTER. I TRUST YOU'VE FURNISHED US WITH ALL THE DETAILS OF YOUR LITTLE ISLAND?
OF COURSE. THERE WERE CERTAIN MATERIALS SECRETED ON THE ISLAND WHEN WE ENDED OUR RECENT SEQUENCE OF NUCLEAR TESTING AND THOSE TERRORIST SCUM--
DON'T GET CARRIED AWAY, SIR. A PENTACLE CHOIR IS NOT YOUR USUAL TERRORIST.
WHAT IS THIS "PENTACLE CHOIR"? MY ADVISORS CANNOT EXPLAIN PROPERLY--
A PENTACLE CHOIR IS A RADICAL OFFSHOOT OF AN AMERICAN CYBORG RELIGION, THE CHURCH OF GORT.
FIVE CYBORG HERETICS LINK THEMSELVES INTO A GESTALT ENTITY--FIVE BODIES, ONE MIND--IN ORDER TO SERVE AN IDEAL OF CYBORG FUNDAMENTALISM.
IF THEY FIND NUCLEAR MATERIALS ON MUNULOA ATOLL, YOU CAN BE CERTAIN THEY WILL USE THEM.

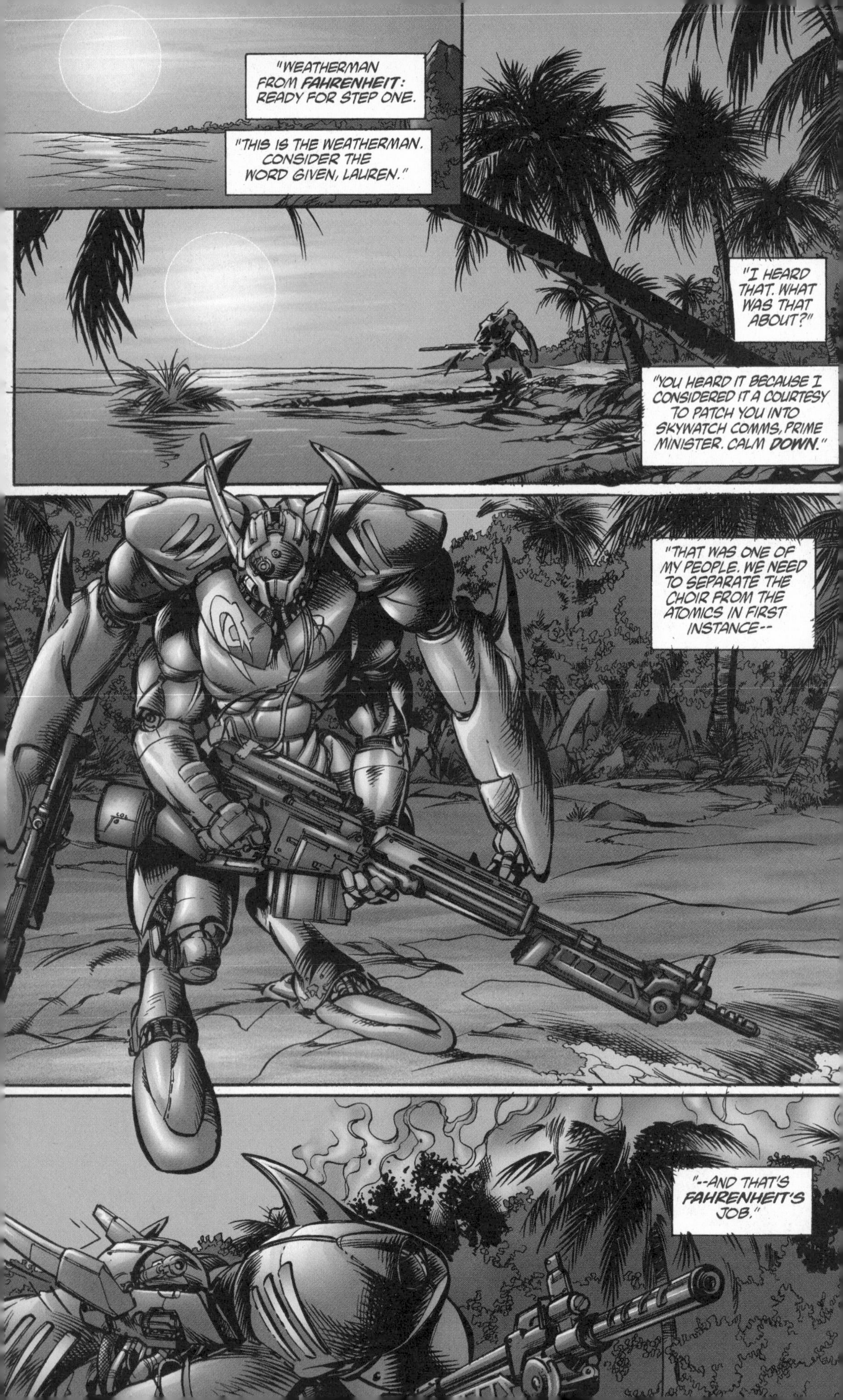
"WEATHERMAN FROM FAHRENHEIT: READY FOR STEP ONE.
"THIS IS THE WEATHERMAN. CONSIDER THE WORD GIVEN, LAUREN."
"I HEARD THAT. WHAT WAS THAT ABOUT?"
"YOU HEARD IT BECAUSE I CONSIDERED IT A COURTESY TO PATCH YOU INTO SKYWATCH COMMS, PRIME MINISTER. CALM DOWN."
"THAT WAS ONE OF MY PEOPLE. WE NEED TO SEPARATE THE CHOIR FROM THE ATOMICS IN FIRST INSTANCE--
"--AND THAT'S FAHRENHEIT'S JOB."

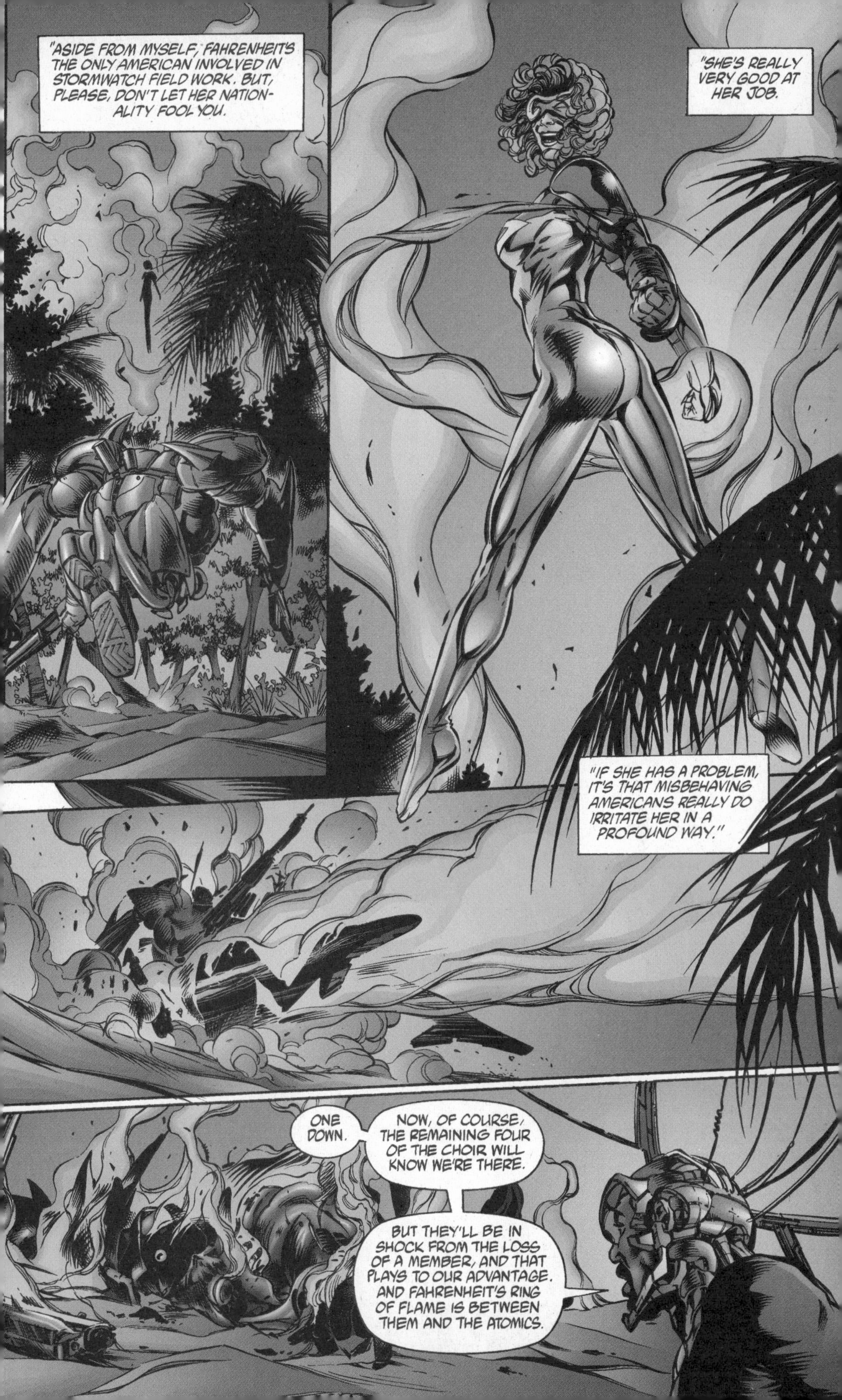
"ASIDE FROM MYSELF, FAHRENHEIT'S THE ONLY AMERICAN INVOLVED IN STORMWATCH FIELD WORK. BUT, PLEASE, DON'T LET HER NATIONALITY FOOL YOU.
"SHE'S REALLY VERY GOOD AT HER JOB.
"IF SHE HAS A PROBLEM, IT'S THAT MISBEHAVING AMERICANS REALLY DO IRRITATE HER IN A PROFOUND WAY."
ONE DOWN.
NOW, OF COURSE, THE REMAINING FOUR OF THE CHOIR WILL KNOW WE'RE THERE.
BUT THEY'LL BE IN SHOCK FROM THE LOSS OF A MEMBER, AND THAT PLAYS TO OUR ADVANTAGE. AND FAHRENHEIT'S RING OF FLAME IS BETWEEN THEM AND THE ATOMICS.

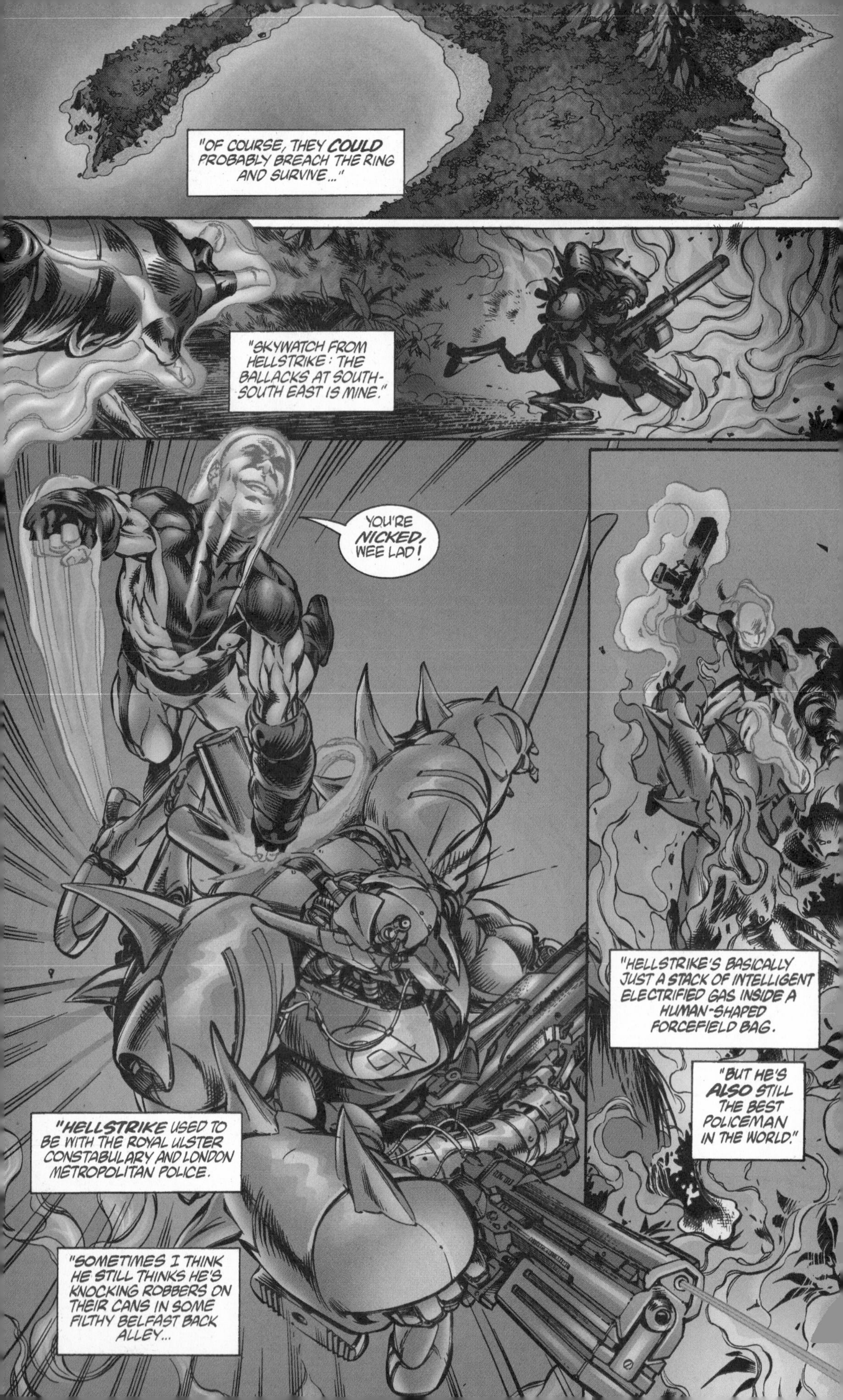
"OF COURSE, THEY COULD PROBABLY BREACH THE RING AND SURVIVE..."
"SKYWATCH FROM HELLSTRIKE: THE BALLACKS AT SOUTH-SOUTH EAST IS MINE."
YOU'RE NICKED, WEE LAD!
"HELLSTRIKE USED TO BE WITH THE ROYAL ULSTER CONSTABULARY AND LONDON METROPOLITAN POLICE.
"SOMETIMES I THINK HE STILL THINKS HE'S KNOCKING ROBBERS ON THEIR CANS IN SOME FILTHY BELFAST BACK ALLEY...
"HELLSTRIKE'S BASICALLY JUST A STACK OF INTELLIGENT ELECTRIFIED GAS INSIDE A HUMAN-SHAPED FORCEFIELD BAG.
"BUT HE'S ALSO STILL THE BEST POLICEMAN IN THE WORLD."

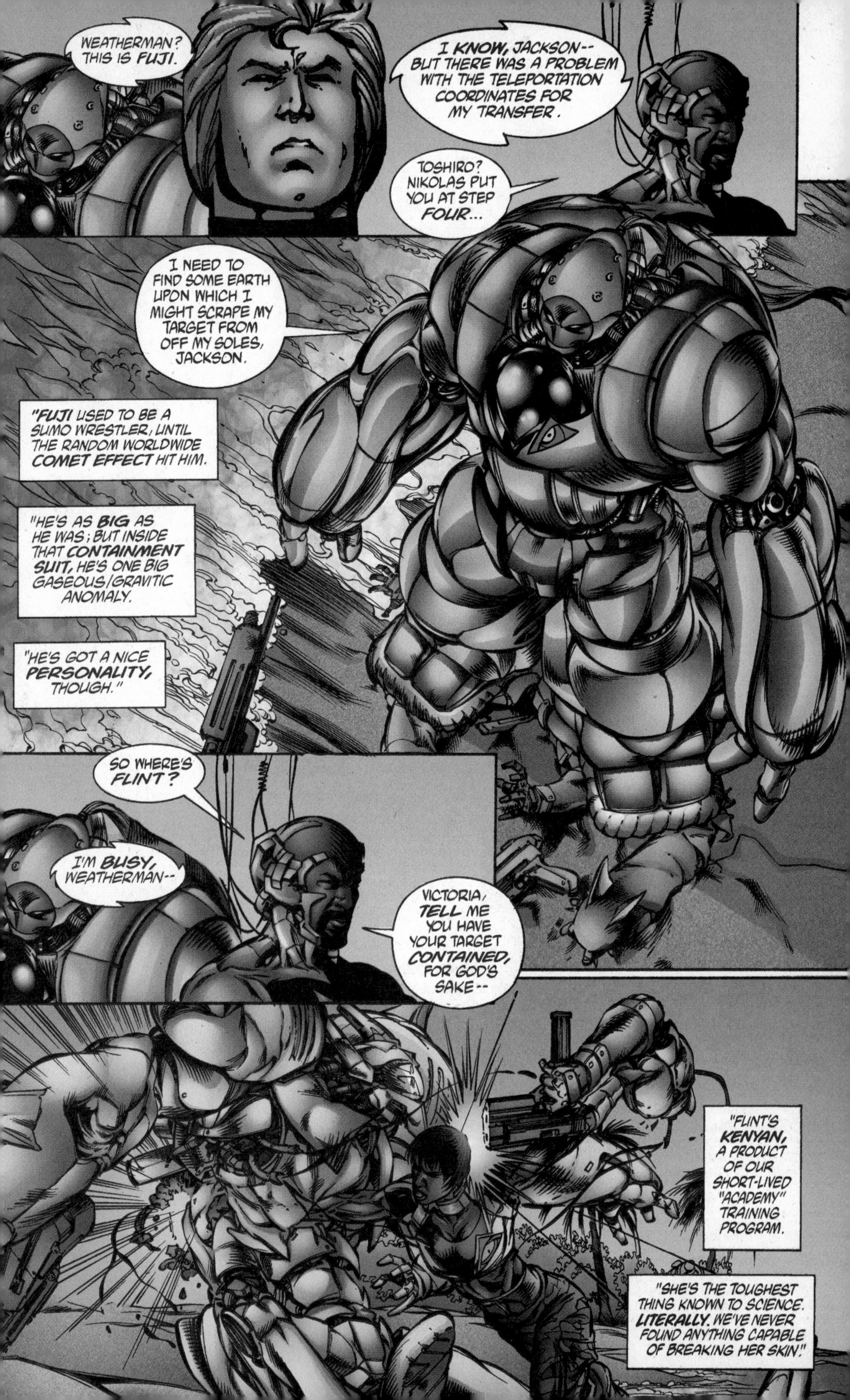

WEATHERMAN? THIS IS FUJI.
I KNOW, JACKSON-- BUT THERE WAS A PROBLEM WITH THE TELEPORTATION COORDINATES FOR MY TRANSFER.
TOSHIRO? NIKOLAS PUT YOU AT STEP FOUR...
I NEED TO FIND SOME EARTH UPON WHICH I MIGHT SCRAPE MY TARGET FROM OFF MY SOLES, JACKSON.
"FUJI USED TO BE A SUMO WRESTLER, UNTIL THE RANDOM WORLDWIDE COMET EFFECT HIT HIM.
"HE'S AS BIG AS HE WAS; BUT INSIDE THAT CONTAINMENT SUIT, HE'S ONE BIG GASEOUS/GRAVITIC ANOMALY.
"HE'S GOT A NICE PERSONALITY, THOUGH."
SO WHERE'S FLINT?
I'M BUSY, WEATHERMAN--
VICTORIA, TELL ME YOU HAVE YOUR TARGET CONTAINED, FOR GOD'S SAKE--
"FLINT'S KENYAN, A PRODUCT OF OUR SHORT-LIVED "ACADEMY" TRAINING PROGRAM.
"SHE'S THE TOUGHEST THING KNOWN TO SCIENCE. LITERALLY. WE'VE NEVER FOUND ANYTHING CAPABLE OF BREAKING HER SKIN."

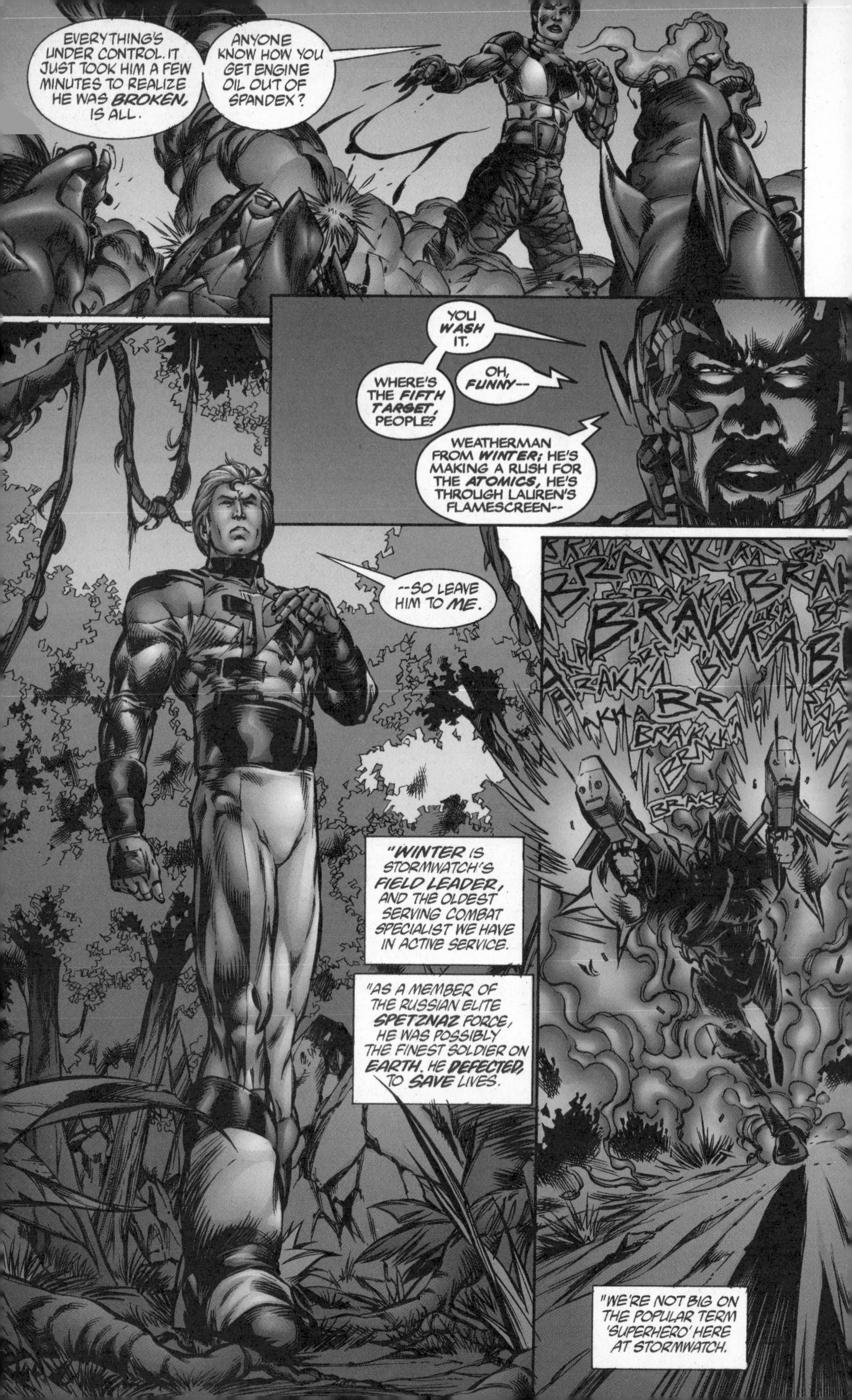
EVERYTHING'S UNDER CONTROL. IT JUST TOOK HIM A FEW MINUTES TO REALIZE HE WAS BROKEN, IS ALL.
ANYONE KNOW HOW YOU GET ENGINE OIL OUT OF SPANDEX?
YOU WASH IT.
OH, FUNNY--
WHERE'S THE FIFTH TARGET, PEOPLE?
WEATHERMAN FROM WINTER; HE'S MAKING A RUSH FOR THE ATOMICS, HE'S THROUGH LAUREN'S FLAMESCREEN--
--SO LEAVE HIM TO ME.
BRAKKA
"WINTER IS STORMWATCH'S FIELD LEADER, AND THE OLDEST SERVING COMBAT SPECIALIST WE HAVE IN ACTIVE SERVICE.
"AS A MEMBER OF THE RUSSIAN ELITE SPETZNAZ FORCE, HE WAS POSSIBLY THE FINEST SOLDIER ON EARTH. HE DEFECTED, TO SAVE LIVES.
"WE'RE NOT BIG ON THE POPULAR TERM 'SUPERHERO' HERE AT STORMWATCH.

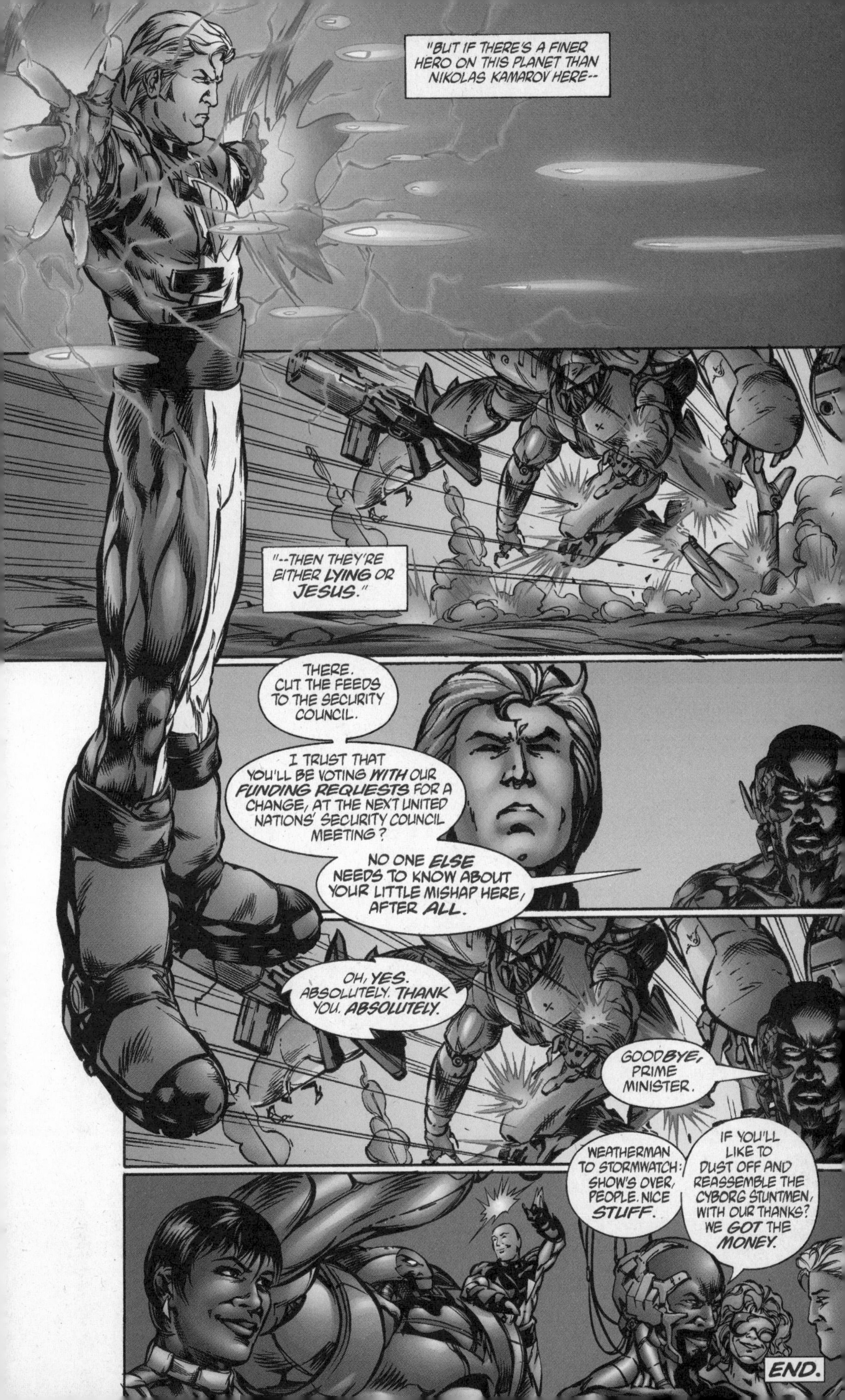
"BUT IF THERE'S A FINER HERO ON THIS PLANET THAN NIKOLAS KAMAROV HERE--
"--THEN THEY'RE EITHER LYING OR JESUS."
THERE. CUT THE FEEDS TO THE SECURITY COUNCIL.
I TRUST THAT YOU'LL BE VOTING WITH OUR FUNDING REQUESTS FOR A CHANGE, AT THE NEXT UNITED NATIONS' SECURITY COUNCIL MEETING?
NO ONE ELSE NEEDS TO KNOW ABOUT YOUR LITTLE MISHAP HERE, AFTER ALL.
OH, YES. ABSOLUTELY. THANK YOU. ABSOLUTELY.
GOODBYE, PRIME MINISTER.
WEATHERMAN TO STORMWATCH: SHOW'S OVER, PEOPLE. NICE STUFF.
IF YOU'LL LIKE TO DUST OFF AND REASSEMBLE THE CYBORG STUNTMEN, WITH OUR THANKS? WE GOT THE MONEY.
END.

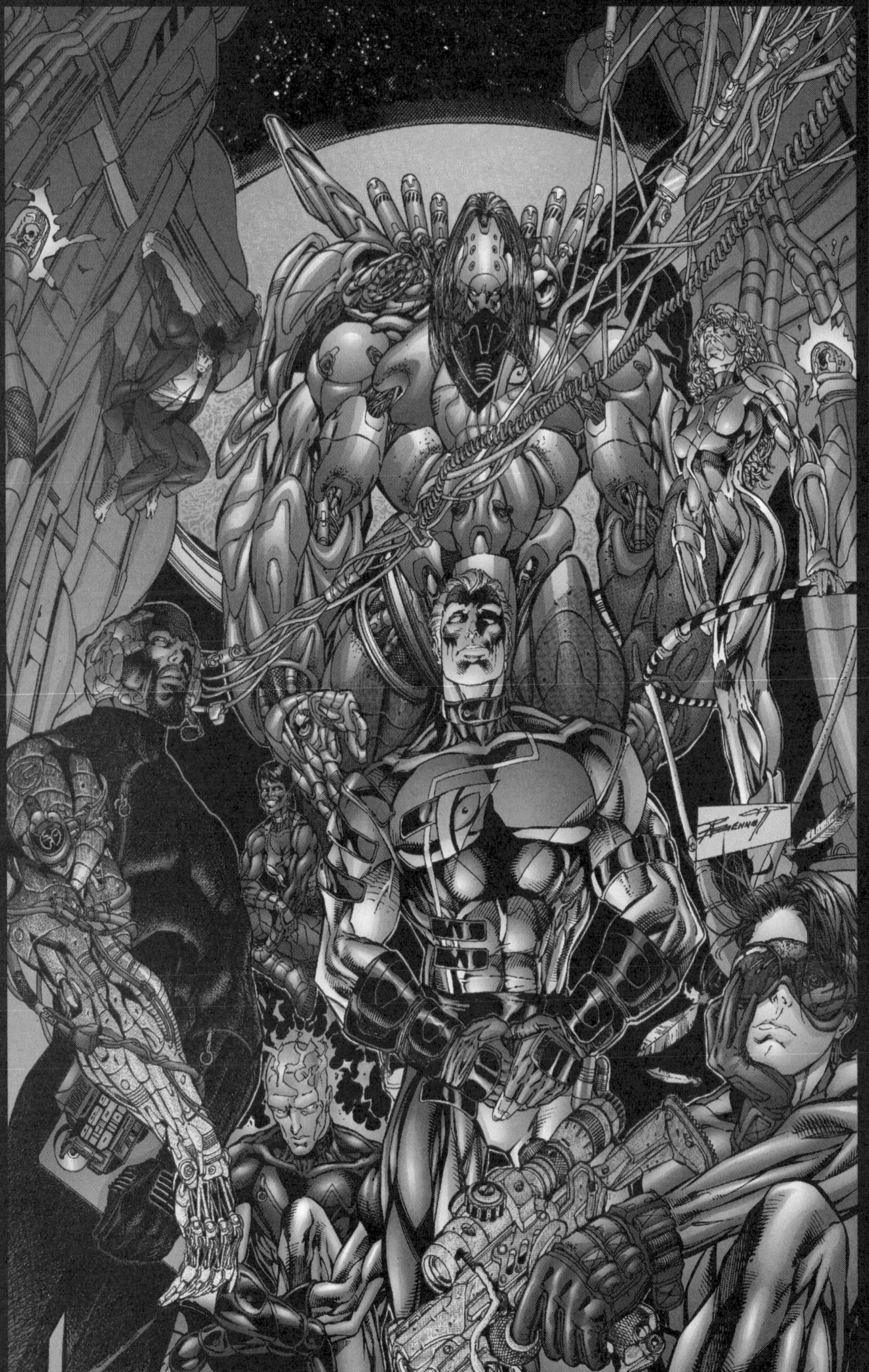

ART BY RICHARD BENNETT, COLOR BY WILDSTORM FX

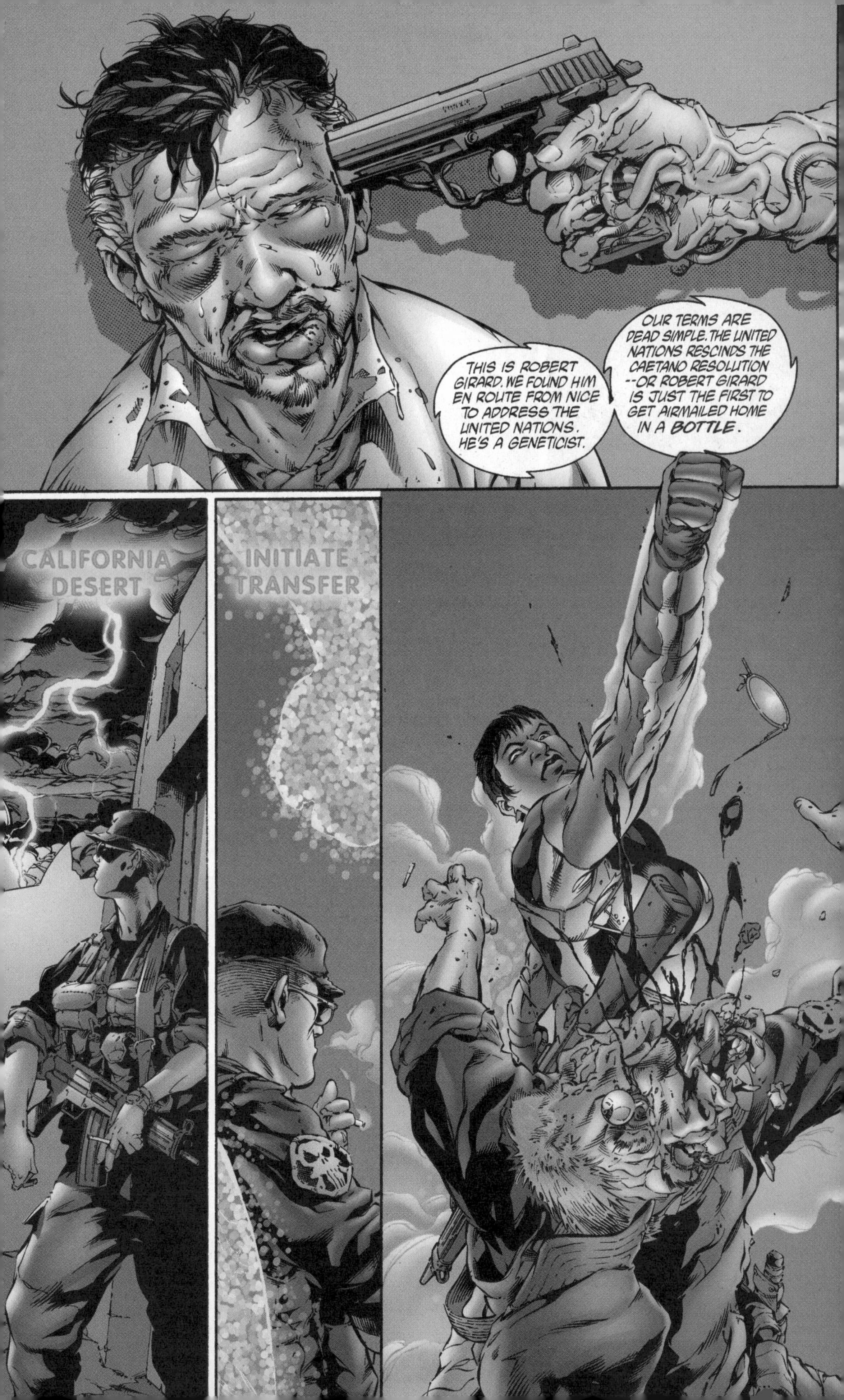
THIS IS ROBERT GIRARD. WE FOUND HIM EN ROUTE FROM NICE TO ADDRESS THE UNITED NATIONS. HE'S A GENETICIST.
OUR TERMS ARE DEAD SIMPLE. THE UNITED NATIONS RESCINDS THE CAETANO RESOLUTION --OR ROBERT GIRARD IS JUST THE FIRST TO GET AIRMAILED HOME IN A BOTTLE.
CALIFORNIA DESERT
INITIATE TRANSFER

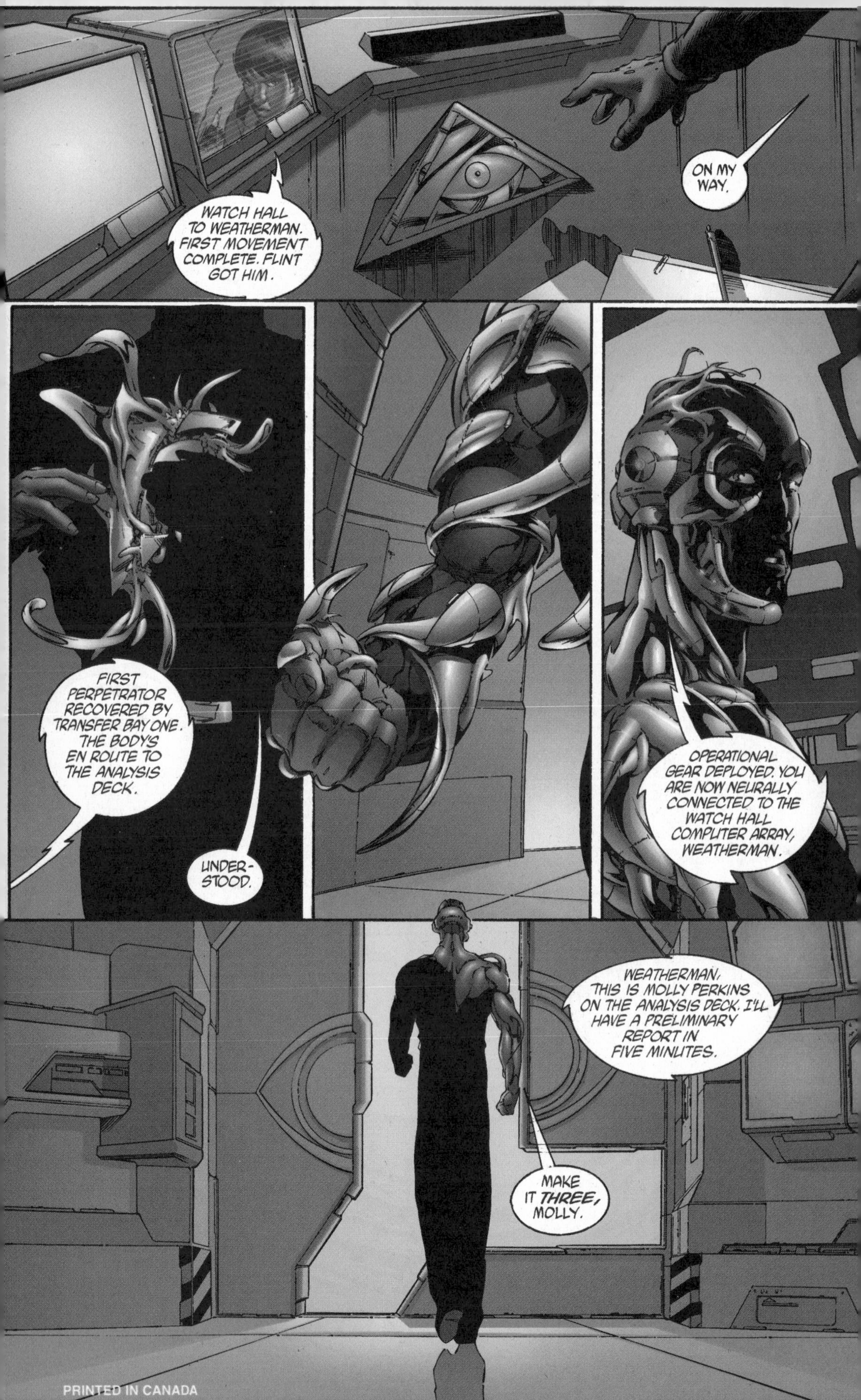

WATCH HALL TO WEATHERMAN. FIRST MOVEMENT COMPLETE. FLINT GOT HIM.
ON MY WAY.
FIRST PERPETRATOR RECOVERED BY TRANSFER BAY ONE. THE BODY'S EN ROUTE TO THE ANALYSIS DECK.
UNDER-STOOD.
OPERATIONAL GEAR DEPLOYED. YOU ARE NOW NEURALLY CONNECTED TO THE WATCH HALL COMPUTER ARRAY, WEATHERMAN.
WEATHERMAN, THIS IS MOLLY PERKINS ON THE ANALYSIS DECK. I'LL HAVE A PRELIMINARY REPORT IN FIVE MINUTES.
MAKE IT *THREE,* MOLLY.

PRINTED IN CANADA

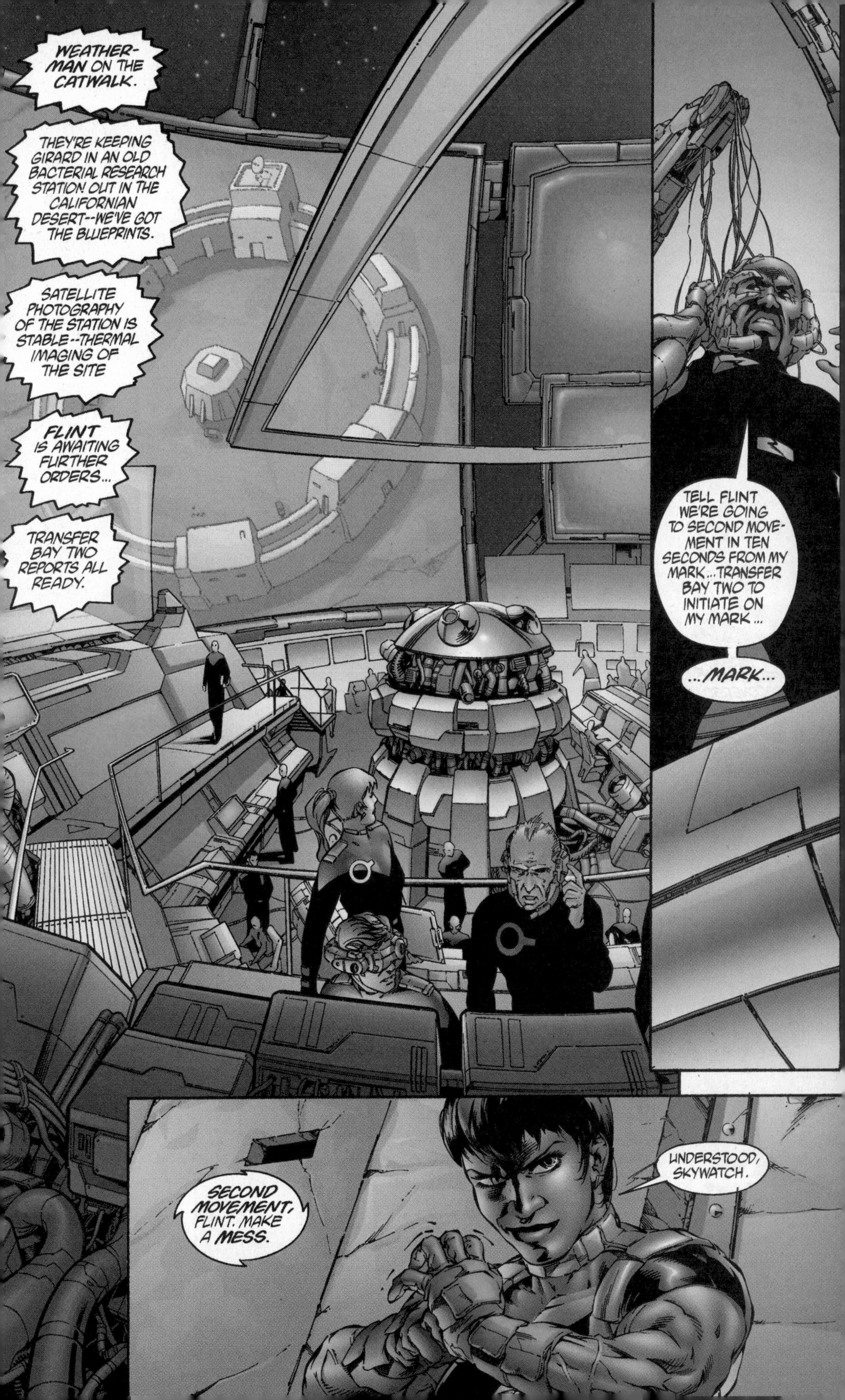
WEATHER-MAN ON THE CATWALK.
THEY'RE KEEPING GIRARD IN AN OLD BACTERIAL RESEARCH STATION OUT IN THE CALIFORNIAN DESERT--WE'VE GOT THE BLUEPRINTS.
SATELLITE PHOTOGRAPHY OF THE STATION IS STABLE--THERMAL IMAGING OF THE SITE
FLINT IS AWAITING FURTHER ORDERS...
TRANSFER BAY TWO REPORTS ALL READY.
TELL FLINT WE'RE GOING TO SECOND MOVE-MENT IN TEN SECONDS FROM MY MARK...TRANSFER BAY TWO TO INITIATE ON MY MARK...
...MARK...
SECOND MOVEMENT, FLINT. MAKE A MESS.
UNDERSTOOD, SKYWATCH.

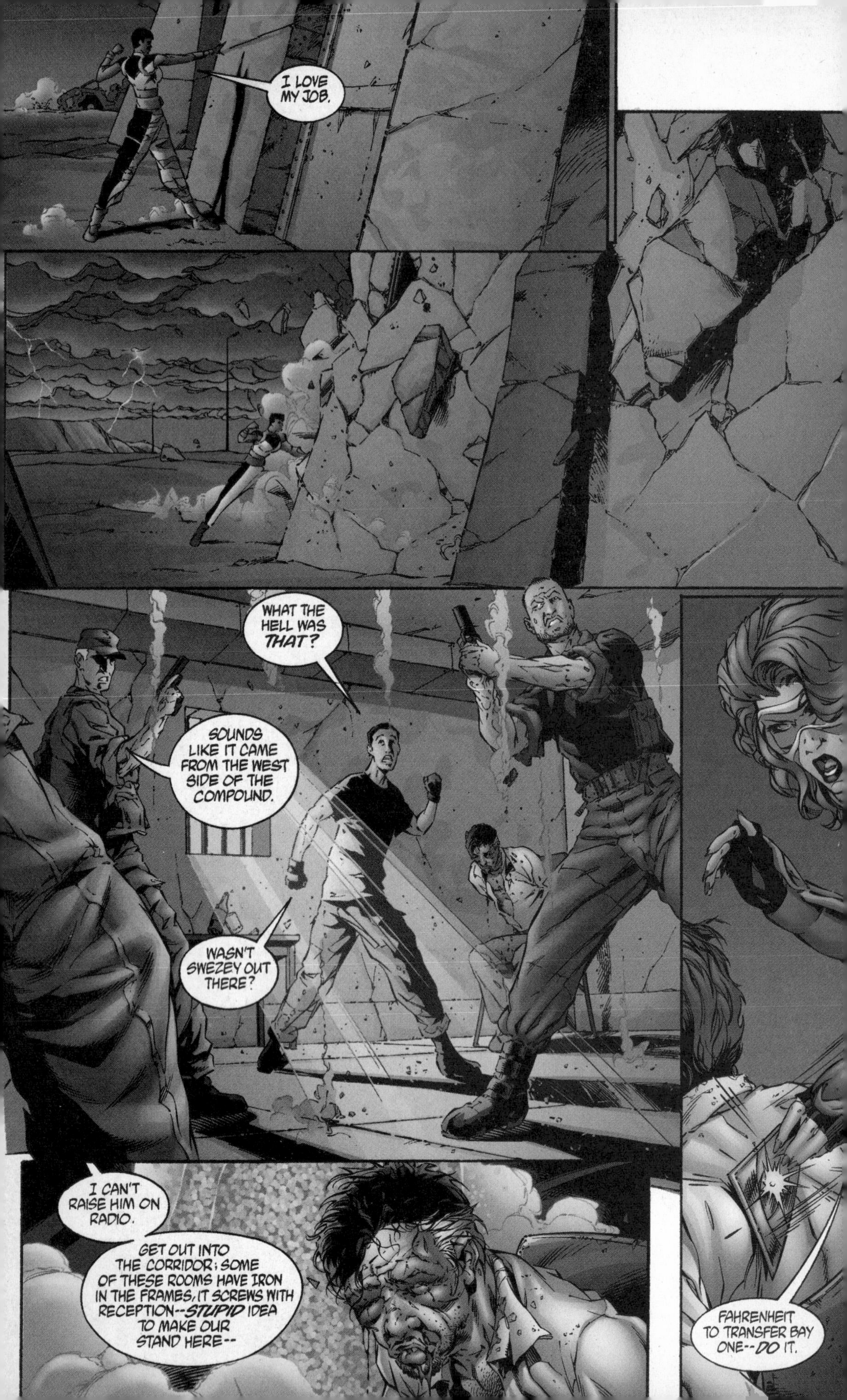
I LOVE MY JOB.
WHAT THE HELL WAS *THAT*?
SOUNDS LIKE IT CAME FROM THE WEST SIDE OF THE COMPOUND.
WASN'T SWEZEY OUT THERE?
I CAN'T RAISE HIM ON RADIO.
GET OUT INTO THE CORRIDOR; SOME OF THESE ROOMS HAVE IRON IN THE FRAMES, IT SCREWS WITH RECEPTION--*STUPID* IDEA TO MAKE OUR STAND HERE--
FAHRENHEIT TO TRANSFER BAY ONE--*DO* IT.

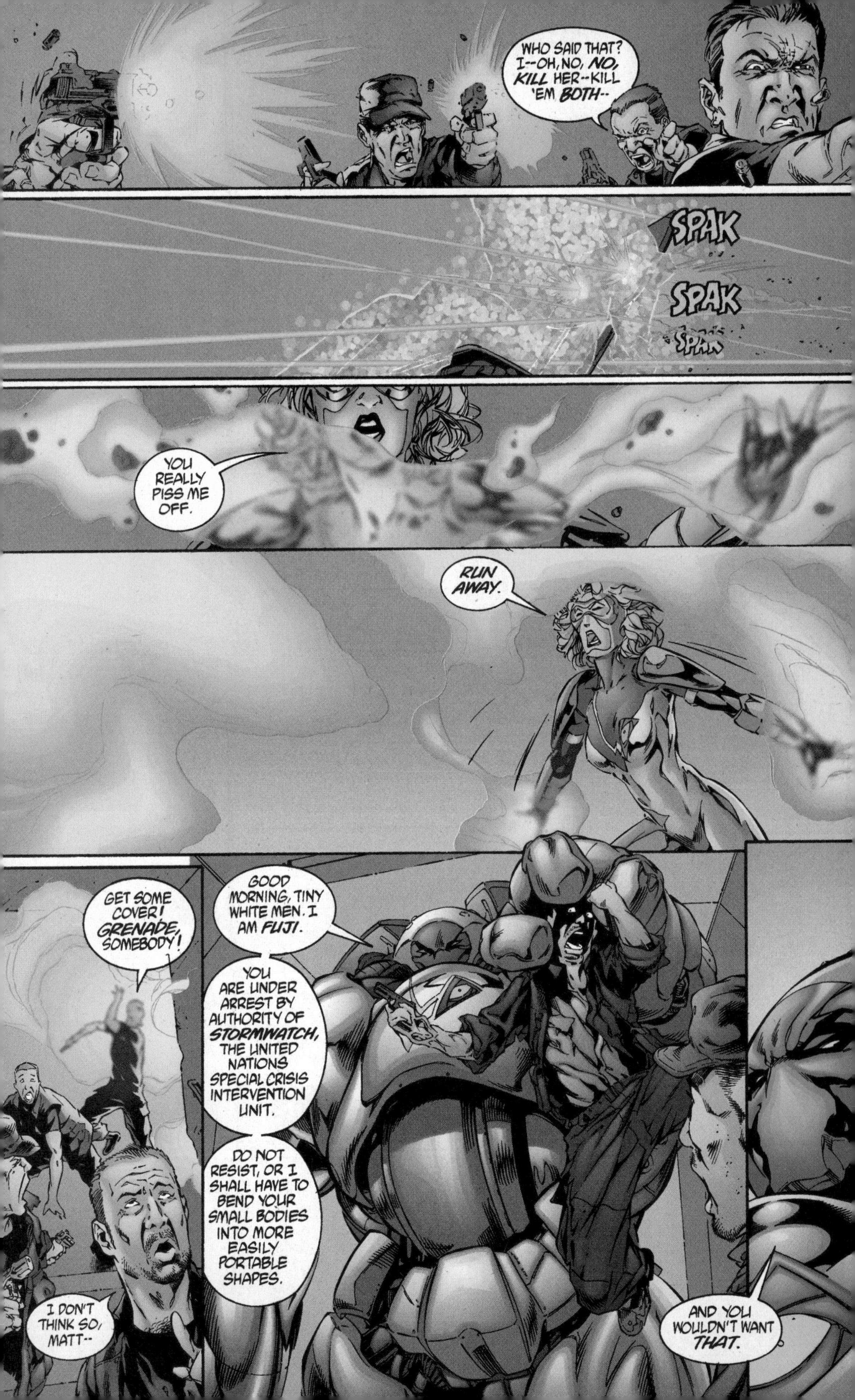
WHO SAID THAT? I--OH, NO, NO, KILL HER--KILL 'EM BOTH--
SPAK
SPAK
SPAK
YOU REALLY PISS ME OFF.
RUN AWAY.
GET SOME COVER! GRENADE, SOMEBODY!
GOOD MORNING, TINY WHITE MEN. I AM FUJI.
YOU ARE UNDER ARREST BY AUTHORITY OF STORMWATCH, THE UNITED NATIONS SPECIAL CRISIS INTERVENTION UNIT.
DO NOT RESIST, OR I SHALL HAVE TO BEND YOUR SMALL BODIES INTO MORE EASILY PORTABLE SHAPES.
I DON'T THINK SO, MATT--
AND YOU WOULDN'T WANT THAT.

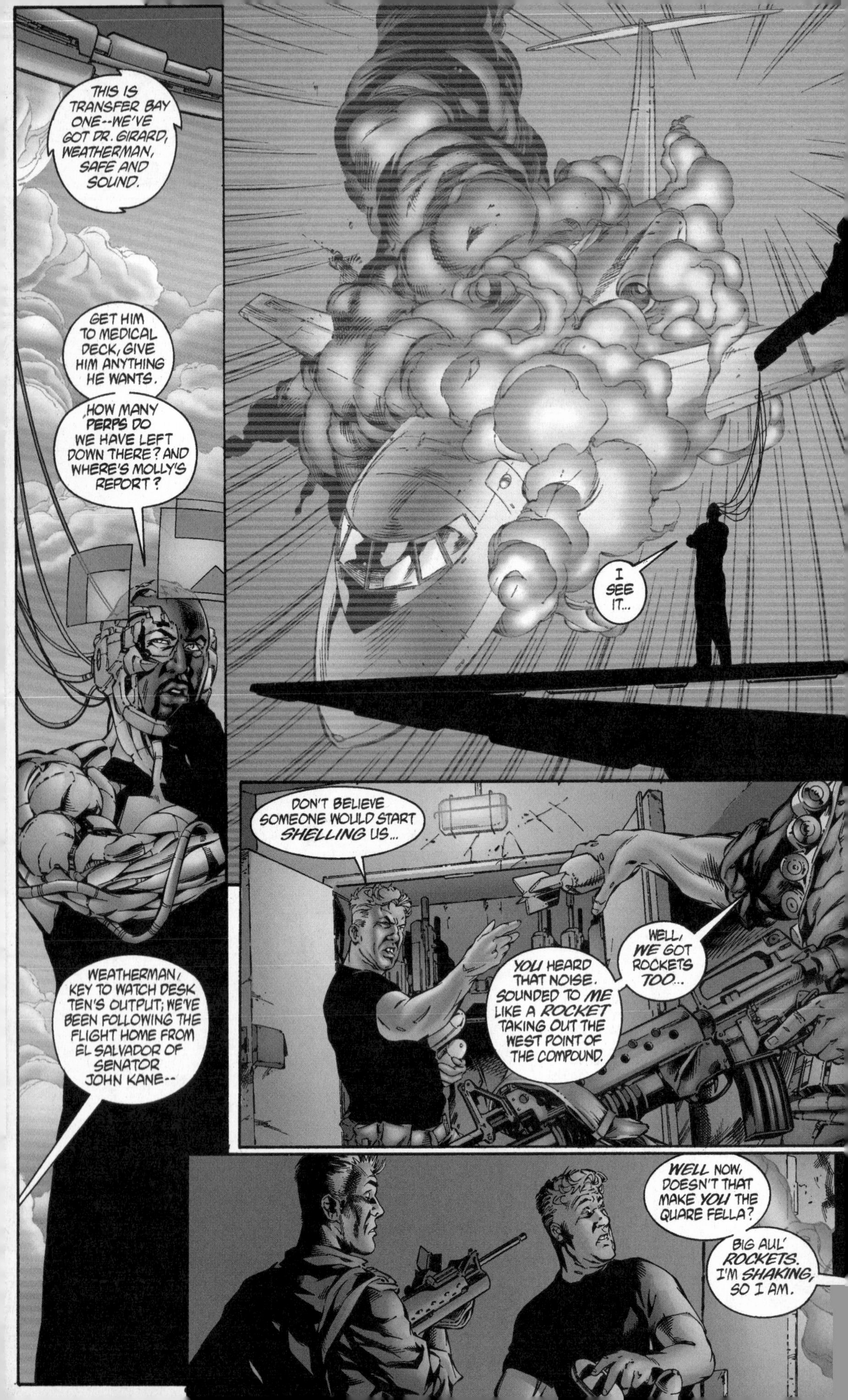
THIS IS TRANSFER BAY ONE--WE'VE GOT DR. GIRARD, WEATHERMAN, SAFE AND SOUND.
GET HIM TO MEDICAL DECK, GIVE HIM ANYTHING HE WANTS.
HOW MANY PERPS DO WE HAVE LEFT DOWN THERE? AND WHERE'S MOLLY'S REPORT?
I SEE IT...
WEATHERMAN, KEY TO WATCH DESK TEN'S OUTPUT; WE'VE BEEN FOLLOWING THE FLIGHT HOME FROM EL SALVADOR OF SENATOR JOHN KANE--
DON'T BELIEVE SOMEONE WOULD START SHELLING US...
YOU HEARD THAT NOISE. SOUNDED TO ME LIKE A ROCKET TAKING OUT THE WEST POINT OF THE COMPOUND.
WELL, WE GOT ROCKETS TOO...
WELL NOW, DOESN'T THAT MAKE YOU THE QUARE FELLA?
BIG AUL' ROCKETS. I'M SHAKING, SO I AM.

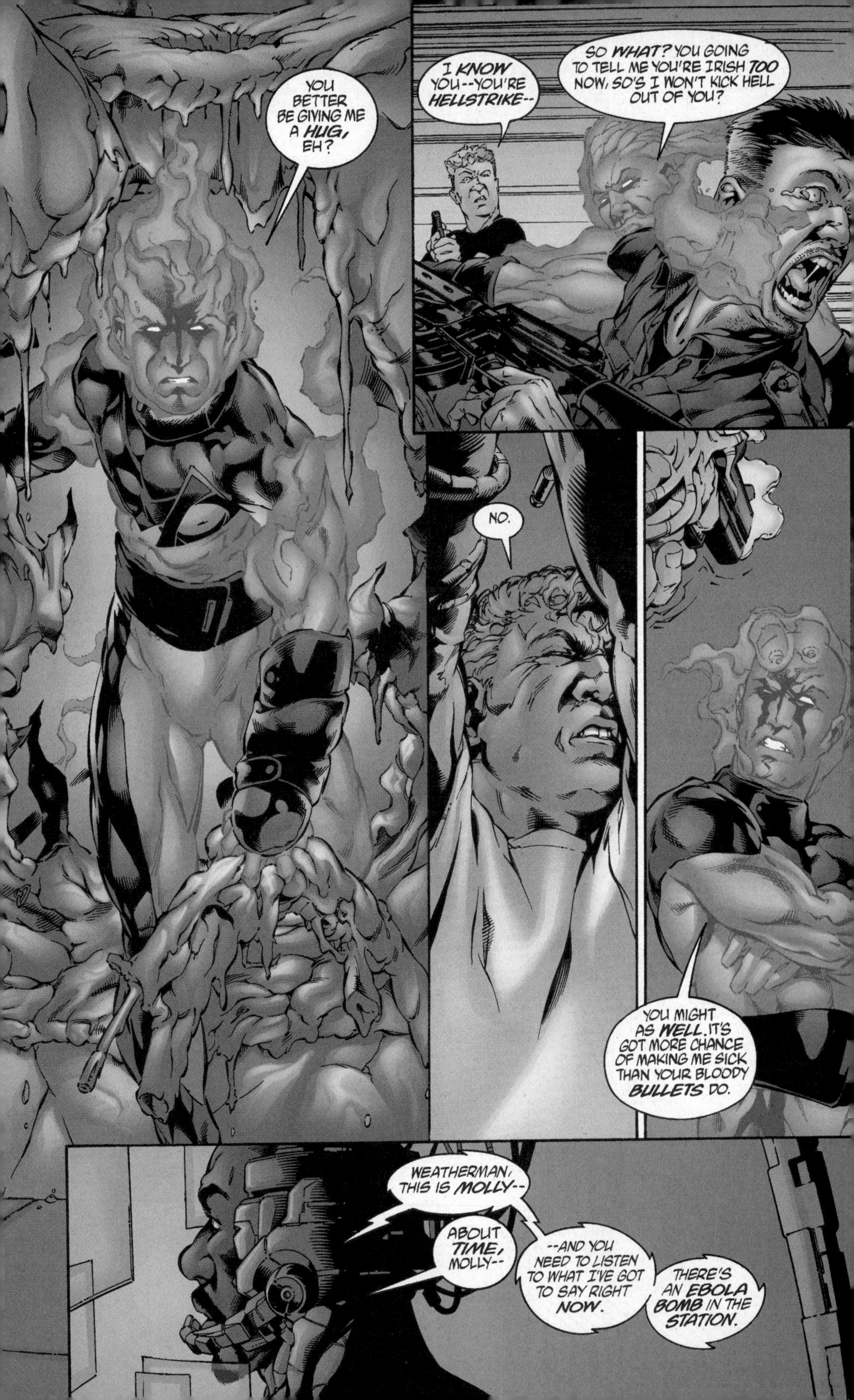
YOU BETTER BE GIVING ME A HUG, EH?
I KNOW YOU--YOU'RE HELLSTRIKE--
SO WHAT? YOU GOING TO TELL ME YOU'RE IRISH TOO NOW, SO'S I WON'T KICK HELL OUT OF YOU?
NO.
YOU MIGHT AS WELL. IT'S GOT MORE CHANCE OF MAKING ME SICK THAN YOUR BLOODY BULLETS DO.
WEATHERMAN, THIS IS MOLLY--
ABOUT TIME, MOLLY--
--AND YOU NEED TO LISTEN TO WHAT I'VE GOT TO SAY RIGHT NOW.
THERE'S AN EBOLA BOMB IN THE STATION.

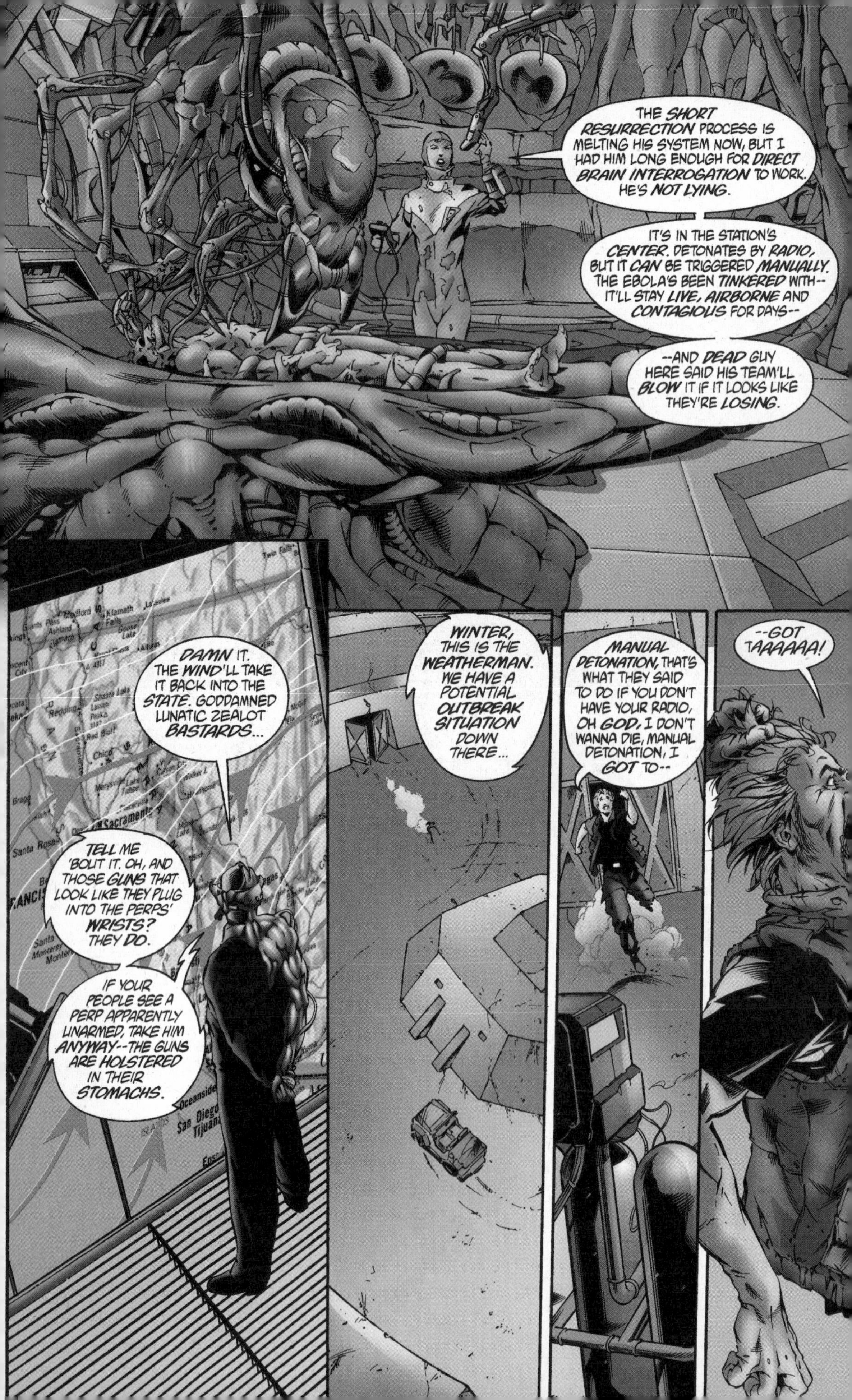
THE SHORT RESURRECTION PROCESS IS MELTING HIS SYSTEM NOW, BUT I HAD HIM LONG ENOUGH FOR DIRECT BRAIN INTERROGATION TO WORK. HE'S NOT LYING.
IT'S IN THE STATION'S CENTER. DETONATES BY RADIO, BUT IT CAN BE TRIGGERED MANUALLY. THE EBOLA'S BEEN TINKERED WITH-- IT'LL STAY LIVE, AIRBORNE AND CONTAGIOUS FOR DAYS--
--AND DEAD GUY HERE SAID HIS TEAM'LL BLOW IT IF IT LOOKS LIKE THEY'RE LOSING.
DAMN IT. THE WIND'LL TAKE IT BACK INTO THE STATE. GODDAMNED LUNATIC ZEALOT BASTARDS...
TELL ME 'BOUT IT. OH, AND THOSE GUNS THAT LOOK LIKE THEY PLUG INTO THE PERPS' WRISTS? THEY DO.
IF YOUR PEOPLE SEE A PERP APPARENTLY UNARMED, TAKE HIM ANYWAY--THE GUNS ARE HOLSTERED IN THEIR STOMACHS.
WINTER, THIS IS THE WEATHERMAN. WE HAVE A POTENTIAL OUTBREAK SITUATION DOWN THERE...
MANUAL DETONATION, THAT'S WHAT THEY SAID TO DO IF YOU DON'T HAVE YOUR RADIO, OH GOD, I DON'T WANNA DIE, MANUAL DETONATION, I GOT TO--
--GOT TAAAAAA!

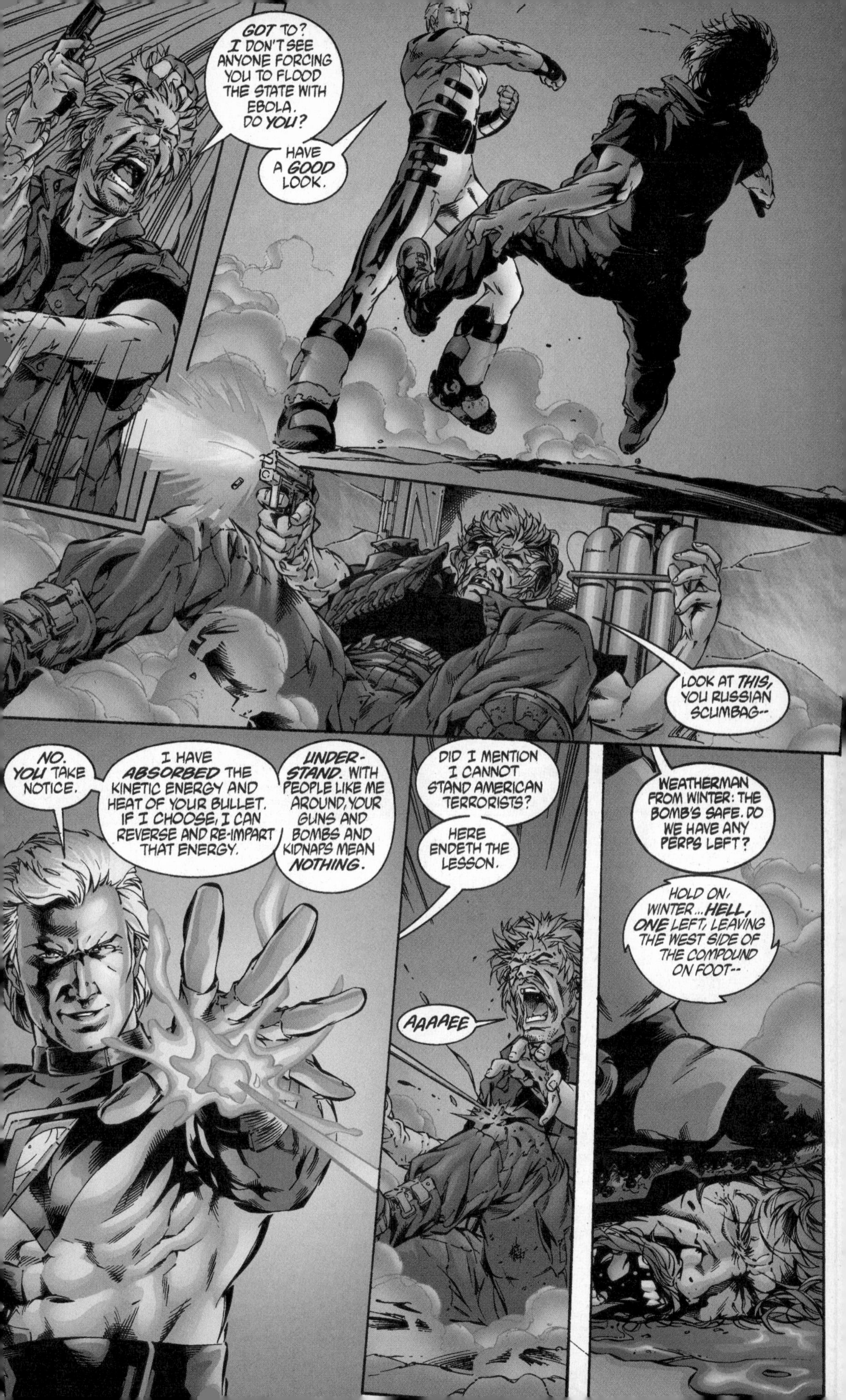
GOT TO? I DON'T SEE ANYONE FORCING YOU TO FLOOD THE STATE WITH EBOLA. DO YOU?
HAVE A GOOD LOOK.
LOOK AT THIS, YOU RUSSIAN SCUMBAG--
NO. YOU TAKE NOTICE.
I HAVE ABSORBED THE KINETIC ENERGY AND HEAT OF YOUR BULLET. IF I CHOOSE, I CAN REVERSE AND RE-IMPART THAT ENERGY.
UNDER-STAND. WITH PEOPLE LIKE ME AROUND, YOUR GUNS AND BOMBS AND KIDNAPS MEAN NOTHING.
DID I MENTION I CANNOT STAND AMERICAN TERRORISTS?
HERE ENDETH THE LESSON.
AAAAEE
WEATHERMAN FROM WINTER: THE BOMB'S SAFE. DO WE HAVE ANY PERPS LEFT?
HOLD ON, WINTER... HELL, ONE LEFT, LEAVING THE WEST SIDE OF THE COMPOUND ON FOOT--

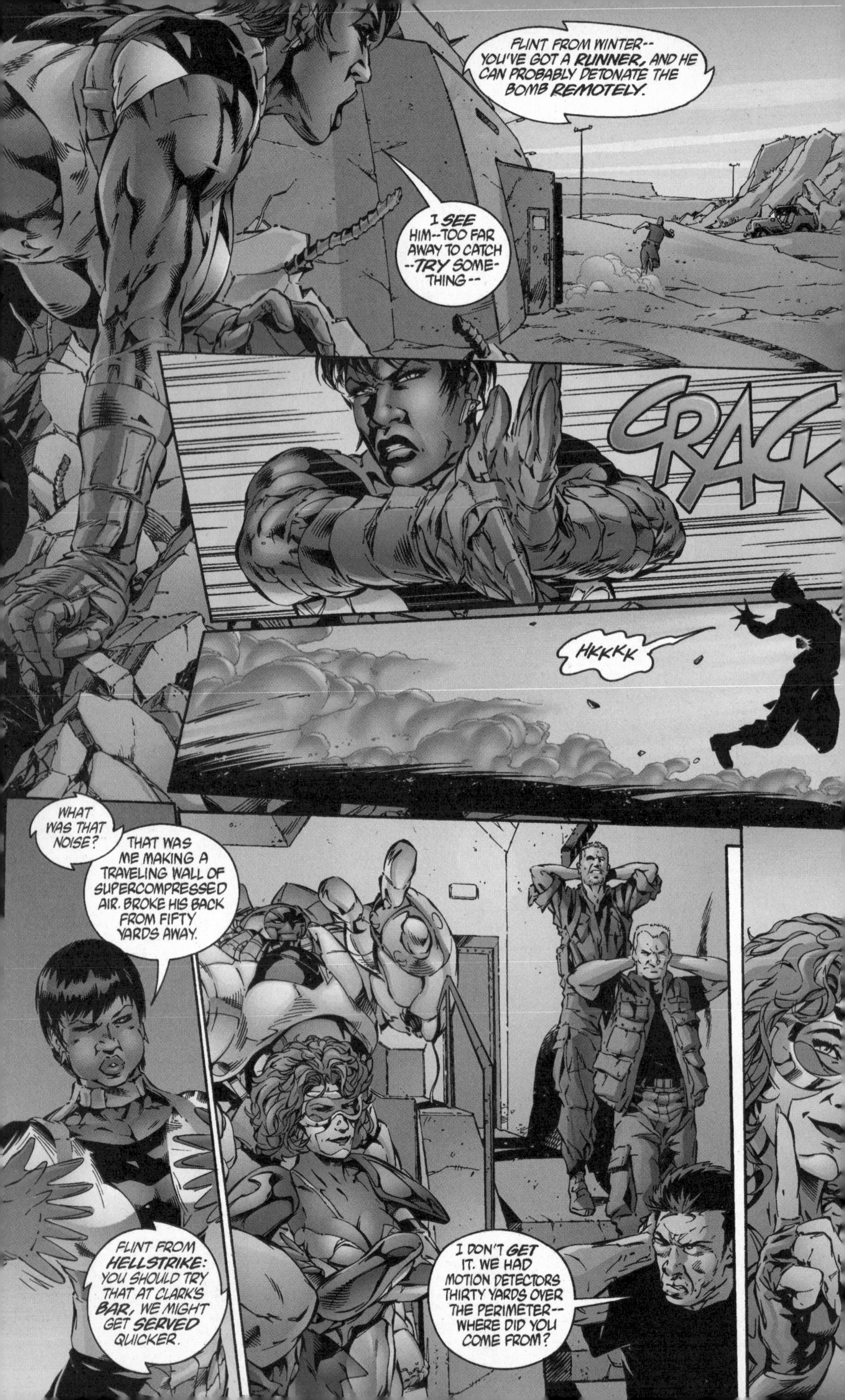
FLINT FROM WINTER-- YOU'VE GOT A RUNNER, AND HE CAN PROBABLY DETONATE THE BOMB REMOTELY.
I SEE HIM--TOO FAR AWAY TO CATCH --TRY SOME-THING--
CRACK
HKKKK
WHAT WAS THAT NOISE?
THAT WAS ME MAKING A TRAVELING WALL OF SUPERCOMPRESSED AIR. BROKE HIS BACK FROM FIFTY YARDS AWAY.
FLINT FROM HELLSTRIKE: YOU SHOULD TRY THAT AT CLARK'S BAR, WE MIGHT GET SERVED QUICKER.
I DON'T GET IT. WE HAD MOTION DETECTORS THIRTY YARDS OVER THE PERIMETER-- WHERE DID YOU COME FROM?

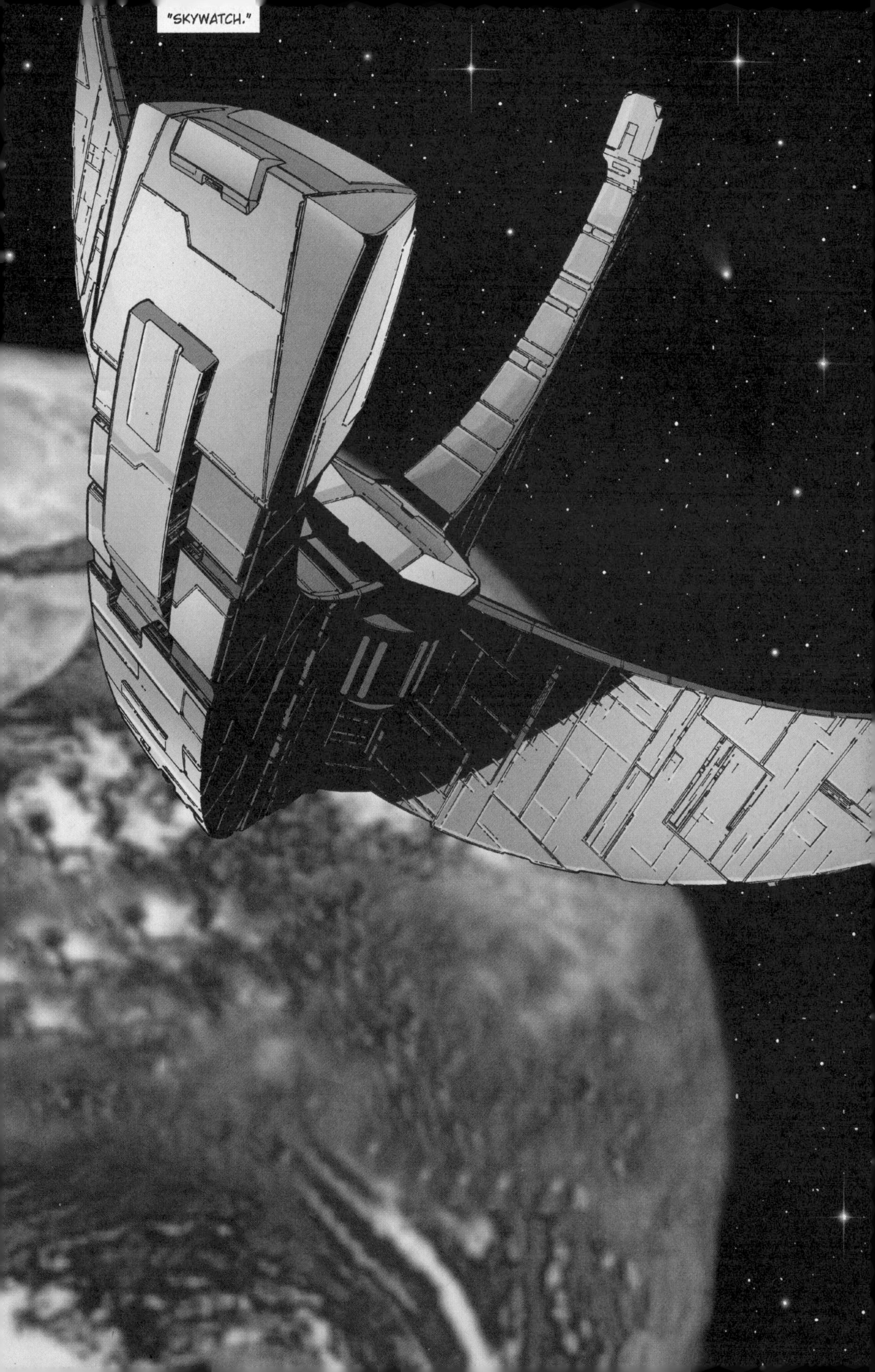
"SKYWATCH."

SO YOU WANT TO KNOW HOW IT STARTED?
-COUGH-
SORRY. DID I GET BLOOD ON YOU?
SORRY. THEY TELL ME I DON'T HAVE LONG.
THEY'VE BEEN WASHING MY D.N.A. TO TRY AND PRESERVE THE GENETIC SEQUENCING.
IT'S CLEVER. THEY'RE DOING THEIR BEST.
BUT I'M READY TO DIE.
IT STARTED AFTER HENRY BENDIX WENT MAD AND LEFT HIS POST AS WEATHERMAN, COMMANDING OFFICER OF STORMWATCH.
HE WENT INTO HIDING, AND SO A NEW WEATHERMAN WAS APPOINTED. A SOLDIER, BUT INEXPERIENCED IN HIGH COMMAND.
WHICH, AS IT TURNS OUT, IS JUST WHAT HALF THE WORLD WAS WAITING FOR.
THAT'S WHAT DID IT FOR STORMWATCH. HALF A WORLD'S WORTH OF HATE, JUST WAITING FOR RELEASE.

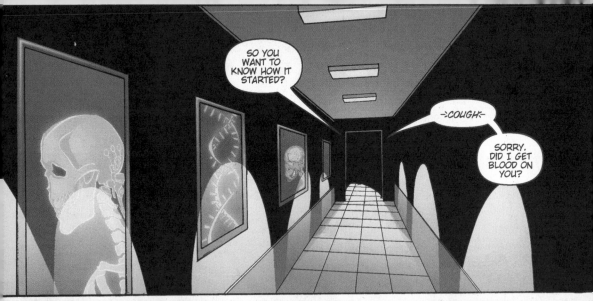

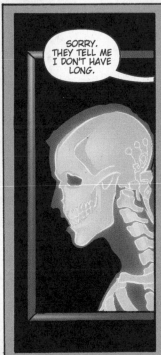

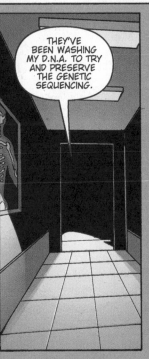

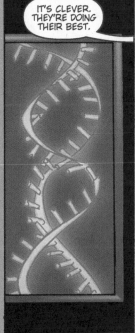

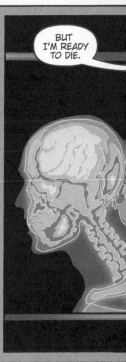

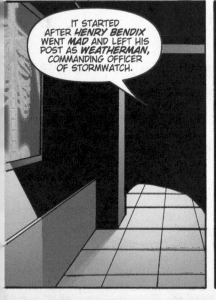

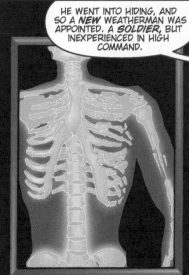

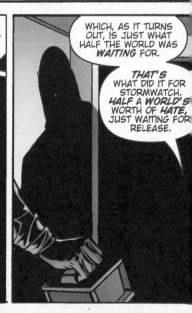

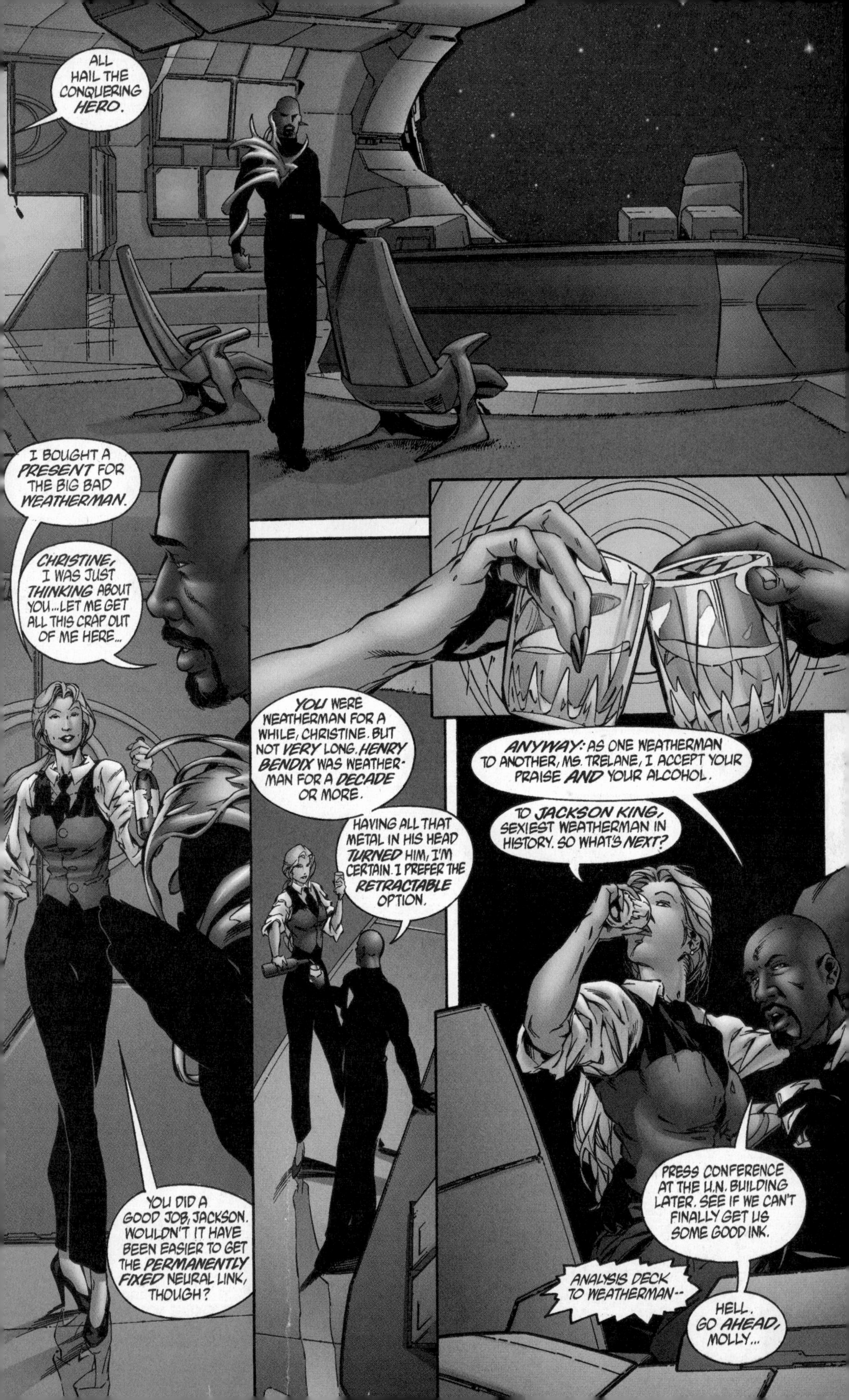
ALL HAIL THE CONQUERING HERO.
I BOUGHT A PRESENT FOR THE BIG BAD WEATHERMAN.
CHRISTINE, I WAS JUST THINKING ABOUT YOU...LET ME GET ALL THIS CRAP OUT OF ME HERE...
YOU DID A GOOD JOB, JACKSON. WOULDN'T IT HAVE BEEN EASIER TO GET THE PERMANENTLY FIXED NEURAL LINK, THOUGH?
YOU WERE WEATHERMAN FOR A WHILE, CHRISTINE. BUT NOT VERY LONG. HENRY BENDIX WAS WEATHER-MAN FOR A DECADE OR MORE.
HAVING ALL THAT METAL IN HIS HEAD TURNED HIM, I'M CERTAIN. I PREFER THE RETRACTABLE OPTION.
ANYWAY: AS ONE WEATHERMAN TO ANOTHER, MS. TRELANE, I ACCEPT YOUR PRAISE AND YOUR ALCOHOL.
TO JACKSON KING, SEXIEST WEATHERMAN IN HISTORY. SO WHAT'S NEXT?
PRESS CONFERENCE AT THE U.N. BUILDING LATER. SEE IF WE CAN'T FINALLY GET US SOME GOOD INK.
ANALYSIS DECK TO WEATHERMAN--
HELL. GO AHEAD, MOLLY...

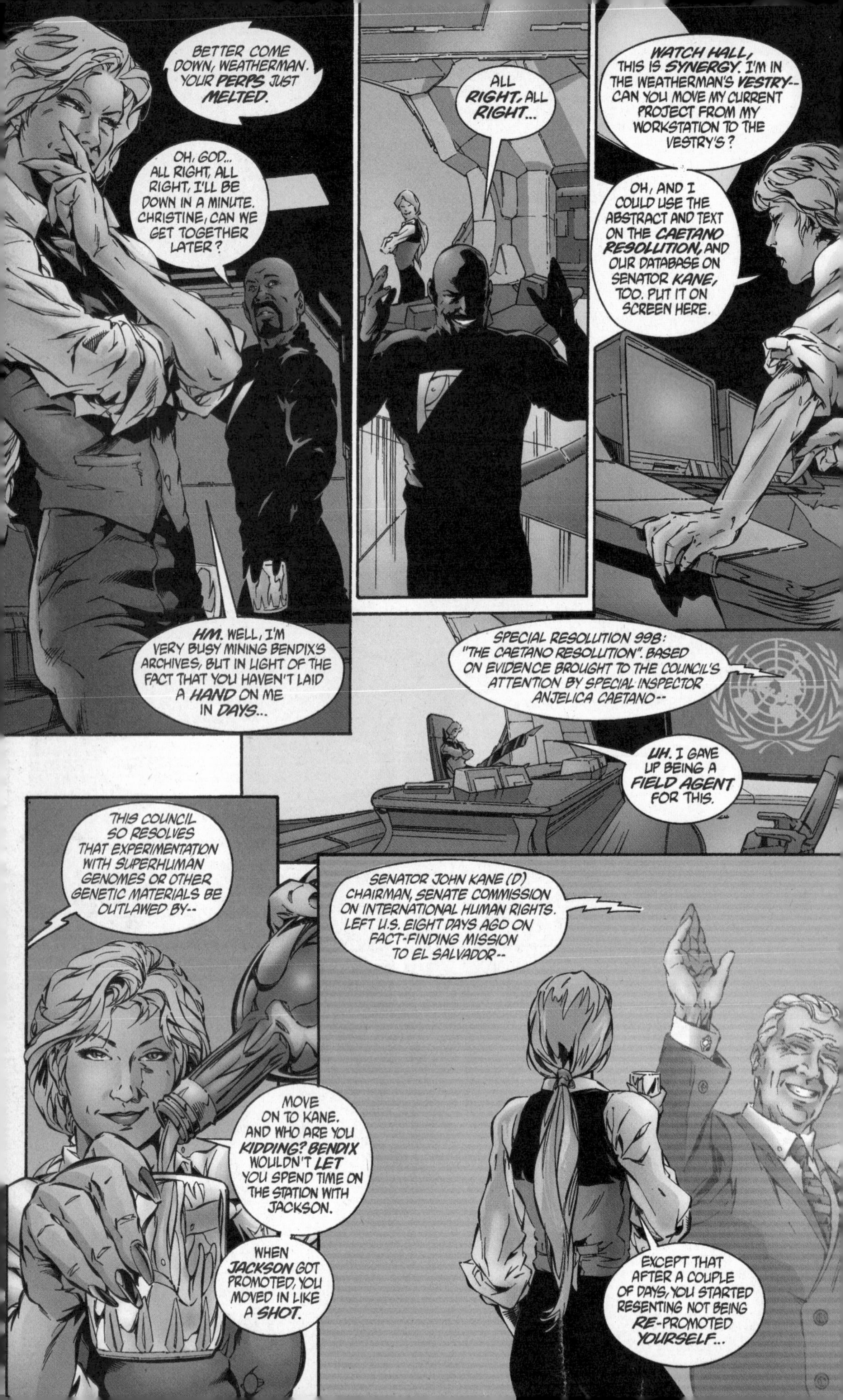

BETTER COME DOWN, WEATHERMAN. YOUR PERPS JUST MELTED.
OH, GOD... ALL RIGHT, ALL RIGHT, I'LL BE DOWN IN A MINUTE. CHRISTINE, CAN WE GET TOGETHER LATER?
HM. WELL, I'M VERY BUSY MINING BENDIX'S ARCHIVES, BUT IN LIGHT OF THE FACT THAT YOU HAVEN'T LAID A HAND ON ME IN DAYS...
ALL RIGHT, ALL RIGHT...
WATCH HALL, THIS IS SYNERGY. I'M IN THE WEATHERMAN'S VESTRY-- CAN YOU MOVE MY CURRENT PROJECT FROM MY WORKSTATION TO THE VESTRY'S?
OH, AND I COULD USE THE ABSTRACT AND TEXT ON THE CAETANO RESOLUTION, AND OUR DATABASE ON SENATOR KANE, TOO. PUT IT ON SCREEN HERE.
SPECIAL RESOLUTION 998: "THE CAETANO RESOLUTION". BASED ON EVIDENCE BROUGHT TO THE COUNCIL'S ATTENTION BY SPECIAL INSPECTOR ANJELICA CAETANO--
UH. I GAVE UP BEING A FIELD AGENT FOR THIS.
THIS COUNCIL SO RESOLVES THAT EXPERIMENTATION WITH SUPERHUMAN GENOMES OR OTHER GENETIC MATERIALS BE OUTLAWED BY--
MOVE ON TO KANE. AND WHO ARE YOU KIDDING? BENDIX WOULDN'T LET YOU SPEND TIME ON THE STATION WITH JACKSON.
WHEN JACKSON GOT PROMOTED, YOU MOVED IN LIKE A SHOT.
SENATOR JOHN KANE (D) CHAIRMAN, SENATE COMMISSION ON INTERNATIONAL HUMAN RIGHTS. LEFT U.S. EIGHT DAYS AGO ON FACT-FINDING MISSION TO EL SALVADOR--
EXCEPT THAT AFTER A COUPLE OF DAYS, YOU STARTED RESENTING NOT BEING RE-PROMOTED YOURSELF...

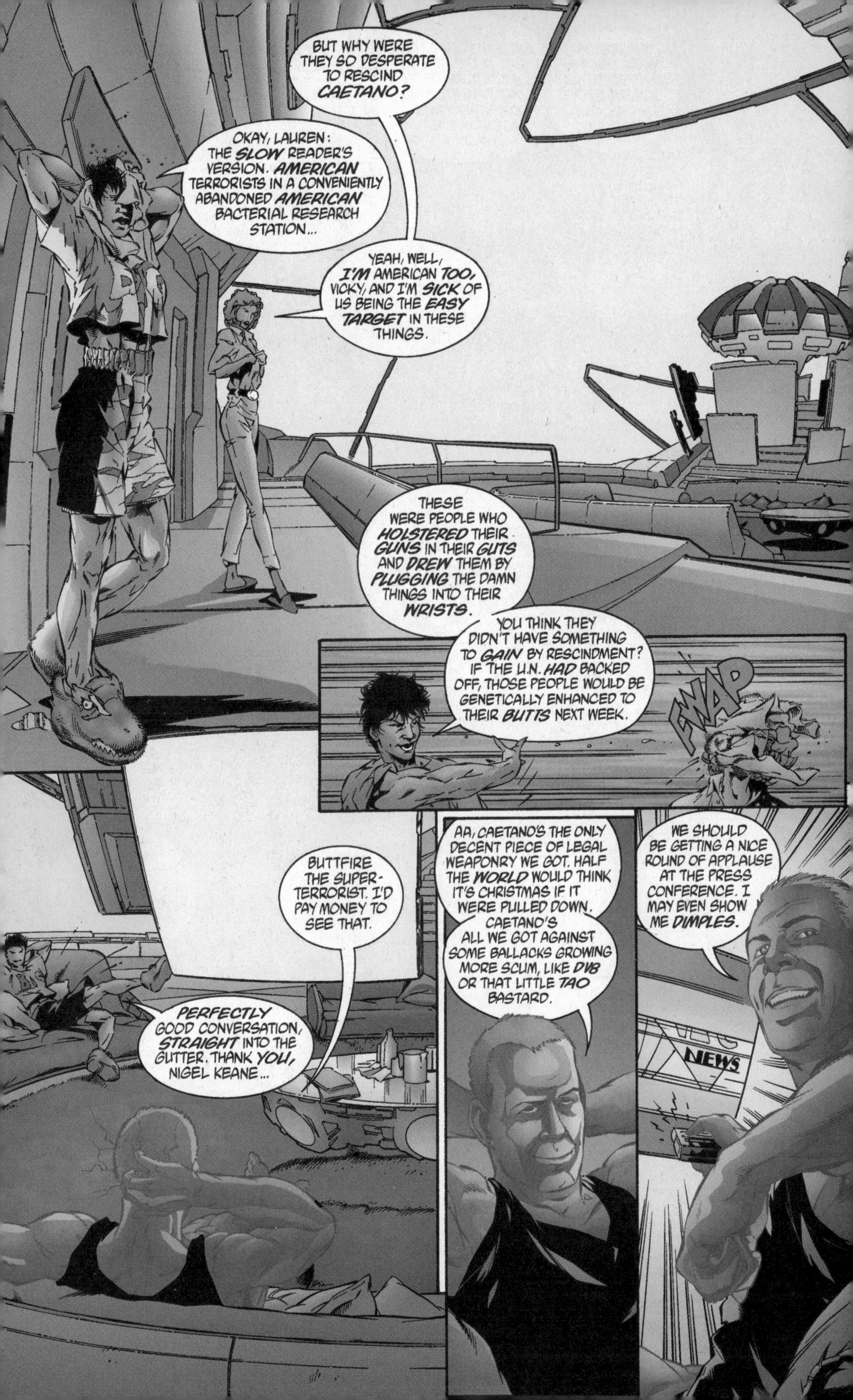
BUT WHY WERE THEY SO DESPERATE TO RESCIND CAETANO?
OKAY, LAUREN: THE SLOW READER'S VERSION. AMERICAN TERRORISTS IN A CONVENIENTLY ABANDONED AMERICAN BACTERIAL RESEARCH STATION...
YEAH, WELL, I'M AMERICAN TOO, VICKY, AND I'M SICK OF US BEING THE EASY TARGET IN THESE THINGS.
THESE WERE PEOPLE WHO HOLSTERED THEIR GUNS IN THEIR GUTS AND DREW THEM BY PLUGGING THE DAMN THINGS INTO THEIR WRISTS.
YOU THINK THEY DIDN'T HAVE SOMETHING TO GAIN BY RESCINDMENT? IF THE U.N. HAD BACKED OFF, THOSE PEOPLE WOULD BE GENETICALLY ENHANCED TO THEIR BUTTS NEXT WEEK.
FWAP
BUTTFIRE THE SUPER-TERRORIST. I'D PAY MONEY TO SEE THAT.
PERFECTLY GOOD CONVERSATION, STRAIGHT INTO THE GUTTER. THANK YOU, NIGEL KEANE...
AA, CAETANO'S THE ONLY DECENT PIECE OF LEGAL WEAPONRY WE GOT. HALF THE WORLD WOULD THINK IT'S CHRISTMAS IF IT WERE PULLED DOWN.
CAETANO'S ALL WE GOT AGAINST SOME BALLACKS GROWING MORE SCUM, LIKE DVB OR THAT LITTLE TAO BASTARD.
WE SHOULD BE GETTING A NICE ROUND OF APPLAUSE AT THE PRESS CONFERENCE. I MAY EVEN SHOW ME DIMPLES.
NEWS

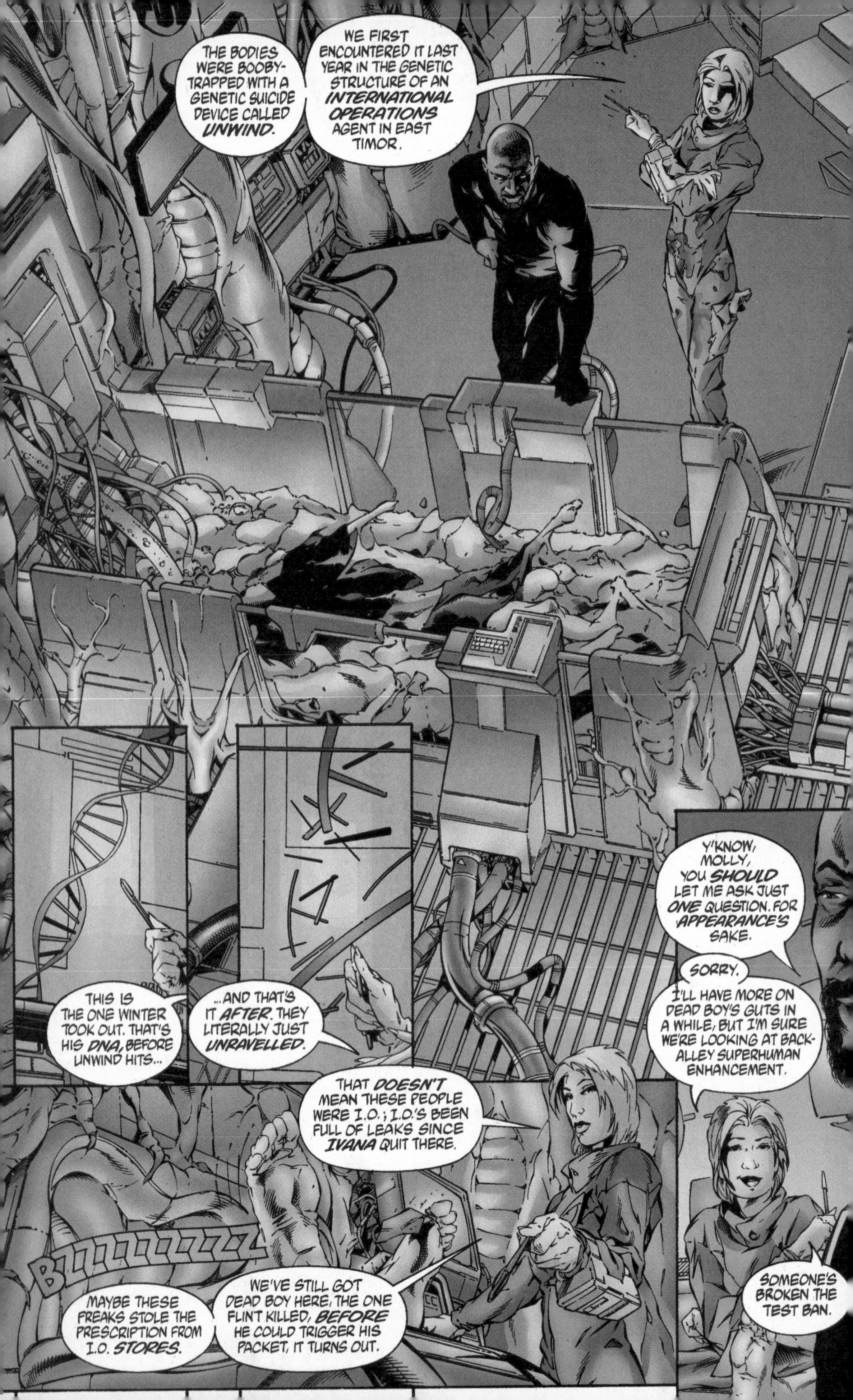
THE BODIES WERE BOOBY-TRAPPED WITH A GENETIC SUICIDE DEVICE CALLED UNWIND.
WE FIRST ENCOUNTERED IT LAST YEAR IN THE GENETIC STRUCTURE OF AN INTERNATIONAL OPERATIONS AGENT IN EAST TIMOR.
THIS IS THE ONE WINTER TOOK OUT. THAT'S HIS DNA, BEFORE UNWIND HITS...
...AND THAT'S IT AFTER. THEY LITERALLY JUST UNRAVELLED.
Y'KNOW, MOLLY, YOU SHOULD LET ME ASK JUST ONE QUESTION. FOR APPEARANCE'S SAKE.
SORRY.
I'LL HAVE MORE ON DEAD BOY'S GUTS IN A WHILE, BUT I'M SURE WE'RE LOOKING AT BACK-ALLEY SUPERHUMAN ENHANCEMENT.
THAT DOESN'T MEAN THESE PEOPLE WERE I.O.; I.O.'S BEEN FULL OF LEAKS SINCE IVANA QUIT THERE.
BZZZZZZZZZZZ
MAYBE THESE FREAKS STOLE THE PRESCRIPTION FROM I.O. STORES.
WE'VE STILL GOT DEAD BOY HERE, THE ONE FLINT KILLED, BEFORE HE COULD TRIGGER HIS PACKET, IT TURNS OUT.
SOMEONE'S BROKEN THE TEST BAN.

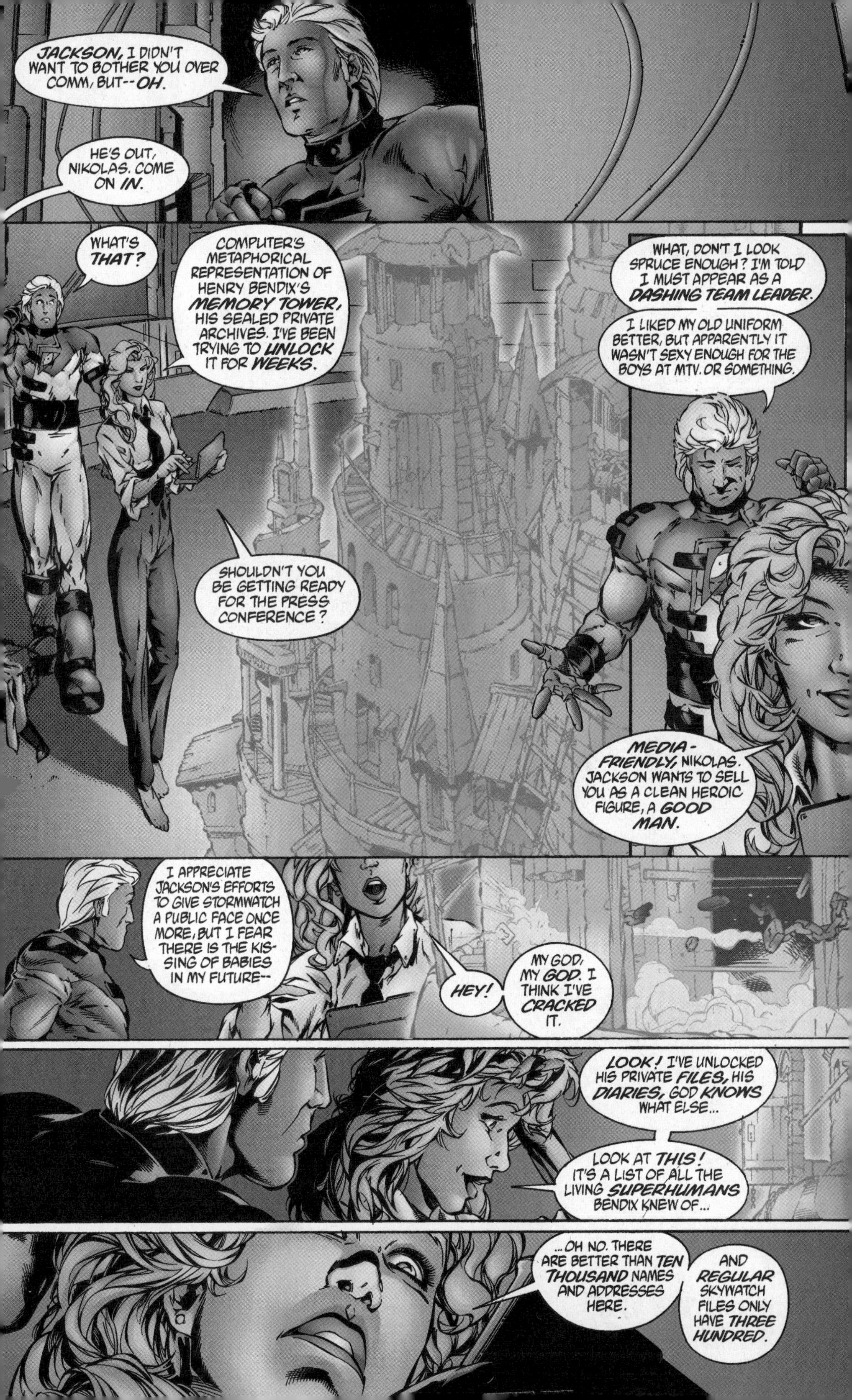
JACKSON, I DIDN'T WANT TO BOTHER YOU OVER COMM, BUT--OH.
HE'S OUT, NIKOLAS. COME ON IN.
WHAT'S THAT?
COMPUTER'S METAPHORICAL REPRESENTATION OF HENRY BENDIX'S MEMORY TOWER, HIS SEALED PRIVATE ARCHIVES. I'VE BEEN TRYING TO UNLOCK IT FOR WEEKS.
SHOULDN'T YOU BE GETTING READY FOR THE PRESS CONFERENCE?
WHAT, DON'T I LOOK SPRUCE ENOUGH? I'M TOLD I MUST APPEAR AS A DASHING TEAM LEADER.
I LIKED MY OLD UNIFORM BETTER, BUT APPARENTLY IT WASN'T SEXY ENOUGH FOR THE BOYS AT MTV. OR SOMETHING.
MEDIA-FRIENDLY, NIKOLAS. JACKSON WANTS TO SELL YOU AS A CLEAN HEROIC FIGURE, A GOOD MAN.
I APPRECIATE JACKSON'S EFFORTS TO GIVE STORMWATCH A PUBLIC FACE ONCE MORE, BUT I FEAR THERE IS THE KISSING OF BABIES IN MY FUTURE--
HEY!
MY GOD, MY GOD. I THINK I'VE CRACKED IT.
LOOK! I'VE UNLOCKED HIS PRIVATE FILES, HIS DIARIES, GOD KNOWS WHAT ELSE...
LOOK AT THIS! IT'S A LIST OF ALL THE LIVING SUPERHUMANS BENDIX KNEW OF...
...OH NO. THERE ARE BETTER THAN TEN THOUSAND NAMES AND ADDRESSES HERE.
AND REGULAR SKYWATCH FILES ONLY HAVE THREE HUNDRED.

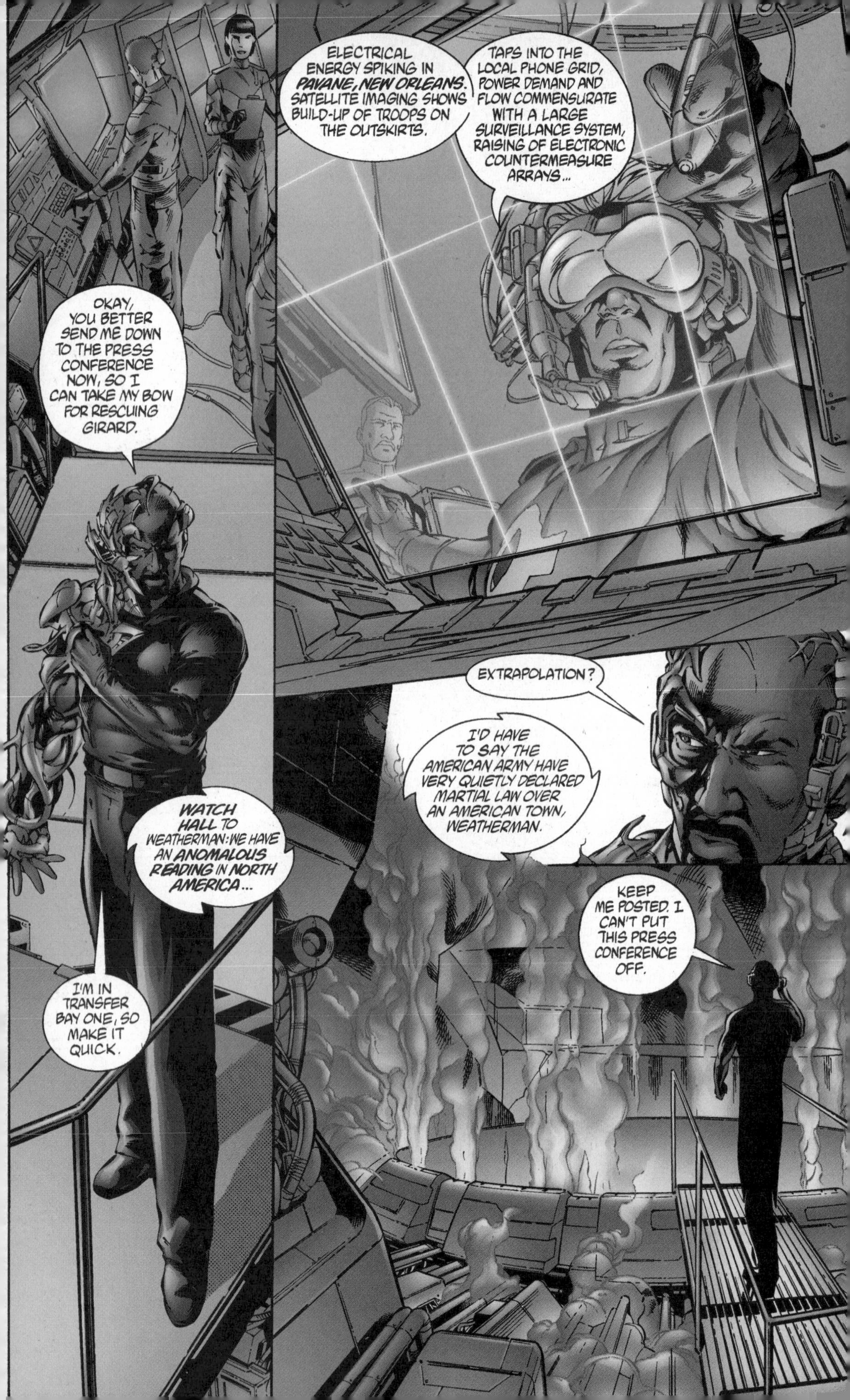
ELECTRICAL ENERGY SPIKING IN PAVANE, NEW ORLEANS. SATELLITE IMAGING SHOWS BUILD-UP OF TROOPS ON THE OUTSKIRTS.
TAPS INTO THE LOCAL PHONE GRID, POWER DEMAND AND FLOW COMMENSURATE WITH A LARGE SURVEILLANCE SYSTEM, RAISING OF ELECTRONIC COUNTERMEASURE ARRAYS...
OKAY, YOU BETTER SEND ME DOWN TO THE PRESS CONFERENCE NOW, SO I CAN TAKE MY BOW FOR RESCUING GIRARD.
EXTRAPOLATION?
I'D HAVE TO SAY THE AMERICAN ARMY HAVE VERY QUIETLY DECLARED MARTIAL LAW OVER AN AMERICAN TOWN, WEATHERMAN.
WATCH HALL TO WEATHERMAN: WE HAVE AN ANOMALOUS READING IN NORTH AMERICA...
I'M IN TRANSFER BAY ONE, SO MAKE IT QUICK.
KEEP ME POSTED. I CAN'T PUT THIS PRESS CONFERENCE OFF.

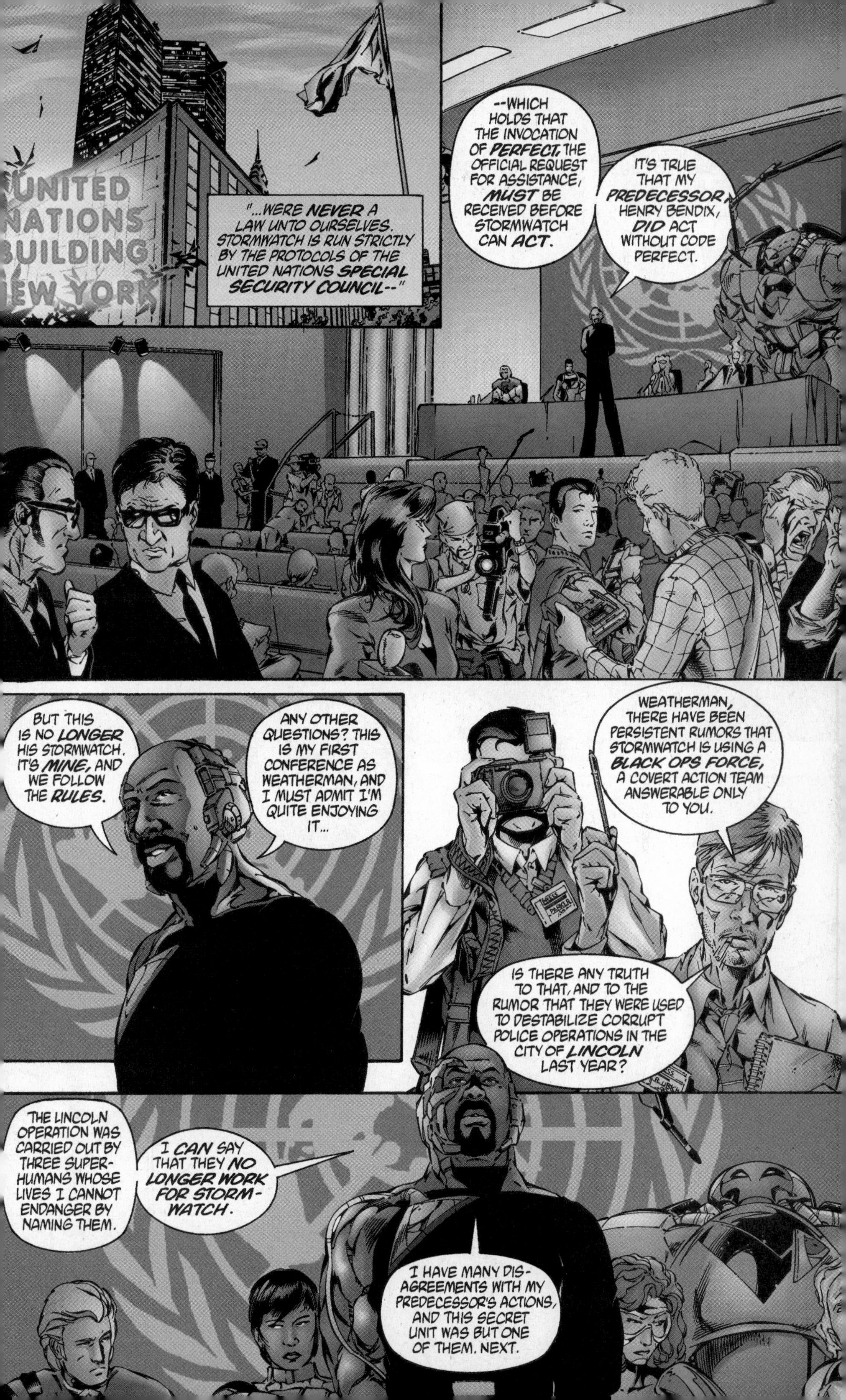
UNITED NATIONS BUILDING NEW YORK
"...WERE NEVER A LAW UNTO OURSELVES. STORMWATCH IS RUN STRICTLY BY THE PROTOCOLS OF THE UNITED NATIONS SPECIAL SECURITY COUNCIL--"
--WHICH HOLDS THAT THE INVOCATION OF PERFECT, THE OFFICIAL REQUEST FOR ASSISTANCE, MUST BE RECEIVED BEFORE STORMWATCH CAN ACT.
IT'S TRUE THAT MY PREDECESSOR, HENRY BENDIX, DID ACT WITHOUT CODE PERFECT.
BUT THIS IS NO LONGER HIS STORMWATCH. IT'S MINE, AND WE FOLLOW THE RULES.
ANY OTHER QUESTIONS? THIS IS MY FIRST CONFERENCE AS WEATHERMAN, AND I MUST ADMIT I'M QUITE ENJOYING IT...
WEATHERMAN, THERE HAVE BEEN PERSISTENT RUMORS THAT STORMWATCH IS USING A BLACK OPS FORCE, A COVERT ACTION TEAM ANSWERABLE ONLY TO YOU.
IS THERE ANY TRUTH TO THAT, AND TO THE RUMOR THAT THEY WERE USED TO DESTABILIZE CORRUPT POLICE OPERATIONS IN THE CITY OF LINCOLN LAST YEAR?
THE LINCOLN OPERATION WAS CARRIED OUT BY THREE SUPER-HUMANS WHOSE LIVES I CANNOT ENDANGER BY NAMING THEM.
I CAN SAY THAT THEY NO LONGER WORK FOR STORM-WATCH.
I HAVE MANY DIS-AGREEMENTS WITH MY PREDECESSOR'S ACTIONS, AND THIS SECRET UNIT WAS BUT ONE OF THEM. NEXT.

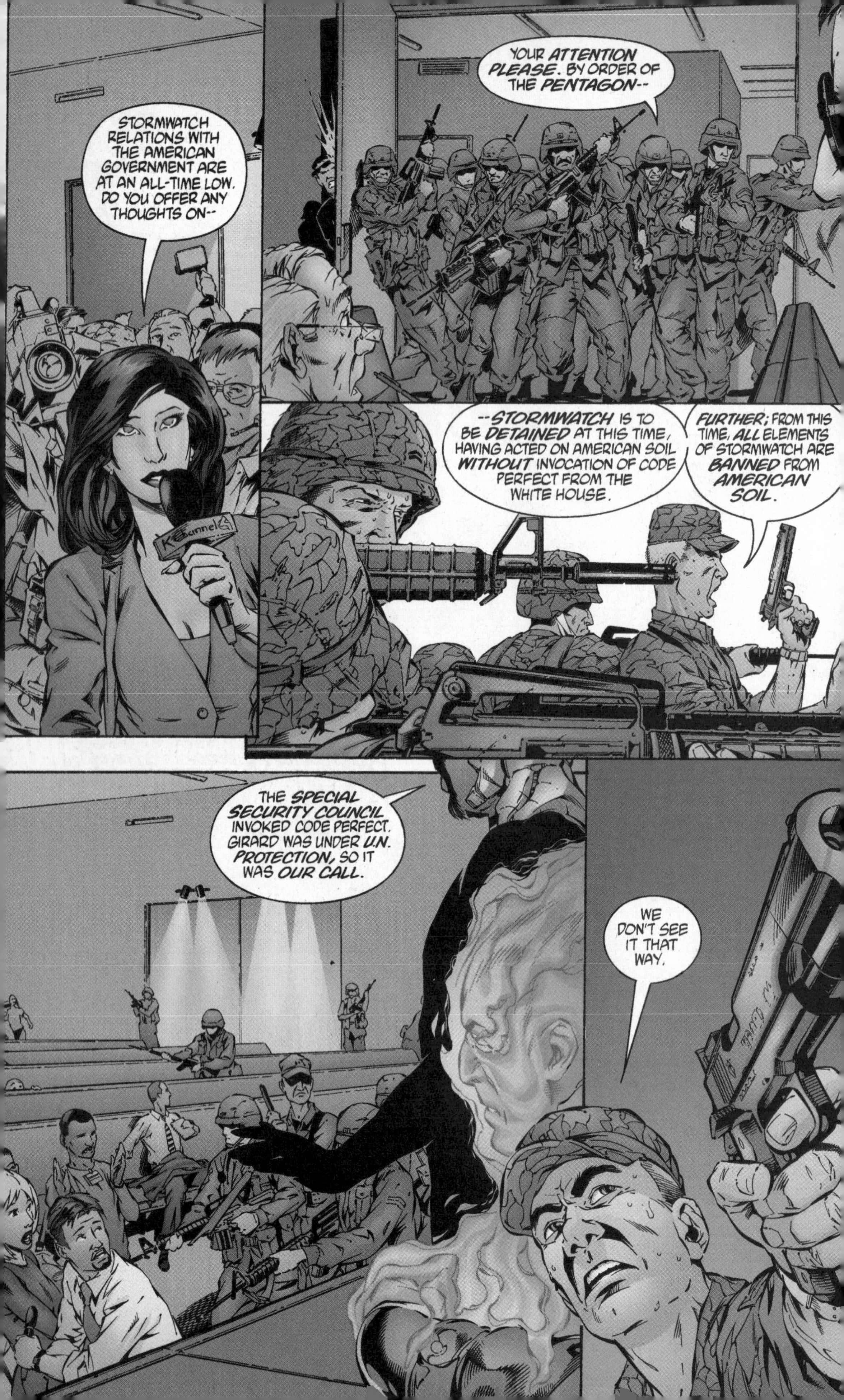
STORMWATCH RELATIONS WITH THE AMERICAN GOVERNMENT ARE AT AN ALL-TIME LOW. DO YOU OFFER ANY THOUGHTS ON--
YOUR ATTENTION PLEASE. BY ORDER OF THE PENTAGON--
--STORMWATCH IS TO BE DETAINED AT THIS TIME, HAVING ACTED ON AMERICAN SOIL WITHOUT INVOCATION OF CODE PERFECT FROM THE WHITE HOUSE.
FURTHER; FROM THIS TIME, ALL ELEMENTS OF STORMWATCH ARE BANNED FROM AMERICAN SOIL.
THE SPECIAL SECURITY COUNCIL INVOKED CODE PERFECT. GIRARD WAS UNDER U.N. PROTECTION, SO IT WAS OUR CALL.
WE DON'T SEE IT THAT WAY.

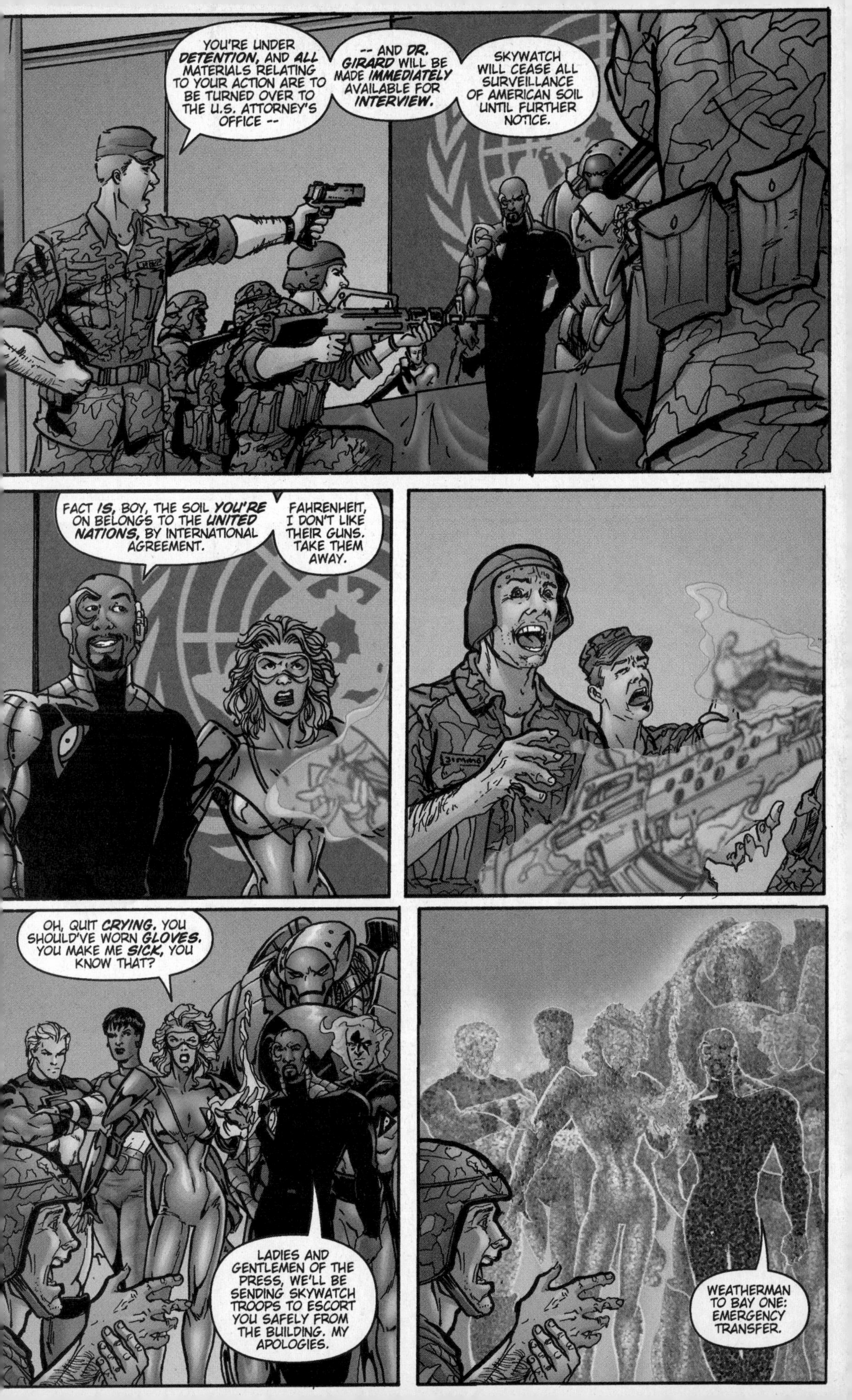
YOU'RE UNDER DETENTION, AND ALL MATERIALS RELATING TO YOUR ACTION ARE TO BE TURNED OVER TO THE U.S. ATTORNEY'S OFFICE --
-- AND DR. GIRARD WILL BE MADE IMMEDIATELY AVAILABLE FOR INTERVIEW.
SKYWATCH WILL CEASE ALL SURVEILLANCE OF AMERICAN SOIL UNTIL FURTHER NOTICE.
FACT IS, BOY, THE SOIL YOU'RE ON BELONGS TO THE UNITED NATIONS, BY INTERNATIONAL AGREEMENT.
FAHRENHEIT, I DON'T LIKE THEIR GUNS. TAKE THEM AWAY.
OH, QUIT CRYING. YOU SHOULD'VE WORN GLOVES. YOU MAKE ME SICK, YOU KNOW THAT?
LADIES AND GENTLEMEN OF THE PRESS, WE'LL BE SENDING SKYWATCH TROOPS TO ESCORT YOU SAFELY FROM THE BUILDING. MY APOLOGIES.
WEATHERMAN TO BAY ONE: EMERGENCY TRANSFER.

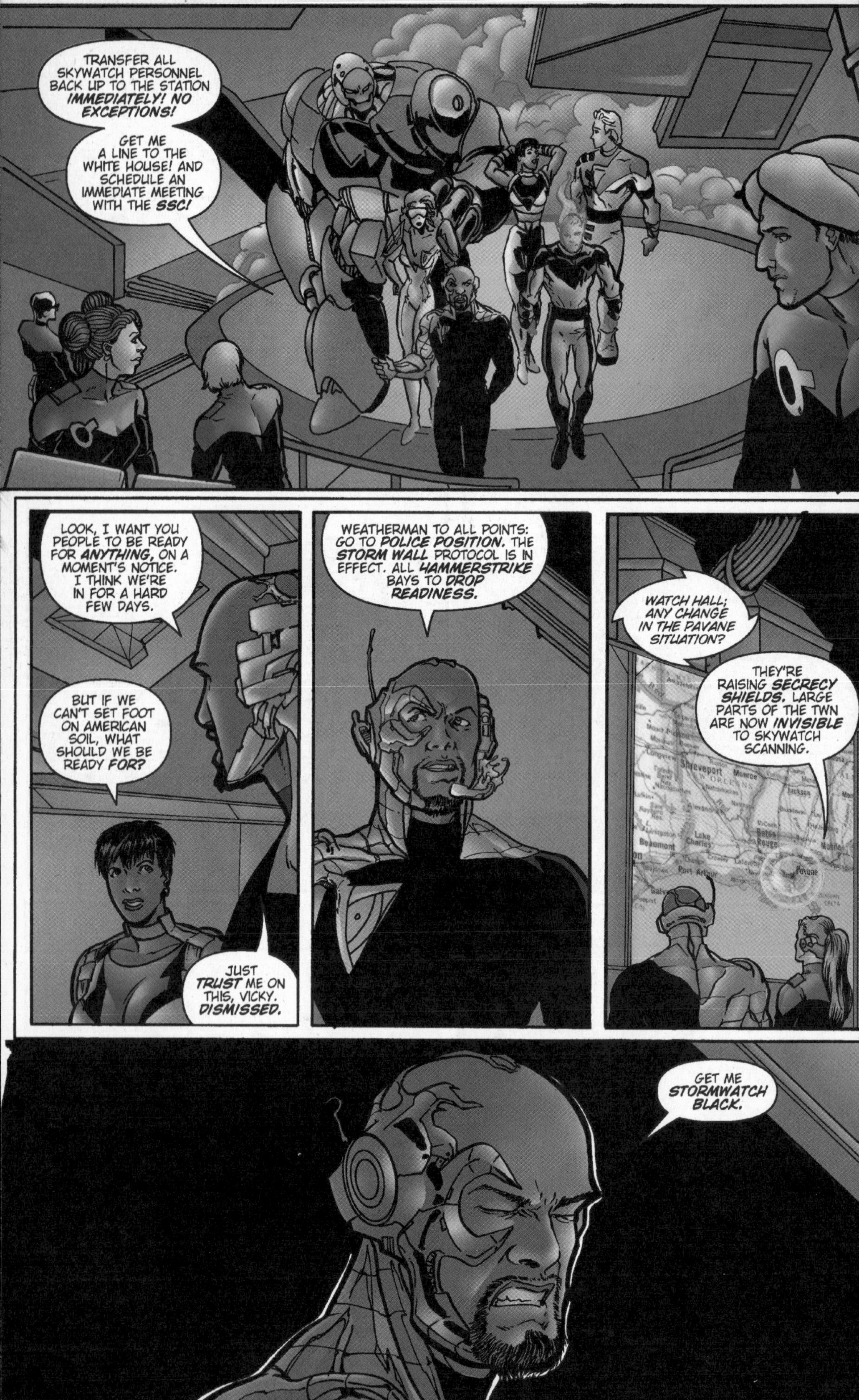
TRANSFER ALL SKYWATCH PERSONNEL BACK UP TO THE STATION IMMEDIATELY! NO EXCEPTIONS!
GET ME A LINE TO THE WHITE HOUSE! AND SCHEDULE AN IMMEDIATE MEETING WITH THE SSC!
LOOK, I WANT YOU PEOPLE TO BE READY FOR ANYTHING, ON A MOMENT'S NOTICE. I THINK WE'RE IN FOR A HARD FEW DAYS.
BUT IF WE CAN'T SET FOOT ON AMERICAN SOIL, WHAT SHOULD WE BE READY FOR?
JUST TRUST ME ON THIS, VICKY. DISMISSED.
WEATHERMAN TO ALL POINTS: GO TO POLICE POSITION. THE STORM WALL PROTOCOL IS IN EFFECT. ALL HAMMERSTRIKE BAYS TO DROP READINESS.
WATCH HALL; ANY CHANGE IN THE PAVANE SITUATION?
THEY'RE RAISING SECRECY SHIELDS. LARGE PARTS OF THE TWN ARE NOW INVISIBLE TO SKYWATCH SCANNING.
GET ME STORMWATCH BLACK.

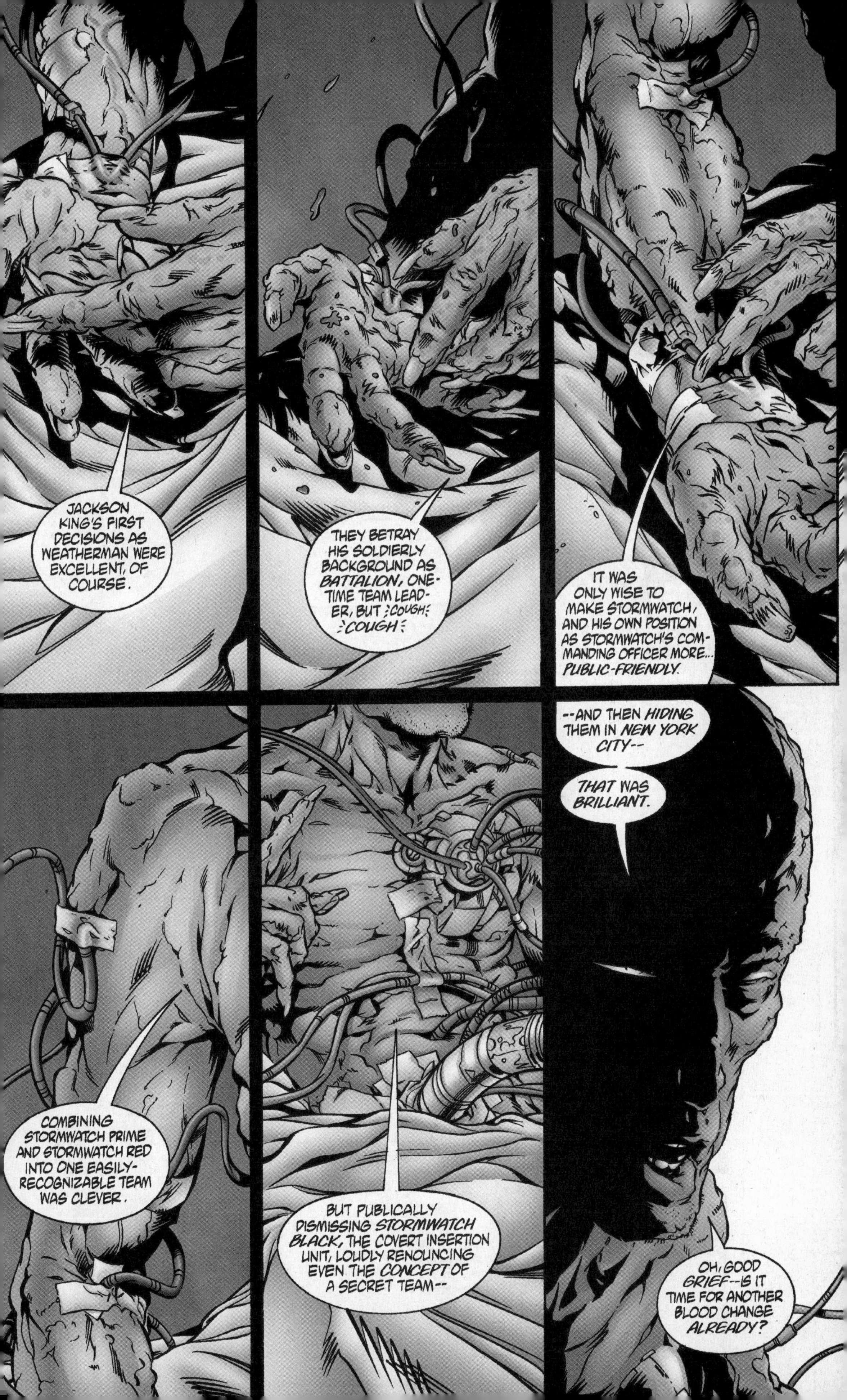

JACKSON KING'S FIRST DECISIONS AS WEATHERMAN WERE EXCELLENT, OF COURSE.
THEY BETRAY HIS SOLDIERLY BACKGROUND AS BATTALION, ONE-TIME TEAM LEADER, BUT :COUGH: :COUGH:
IT WAS ONLY WISE TO MAKE STORMWATCH, AND HIS OWN POSITION AS STORMWATCH'S COMMANDING OFFICER MORE... PUBLIC-FRIENDLY.
COMBINING STORMWATCH PRIME AND STORMWATCH RED INTO ONE EASILY-RECOGNIZABLE TEAM WAS CLEVER.
BUT PUBLICALLY DISMISSING STORMWATCH BLACK, THE COVERT INSERTION UNIT, LOUDLY RENOUNCING EVEN THE CONCEPT OF A SECRET TEAM--
--AND THEN HIDING THEM IN NEW YORK CITY--
THAT WAS BRILLIANT.
OH, GOOD GRIEF--IS IT TIME FOR ANOTHER BLOOD CHANGE ALREADY?

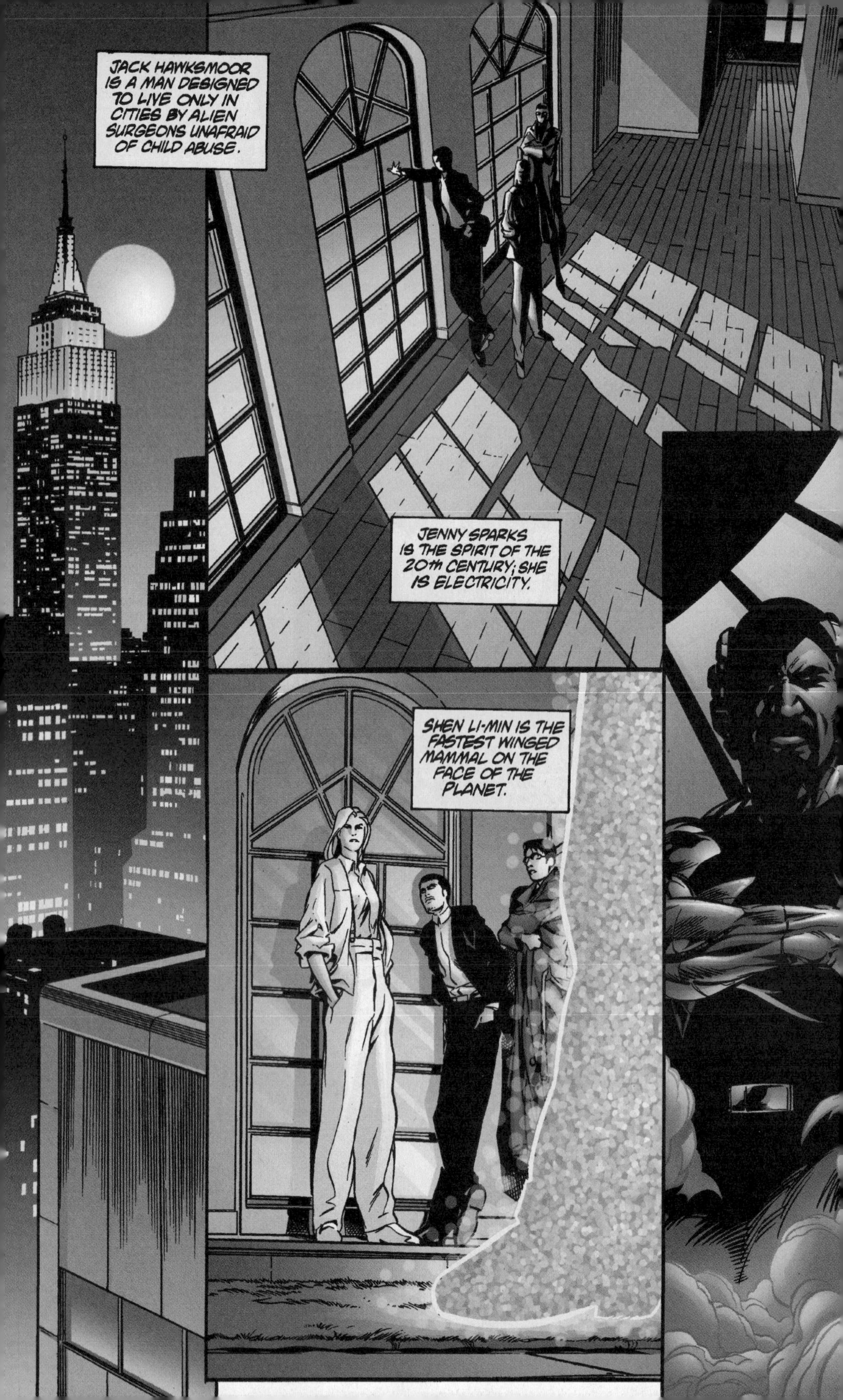
JACK HAWKSMOOR IS A MAN DESIGNED TO LIVE ONLY IN CITIES BY ALIEN SURGEONS UNAFRAID OF CHILD ABUSE.
JENNY SPARKS IS THE SPIRIT OF THE 20th CENTURY; SHE IS ELECTRICITY.
SHEN LI-MIN IS THE FASTEST WINGED MAMMAL ON THE FACE OF THE PLANET.

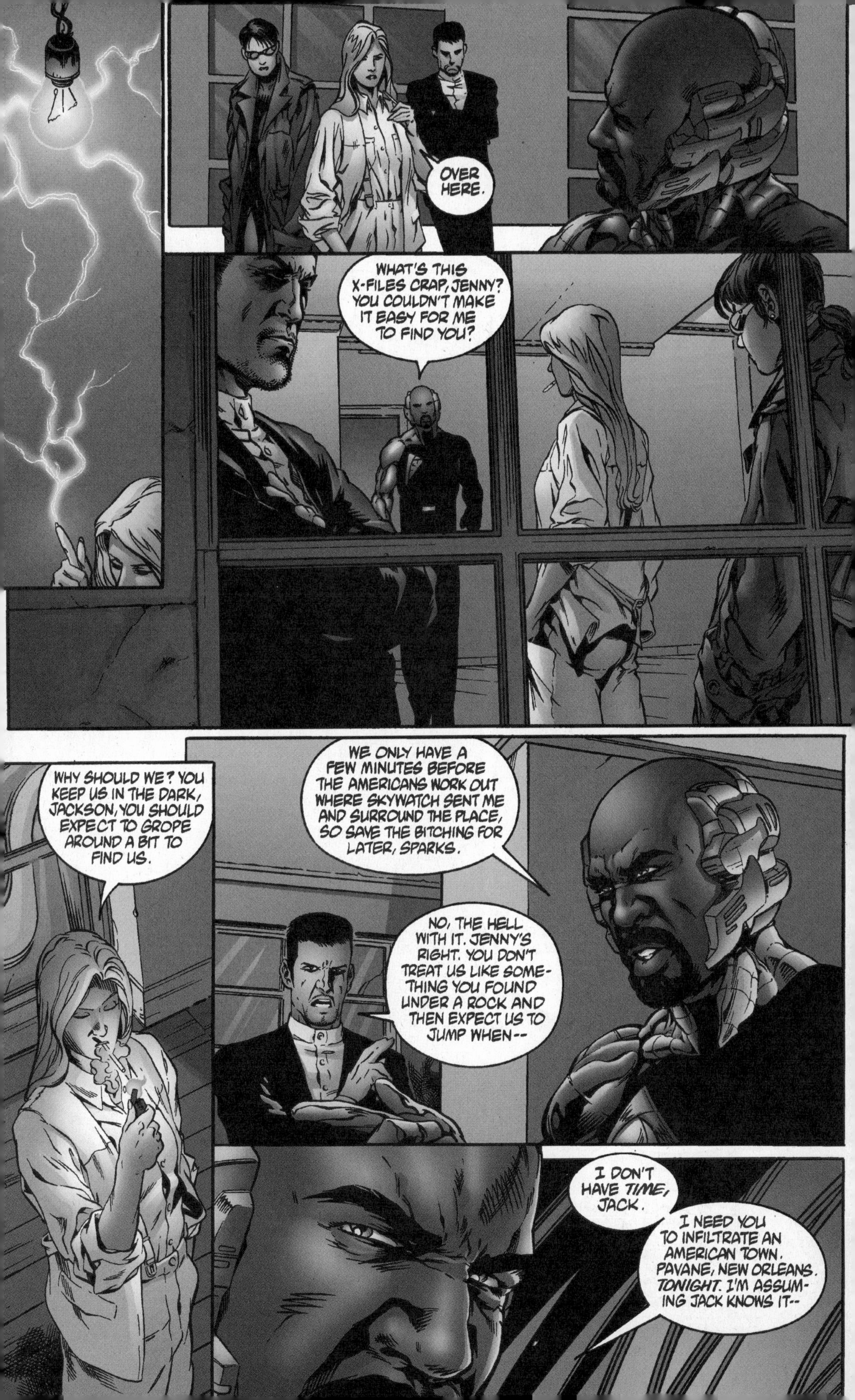
OVER HERE.
WHAT'S THIS X-FILES CRAP, JENNY? YOU COULDN'T MAKE IT EASY FOR ME TO FIND YOU?
WHY SHOULD WE? YOU KEEP US IN THE DARK, JACKSON, YOU SHOULD EXPECT TO GROPE AROUND A BIT TO FIND US.
WE ONLY HAVE A FEW MINUTES BEFORE THE AMERICANS WORK OUT WHERE SKYWATCH SENT ME AND SURROUND THE PLACE, SO SAVE THE BITCHING FOR LATER, SPARKS.
NO, THE HELL WITH IT. JENNY'S RIGHT. YOU DON'T TREAT US LIKE SOME-THING YOU FOUND UNDER A ROCK AND THEN EXPECT US TO JUMP WHEN--
I DON'T HAVE *TIME*, JACK.
I NEED YOU TO INFILTRATE AN AMERICAN TOWN. PAVANE, NEW ORLEANS. *TONIGHT*. I'M ASSUM-ING JACK KNOWS IT--

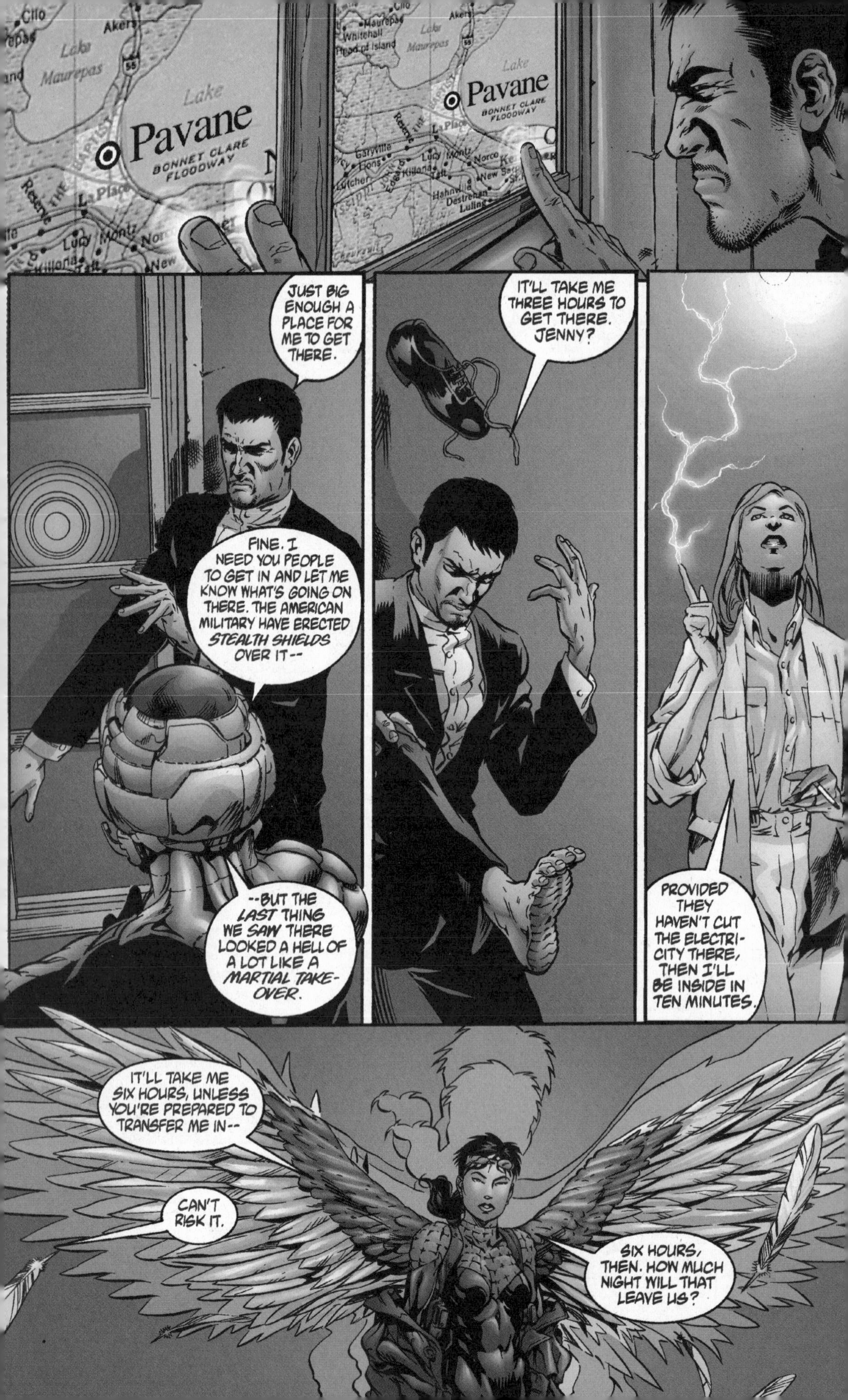
Pavane
BONNET CLARE FLOODWAY
JUST BIG ENOUGH A PLACE FOR ME TO GET THERE.
FINE. I NEED YOU PEOPLE TO GET IN AND LET ME KNOW WHAT'S GOING ON THERE. THE AMERICAN MILITARY HAVE ERECTED STEALTH SHIELDS OVER IT--
--BUT THE LAST THING WE SAW THERE LOOKED A HELL OF A LOT LIKE A MARTIAL TAKE-OVER.
IT'LL TAKE ME THREE HOURS TO GET THERE. JENNY?
PROVIDED THEY HAVEN'T CUT THE ELECTRICITY THERE, THEN I'LL BE INSIDE IN TEN MINUTES.
IT'LL TAKE ME SIX HOURS, UNLESS YOU'RE PREPARED TO TRANSFER ME IN--
CAN'T RISK IT.
SIX HOURS, THEN. HOW MUCH NIGHT WILL THAT LEAVE US?

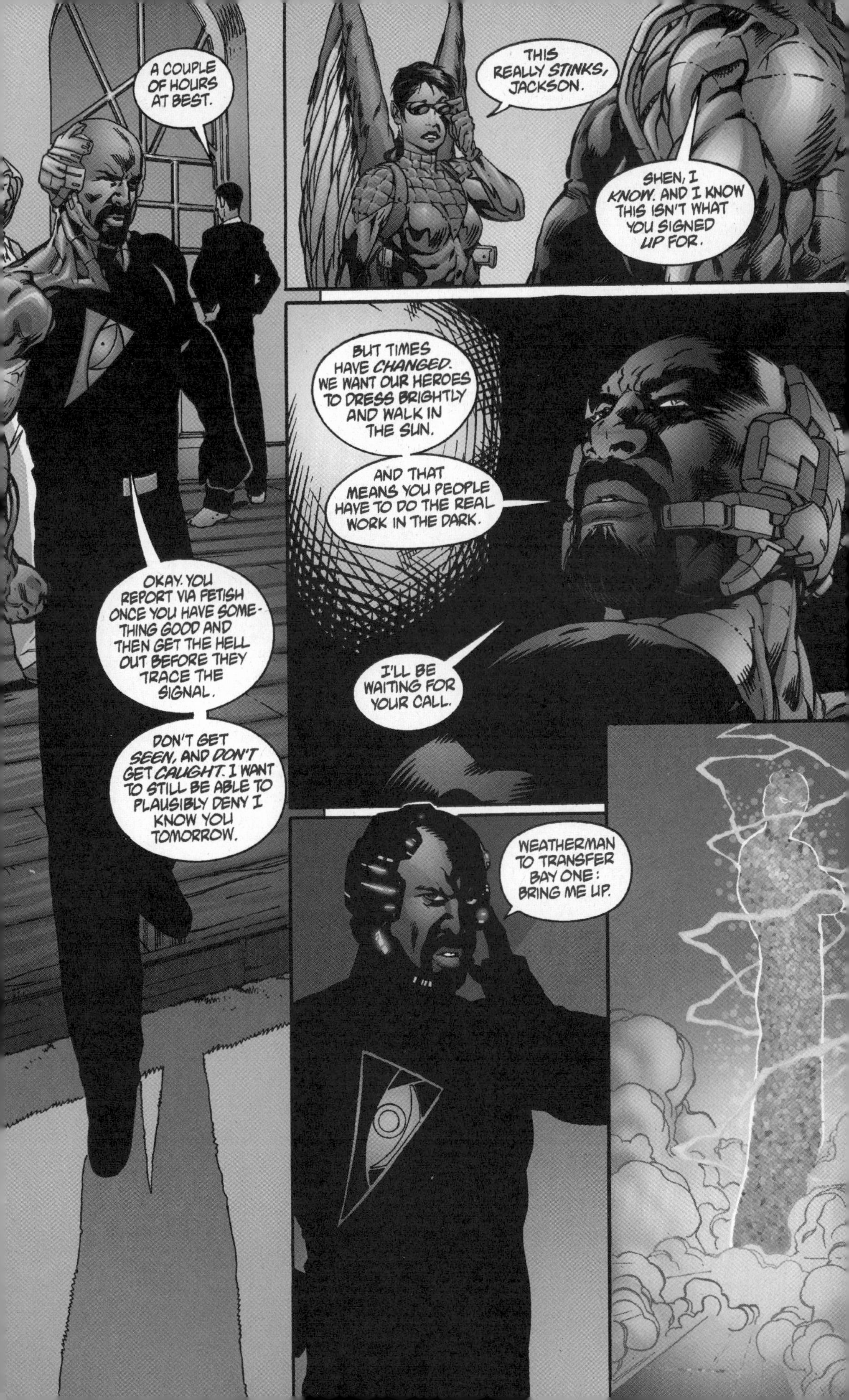
A COUPLE OF HOURS AT BEST.
THIS REALLY STINKS, JACKSON.
SHEN, I KNOW. AND I KNOW THIS ISN'T WHAT YOU SIGNED UP FOR.
BUT TIMES HAVE CHANGED. WE WANT OUR HEROES TO DRESS BRIGHTLY AND WALK IN THE SUN.
AND THAT MEANS YOU PEOPLE HAVE TO DO THE REAL WORK IN THE DARK.
I'LL BE WAITING FOR YOUR CALL.
OKAY. YOU REPORT VIA FETISH ONCE YOU HAVE SOME-THING GOOD AND THEN GET THE HELL OUT BEFORE THEY TRACE THE SIGNAL.
DON'T GET SEEN, AND DON'T GET CAUGHT. I WANT TO STILL BE ABLE TO PLAUSIBLY DENY I KNOW YOU TOMORROW.
WEATHERMAN TO TRANSFER BAY ONE: BRING ME UP.

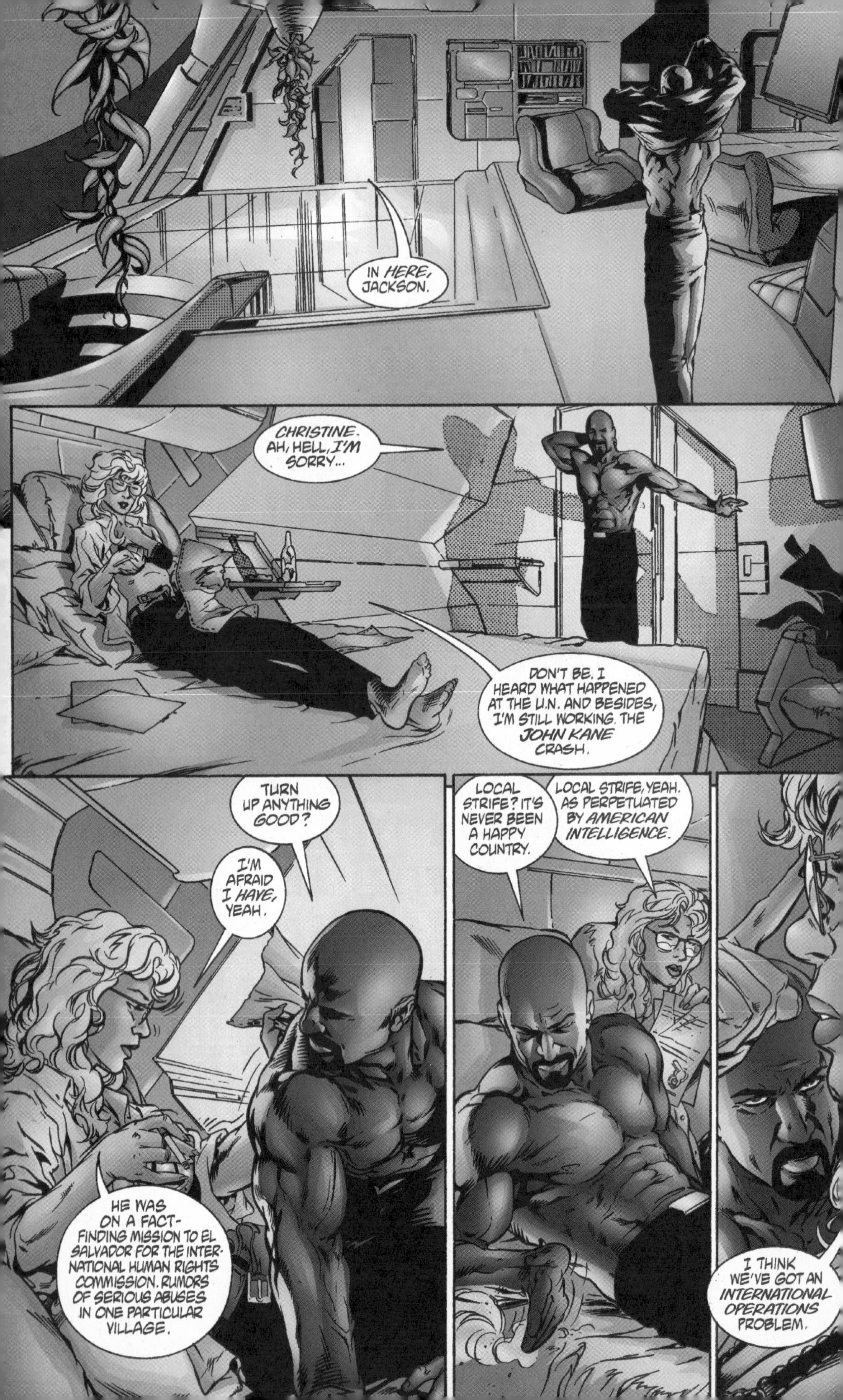
IN HERE, JACKSON.
CHRISTINE. AH, HELL, I'M SORRY...
DON'T BE. I HEARD WHAT HAPPENED AT THE U.N. AND BESIDES, I'M STILL WORKING. THE JOHN KANE CRASH.
TURN UP ANYTHING GOOD?
I'M AFRAID I HAVE, YEAH.
HE WAS ON A FACT-FINDING MISSION TO EL SALVADOR FOR THE INTERNATIONAL HUMAN RIGHTS COMMISSION. RUMORS OF SERIOUS ABUSES IN ONE PARTICULAR VILLAGE.
LOCAL STRIFE? IT'S NEVER BEEN A HAPPY COUNTRY.
LOCAL STRIFE, YEAH. AS PERPETUATED BY AMERICAN INTELLIGENCE.
I THINK WE'VE GOT AN INTERNATIONAL OPERATIONS PROBLEM.

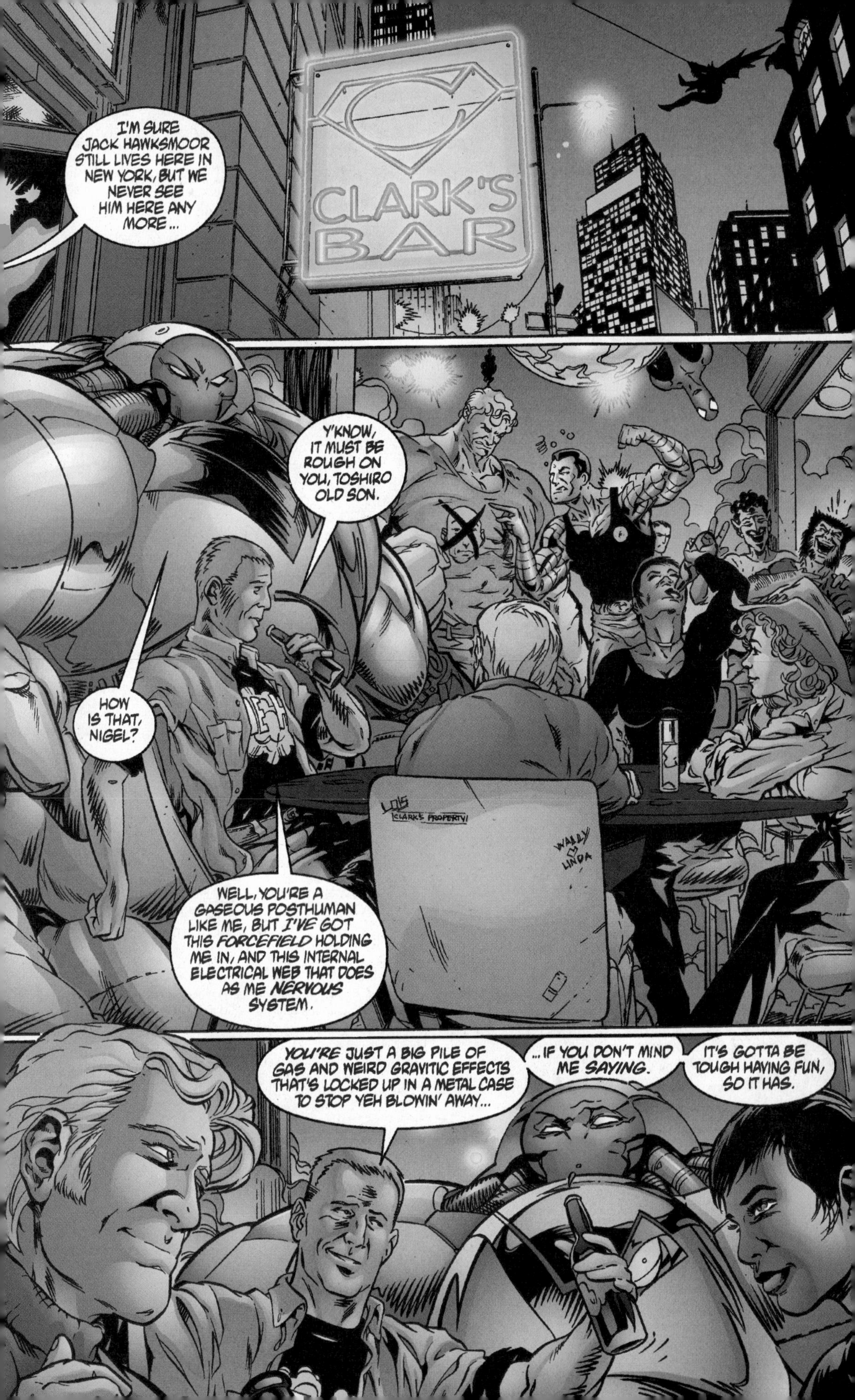
I'M SURE JACK HAWKSMOOR STILL LIVES HERE IN NEW YORK, BUT WE NEVER SEE HIM HERE ANY MORE...
CLARK'S BAR
Y'KNOW, IT MUST BE ROUGH ON YOU, TOSHIRO OLD SON.
HOW IS THAT, NIGEL?
WELL, YOU'RE A GASEOUS POSTHUMAN LIKE ME, BUT I'VE GOT THIS FORCEFIELD HOLDING ME IN, AND THIS INTERNAL ELECTRICAL WEB THAT DOES AS ME NERVOUS SYSTEM.
LOIS
CLARK'S PROPERTY!
WALLY LINDA
YOU'RE JUST A BIG PILE OF GAS AND WEIRD GRAVITIC EFFECTS THAT'S LOCKED UP IN A METAL CASE TO STOP YEH BLOWIN' AWAY...
...IF YOU DON'T MIND ME SAYING.
IT'S GOTTA BE TOUGH HAVING FUN, SO IT HAS.

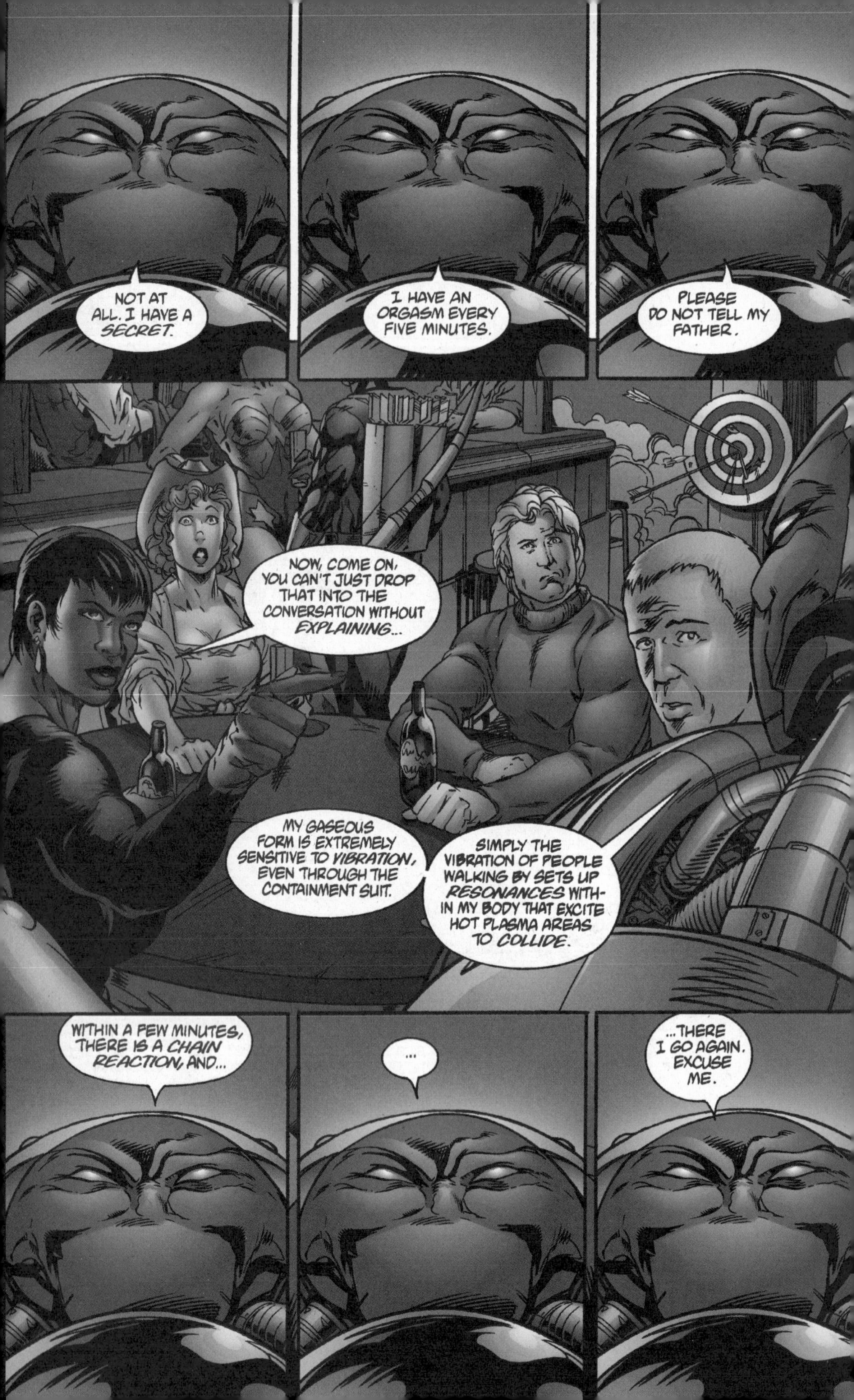
NOT AT ALL. I HAVE A SECRET.
I HAVE AN ORGASM EVERY FIVE MINUTES.
PLEASE DO NOT TELL MY FATHER.
NOW, COME ON, YOU CAN'T JUST DROP THAT INTO THE CONVERSATION WITHOUT EXPLAINING...
MY GASEOUS FORM IS EXTREMELY SENSITIVE TO VIBRATION, EVEN THROUGH THE CONTAINMENT SUIT.
SIMPLY THE VIBRATION OF PEOPLE WALKING BY SETS UP RESONANCES WITHIN MY BODY THAT EXCITE HOT PLASMA AREAS TO COLLIDE.
WITHIN A FEW MINUTES, THERE IS A CHAIN REACTION, AND...
...
...THERE I GO AGAIN. EXCUSE ME.

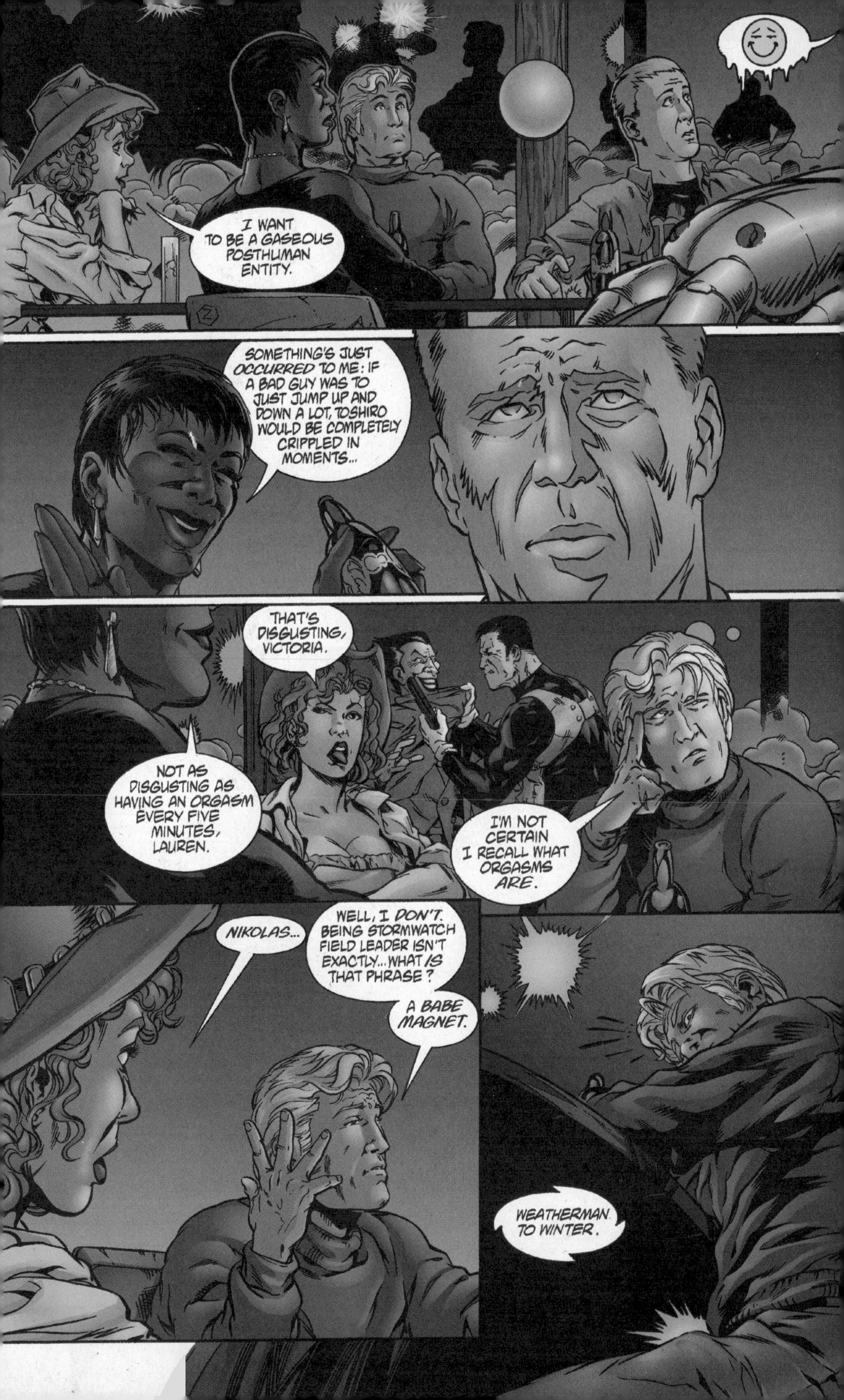
I WANT TO BE A GASEOUS POSTHUMAN ENTITY.
SOMETHING'S JUST OCCURRED TO ME: IF A BAD GUY WAS TO JUST JUMP UP AND DOWN A LOT, TOSHIRO WOULD BE COMPLETELY CRIPPLED IN MOMENTS...
THAT'S DISGUSTING, VICTORIA.
NOT AS DISGUSTING AS HAVING AN ORGASM EVERY FIVE MINUTES, LAUREN.
I'M NOT CERTAIN I RECALL WHAT ORGASMS ARE.
NIKOLAS...
WELL, I DON'T. BEING STORMWATCH FIELD LEADER ISN'T EXACTLY... WHAT IS THAT PHRASE?
A BABE MAGNET.
WEATHERMAN TO WINTER.

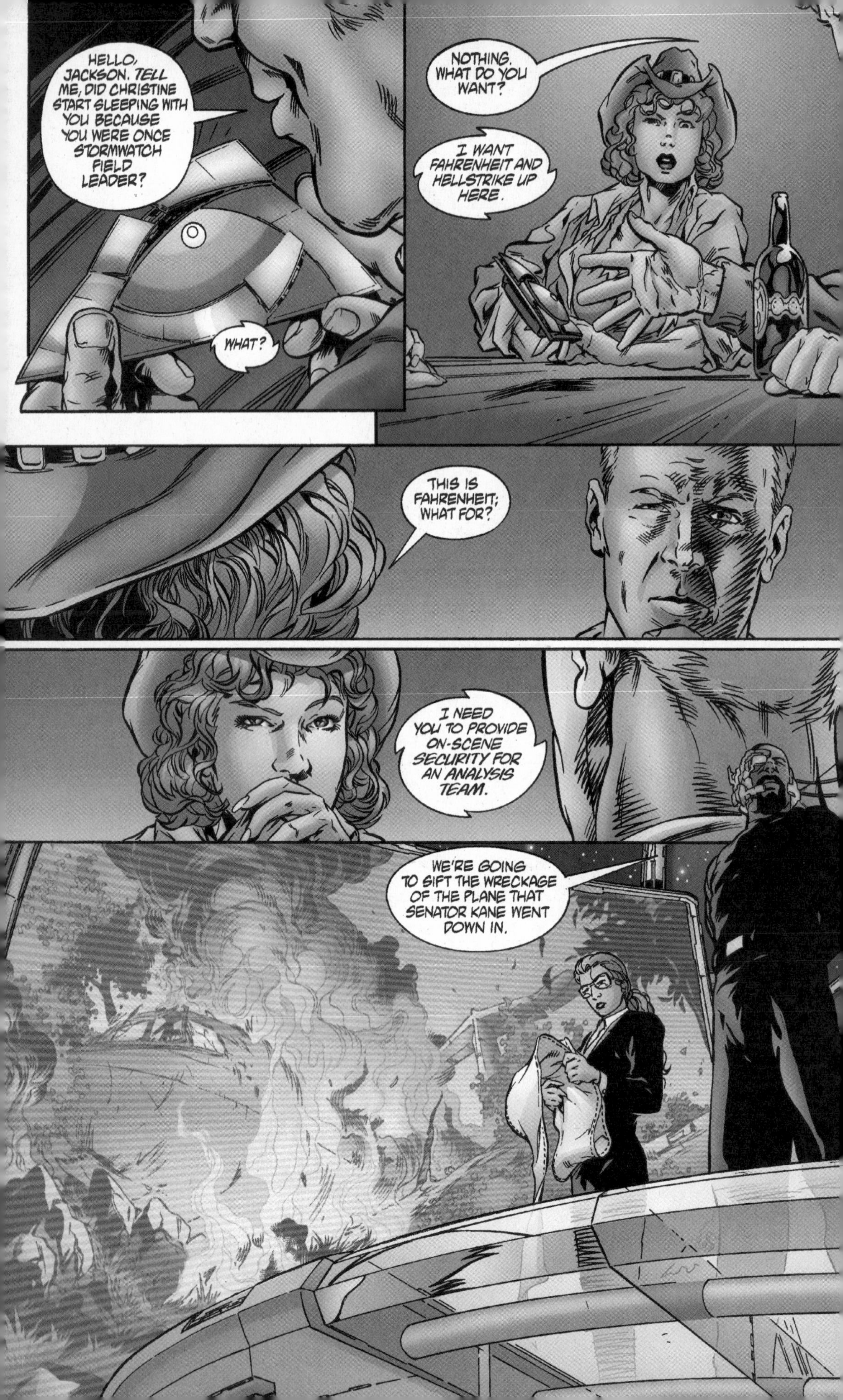
HELLO, JACKSON. TELL ME, DID CHRISTINE START SLEEPING WITH YOU BECAUSE YOU WERE ONCE STORMWATCH FIELD LEADER?
WHAT?
NOTHING. WHAT DO YOU WANT?
I WANT FAHRENHEIT AND HELLSTRIKE UP HERE.
THIS IS FAHRENHEIT; WHAT FOR?
I NEED YOU TO PROVIDE ON-SCENE SECURITY FOR AN ANALYSIS TEAM.
WE'RE GOING TO SIFT THE WRECKAGE OF THE PLANE THAT SENATOR KANE WENT DOWN IN.

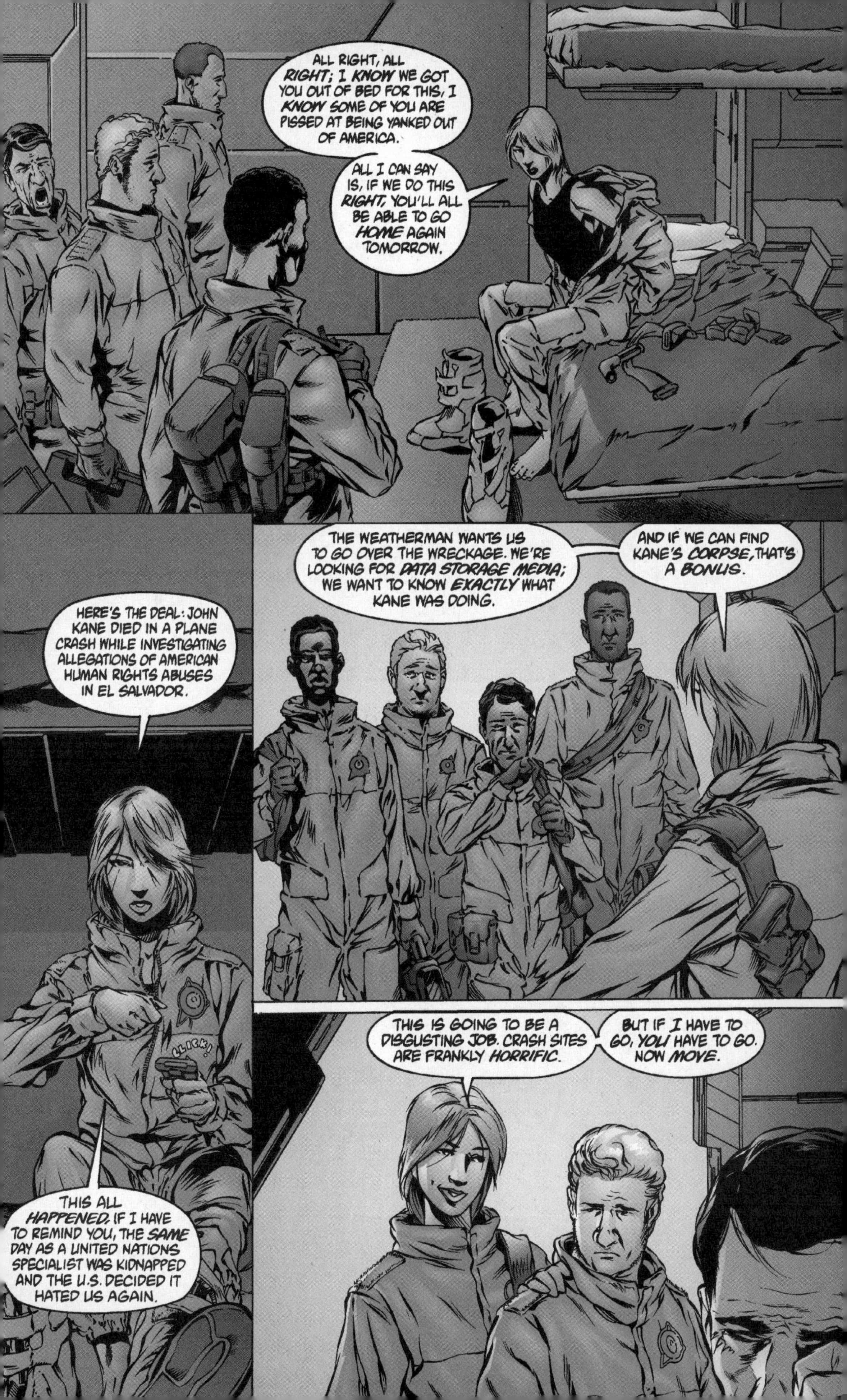
ALL RIGHT, ALL RIGHT; I KNOW WE GOT YOU OUT OF BED FOR THIS, I KNOW SOME OF YOU ARE PISSED AT BEING YANKED OUT OF AMERICA.
ALL I CAN SAY IS, IF WE DO THIS RIGHT, YOU'LL ALL BE ABLE TO GO HOME AGAIN TOMORROW.
HERE'S THE DEAL: JOHN KANE DIED IN A PLANE CRASH WHILE INVESTIGATING ALLEGATIONS OF AMERICAN HUMAN RIGHTS ABUSES IN EL SALVADOR.
CLICK!
THIS ALL HAPPENED, IF I HAVE TO REMIND YOU, THE SAME DAY AS A UNITED NATIONS SPECIALIST WAS KIDNAPPED AND THE U.S. DECIDED IT HATED US AGAIN.
THE WEATHERMAN WANTS US TO GO OVER THE WRECKAGE. WE'RE LOOKING FOR DATA STORAGE MEDIA; WE WANT TO KNOW EXACTLY WHAT KANE WAS DOING.
AND IF WE CAN FIND KANE'S CORPSE, THAT'S A BONUS.
THIS IS GOING TO BE A DISGUSTING JOB. CRASH SITES ARE FRANKLY HORRIFIC.
BUT IF I HAVE TO GO, YOU HAVE TO GO. NOW MOVE.

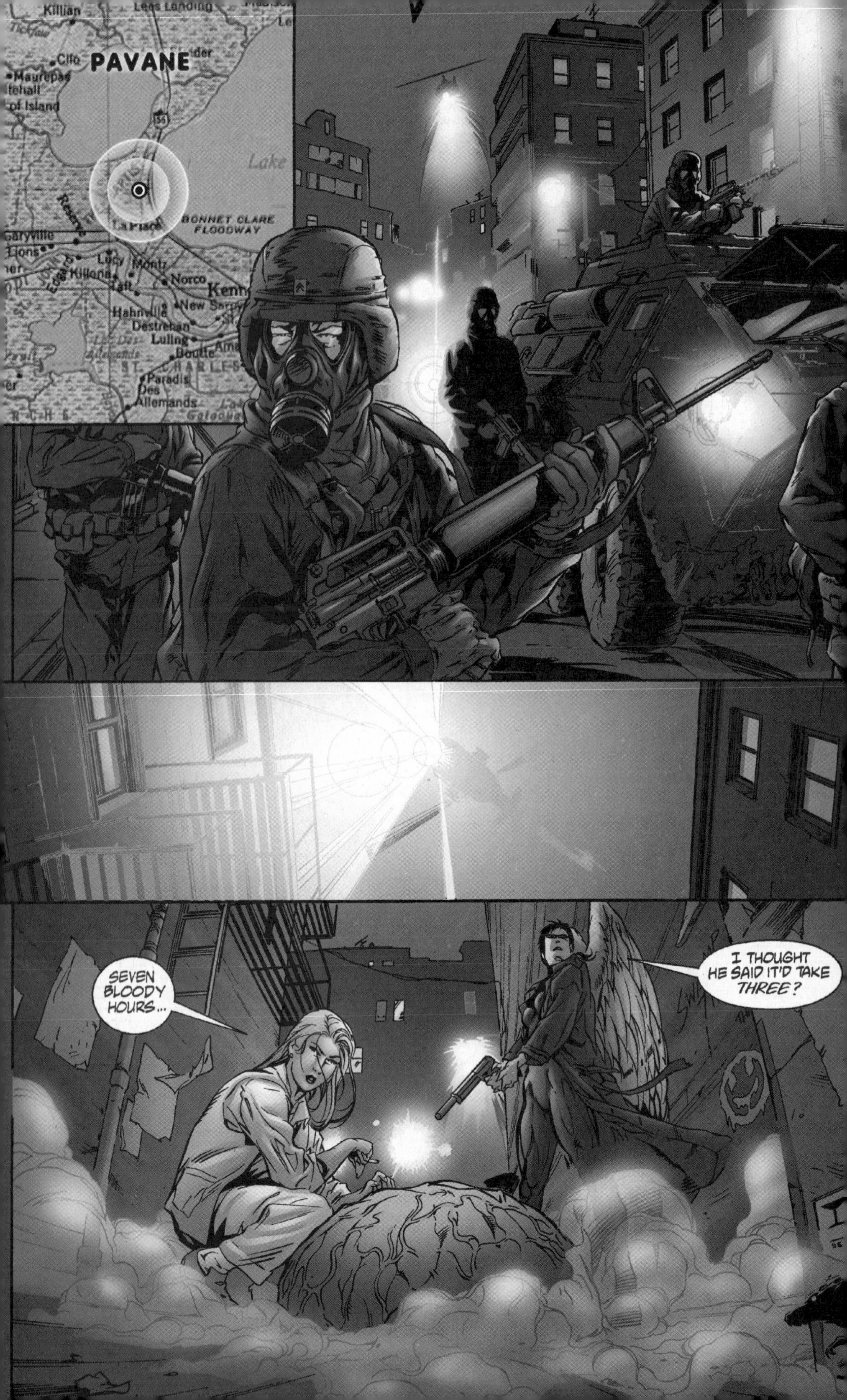
PAVANE
Killian
Clio
Maurepas
Lake
BONNET CLARE
FLOODWAY
Garyville
Lions
Lucy
Montz
Killona
Taft
Norco
Hahnville
Destrehan
Luling
Boutte
Paradis
Des
Allemands
SEVEN BLOODY HOURS...
I THOUGHT HE SAID IT'D TAKE THREE?

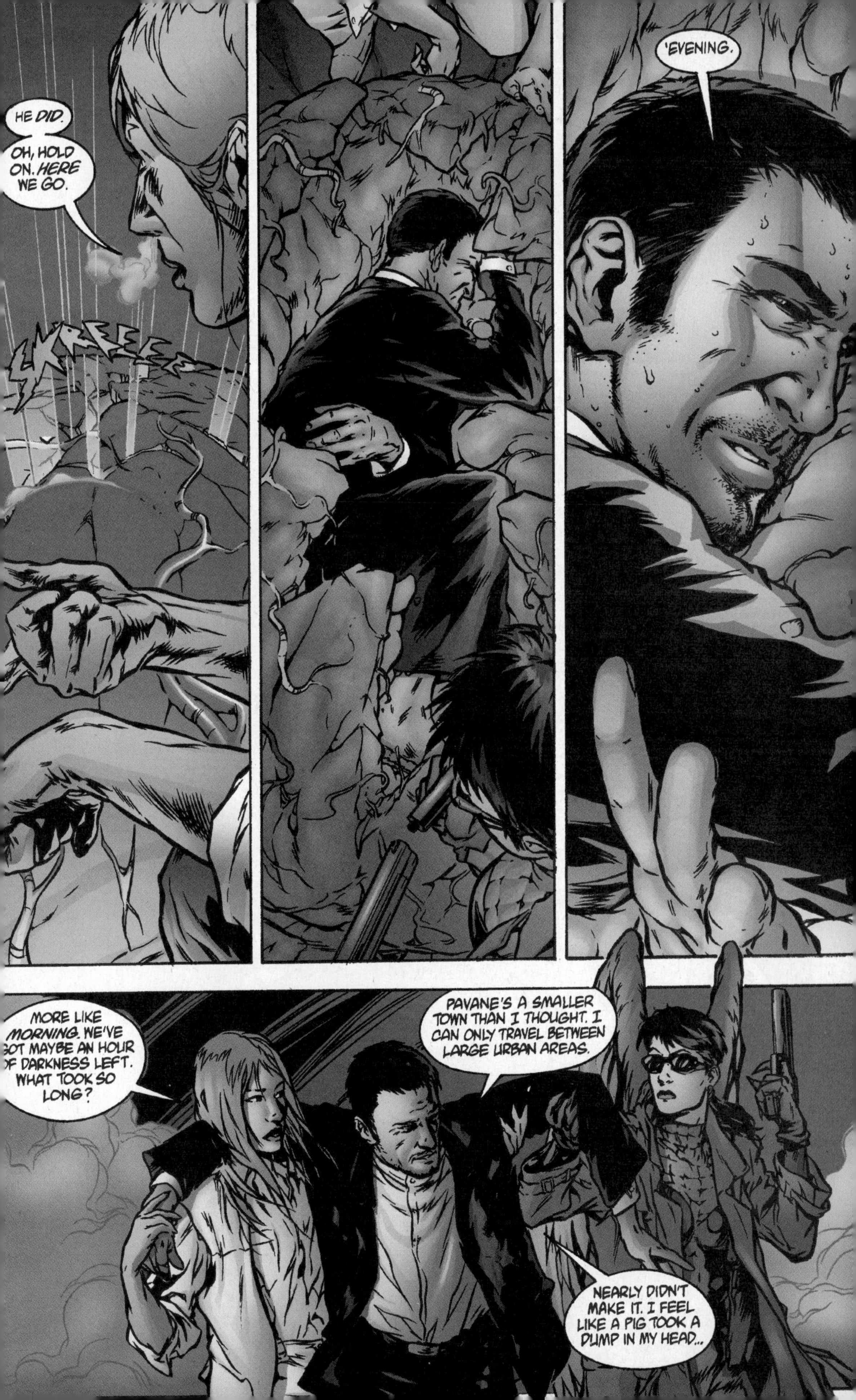
HE DID.
OH, HOLD ON. HERE WE GO.
SKREEEE
'EVENING.
MORE LIKE MORNING. WE'VE GOT MAYBE AN HOUR OF DARKNESS LEFT. WHAT TOOK SO LONG?
PAVANE'S A SMALLER TOWN THAN I THOUGHT. I CAN ONLY TRAVEL BETWEEN LARGE URBAN AREAS.
NEARLY DIDN'T MAKE IT. I FEEL LIKE A PIG TOOK A DUMP IN MY HEAD...

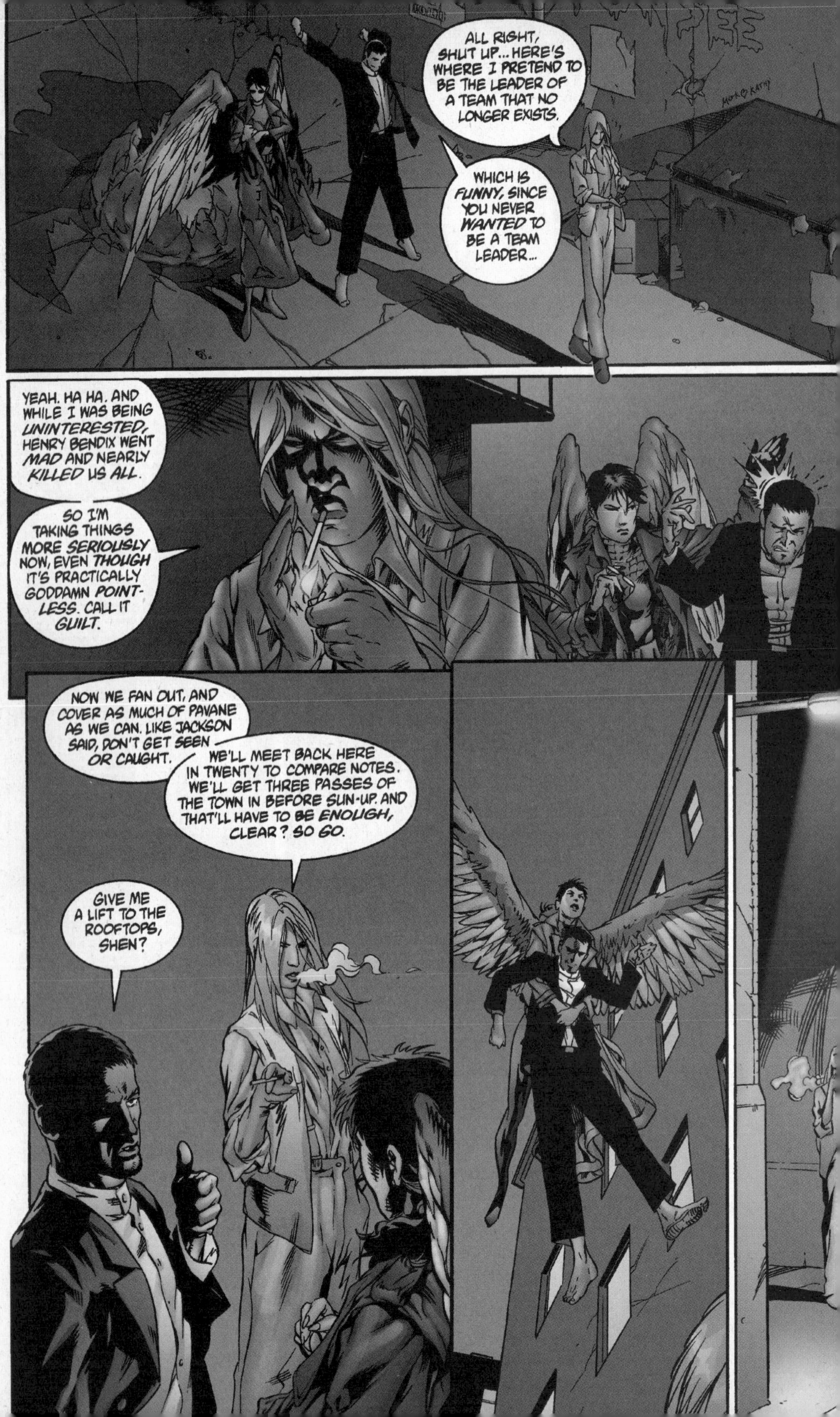
ALL RIGHT, SHUT UP... HERE'S WHERE I PRETEND TO BE THE LEADER OF A TEAM THAT NO LONGER EXISTS.
WHICH IS FUNNY, SINCE YOU NEVER WANTED TO BE A TEAM LEADER...
YEAH. HA HA. AND WHILE I WAS BEING UNINTERESTED, HENRY BENDIX WENT MAD AND NEARLY KILLED US ALL.
SO I'M TAKING THINGS MORE SERIOUSLY NOW, EVEN THOUGH IT'S PRACTICALLY GODDAMN POINTLESS. CALL IT GUILT.
NOW WE FAN OUT, AND COVER AS MUCH OF PAVANE AS WE CAN. LIKE JACKSON SAID, DON'T GET SEEN OR CAUGHT.
WE'LL MEET BACK HERE IN TWENTY TO COMPARE NOTES. WE'LL GET THREE PASSES OF THE TOWN IN BEFORE SUN-UP. AND THAT'LL HAVE TO BE ENOUGH, CLEAR? SO GO.
GIVE ME A LIFT TO THE ROOFTOPS, SHEN?

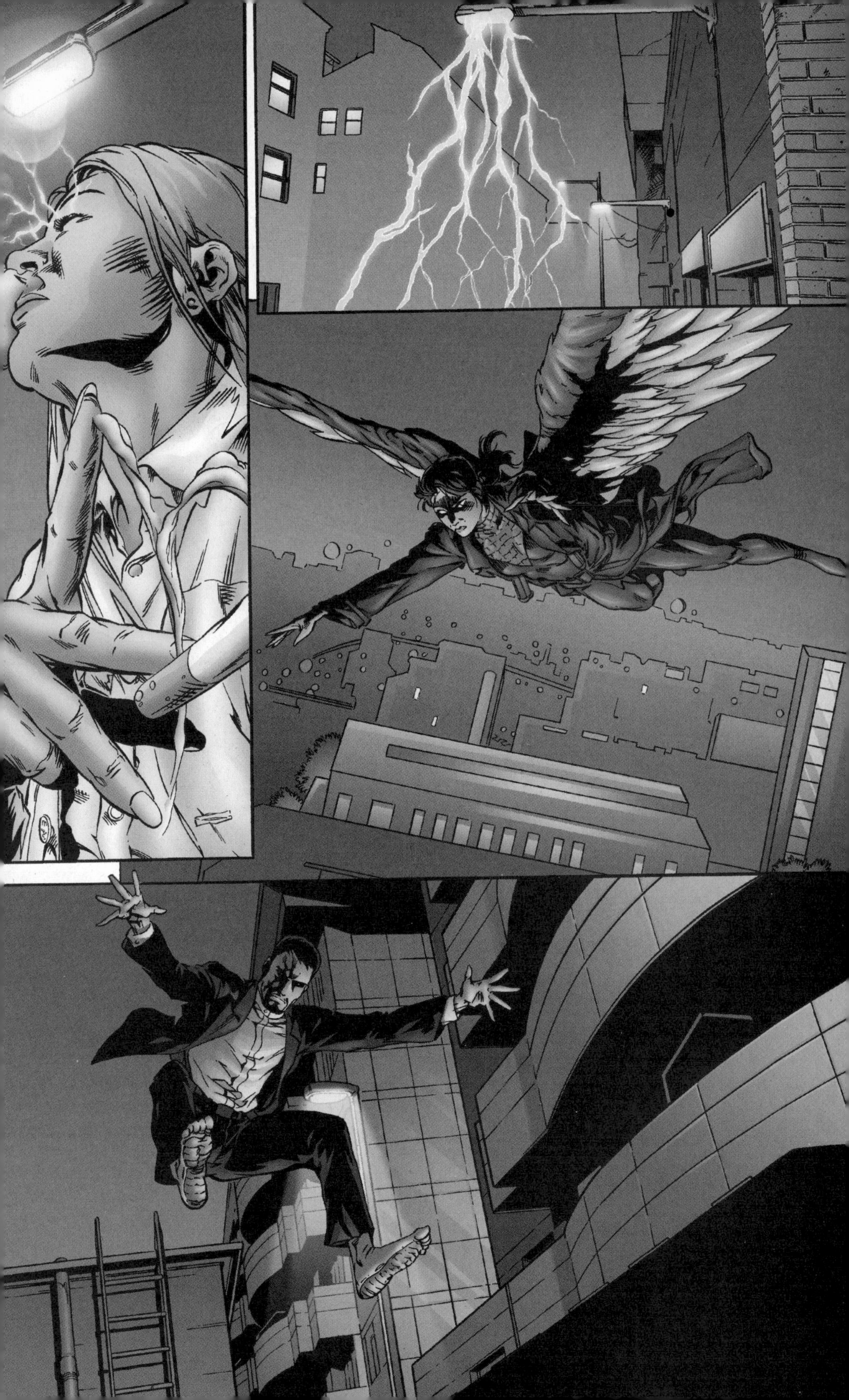

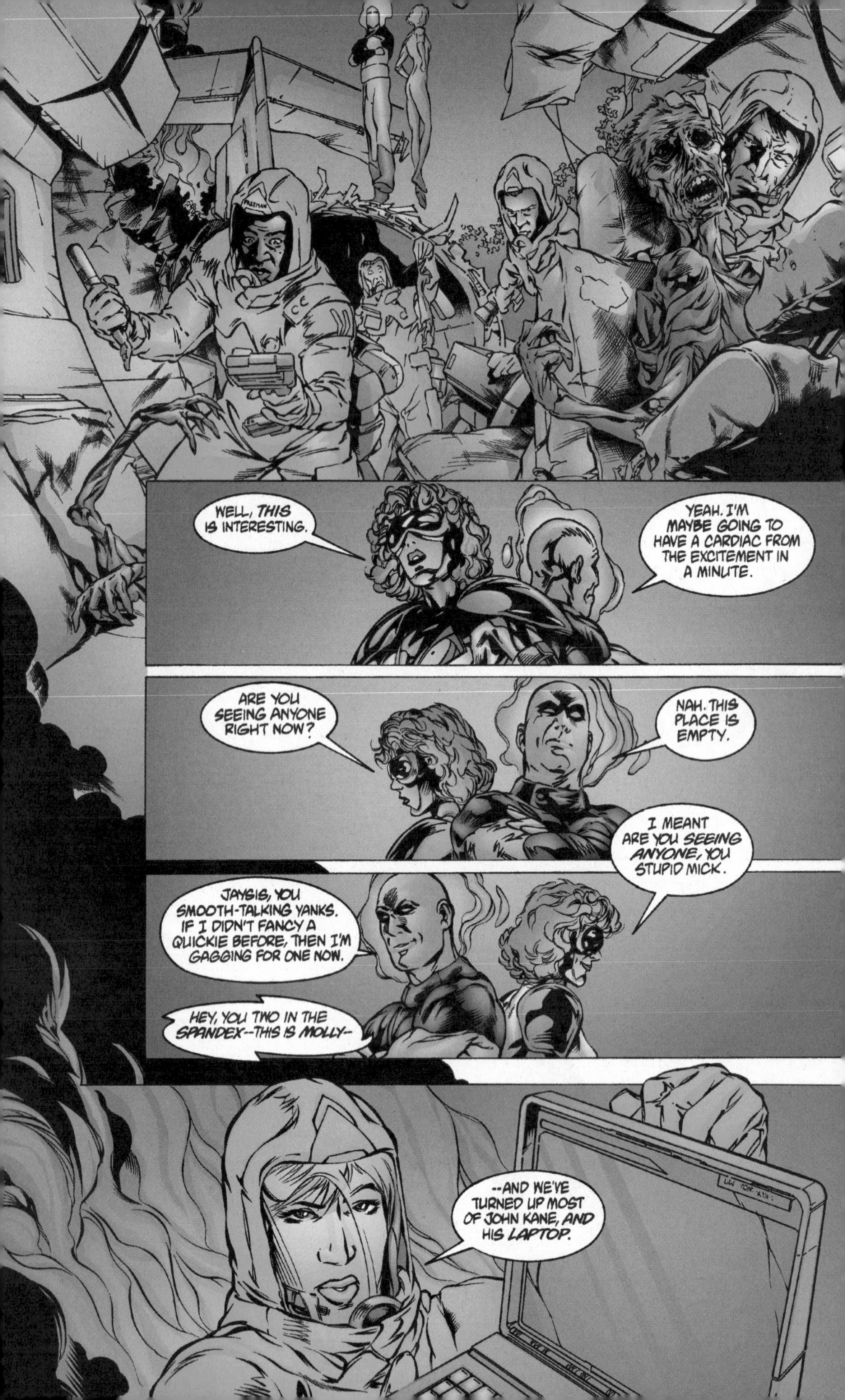
WELL, THIS IS INTERESTING.
YEAH. I'M MAYBE GOING TO HAVE A CARDIAC FROM THE EXCITEMENT IN A MINUTE.
ARE YOU SEEING ANYONE RIGHT NOW?
NAH. THIS PLACE IS EMPTY.
I MEANT ARE YOU SEEING ANYONE, YOU STUPID MICK.
JAYSIS, YOU SMOOTH-TALKING YANKS. IF I DIDN'T FANCY A QUICKIE BEFORE, THEN I'M GAGGING FOR ONE NOW.
HEY, YOU TWO IN THE SPANDEX--THIS IS MOLLY--
--AND WE'VE TURNED UP MOST OF JOHN KANE, AND HIS LAPTOP.

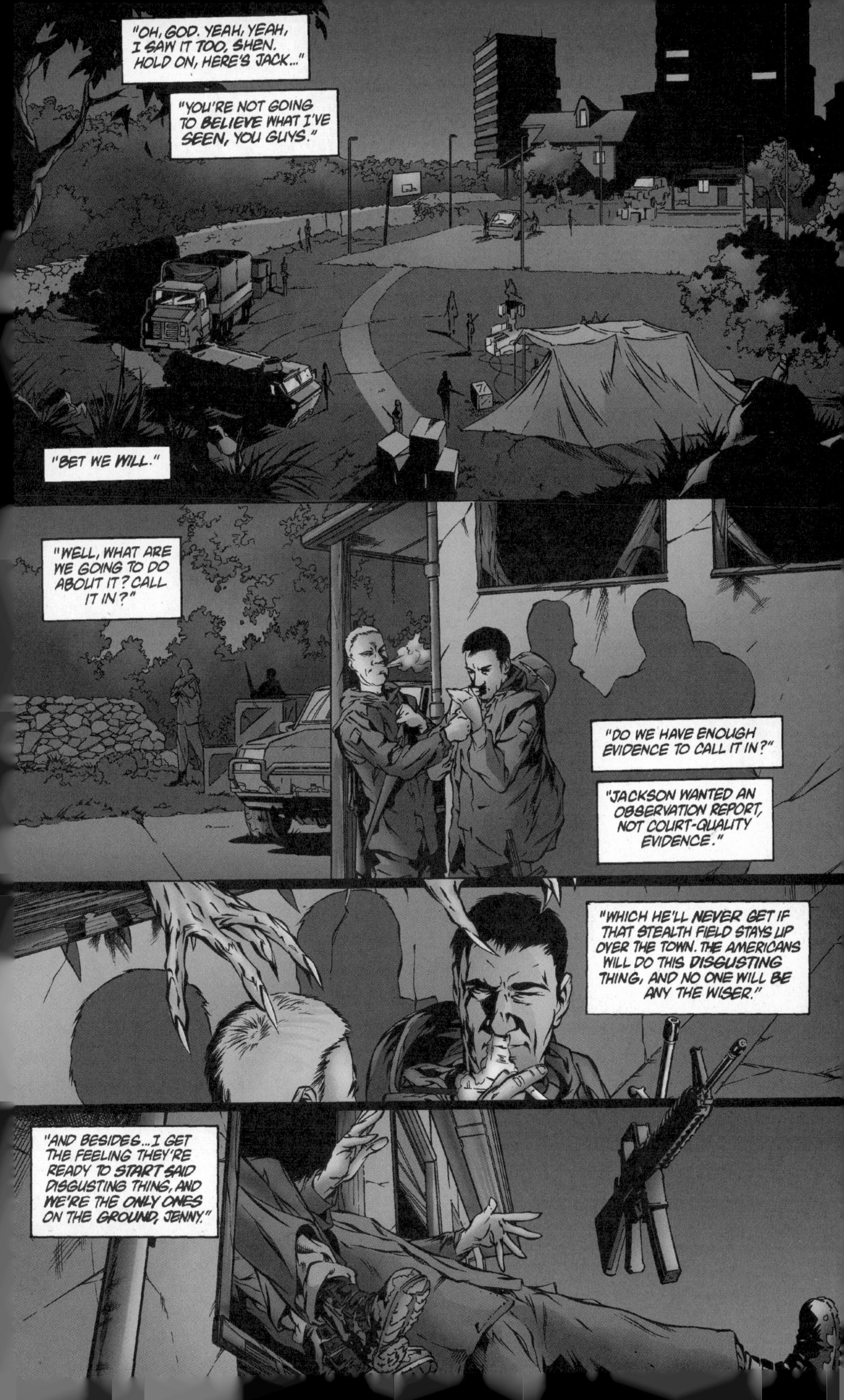
"OH, GOD. YEAH, YEAH, I SAW IT TOO, SHEN. HOLD ON, HERE'S JACK..."
"YOU'RE NOT GOING TO BELIEVE WHAT I'VE SEEN, YOU GUYS."
"BET WE WILL."
"WELL, WHAT ARE WE GOING TO DO ABOUT IT? CALL IT IN?"
"DO WE HAVE ENOUGH EVIDENCE TO CALL IT IN?"
"JACKSON WANTED AN OBSERVATION REPORT, NOT COURT-QUALITY EVIDENCE."
"WHICH HE'LL NEVER GET IF THAT STEALTH FIELD STAYS UP OVER THE TOWN. THE AMERICANS WILL DO THIS DISGUSTING THING, AND NO ONE WILL BE ANY THE WISER."
"AND BESIDES... I GET THE FEELING THEY'RE READY TO START SAID DISGUSTING THING, AND WE'RE THE ONLY ONES ON THE GROUND, JENNY."

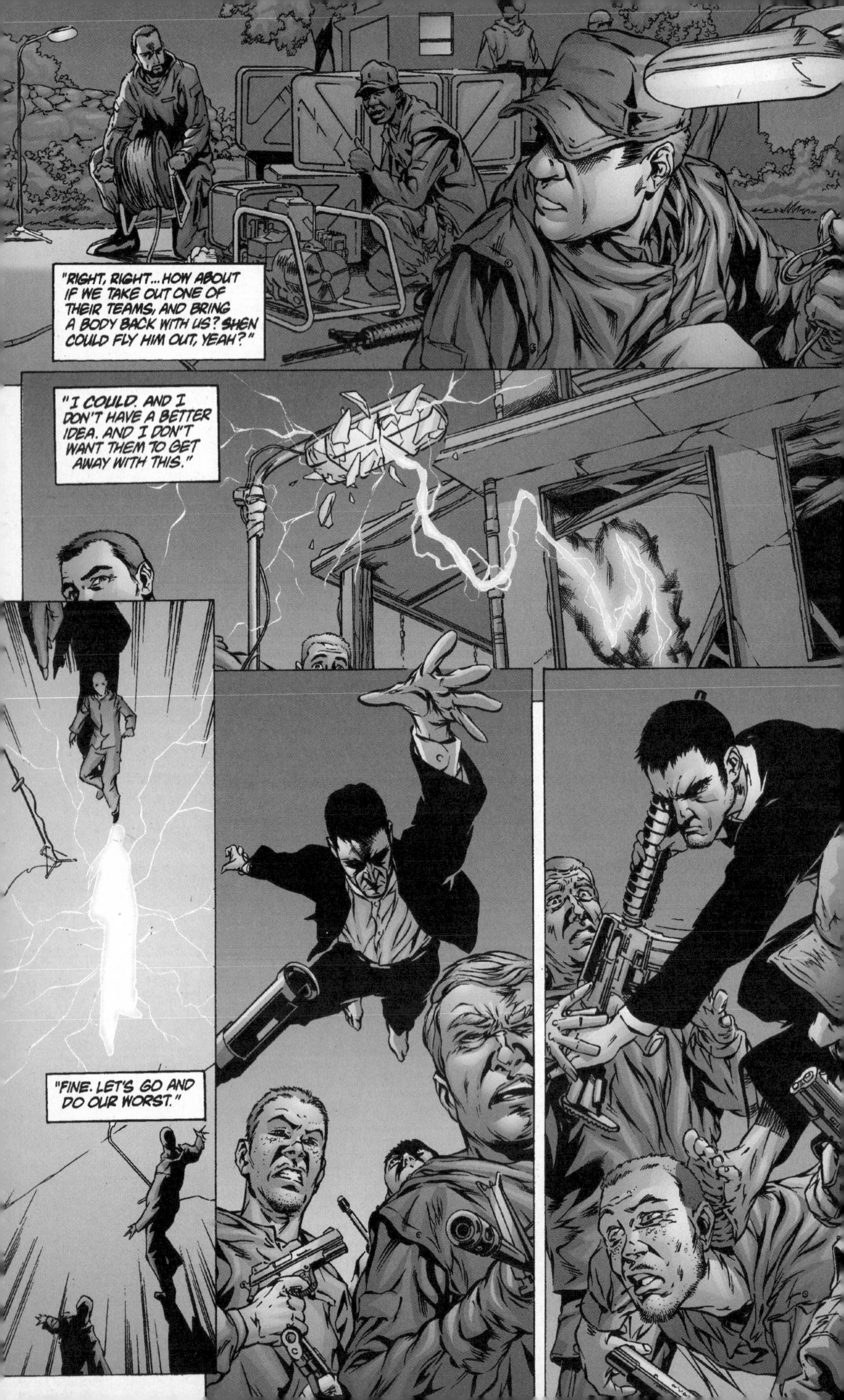
"RIGHT, RIGHT... HOW ABOUT IF WE TAKE OUT ONE OF THEIR TEAMS, AND BRING A BODY BACK WITH US? SHEN COULD FLY HIM OUT, YEAH?"
"I COULD. AND I DON'T HAVE A BETTER IDEA. AND I DON'T WANT THEM TO GET AWAY WITH THIS."
"FINE. LET'S GO AND DO OUR WORST."

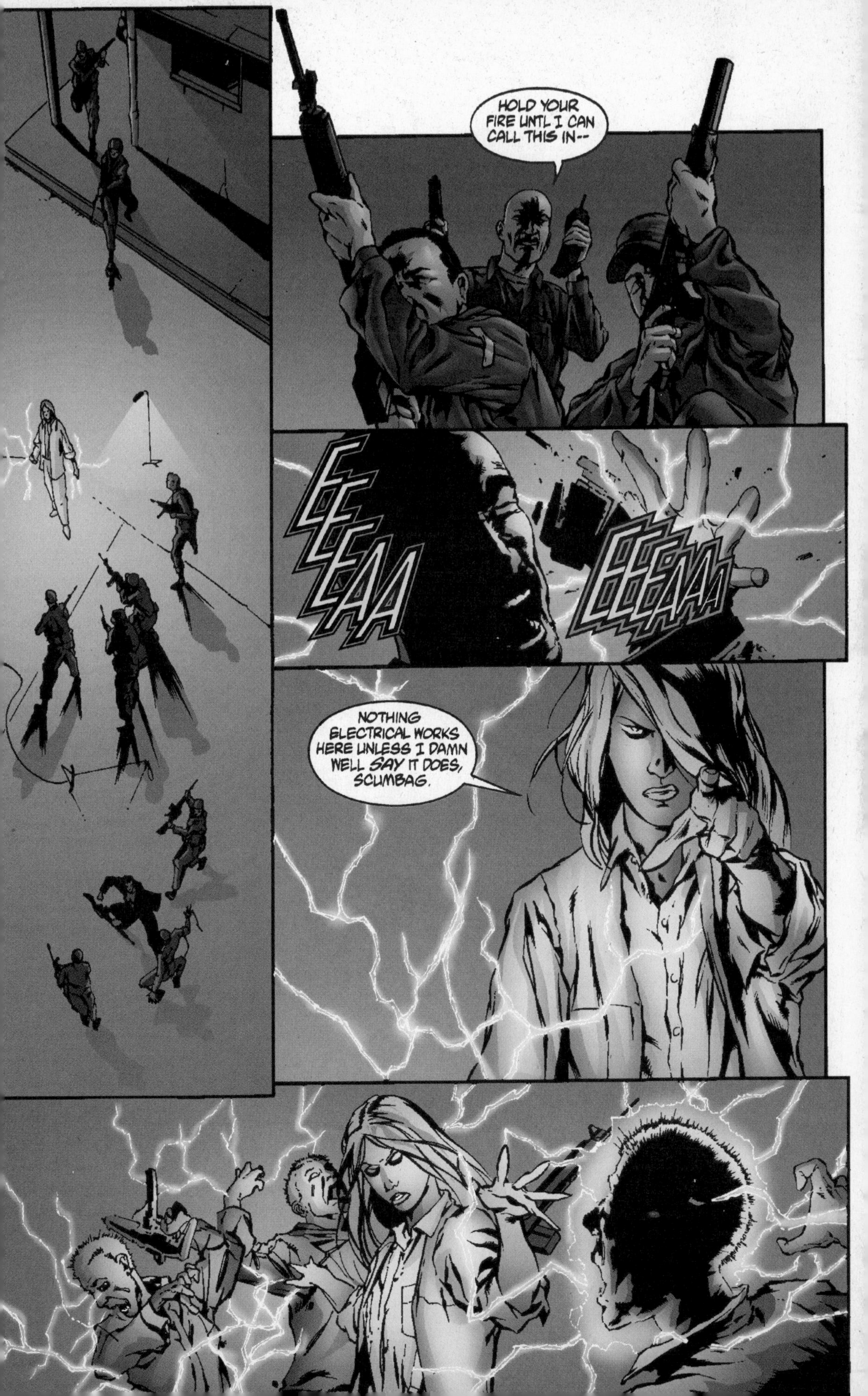
HOLD YOUR FIRE UNTL I CAN CALL THIS IN--
EEEEAA
EEEEAAAA
NOTHING ELECTRICAL WORKS HERE UNLESS I DAMN WELL SAY IT DOES, SCUMBAG.

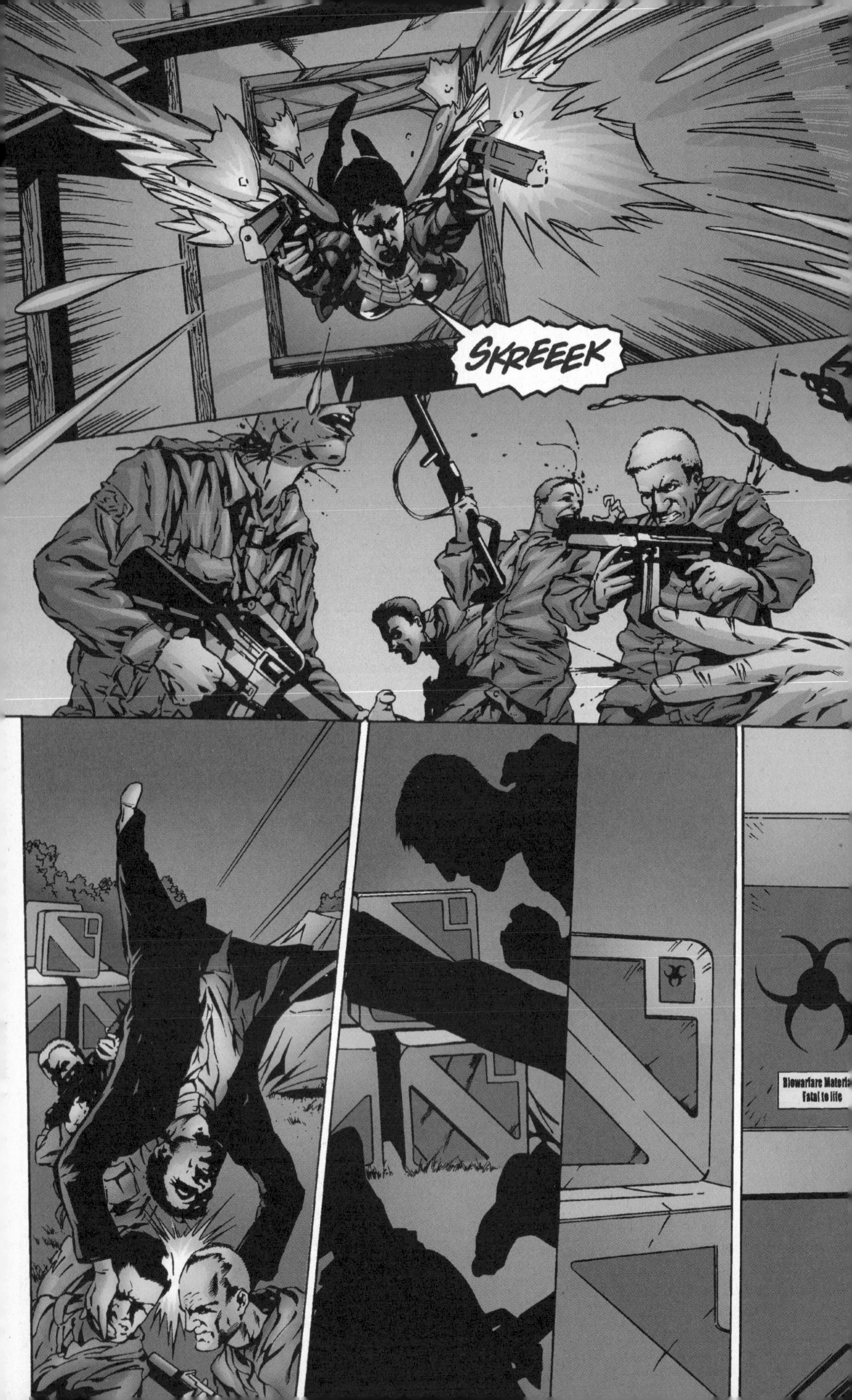
SKREEEK
Biowarfare Materia
Fatal to life

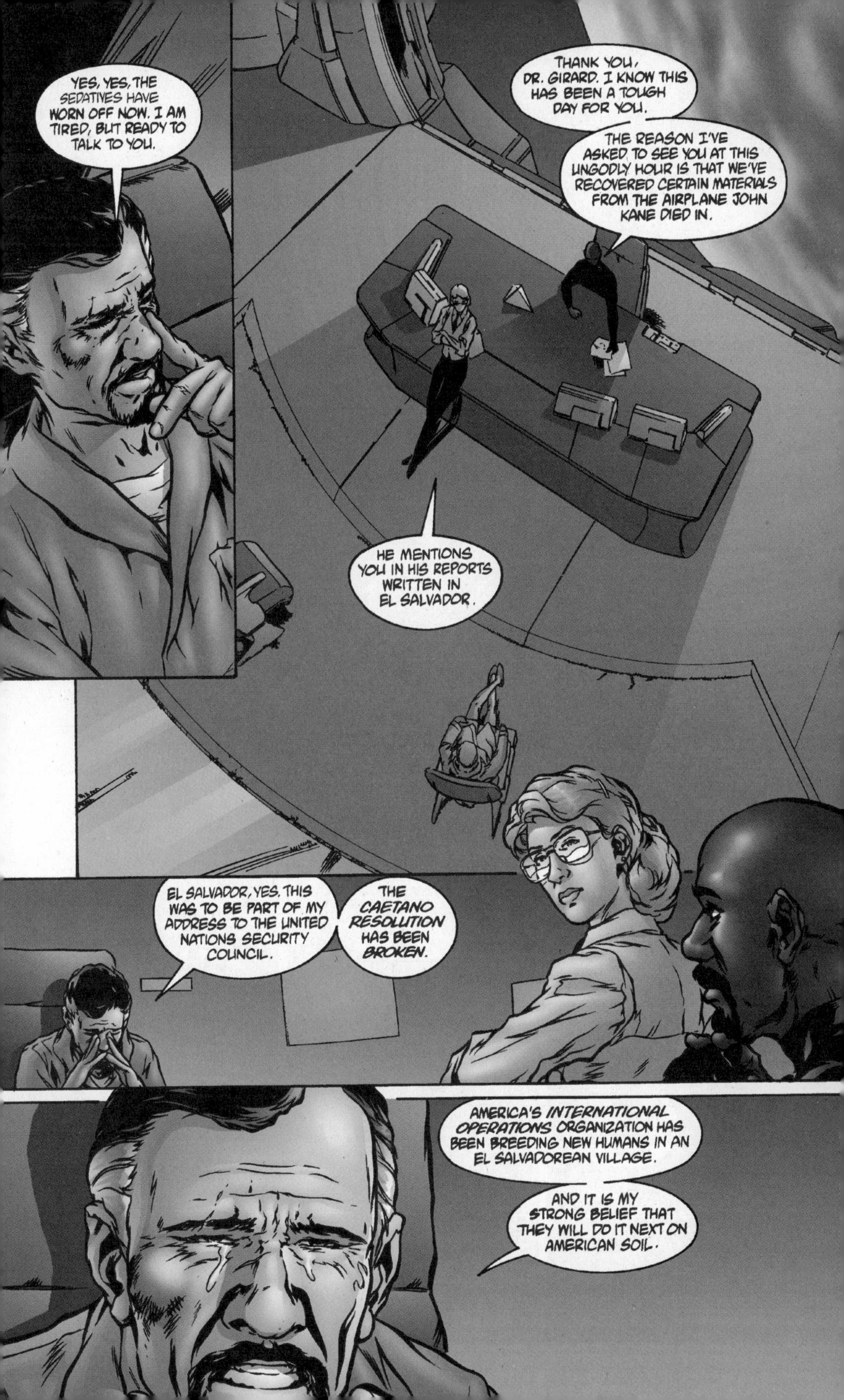
YES, YES, THE SEDATIVES HAVE WORN OFF NOW. I AM TIRED, BUT READY TO TALK TO YOU.
THANK YOU, DR. GIRARD. I KNOW THIS HAS BEEN A TOUGH DAY FOR YOU.
THE REASON I'VE ASKED TO SEE YOU AT THIS UNGODLY HOUR IS THAT WE'VE RECOVERED CERTAIN MATERIALS FROM THE AIRPLANE JOHN KANE DIED IN.
HE MENTIONS YOU IN HIS REPORTS WRITTEN IN EL SALVADOR.
EL SALVADOR, YES. THIS WAS TO BE PART OF MY ADDRESS TO THE UNITED NATIONS SECURITY COUNCIL.
THE *CAETANO RESOLUTION* HAS BEEN *BROKEN*.
AMERICA'S *INTERNATIONAL OPERATIONS* ORGANIZATION HAS BEEN BREEDING NEW HUMANS IN AN EL SALVADOREAN VILLAGE.
AND IT IS MY STRONG BELIEF THAT THEY WILL DO IT NEXT ON AMERICAN SOIL.

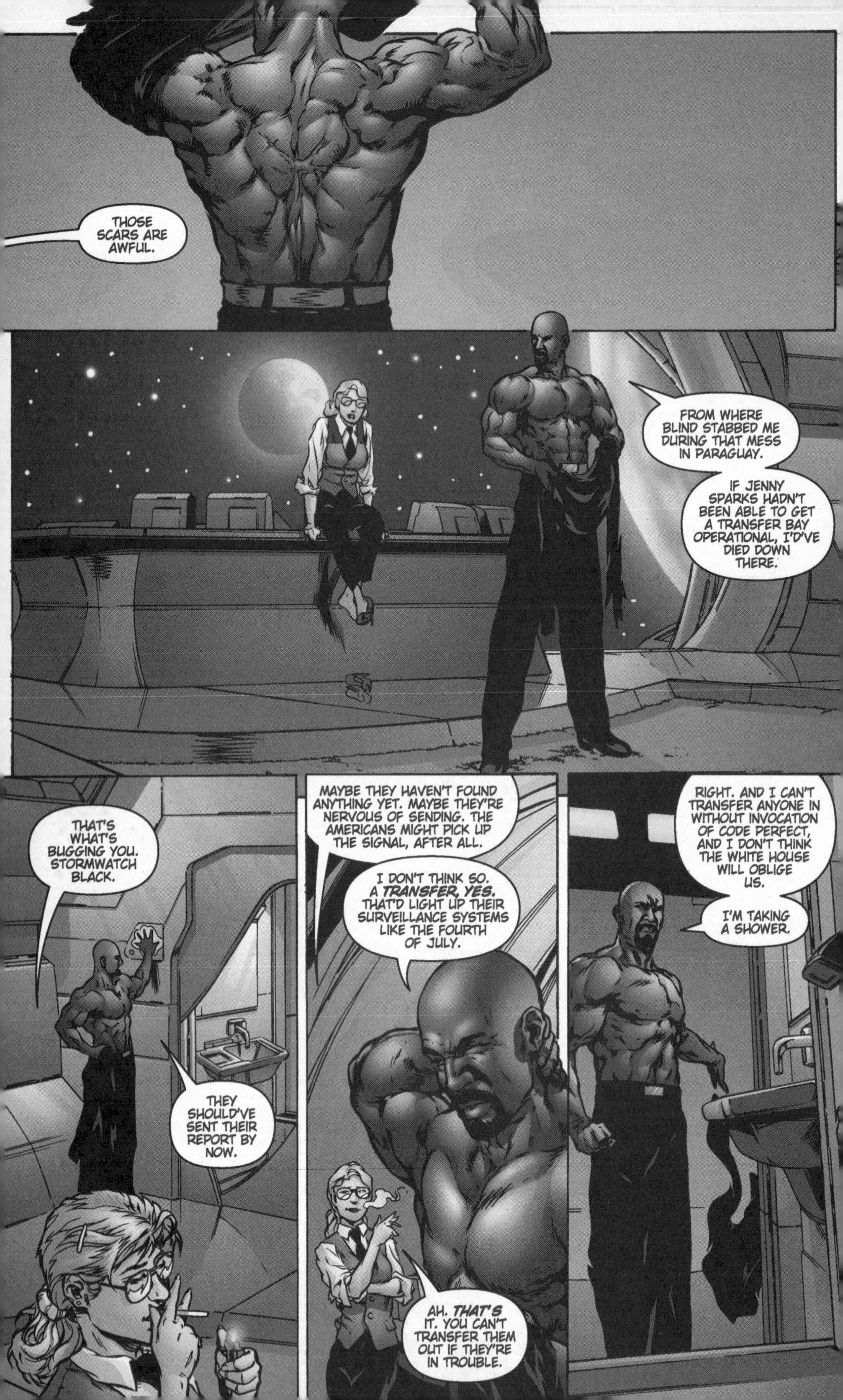
THOSE SCARS ARE AWFUL.
FROM WHERE BLIND STABBED ME DURING THAT MESS IN PARAGUAY.
IF JENNY SPARKS HADN'T BEEN ABLE TO GET A TRANSFER BAY OPERATIONAL, I'D'VE DIED DOWN THERE.
THAT'S WHAT'S BUGGING YOU. STORMWATCH BLACK.
THEY SHOULD'VE SENT THEIR REPORT BY NOW.
MAYBE THEY HAVEN'T FOUND ANYTHING YET. MAYBE THEY'RE NERVOUS OF SENDING. THE AMERICANS MIGHT PICK UP THE SIGNAL, AFTER ALL.
I DON'T THINK SO. A *TRANSFER, YES.* THAT'D LIGHT UP THEIR SURVEILLANCE SYSTEMS LIKE THE FOURTH OF JULY.
AH. *THAT'S* IT. YOU CAN'T TRANSFER THEM OUT IF THEY'RE IN TROUBLE.
RIGHT. AND I CAN'T TRANSFER ANYONE IN WITHOUT INVOCATION OF CODE PERFECT, AND I DON'T THINK THE WHITE HOUSE WILL OBLIGE US.
I'M TAKING A SHOWER.

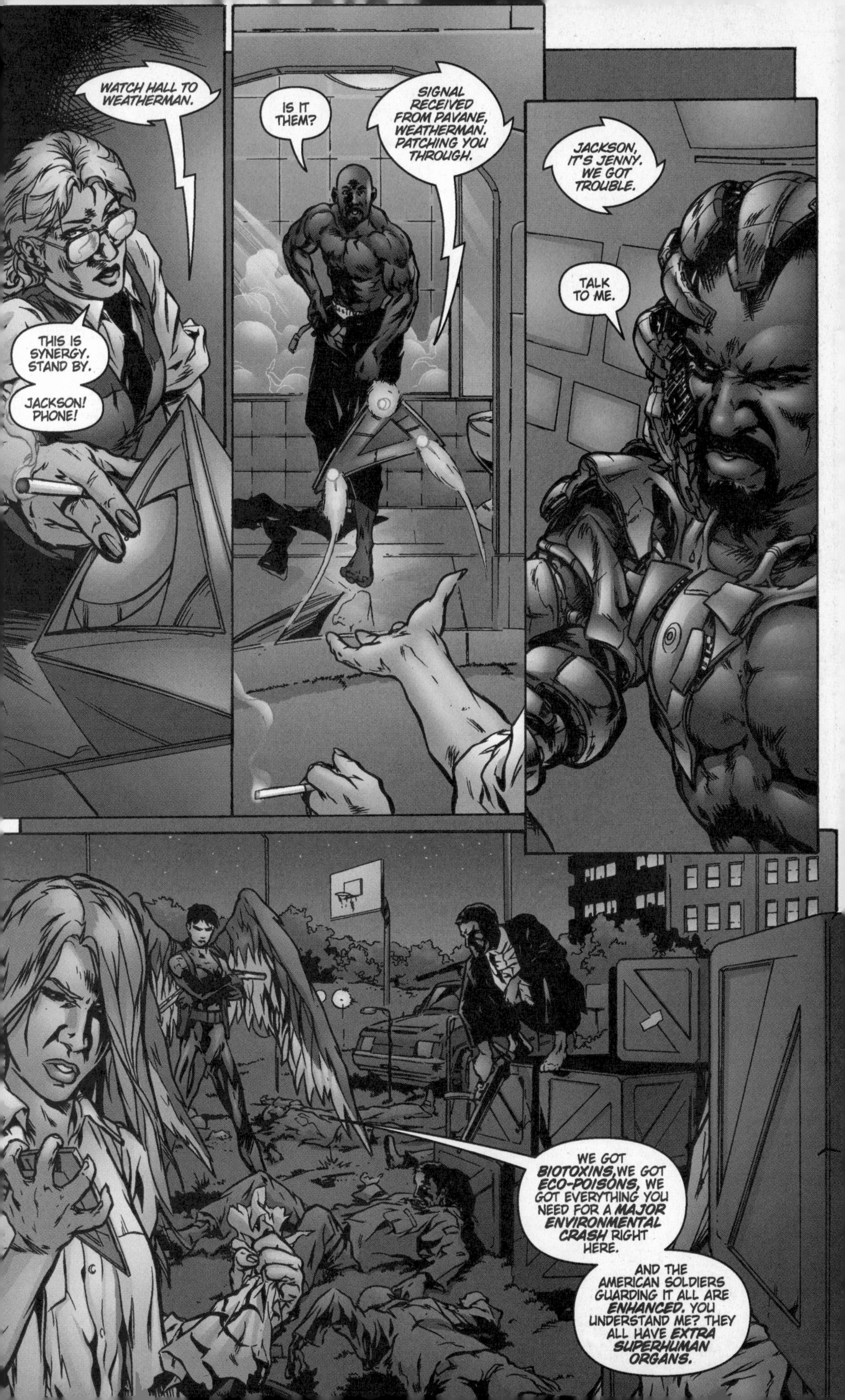
WATCH HALL TO WEATHERMAN.
THIS IS SYNERGY. STAND BY.
JACKSON! PHONE!
IS IT THEM?
SIGNAL RECEIVED FROM PAVANE, WEATHERMAN. PATCHING YOU THROUGH.
JACKSON, IT'S JENNY. WE GOT TROUBLE.
TALK TO ME.
WE GOT BIOTOXINS, WE GOT ECO-POISONS, WE GOT EVERYTHING YOU NEED FOR A MAJOR ENVIRONMENTAL CRASH RIGHT HERE.
AND THE AMERICAN SOLDIERS GUARDING IT ALL ARE ENHANCED. YOU UNDERSTAND ME? THEY ALL HAVE EXTRA SUPERHUMAN ORGANS.

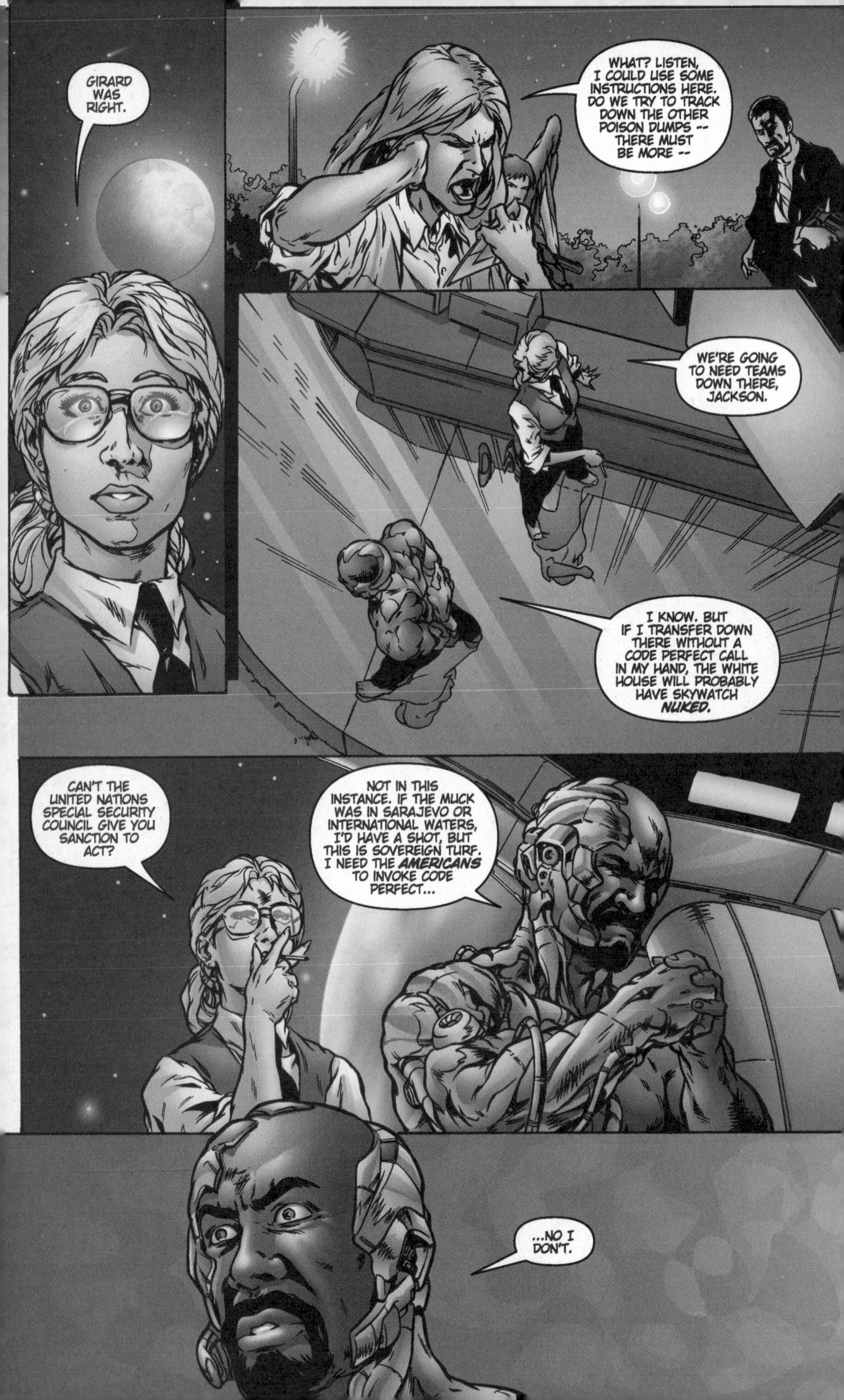
GIRARD WAS RIGHT.
WHAT? LISTEN, I COULD USE SOME INSTRUCTIONS HERE. DO WE TRY TO TRACK DOWN THE OTHER POISON DUMPS -- THERE MUST BE MORE --
WE'RE GOING TO NEED TEAMS DOWN THERE, JACKSON.
I KNOW. BUT IF I TRANSFER DOWN THERE WITHOUT A CODE PERFECT CALL IN MY HAND, THE WHITE HOUSE WILL PROBABLY HAVE SKYWATCH *NUKED*.
CAN'T THE UNITED NATIONS SPECIAL SECURITY COUNCIL GIVE YOU SANCTION TO ACT?
NOT IN THIS INSTANCE. IF THE MUCK WAS IN SARAJEVO OR INTERNATIONAL WATERS, I'D HAVE A SHOT, BUT THIS IS SOVEREIGN TURF. I NEED THE *AMERICANS* TO INVOKE CODE PERFECT...
...NO I DON'T.

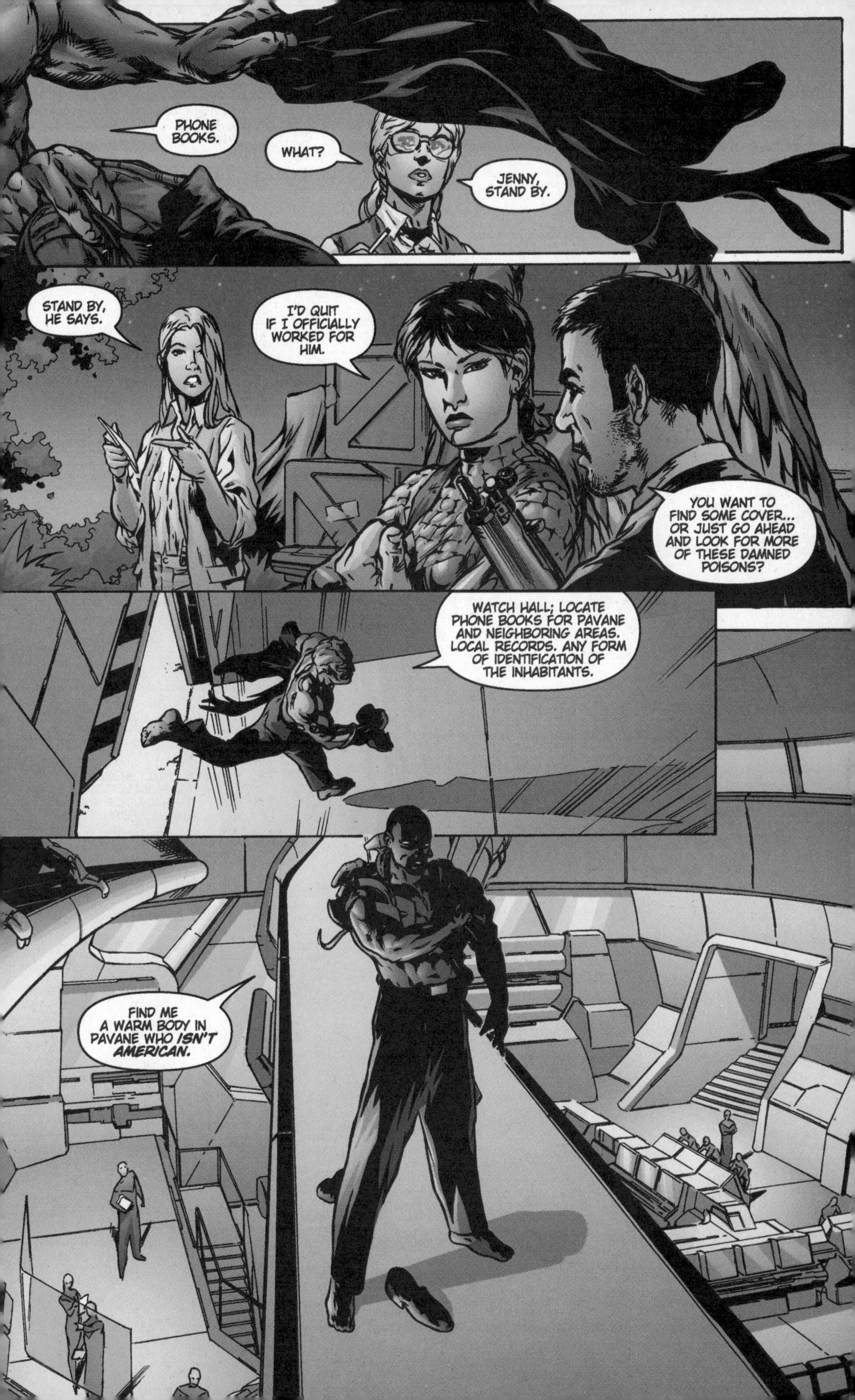
PHONE BOOKS.
WHAT?
JENNY, STAND BY.
STAND BY, HE SAYS.
I'D QUIT IF I OFFICIALLY WORKED FOR HIM.
YOU WANT TO FIND SOME COVER... OR JUST GO AHEAD AND LOOK FOR MORE OF THESE DAMNED POISONS?
WATCH HALL; LOCATE PHONE BOOKS FOR PAVANE AND NEIGHBORING AREAS. LOCAL RECORDS. ANY FORM OF IDENTIFICATION OF THE INHABITANTS.
FIND ME A WARM BODY IN PAVANE WHO ISN'T AMERICAN.

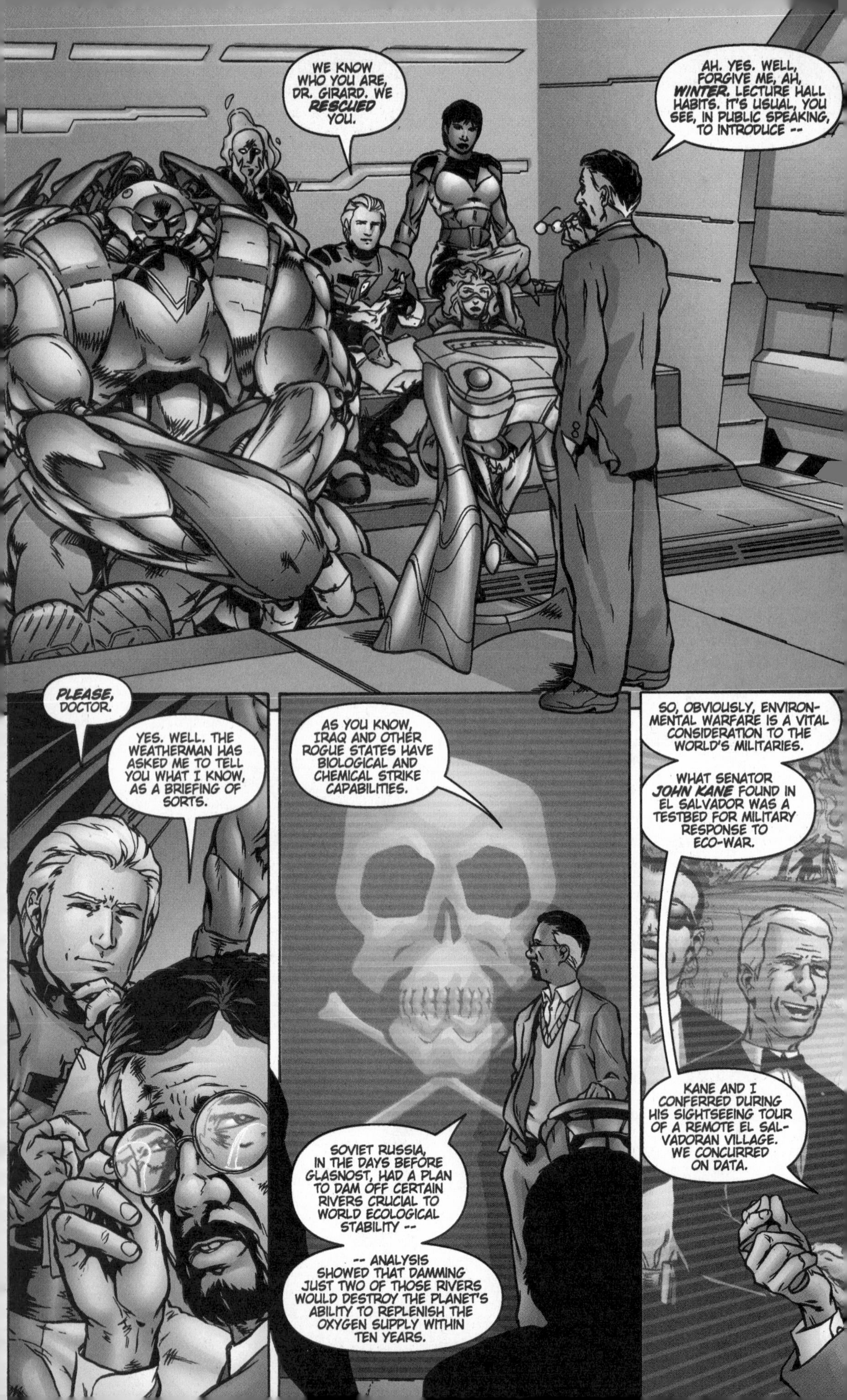

WE KNOW WHO YOU ARE, DR. GIRARD. WE RESCUED YOU.
AH. YES. WELL, FORGIVE ME, AH, WINTER. LECTURE HALL HABITS. IT'S USUAL, YOU SEE, IN PUBLIC SPEAKING, TO INTRODUCE --
PLEASE, DOCTOR.
YES. WELL. THE WEATHERMAN HAS ASKED ME TO TELL YOU WHAT I KNOW, AS A BRIEFING OF SORTS.
AS YOU KNOW, IRAQ AND OTHER ROGUE STATES HAVE BIOLOGICAL AND CHEMICAL STRIKE CAPABILITIES.
SOVIET RUSSIA, IN THE DAYS BEFORE GLASNOST, HAD A PLAN TO DAM OFF CERTAIN RIVERS CRUCIAL TO WORLD ECOLOGICAL STABILITY --
-- ANALYSIS SHOWED THAT DAMMING JUST TWO OF THOSE RIVERS WOULD DESTROY THE PLANET'S ABILITY TO REPLENISH THE OXYGEN SUPPLY WITHIN TEN YEARS.
SO, OBVIOUSLY, ENVIRONMENTAL WARFARE IS A VITAL CONSIDERATION TO THE WORLD'S MILITARIES.
WHAT SENATOR JOHN KANE FOUND IN EL SALVADOR WAS A TESTBED FOR MILITARY RESPONSE TO ECO-WAR.
KANE AND I CONFERRED DURING HIS SIGHTSEEING TOUR OF A REMOTE EL SALVADORAN VILLAGE. WE CONCURRED ON DATA.

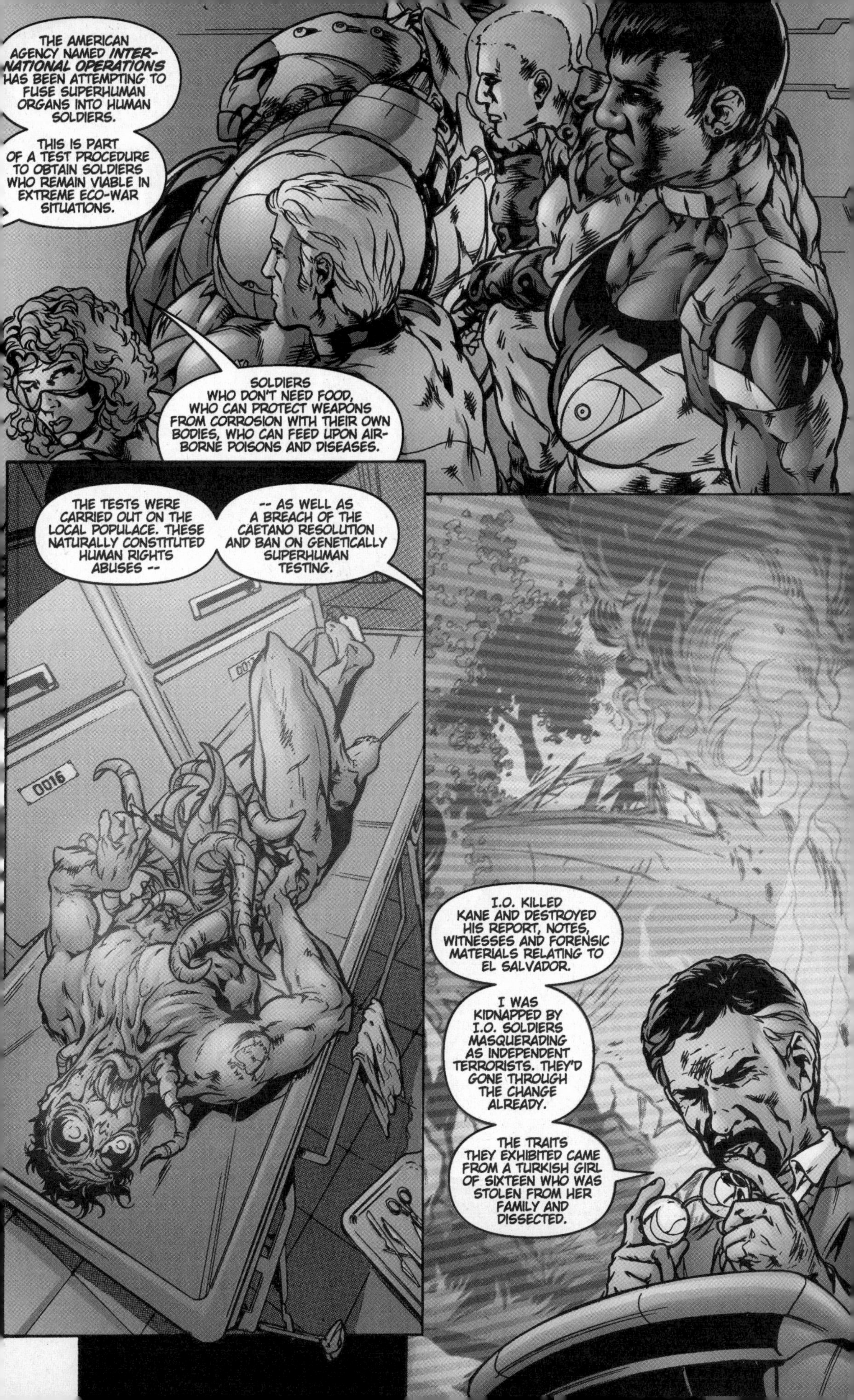
THE AMERICAN AGENCY NAMED *INTERNATIONAL OPERATIONS* HAS BEEN ATTEMPTING TO FUSE SUPERHUMAN ORGANS INTO HUMAN SOLDIERS.
THIS IS PART OF A TEST PROCEDURE TO OBTAIN SOLDIERS WHO REMAIN VIABLE IN EXTREME ECO-WAR SITUATIONS.
SOLDIERS WHO DON'T NEED FOOD, WHO CAN PROTECT WEAPONS FROM CORROSION WITH THEIR OWN BODIES, WHO CAN FEED UPON AIRBORNE POISONS AND DISEASES.
THE TESTS WERE CARRIED OUT ON THE LOCAL POPULACE. THESE NATURALLY CONSTITUTED HUMAN RIGHTS ABUSES --
-- AS WELL AS A BREACH OF THE CAETANO RESOLUTION AND BAN ON GENETICALLY SUPERHUMAN TESTING.
0016
I.O. KILLED KANE AND DESTROYED HIS REPORT, NOTES, WITNESSES AND FORENSIC MATERIALS RELATING TO EL SALVADOR.
I WAS KIDNAPPED BY I.O. SOLDIERS MASQUERADING AS INDEPENDENT TERRORISTS. THEY'D GONE THROUGH THE CHANGE ALREADY.
THE TRAITS THEY EXHIBITED CAME FROM A TURKISH GIRL OF SIXTEEN WHO WAS STOLEN FROM HER FAMILY AND DISSECTED.

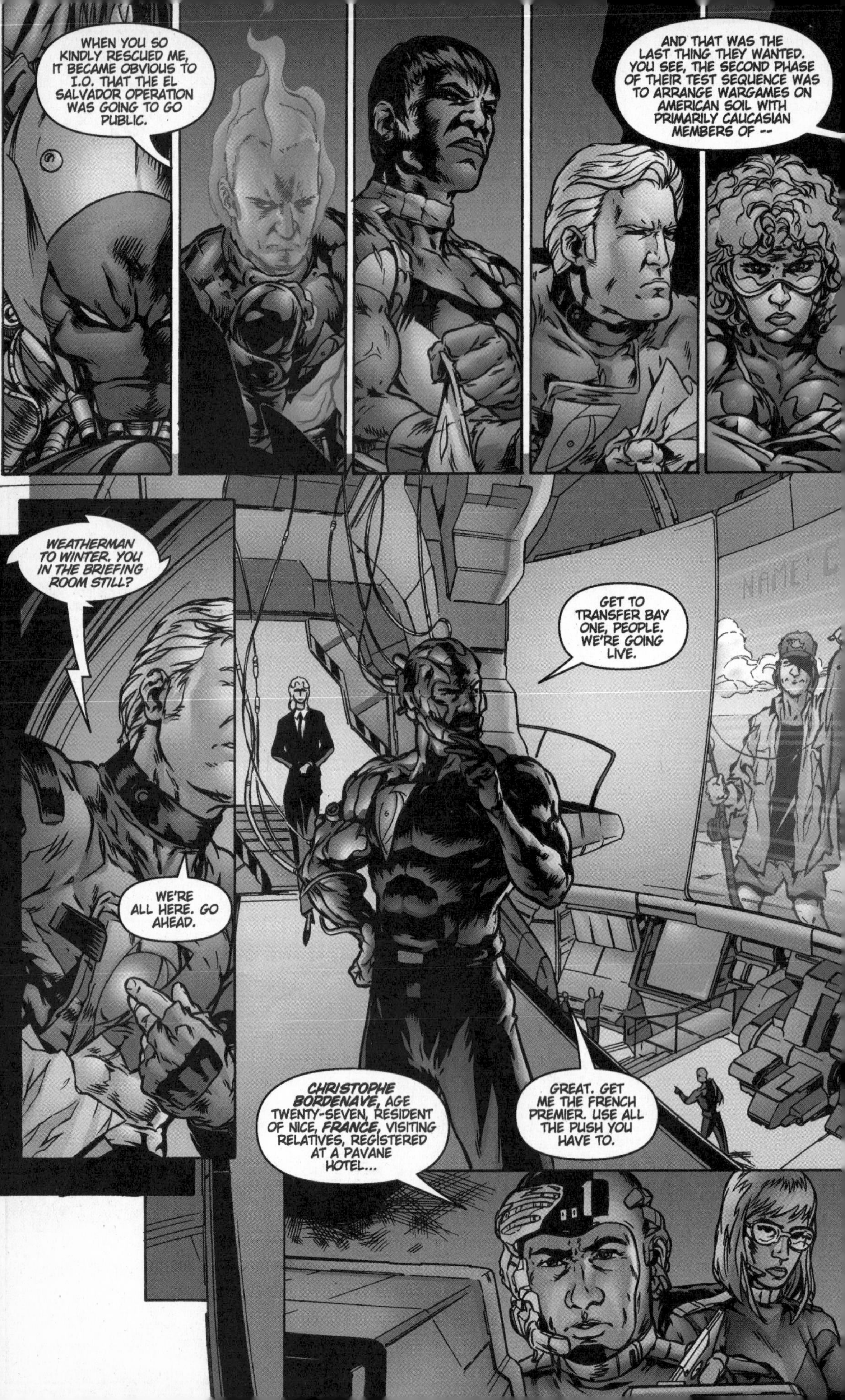
WHEN YOU SO KINDLY RESCUED ME, IT BECAME OBVIOUS TO I.O. THAT THE EL SALVADOR OPERATION WAS GOING TO GO PUBLIC.
AND THAT WAS THE LAST THING THEY WANTED. YOU SEE, THE SECOND PHASE OF THEIR TEST SEQUENCE WAS TO ARRANGE WARGAMES ON AMERICAN SOIL WITH PRIMARILY CAUCASIAN MEMBERS OF --
WEATHERMAN TO WINTER. YOU IN THE BRIEFING ROOM STILL?
WE'RE ALL HERE. GO AHEAD.
GET TO TRANSFER BAY ONE, PEOPLE. WE'RE GOING LIVE.
NAME: C
CHRISTOPHE BORDENAVE, AGE TWENTY-SEVEN, RESIDENT OF NICE, FRANCE, VISITING RELATIVES, REGISTERED AT A PAVANE HOTEL...
GREAT. GET ME THE FRENCH PREMIER. USE ALL THE PUSH YOU HAVE TO.

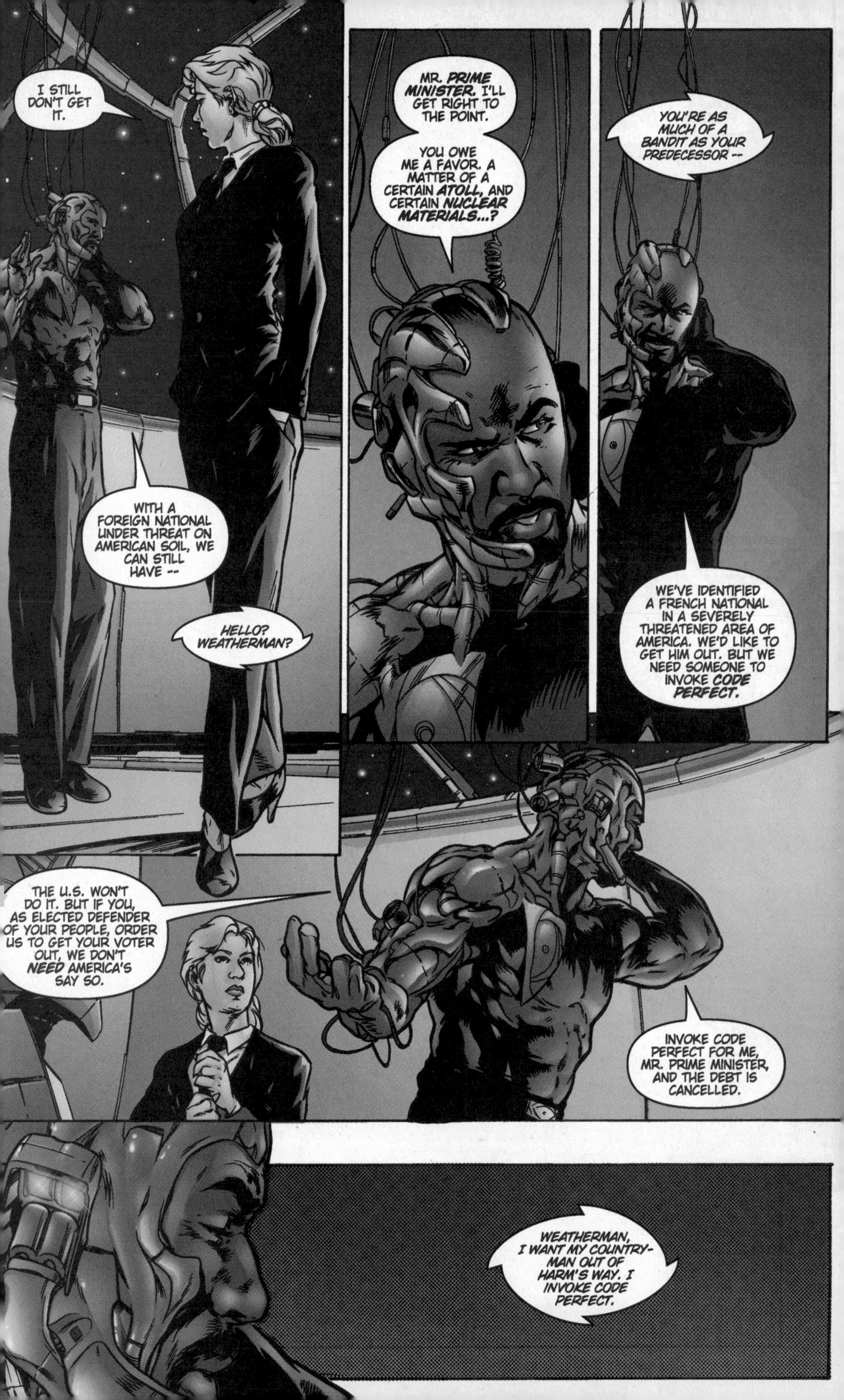
I STILL DON'T GET IT.
MR. PRIME MINISTER. I'LL GET RIGHT TO THE POINT.
YOU OWE ME A FAVOR. A MATTER OF A CERTAIN ATOLL, AND CERTAIN NUCLEAR MATERIALS...?
YOU'RE AS MUCH OF A BANDIT AS YOUR PREDECESSOR --
WITH A FOREIGN NATIONAL UNDER THREAT ON AMERICAN SOIL, WE CAN STILL HAVE --
HELLO? WEATHERMAN?
WE'VE IDENTIFIED A FRENCH NATIONAL IN A SEVERELY THREATENED AREA OF AMERICA. WE'D LIKE TO GET HIM OUT. BUT WE NEED SOMEONE TO INVOKE CODE PERFECT.
THE U.S. WON'T DO IT. BUT IF YOU, AS ELECTED DEFENDER OF YOUR PEOPLE, ORDER US TO GET YOUR VOTER OUT, WE DON'T NEED AMERICA'S SAY SO.
INVOKE CODE PERFECT FOR ME, MR. PRIME MINISTER, AND THE DEBT IS CANCELLED.
WEATHERMAN, I WANT MY COUNTRY-MAN OUT OF HARM'S WAY. I INVOKE CODE PERFECT.

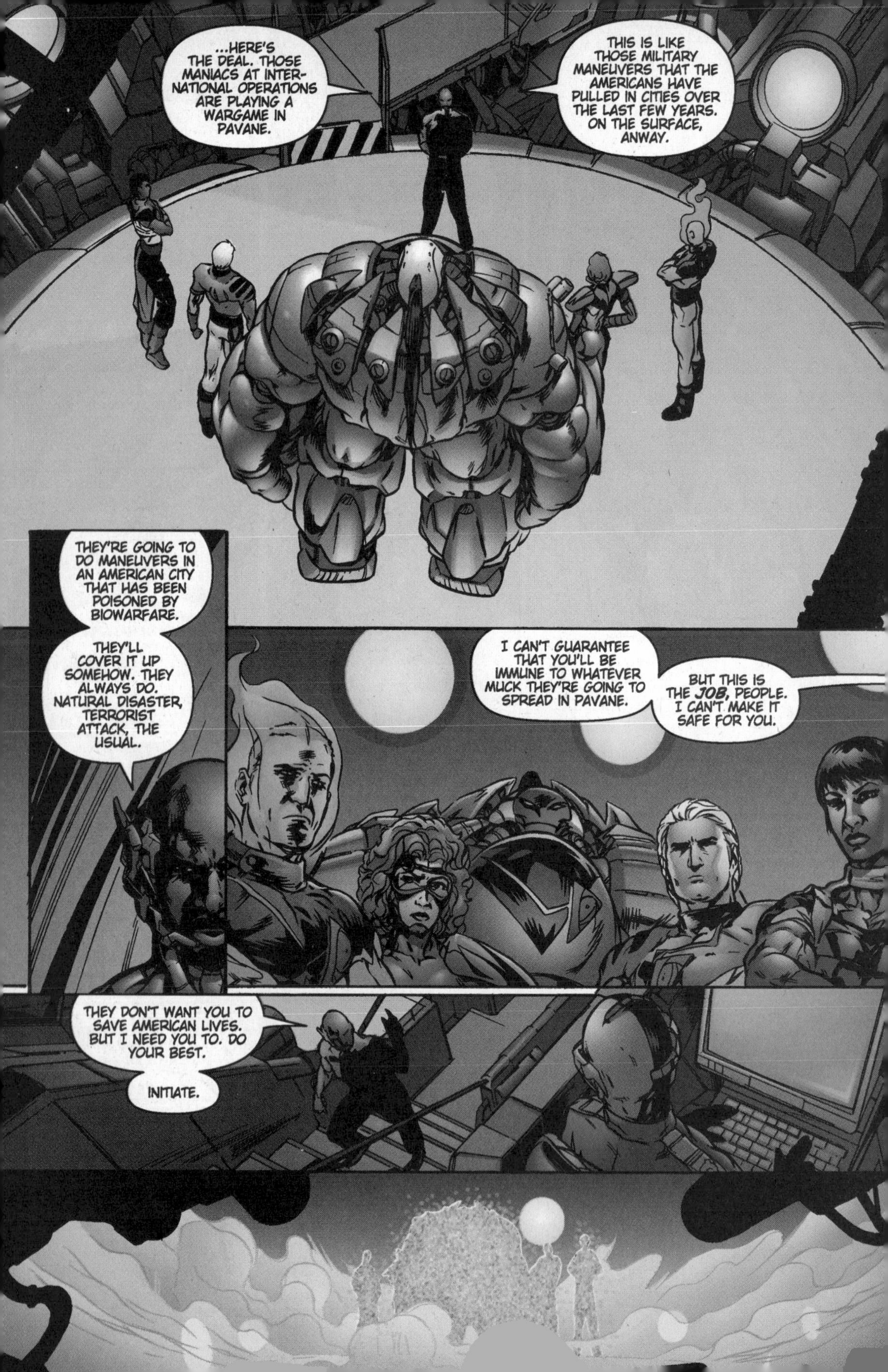

...HERE'S THE DEAL. THOSE MANIACS AT INTER-NATIONAL OPERATIONS ARE PLAYING A WARGAME IN PAVANE.
THIS IS LIKE THOSE MILITARY MANEUVERS THAT THE AMERICANS HAVE PULLED IN CITIES OVER THE LAST FEW YEARS. ON THE SURFACE, ANWAY.
THEY'RE GOING TO DO MANEUVERS IN AN AMERICAN CITY THAT HAS BEEN POISONED BY BIOWARFARE.
THEY'LL COVER IT UP SOMEHOW. THEY ALWAYS DO. NATURAL DISASTER, TERRORIST ATTACK, THE USUAL.
I CAN'T GUARANTEE THAT YOU'LL BE IMMUNE TO WHATEVER MUCK THEY'RE GOING TO SPREAD IN PAVANE.
BUT THIS IS THE JOB, PEOPLE. I CAN'T MAKE IT SAFE FOR YOU.
THEY DON'T WANT YOU TO SAVE AMERICAN LIVES. BUT I NEED YOU TO. DO YOUR BEST.
INITIATE.

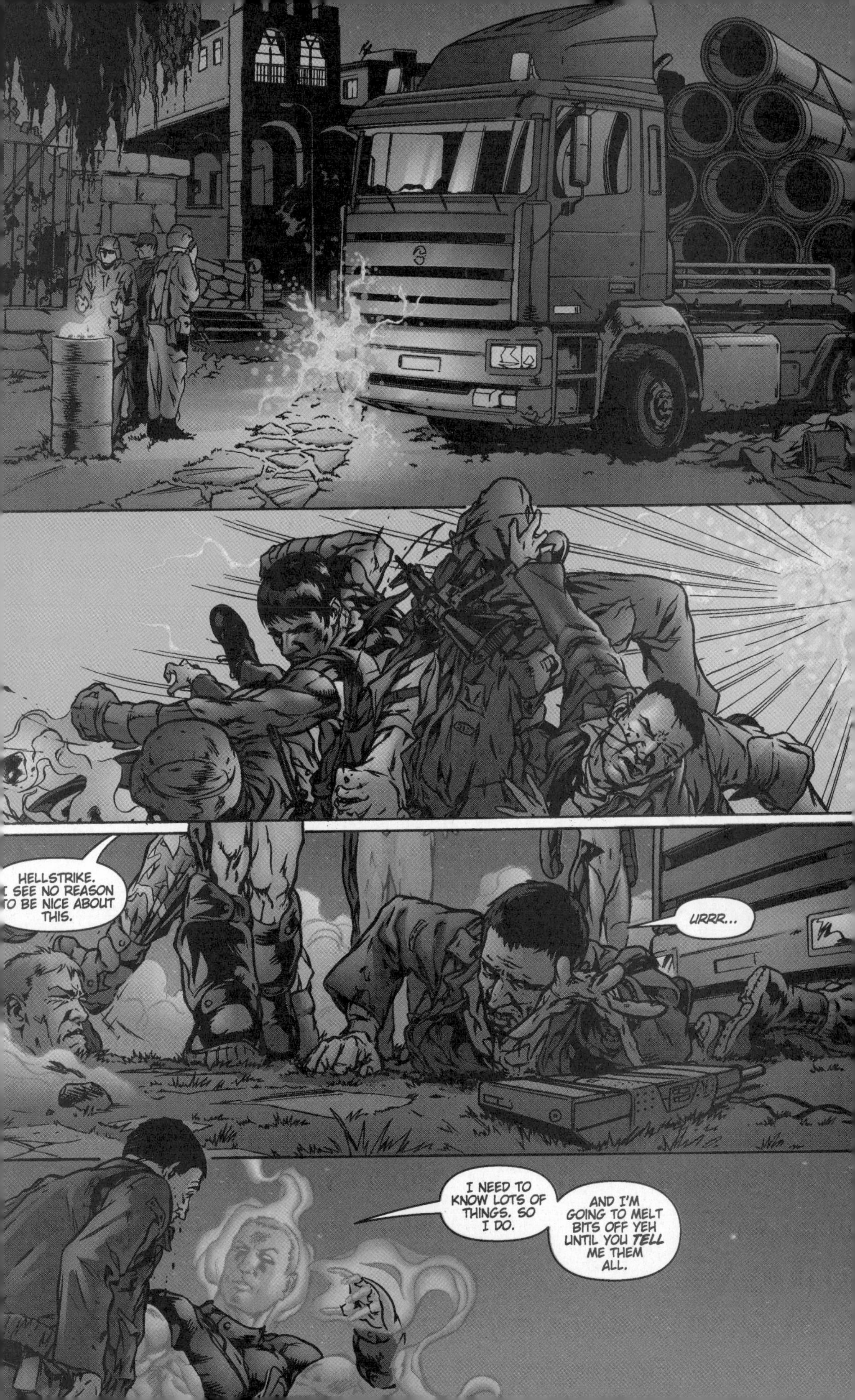
HELLSTRIKE. I SEE NO REASON TO BE NICE ABOUT THIS.
URRR...
I NEED TO KNOW LOTS OF THINGS. SO I DO.
AND I'M GOING TO MELT BITS OFF YEH UNTIL YOU *TELL* ME THEM ALL.

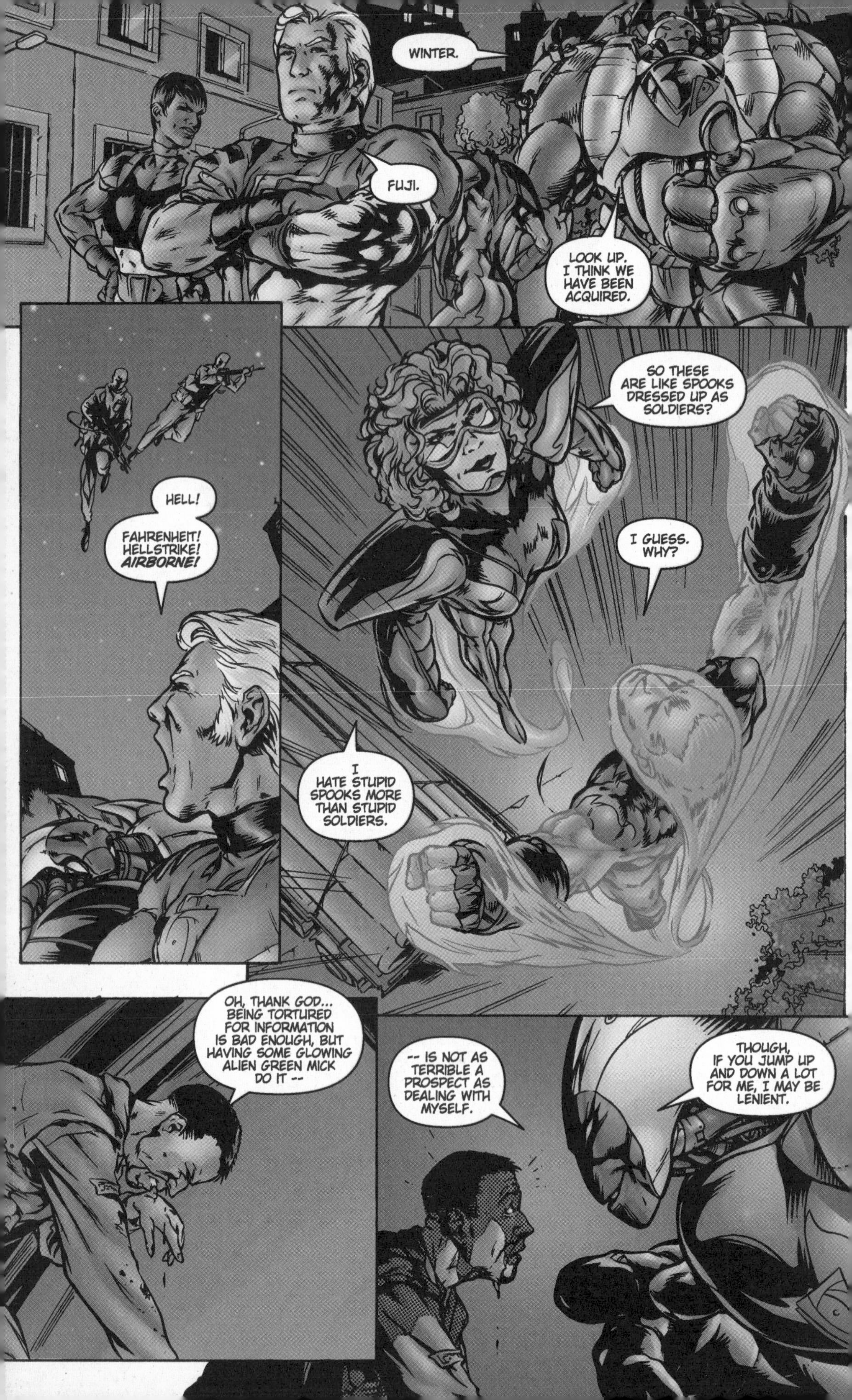
WINTER.
FUJI.
LOOK UP. I THINK WE HAVE BEEN ACQUIRED.
HELL!
FAHRENHEIT! HELLSTRIKE! AIRBORNE!
SO THESE ARE LIKE SPOOKS DRESSED UP AS SOLDIERS?
I GUESS. WHY?
I HATE STUPID SPOOKS MORE THAN STUPID SOLDIERS.
OH, THANK GOD... BEING TORTURED FOR INFORMATION IS BAD ENOUGH, BUT HAVING SOME GLOWING ALIEN GREEN MICK DO IT --
-- IS NOT AS TERRIBLE A PROSPECT AS DEALING WITH MYSELF.
THOUGH, IF YOU JUMP UP AND DOWN A LOT FOR ME, I MAY BE LENIENT.

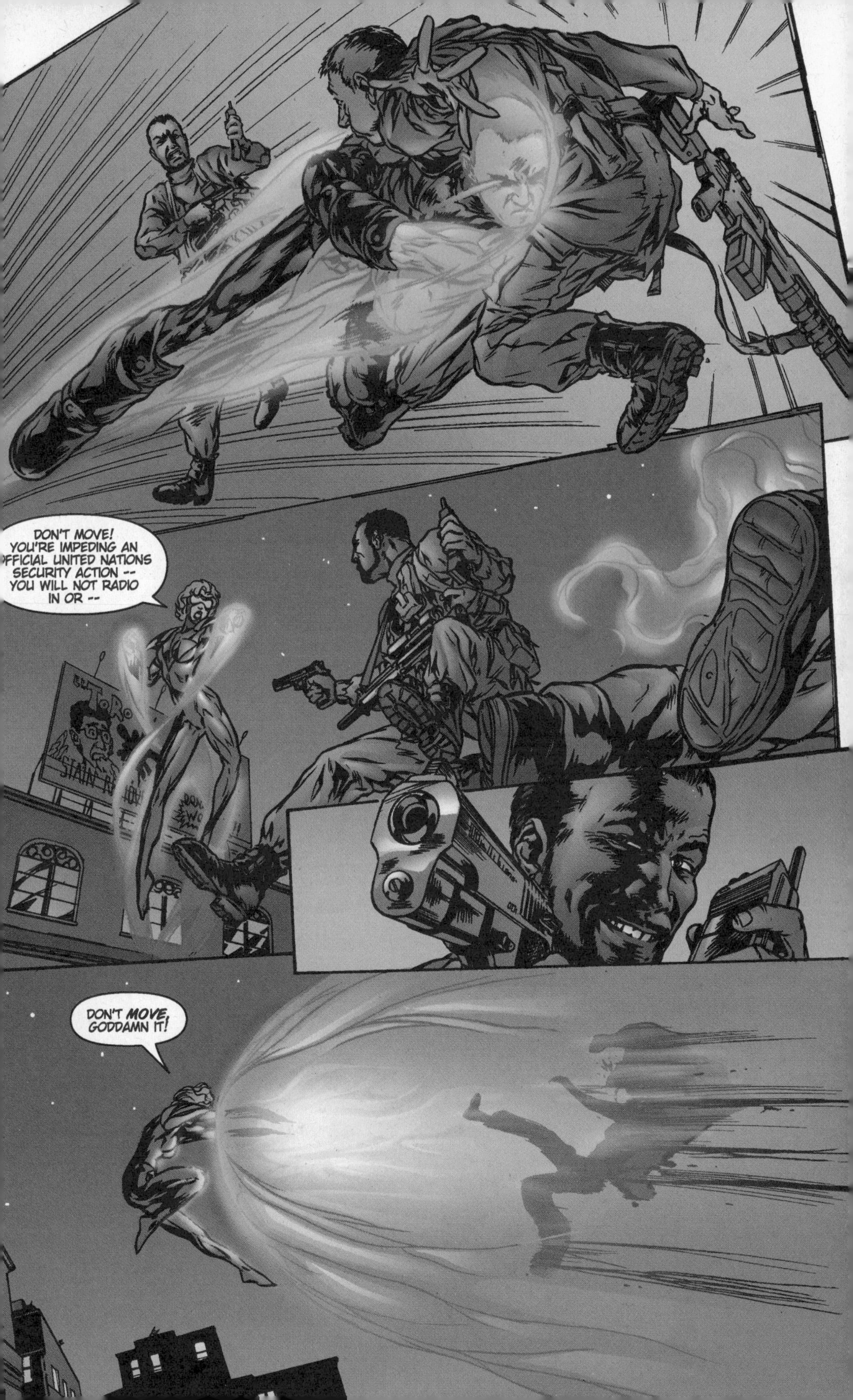
DON'T MOVE! YOU'RE IMPEDING AN OFFICIAL UNITED NATIONS SECURITY ACTION -- YOU WILL NOT RADIO IN OR --
DON'T MOVE, GODDAMN IT!

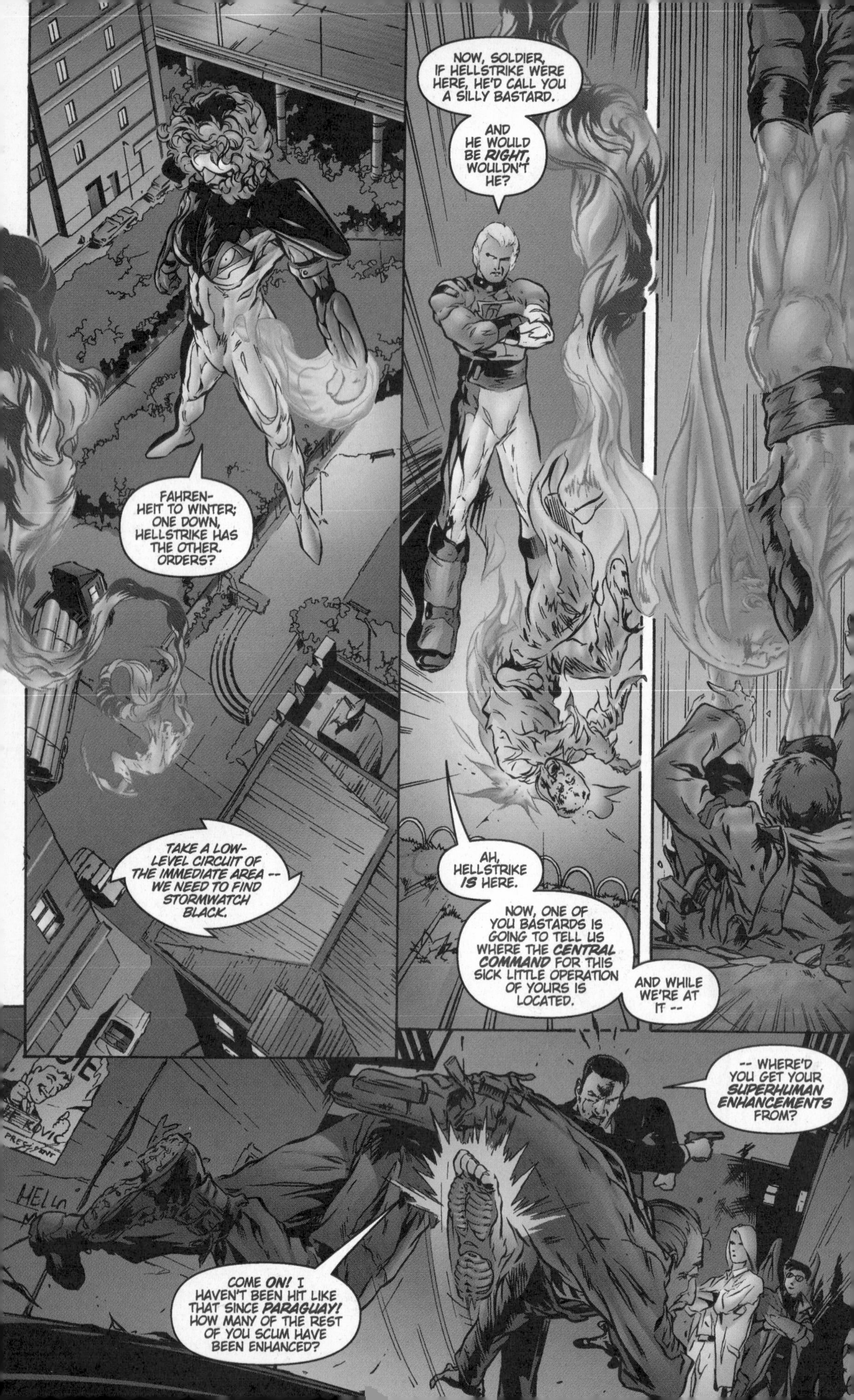
FAHREN-HEIT TO WINTER; ONE DOWN, HELLSTRIKE HAS THE OTHER. ORDERS?
TAKE A LOW-LEVEL CIRCUIT OF THE IMMEDIATE AREA -- WE NEED TO FIND STORMWATCH BLACK.
NOW, SOLDIER, IF HELLSTRIKE WERE HERE, HE'D CALL YOU A SILLY BASTARD.
AND HE WOULD BE RIGHT, WOULDN'T HE?
AH, HELLSTRIKE IS HERE.
NOW, ONE OF YOU BASTARDS IS GOING TO TELL US WHERE THE CENTRAL COMMAND FOR THIS SICK LITTLE OPERATION OF YOURS IS LOCATED.
AND WHILE WE'RE AT IT --
-- WHERE'D YOU GET YOUR SUPERHUMAN ENHANCEMENTS FROM?
COME ON! I HAVEN'T BEEN HIT LIKE THAT SINCE PARAGUAY! HOW MANY OF THE REST OF YOU SCUM HAVE BEEN ENHANCED?

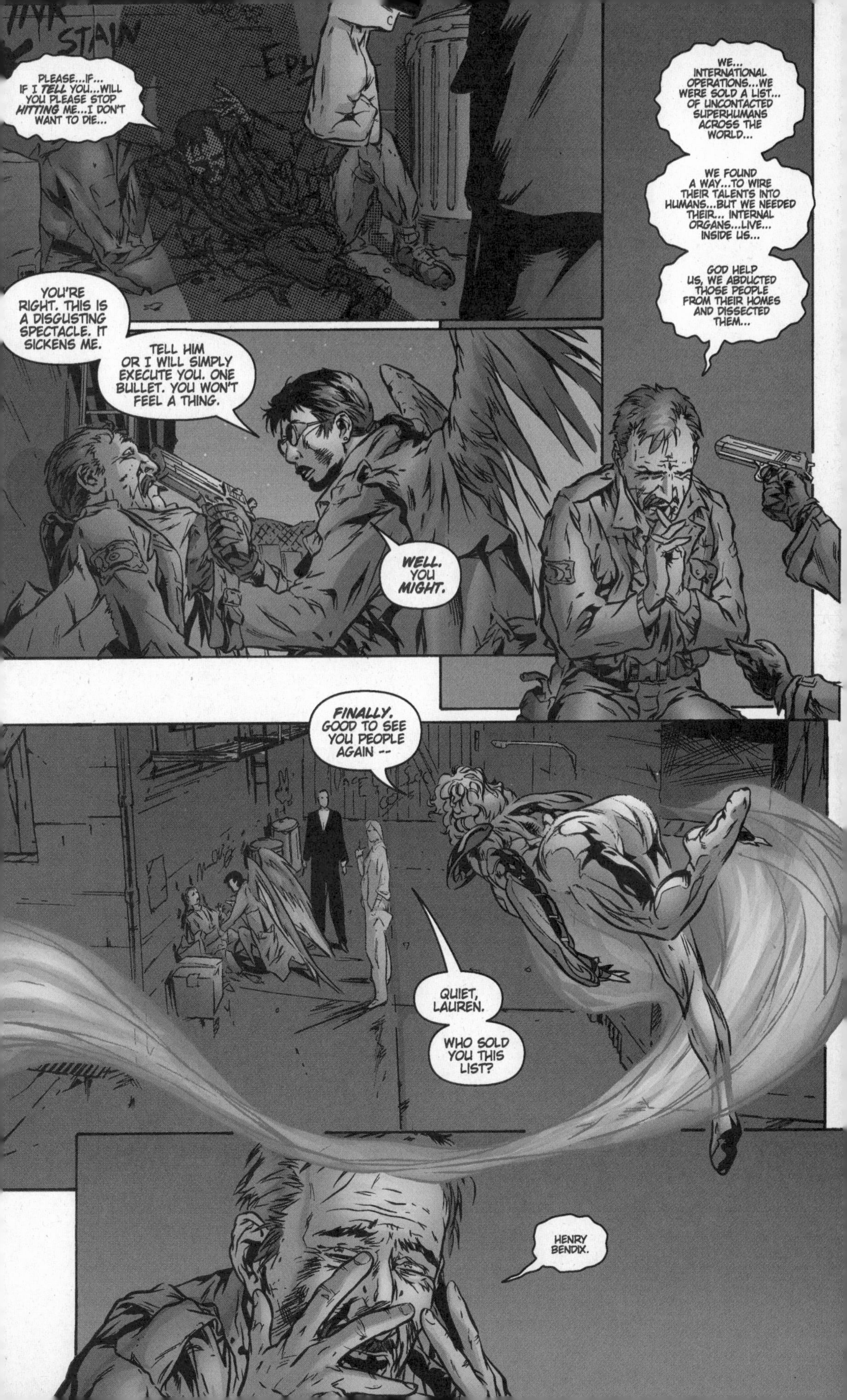

PLEASE...IF... IF I TELL YOU...WILL YOU PLEASE STOP HITTING ME...I DON'T WANT TO DIE...
WE... INTERNATIONAL OPERATIONS...WE WERE SOLD A LIST... OF UNCONTACTED SUPERHUMANS ACROSS THE WORLD...
WE FOUND A WAY...TO WIRE THEIR TALENTS INTO HUMANS...BUT WE NEEDED THEIR... INTERNAL ORGANS...LIVE... INSIDE US...
GOD HELP US, WE ABDUCTED THOSE PEOPLE FROM THEIR HOMES AND DISSECTED THEM...
YOU'RE RIGHT. THIS IS A DISGUSTING SPECTACLE. IT SICKENS ME.
TELL HIM OR I WILL SIMPLY EXECUTE YOU. ONE BULLET. YOU WON'T FEEL A THING.
WELL. YOU MIGHT.
FINALLY. GOOD TO SEE YOU PEOPLE AGAIN --
QUIET, LAUREN.
WHO SOLD YOU THIS LIST?
HENRY BENDIX.

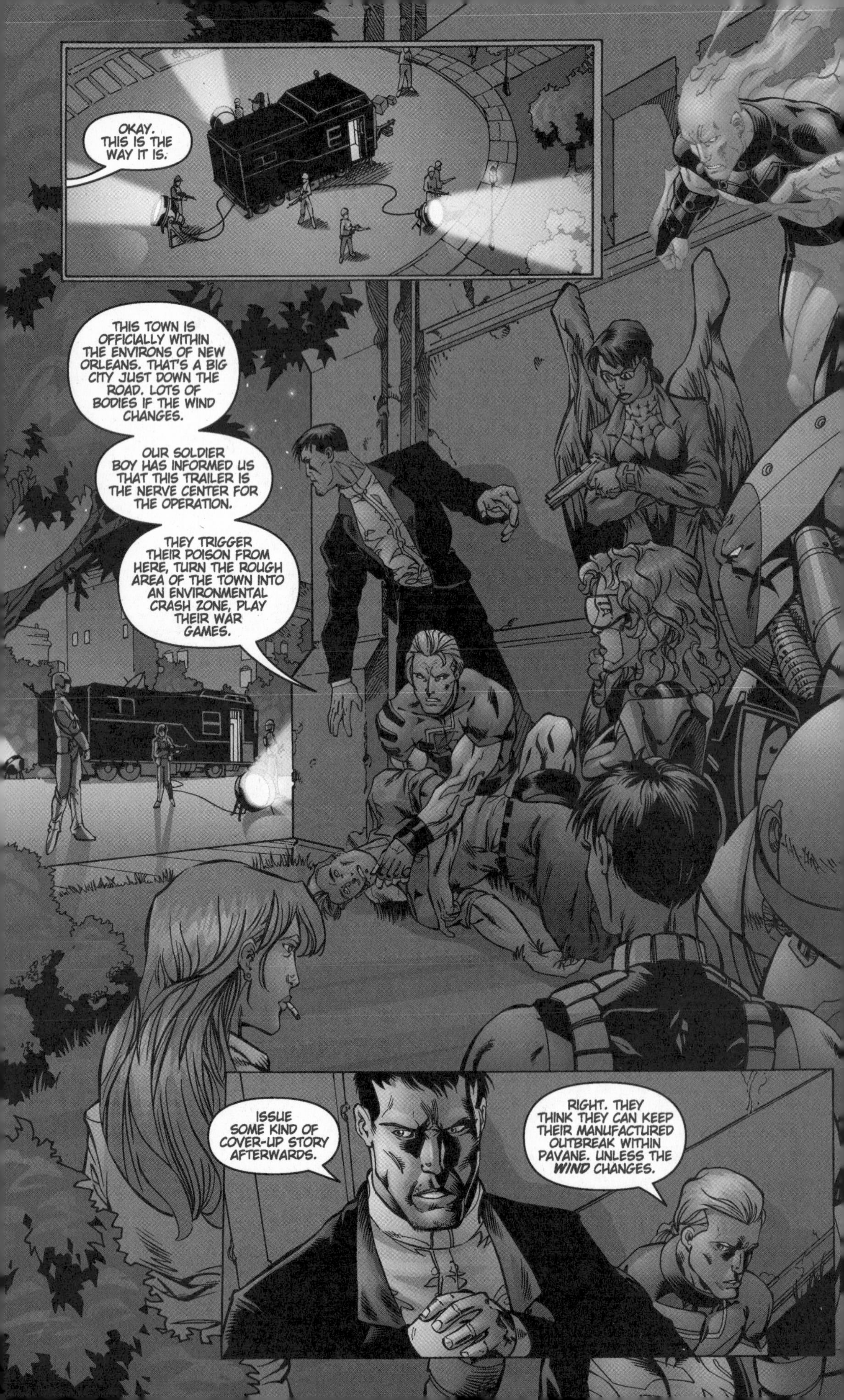
OKAY. THIS IS THE WAY IT IS.
THIS TOWN IS OFFICIALLY WITHIN THE ENVIRONS OF NEW ORLEANS. THAT'S A BIG CITY JUST DOWN THE ROAD. LOTS OF BODIES IF THE WIND CHANGES.
OUR SOLDIER BOY HAS INFORMED US THAT THIS TRAILER IS THE NERVE CENTER FOR THE OPERATION.
THEY TRIGGER THEIR POISON FROM HERE, TURN THE ROUGH AREA OF THE TOWN INTO AN ENVIRONMENTAL CRASH ZONE, PLAY THEIR WAR GAMES.
ISSUE SOME KIND OF COVER-UP STORY AFTERWARDS.
RIGHT. THEY THINK THEY CAN KEEP THEIR MANUFACTURED OUTBREAK WITHIN PAVANE. UNLESS THE *WIND* CHANGES.

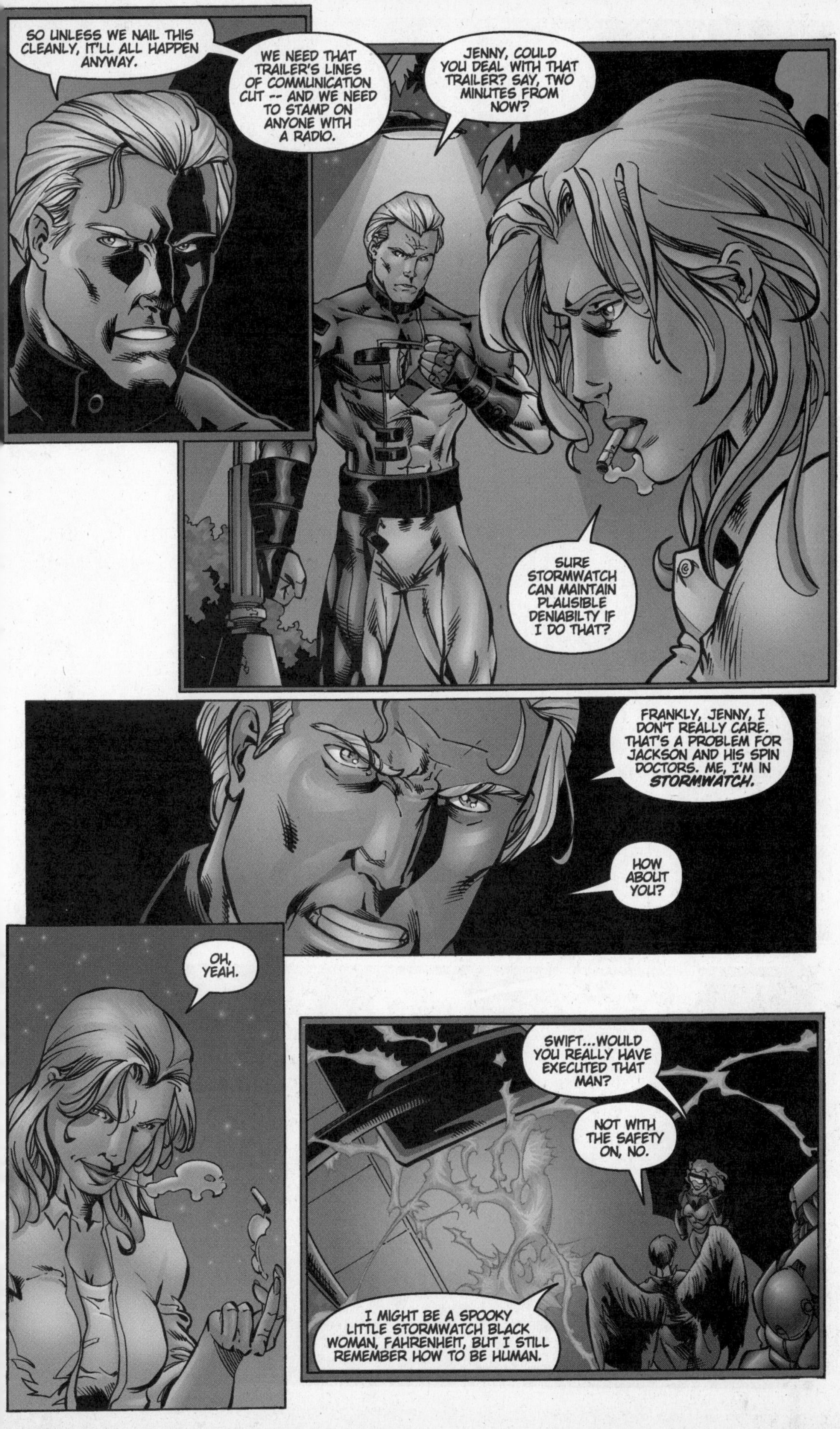
SO UNLESS WE NAIL THIS CLEANLY, IT'LL ALL HAPPEN ANYWAY.
WE NEED THAT TRAILER'S LINES OF COMMUNICATION CUT -- AND WE NEED TO STAMP ON ANYONE WITH A RADIO.
JENNY, COULD YOU DEAL WITH THAT TRAILER? SAY, TWO MINUTES FROM NOW?
SURE STORMWATCH CAN MAINTAIN PLAUSIBLE DENIABILTY IF I DO THAT?
FRANKLY, JENNY, I DON'T REALLY CARE. THAT'S A PROBLEM FOR JACKSON AND HIS SPIN DOCTORS. ME, I'M IN *STORMWATCH.*
HOW ABOUT YOU?
OH, YEAH.
SWIFT...WOULD YOU REALLY HAVE EXECUTED THAT MAN?
NOT WITH THE SAFETY ON, NO.
I MIGHT BE A SPOOKY LITTLE STORMWATCH BLACK WOMAN, FAHRENHEIT, BUT I STILL REMEMBER HOW TO BE HUMAN.

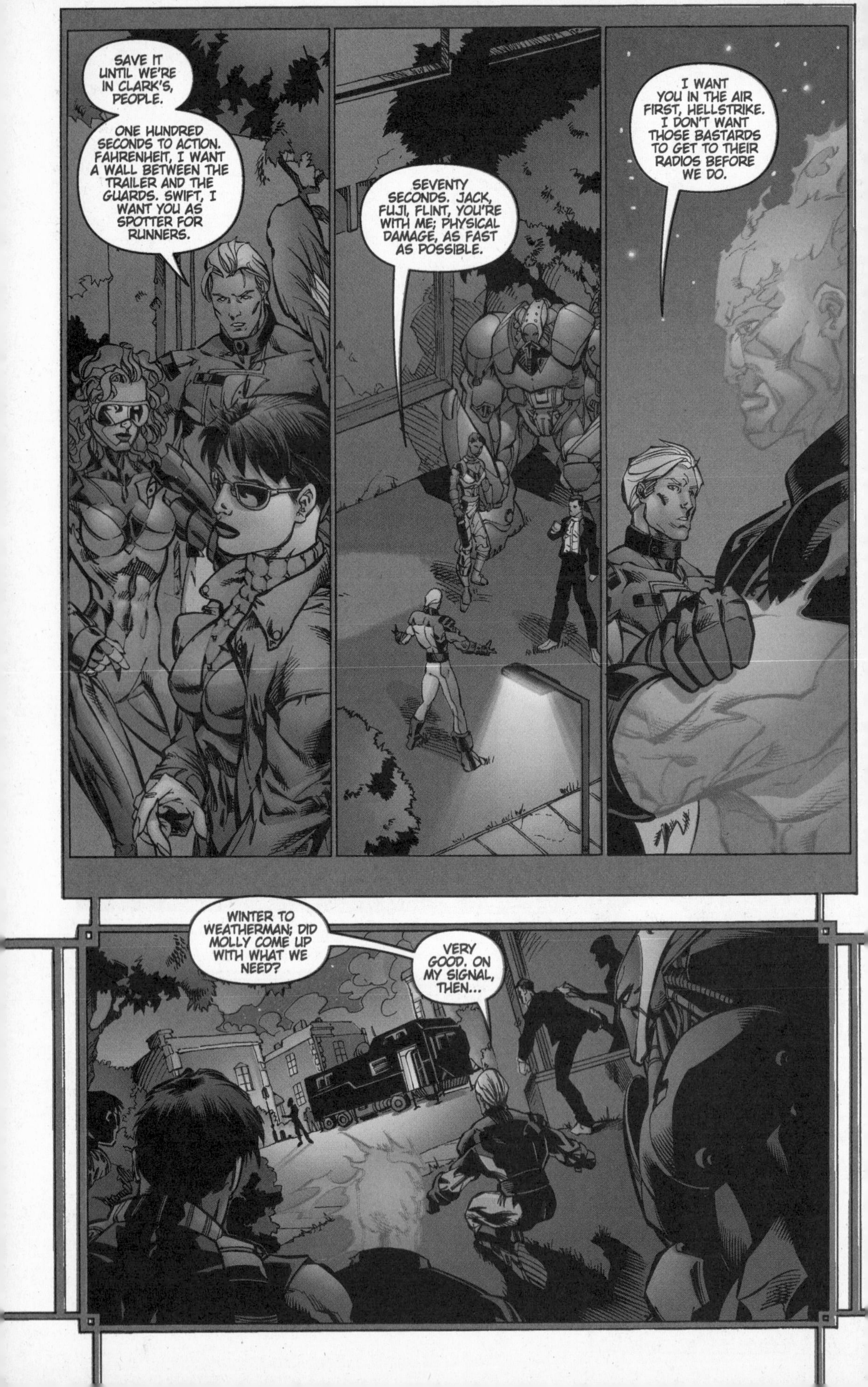
SAVE IT UNTIL WE'RE IN CLARK'S, PEOPLE.
ONE HUNDRED SECONDS TO ACTION. FAHRENHEIT, I WANT A WALL BETWEEN THE TRAILER AND THE GUARDS. SWIFT, I WANT YOU AS SPOTTER FOR RUNNERS.
SEVENTY SECONDS. JACK, FUJI, FLINT, YOU'RE WITH ME; PHYSICAL DAMAGE, AS FAST AS POSSIBLE.
I WANT YOU IN THE AIR FIRST, HELLSTRIKE. I DON'T WANT THOSE BASTARDS TO GET TO THEIR RADIOS BEFORE WE DO.
WINTER TO WEATHERMAN; DID MOLLY COME UP WITH WHAT WE NEED?
VERY GOOD. ON MY SIGNAL, THEN...

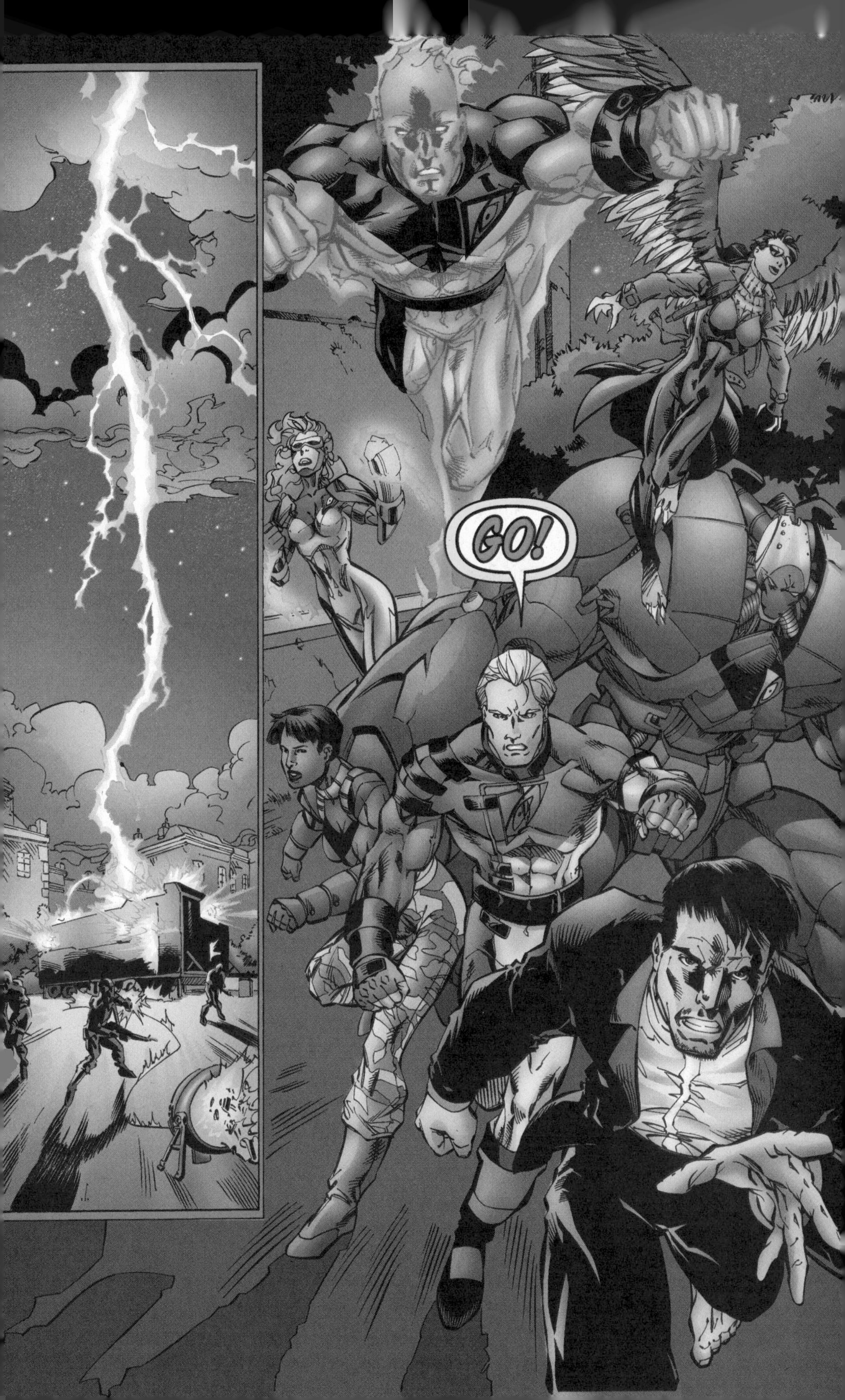
GO!

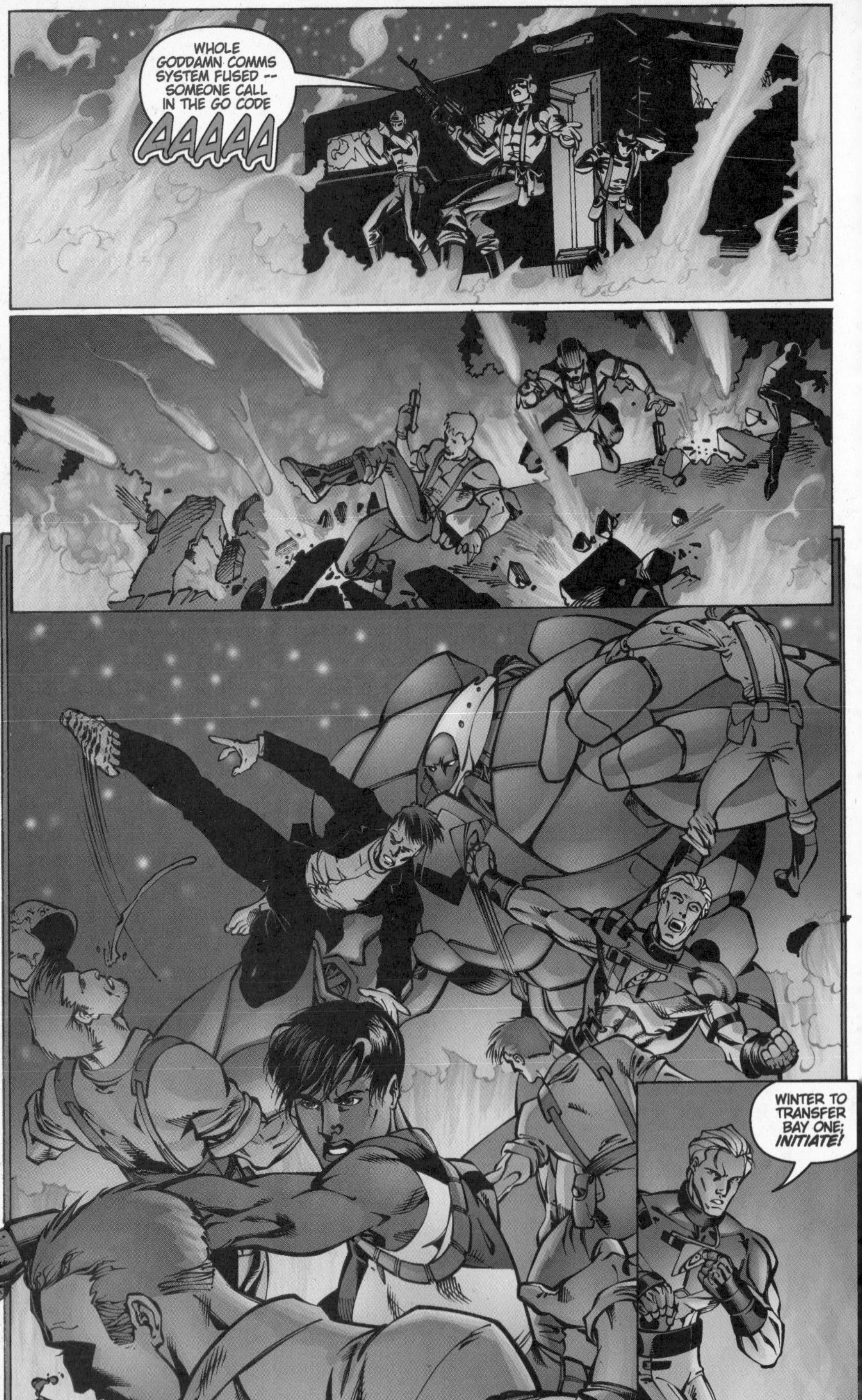
WHOLE GODDAMN COMMS SYSTEM FUSED -- SOMEONE CALL IN THE GO CODE
AAAAA
WINTER TO TRANSFER BAY ONE; *INITIATE!*

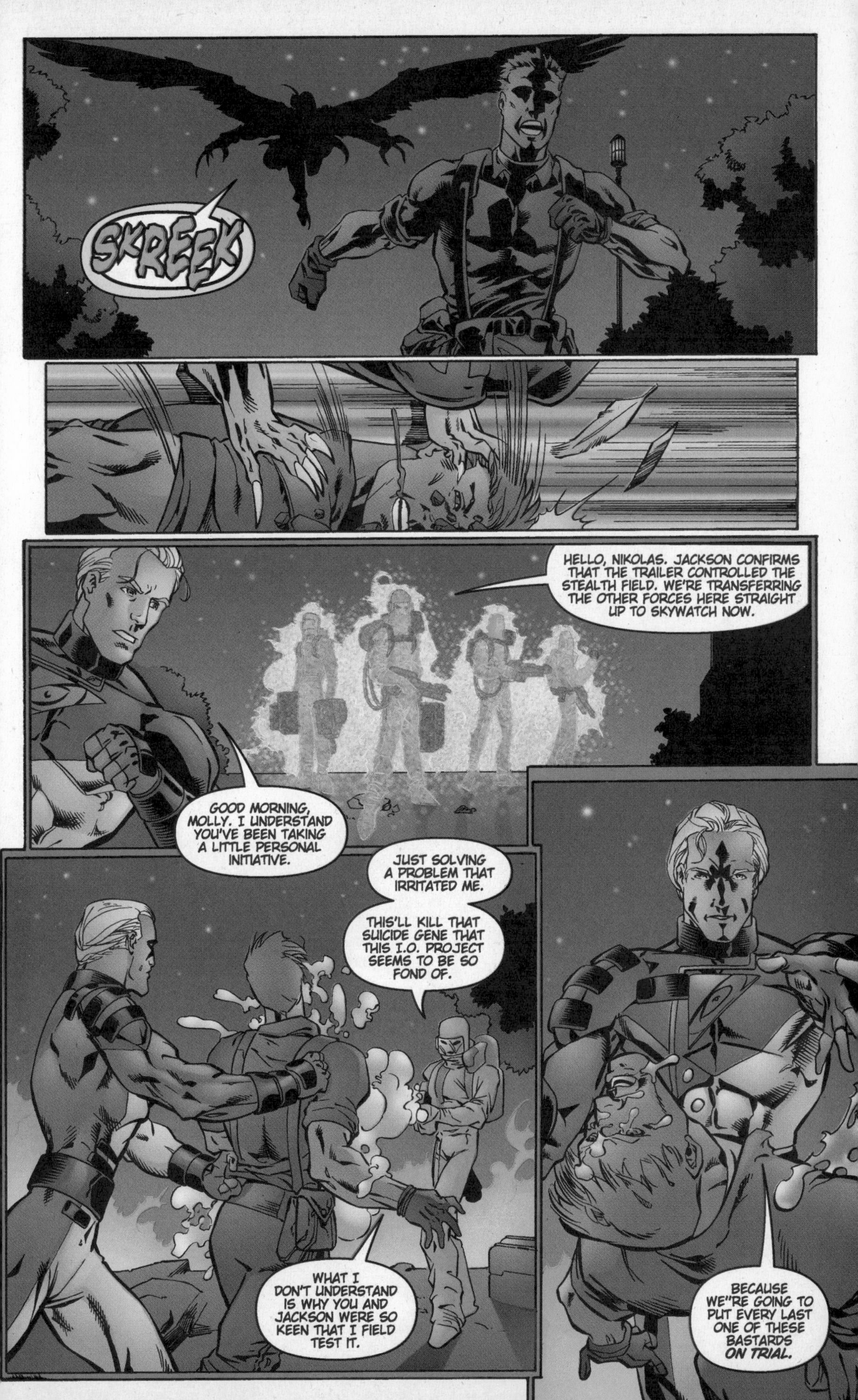
SKREEK
HELLO, NIKOLAS. JACKSON CONFIRMS THAT THE TRAILER CONTROLLED THE STEALTH FIELD. WE'RE TRANSFERRING THE OTHER FORCES HERE STRAIGHT UP TO SKYWATCH NOW.
GOOD MORNING, MOLLY. I UNDERSTAND YOU'VE BEEN TAKING A LITTLE PERSONAL INITIATIVE.
JUST SOLVING A PROBLEM THAT IRRITATED ME.
THIS'LL KILL THAT SUICIDE GENE THAT THIS I.O. PROJECT SEEMS TO BE SO FOND OF.
WHAT I DON'T UNDERSTAND IS WHY YOU AND JACKSON WERE SO KEEN THAT I FIELD TEST IT.
BECAUSE WE"RE GOING TO PUT EVERY LAST ONE OF THESE BASTARDS *ON TRIAL.*

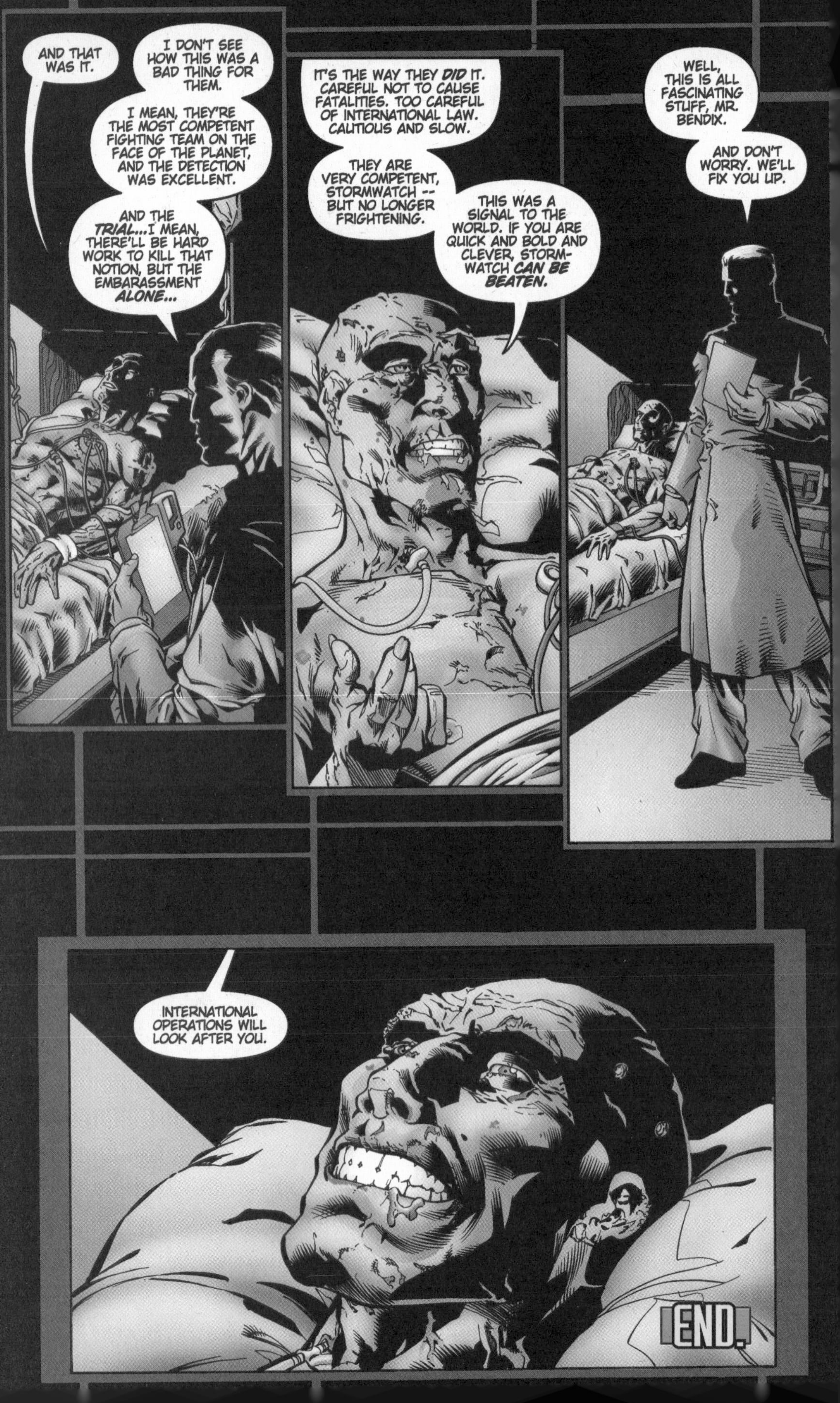
AND THAT WAS IT.
I DON'T SEE HOW THIS WAS A BAD THING FOR THEM.
I MEAN, THEY'RE THE MOST COMPETENT FIGHTING TEAM ON THE FACE OF THE PLANET, AND THE DETECTION WAS EXCELLENT.
AND THE TRIAL...I MEAN, THERE'LL BE HARD WORK TO KILL THAT NOTION, BUT THE EMBARASSMENT ALONE...
IT'S THE WAY THEY DID IT. CAREFUL NOT TO CAUSE FATALITIES. TOO CAREFUL OF INTERNATIONAL LAW. CAUTIOUS AND SLOW.
THEY ARE VERY COMPETENT, STORMWATCH -- BUT NO LONGER FRIGHTENING.
THIS WAS A SIGNAL TO THE WORLD. IF YOU ARE QUICK AND BOLD AND CLEVER, STORM-WATCH CAN BE BEATEN.
WELL, THIS IS ALL FASCINATING STUFF, MR. BENDIX.
AND DON'T WORRY. WE'LL FIX YOU UP.
INTERNATIONAL OPERATIONS WILL LOOK AFTER YOU.
END.

COVERS

This piece was originally intended as a triptych for
the covers of STORMWATCH #48, #49, and #50, but
was never used.

PENCILS: Tom Raney
INKS: Randy Elliott
COLORS: WildStorm FX

COVERS

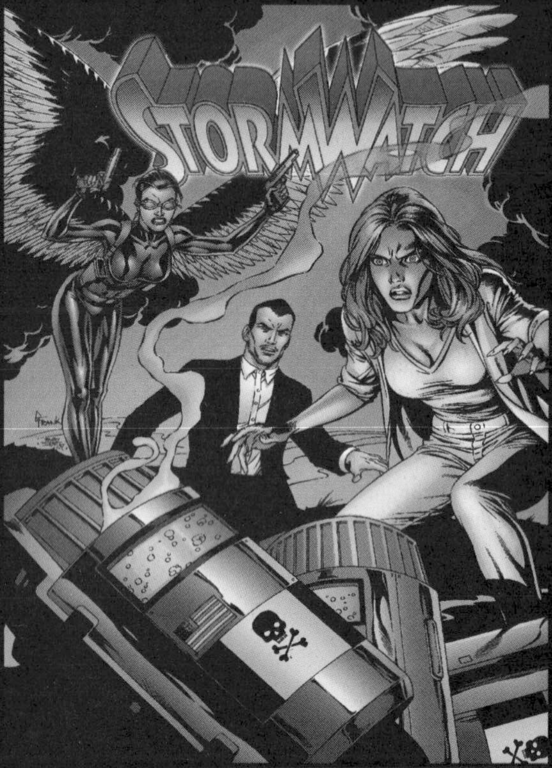
STORMWATCH

STORMWATCH VOL. TWO, #2 COVER
Gary Frank - Randy Elliott - WildStorm FX

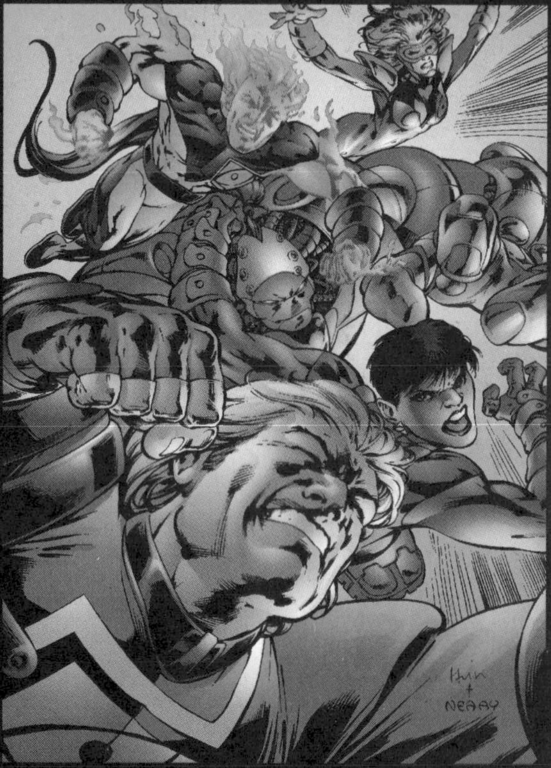

STORMWATCH VOL. TWO, #3 COVER
Bryan Hitch - Paul Neary - WildStorm FX

Following page:
STORMWATCH VOL. TWO, #1 VARIANT COVER
Travis Charest

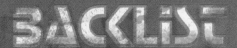

BACKLIST

Look for these other great books from WildStorm and DC:

COLLECTIONS

Battle Chasers: A Gathering of Heroes
Madureira/Sharrieff/McWeeney

Crimson: Loyalty & Loss
Augustyn/Ramos/Hope

Crimson: Heaven & Earth
Augustyn/Ramos/Hope

Deathblow: Sinners and Saints
Choi/Lee/Sale/Scott

Danger Girl: The Dangerous Collection #1-3
Hartnell/Campbell/Garner

Divine Right: Collected Edition #1-3
Lee/Williams

Gen[13]
Choi/Lee/Campbell/Garner

Gen[13]: #13 ABC
Choi/Lee/Campbell/Garner

Gen[13]: Bootleg Vol. 1
Various writers and artists

Gen[13]: Grunge the Movie
Warren

Gen[13]: I Love New York
Arcudi/Frank/Smith

Gen[13]: Interactive Plus
Various writers and artists

Gen[13]: Starting Over
Choi/Lee/Campbell/Garner

Kurt Busiek's Astro City: Life in the Big City
Busiek/Anderson

Kurt Busiek's Astro City: Confession
Busiek/Anderson/Blyberg

Kurt Busiek's Astro City: Family Album
Busiek/Anderson/Blyberg

Kurt Busiek's Astro City: The Tarnished Angel
Busiek/Anderson/Blyberg

Leave It to Chance: Shaman's Rain
Robinson/Smith

Leave It to Chance: Trick or Threat
Robinson/Smith/Freeman

Resident Evil - Collection One
Various writers and artists

Voodoo: Dancing in the Dark
Moore/Lopez/Rio/Various

Wetworks: Rebirth
Portacio/Choi/Williams

StormWatch: Force of Nature
Ellis/Raney/Elliott

StormWatch: Change or Die
Ellis/Raney/Jimenez

StormWatch: A Finer World
Ellis/Hitch/Neary

WildC.A.T.s: Gang War
Moore/Various

WildC.A.T.s: A Gathering of Eagles
Claremont/Lee/Williams

WildC.A.T.s: Homecoming
Moore/Various

WildC.A.T.s/X-Men
Various writers and artists

WildStorm Rising
Windsor-Smith/Various

OTHER COLLECTIONS OF INTEREST

Art of Chiodo
Chiodo

The Batman Adventures: Mad Love
Dini/Timm

Batman: The Dark Knight Returns
Miller/Janson/Varley

Batman: Faces
Wagner

Batman: The Killing Joke
Moore/Bolland/Higgins

Batman: Year One
Miller/Mazzucchelli/Lewis

Camelot 3000
Barr/Bolland

The Golden Age
Robinson/Smith

Green Lantern: Emerald Knights
Marz/Dixon/Banks/Various

Green Lantern: Fear itself
Marz/Parker

JLA: New World Order
Morrison/Porter/Dell

JLA: Rock of Ages
Morrison/Porter/Dell/Various

JLA: Year One
Waid/Augustyn/Kitson

JLA/ WildC.A.T.s
Morrison/Semeiks/Conrad

Justice League of America: The Nail
Davis/Farmer

Kingdom Come
Waid/Ross

Ronin
Miller

Starman: Sins of the Father
Robinson/Harris/Von Grawbadger

Starman: Night and Day
Robinson/Harris/Von Grawbadger

Starman: Times Past
Harris/Jimenez/Weeks/Various

Starman: A Wicked Inclination...
Robinson/Harris/Von Grawbadger/Various

Watchmen
Moore/Gibbons

ARCHIVE EDITIONS

All Star Comics Archives Vols. 1-5
Various writers and artists

The Golden Age Flash Archives Vol. 1
Various writers and artists

The Flash Archives Vol. 1
Various writers and artists

The Golden Age Green Lantern Vol. 1
Various writers and artists

Green Lantern Archives Vols. 1-2
Various writers and artists

Justice League of America Archives Vols. 1-5
Various writers and artists

Legion of Super-Heroes Archives Vols. 1-9
Various writers and artists

For the nearest comics shop carrying collected editions and monthly titles from DC Comics, call 1-888-COMIC BOOK.

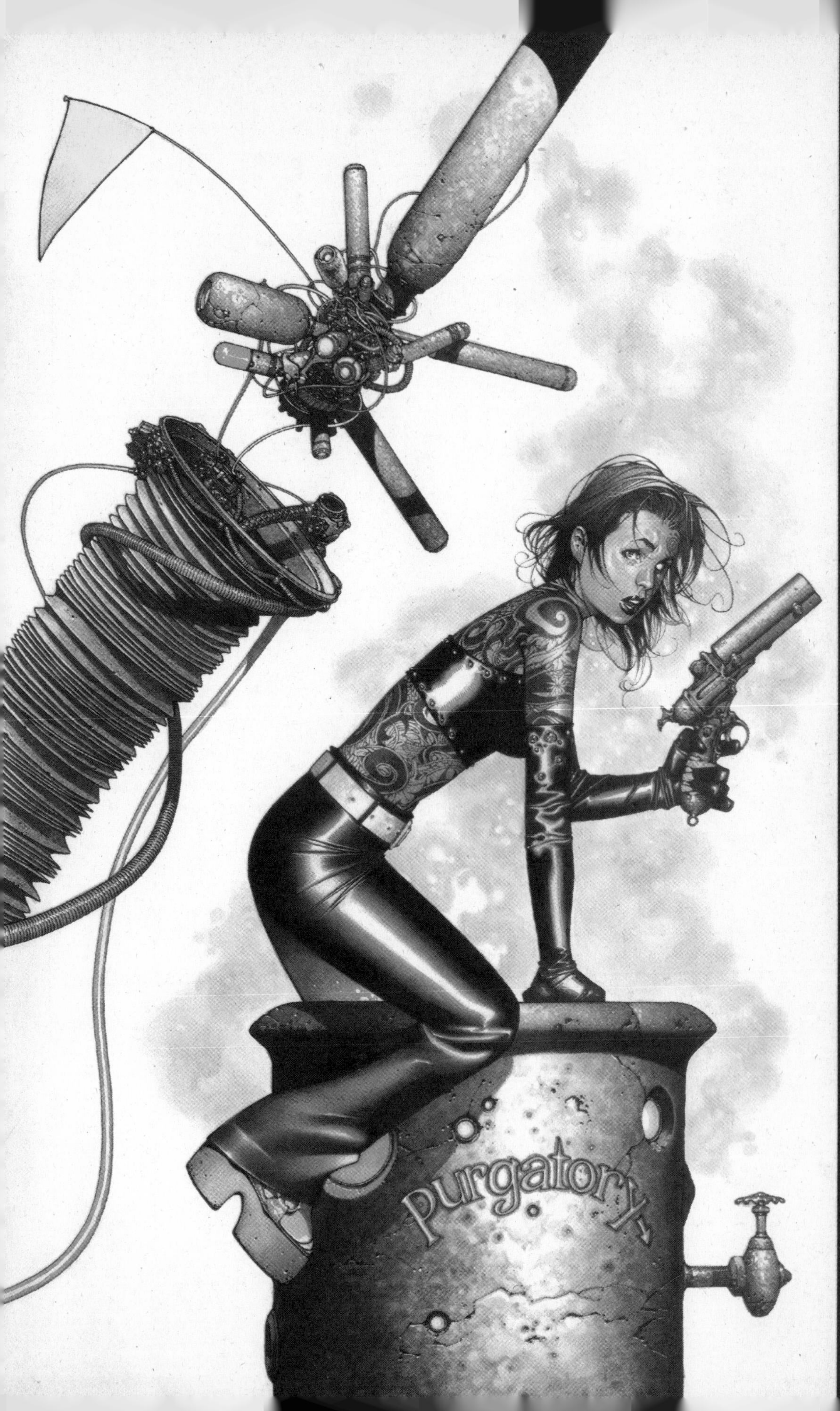
purgatory